This Grim and Savage Game

OSS and the Beginning
of U.S. Covert Operations
in World War II

This Grim and Savage Game

OSS and the Beginning of U.S. Covert Operations in World War II

Tom Moon

DA CAPO PRESS

A CIP catalog record for this book is available from the Library of Congress.
ISBN 0-306-80956-7

First Da Capo Press Edition 2000

Published by Da Capo Press
A Member of the Perseus Books Group
http://www.dacapopress.com

1 2 3 4 5 6 7 8 9 10——04 03 02 01 00

Introduction to the Da Capo Edition

Since earliest recorded history, nations have practiced espionage, covert operations, and even assassinations in their national interests. It has been expected of rogue nations under tyrants, though people of democracies hope their countries will not stoop to that level. But the need to know other nations' plans in the interests of national security is too great to overlook.

In the United States, the art of deception, manipulation, and disinformation was first practiced under George Washington and Benjamin Franklin during the Revolutionary War. President Madison followed suit, strategically altering some dates in negotiations with France for the Louisiana Purchase. Prior to World War II, American men and women serving in outposts in diplomatic and law-enforcement capacities often acted on their own, since America had no official agency devoted to espionage and covert operations. It was U.S. Customs that first copied Japanese codes from a ship off the coast of Hawaii in 1937. It was Customs agent Carl F. Eifler, later head of the first OSS unit (OSS DET 101), who in 1934 uncovered Japanese naval officers in Tijuana, Mexico, and their plans for war with America.

In the cauldron of a total world war America found itself playing a new game—one with no rules other than to win. The brightest and bravest citizens studied and analyzed the minds, habits, and weak points of our enemies. Scientists in research laboratories developed new weapons for the fight. President Roosevelt selected William J. "Wild Bill" Donovan, a decorated hero of World War I, to head the Office of Strategic Services (OSS) organization in 1941. Donovan in turn selected Carl F. Eifler to take command of its first unit to go into action just a few months after the U.S. entered World War II.

Now, more than a half century later, we still fight many of the same battles. It is to the men and women of OSS in World War II, and to those who have since followed in the CIA, the DIA, and NSA, that I would like to dedicate this book.

T. M.
Orange, California
March 2000

Foreword

The stories of bravery, ingenuity, chicanery, daring, dedication and imagination displayed by men and women of the Office of Strategic Services almost boggle the mind. The undisciplined, hodge-podge Americans, whose ancestry embraced every nation we fought with and against, were thrown into the intelligence arena where they had never fought before.

It was bitter sweet irony that the Germans, who originally so ridiculed and maligned America's intelligence ineptness, in the end sought to surrender their troops to many of those same OSS agents.

Many negotiations were attempted by the German SS through OSS operatives to alter the course of the war. The Nazi character was demonstrated in their offer to double cross their Japanese allies if OSS could convince the American armies to slow their pace in the west enough for the Germans to defeat Russia. The American character was demonstrated when the offer was not even considered.

Could Americans fight dirty? For a cause, we proved we could, if conducting unorthodox warfare against a ruthless foe was so considered. It was American ingenuity in espionage, sabotage and propaganda that surprised and ultimately defeated the enemy.

But even prior to Pearl Harbor, patriotic Americans on their own, watching the war clouds form, had made inquiries and taken photographs of what were destined to be American targets. Among them was William J. "Wild Bill" Donovan, decorated hero of WWI who was selected by President Franklin D. Roosevelt to head the new Coordinator of Information, later to become the Office of Strategic Services.

While OSS was criticized for the socialites among its ranks (many called it "Oh So Social") it recruited Americans from all ranks and strata. With no prior experience in covert and intelligence matters Oss had no psychological guidelines for recruitment of the "perfect" or even "good" agent.

Donovan surrounded himself with top administrative men. By chance he hit on an ex-Customs man, Carl F. Eifler, to take the first OSS unit into action. His OSS DET 101 achieved many firsts for unorthodox units. His strength, bravery and dedication inspired all of us who were privileged to serve under him.

While this book is dedicated to all OSS personnel who served world-wide I must especially mention that man who walked and roared like a bear—and won all our respect—Colonel Carl F. Eifler. I am proud to have served under him.

Tom Moon

This Grim and Savage Game

OSS and the Beginning
of U.S. Covert Operations
in World War II

1

On a sultry Spring evening in April, 1934, a husky young American sat on a bar stool in the Foreign Club in Tijuana, Mexico slowly sipping a beer. He appeared to be just another disinterested patron.

Because gambling was the main source of income to the Foreign Club it attracted people from the United States as well as locals. Some American sailors walked between the crap tables and the blackjack dealers. It was just after nine o'clock and the evening was starting to pick up.

Outside, where people walked the mostly unpaved streets, the night air was warm but pleasant. The street vendors selling pots, leather goods and jewelry tried to make a sale to anyone who might look their way. Small boys promised the men a good time with their sisters or mothers.

The burly American, in his late 20's, looked like a man trying to find some action but not caring too much if he didn't. He was dressed to fit the scene in an open neck shirt, cotton slacks that needed a pressing and rubber soled shoes. What was not evident was a badge and ID card in his hip pocket that identified him as U.S. Customs Agent, Carl F. Eifler.

The club was adequately lighted only over the gambling tables. Elsewhere it was dim, as if to hide the bordertown seediness of the place. Sailors walked over to talk with the local prostitutes who plied their trade for a few dollars.

Eifler was not interested in the ladies of the night or who might be gambling. His undercover assignment was to look for bootleggers and others who might be involved in their back scene operations. Mexican locals on his payroll, acting as informants, brought him small bits of information. He knew most of it was manufactured just to get the money he could provide.

To not appear conspicuous, Eifler slowly got off his stool and sauntered over to the black jack table. Laying down a dollar he picked up his cards, took a hit and won the first round. He pulled the dollar back, let the winning money ride and pushed on the next round. For about fifteen minutes he played at a leisurely pace. Finally he quit, picked up his money and walked over to the bar to order another beer. He walked to the front door, looked up and down the street and returned to watch six people shooting craps. He recognized most of the locals and even some of the San Diego based sailors who often frequented the club.

While there were sometimes brawls between the Americans and Mexicans, no one ever bothered Eifler. His weight of 230 pounds and gigantic arms and hands said clearly that fights with him were to be avoided.

Another thirty minutes went by and the action gradually picked up. The hubbub increased as more bodies came in the front door. But suddenly three of those bodies drew Eifler's attention.

They were Japanese—what Eifler considered typical Japanese. They were dressed in casual pants and white shirts. They went immediately to the crap table talking among themselves.

Eifler suddenly felt it incumbent on himself to shoot craps and walked to the same side of the table where the Japanese stood. They were trying to buy chips but having trouble communicating. It was obvious they spoke no Spanish. To see if they knew English, Eifler offered to help. It was immediately apparent they spoke no English either.

Through sign language they made their wishes known and soon began placing bets. They knew the game of craps quite well. Eifler studied their similar haircuts and their comparable builds. He had not seen Japanese in Tijuana before but then many ships put in at Mexican ports and these were no doubt some crewmen out for a good time.

After losing all he felt he could afford Eifler returned to the bar and sat quietly overlooking the enthusiastic crowd. His gaze returned often to the Japanese now at the black jack table.

After about an hour the Japanese conversed among themselves, then headed out the door. Having nothing better to do at the time Eifler followed them at a discreet distance. He had been trained to always follow the unusual and these men were unusual.

Down the dingy streets they went, laughing among themselves and having obviously enjoyed themselves. They never looked back at their American tail.

Several more turns and they were at a small grocery store, the El Eden. Without hesitation they went inside and closed the door. Eifler followed, trying to look in but there were no side windows.

He knew the issue was over and, while he could make nothing of it, it was worth filing in the back of his mind. He returned to his car, drove over the border and went to his home in San Diego for the night.

The next day's operations were similar. While he did not go to

2

the Foreign Club every evening he was somehow drawn back that night.

At almost the same hour a group of noisy sailors came in. Behind them were three quiet, well mannered Japanese. They were not the same ones as the night before, but were dressed similarly. Their gambling activities were much the same as their predecessors. Eifler waited nearly an hour and a half to follow them as they left. They led him to the same grocery store and disappeared.

Intrigued, Eifler made it a definite point to be at the Club the next night. As he sipped his second beer he saw the familiar sight of three Japanese entering. None of them were from the previous nights. Eifler looked them over seeing much the same clothing, body types and haircuts. He felt they had to be military.

He tailed them again, and again they led him to the same grocery store.

Now he was puzzled. He had seen nine different Japanese in three nights. Something definitely was going on—but what?

A Mexican who was on the U.S. payroll as an informant was brought into the picture. "Who are these men and what is going on," Eifler told him to find out.

A few days later he reported that they were all Imperial Navy Officers and part of a task force of 400 such officers camped just south of Tijuana. They had made an artesian well and the area had a natural aerodrome.

Eifler asked himself a thousand questions about what it might mean. Why were they there? For how long?

The next night Eifler reported for his regular meeting with the U.S. Army Reserves in San Diego. They were commanded by a no-nonsense regular line officer, a Lt. Colonel of Infantry. Eifler debated telling him of the puzzle but decided to wait until he had more information.

Through his informants Eifler learned there were Japanese exchange professors in Mexican universities and at different levels of the Mexican government preaching the advantages of economic ties to Japan. For its planned war with America, Japan would need lower Baja for troops and supplies. In return for Mexico's help, at the successful conclusion of the war, Mexico was to be ceded Arizona, New Mexico and California.

Eifler took this startling information to his next-in-command, Leo Stanley. Though maintaining a straight face it was obvious Stanley felt Eifler was taking his job too seriously.

Fellow Customs agents began razzing Eifler. Each time they would spot an Oriental they would say, "Hey, Eifler, isn't that a Jap spy?"

Wanting someone to listen to him Eifler finally went to the commanding officer of his Reserve unit, Lt. Col. Joseph W. Stilwell, with a written report. Stilwell, while on duty in China, had studied the Japanese operations in Manchuria. He realized far ahead of his time that the Japanese were set on a course of war with America. He studied and restudied the Eifler report, then took it to higher authorities where he was rebuffed as Eifler had been. Finally Stilwell took it to a retired Major General in San Diego who had commanded World War I intelligence operations in France. He was impressed with the thoroughness of Eifler's report and investigation. He could do nothing either but tell Stilwell to have his man keep gathering evidence.

Several months passed. Then the Chief Inspector of the Border Patrol, Al Cohen, called Leo Stanley to Los Angeles for a conference.

Stanley said the Japanese government had requested American permission to bring their ships into Long Beach and San Pedro where they might transship their prawns from lower Mexico into Japan. They had been careful to promise not to let their prawns enter American markets.

Customs in Washington, D.C., was intrigued and asked for an investigation. Cohen was at a loss as to how to proceed. Stanley reported he had a young fool under his wing who had spent a lot of time making such a study and had written a report. Cohen asked to see a full report.

Now that he had someone's attention, Eifler took his finger out of the dike and began typing. For seventeen hours he listed names, ranks and locations. Included was his sighting of the German cruiser, Karlsbad, just off Baja engaged in anti-aircraft practice.

Amazingly enough, even with this detailed report, the Japanese were given permission to transship their prawns and enter Long Beach and San Pedro ports. Either the Eifler report was discounted or the United States decided to see just how determined the Japanese were.

America at that time had no central organization to assemble and evaluate such reports. It was impossible to learn what eventually happened to Eifler's report.

He did continue dogging the Japanese on his days off following them to Long Beach and San Pedro. The "fishermen," he noted, all had military bearing.

Fortunately the alliance did not materialize. The Japanese simply disappeared. The threat melted.

President Roosevelt, however, was convinced of Japan's long-range plans of conquest. He had studied Admiral Alfred Mahan's

4

book on the influence of sea power on history. Mahan, who was in contact with Roosevelt, agreed Japan was a major threat to world peace.

In 1920 a Japanese student attending Harvard had told Roosevelt that his nation had a hundred year plan which had been drafted in 1889. It covered annexing Manchuria, establishing a protectorate in north China and acquiring American and British Pacific bases, including Hawaii, plus bases in Mexico and Peru.

In 1934 Roosevelt informed Secretary of War, Henry L. Stimson, of the plot as outlined to him in 1920 by that Japanese student. He added many of its particulars had already been verified. It is most likely Eifler's reports had eventually reached the President's desk.

His brief stint in espionage behind him Eifler turned his immense energies and singleness of mind into his Customs work and the Army Reserves.

Stilwell had resented being given charge of a Reserve unit. In taking charge of it he disagreed with the commanding officer he was relieving who told him it was one of the best units in the army.

With typical aplomb Stilwell had folded his arms and said, "Show me. I was shanghaied in here and someone had better damn well show me." In addition he had referred to the unit as a bunch of "goddamned tinhorn soldiers."

The unit, especially Eifler, decided to show him. Eifler declared that his unit would be the best of all. He attended all programs and lectures given by Stilwell. Stilwell noted the interest and brought in ROTC troops to join his unit in maneuvers.

One night Eifler had set his men out in a defensive perimeter. Several runners failed to return. He needed to know what was going on. Finally he went himself. In the dark he ran into Stilwell.

"Eifler, what the hell are you doing," he asked.

"Colonel, right now I am acting as my own runner," was the reply.

"Good, goddamn it. That's what you'll be doing in combat," snapped the salty Colonel.

As the men ran their maneuvers they noted one of their major problems was communication. Together with the radio operators they tried to find a better way to communicate. Out of their efforts came the walkie-talkie which was to prove itself time and again in World War II.

Stilwell began warming up to his officers. He went into the field with them. At night he sat discussing strategy. He told them of the Japanese military machine and what he thought the Japanese would do in China. As the young officers sat at his feet he could go over the map of China and accurately predict the next Japanese moves.

The lessons Stilwell taught the young officers were the result of long and critical experience of the Chinese people and government. He was first sent to China in 1921 as a language student in Peking. He served in the Shansi province as a construction engineer on a road being built by the Red Cross for famine relief. While in Shansi he chose to live for months with the laborers and peasants.

In 1927, Stilwell was stationed in Tientsin, China. He spent months as an observer with the Chinese army during a civil war. His keen interest in military tactics took him to the front where he observed the troops in combat. Later he was transferred to the U.S. Embassy in Peking as Military Attache. This time he mingled with the upper strata of the Chinese diplomats and the highest ranking military officers.

Few people knew of a serious injury he had suffered that would bother him for the rest of his life. During World War I, at Belrupt, an ammunition dump blew up causing a severe injury to his left eye. He suffered a deformity of the pupil and a growth of a cataract on his lens. The left eye was so badly damaged he could not make out the fingers of his hand from a distance of three feet. His right eye attempted to compensate for the problem. It required a heavy correction and demanded use of glasses from that day on.

In combat, or on maneuvers, where lighting was often poor at night, Stilwell had to make a great extra effort to read reports and maps. Perhaps the trauma from his injury caused the bitter disposition that earned him the nickname "Vinegar Joe." A hand drawn cartoon showing Stilwell drinking from a vinegar bottle was attached to one of the military bulletin boards where he commanded. The actual caption, lost in the passage of time, was to the effect that consumption of this peculiar beverage was what was responsible for the Stilwell tirades.

Recognizing the genius of this very unique officer, Eifler spent every possible minute with him questioning, probing. Eifler wanted to understand the reasoning of the Oriental mind. He knew one day he would be at war with them.

Their time together was short lived. In 1935, Stilwell was transferred back to the Embassy in Peking. With more authority and understanding of the Chinese thinking he saw the same old patterns of corruption and abuse he had seen before. He considered the Chinese grossly underrated and dreamed of the day he could command them and make them into a first rate army. The Chinese army was trained and equipped by the Germans. Their commanding officers got their positions through purchase or political favor. Suffering continual defeats in the field their generalissimo, Chiang Kai-shek, said it was due to bad equipment.

"Not so," blurted Stilwell. "They lack proper leadership, don't know how to maintain their equipment and are not properly commanded."

This was the start of a bitter feud between the two men that was never resolved.

That same year, 1935, Eifler was transferred to a Customs job in San Pedro. He remained there until 1936 when a big promotion came his way. He was offered the job of Chief Inspector in Honolulu. There was some sort of scandal that needed to be cleaned up. He eagerly accepted and was shortly on his way.

He went about his new job with typical hustle and efficiency. He questioned and probed. He transferred men and soon erased all traces of the scandal and corruption that had caused the relief of his predecessor. And all the while he kept an eye open for news of Stilwell, now a full Colonel.

In 1937 the Japanese began their big push into central and north China. Their troops rolled over the untrained and corrupt Chinese forces. America reacted promptly. Women burned their silk stockings in public. Japanese restaurants, banks and streets in America were renamed. Prejudice against Japanese-Americans mounted. Demands were made to restrict trade with Japan and to stop the flow of America's scrap metal into the Japanese war machine.

Public mention was made of the Tanaka Memorial to the Japanese Emperor in 1937 which said, "In order to conquer China we must first conquer Manchuria and Mongolia. In order to conquer the world we must begin by conquering China."

Even with this blueprint plainly laid out many in America doubted both the seriousness of the Japanese and their ability to carry out such grandiose plans. In 1938 Stilwell recognized a marvelous opportunity to study America's future enemy. Using his role as Military Attache he would ride out to the Japanese lines where he was politely received. The Japanese courteously conducted a tour of their lines showing him their equipment and discussing their strategy. Stilwell eagerly made mental notes of everything he saw.

In 1939, Stilwell was again ordered to return home. While his ship was at sea, Eifler heard a newscast that President Roosevelt had appointed Stilwell to the rank of Brigadier General. Anxious to break the news and congratulate him Eifler took a boat out of Honolulu. Twenty miles at sea he intercepted the Stilwell ship, quickly boarded, and sought his friend. Stilwell had already heard the news.

In the brief time Eifler had he asked numerous questions about the approaching war. Eifler reported he had remained active in the Reserves and was now assigned as training officer in the Reserve Officers Association School. He added there was a scarcity of regular army officers to train the men in the school.

"General, will you please see what you can do about this when you get back? If you will get me one regular army officer now I will promise you a hundred good officers by the time the war breaks," he said.

Stilwell agreed to do what he could. Heartened by the promise, Eifler took his leave. In short order he did receive the promised officer.

Another American was also closely monitoring the Japanese and correctly evaluating their intentions. He was Claire Chennault who in that same year, 1939, was in China working with the Nationalist Government in their war with Japan.

The Japanese, facing no resistance, moved with ease. Chennault felt the only way to stop them was with air power. China had no planes, no pilots, no air force. In some manner Chennault knew he had to get America involved. Because the Japanese government was in control of the military who had dreams of conquering all the Pacific, something big, bold and dramatic had to be done. If Japan itself could be bombed it might make the people realize they were not invulnerable and cause their leaders to reconsider their ambitious plans.

Chennault had been forced to retire from the U.S. Air Corps three years earlier. His short temper, insubordination and reputation as a maverick did not wash with the military. He served as a consultant to the Chinese Government at a salary of $15,000. In addition he was given the rank of Colonel.

As he worked out his plan against Japan the war in China showed no signs of letting up. Even with his preoccupation of helping China he also watched the gathering war clouds in Europe. In September, 1939, the German war machine poured over the borders into Poland and World War II began.

Japan declared its neutrality but no one was convinced.

America's war plants began humming as Roosevelt declared her to be the arsenal of democracy.

One year later, in October 1940, Chennault felt it time to come to Washington to present his unorthodox plan. His former commanding officers in the U.S. military scoffed at a man who had spent 20 years in their Air Corps and never rose above the rank of Captain. In their

8

eyes he was a trouble maker.

Members of President Roosevelt's Cabinet listened intently to the plan. They recognized the growing Japanese menace. Chennault's plan was well thought out and carefully detailed.

The bombings were to be carried out by American mercenaries, actually men released by the army and navy. They would be paid by the U.S. through a dummy corporation established for that purpose. The planes would be American but bearing Chinese insignia.

Air Corps brass continued belittling the plan and the man. In Chennault's corner, however, was the powerful China lobby. T. V. Soong, one of the world's wealthiest men, presented the plan to Henry Morgenthau who was sympathetic to the Chinese. The plan required 500 planes piloted and paid for by America which Chennault felt could defeat the Japanese in China and reign terror on the Japanese mainland. Morgenthau was convinced.

On Dec. 10, 1940, Morgenthau called on Cordell Hull, Secretary of State to present the plan. Hull was ahead of him saying we should fly 500 planes from the Aleutians over Japan to "teach them a lesson," and added, "if we could only find some way to drop some bombs on them."

Their enthusiasm growing, they met with President Roosevelt and his Cabinet on December 19.

"Wonderful," was the President's reaction. He then asked Hull, Morgenthau, Secretary of War Stimson and Secretary of the Navy Frank Knox to stay with him and work out the plan. The plan called for utilizing airfields that Chennault had already constructed in anticipation of the bombers. They were 650 miles from Tokyo.

Chennault argued for the four engine B-17 bombers in place of the British Lockheed Hudson planes. The longer range of the B-17s would also allow the bombing of Osaka, Kobe and Nagasaki in addition to Tokyo.

Morgenthau agreed that the crews should be entirely American and that each man should be paid $1,000 per month after release from the Air Corps. The planes would be shipped from the West Coast to Clark Field in the Philippines, assembled there and then flown to China to avoid prying reporters as well as the enemy.

The plan gathered momentum and may have been carried out, but for the intervention of Secretary of War, Stimson. He called a meeting on December 22, 1940, pointing out that the U.S. military would suffer from the depletion of planes and personnel. Further, he called into question the heavy influence of the China lobby on the plan. He noted that the Chinese were not really concerned with America's precarious situation facing a looming world war. General

Marshall expressed his concern that any planes and men we gave China would be taken from the European war and in addition might give Japan an excuse to attack us at a time we were woefully unprepared.

General Marshall's opinions were highly respected. He ultimately changed the thinking of Morgenthau, then the President, and the plan was finally dropped.

As a consolation, and agreeing some help must be given to protect the Burma Road, 100 P40B fighter planes were given to Chennault who used them as the backbone of his AVG, the Flying Tigers.

Thousands of miles away another American was looking into the future and seeing a picture he did not like. He was William J. "Wild Bill" Donovan, highly decorated hero of World War I. He had not only proved his bravery but displayed a love of country that prompted him to do extraordinary things.

He had been passed over for a Cabinet position by President Hoover because of his Catholicism. While earning a very comfortable living as a New York attorney he maintained a sharp look-out for those who would be enemies of America.

In 1932 Donovan had visited Germany and returned to urge America to build up its military strength. At that time the American army had been so depleted it ranked seventeenth in the world in actual strength.

Donovan liked to talk to visiting businessmen, diplomats, educators—anyone who might give him knowledge. From their observations he put together his own scenario. One of his acquaintances was Italian Ambassador Rossi.

In 1935 Mussolini invaded Ethiopia. Donovan wanted to meet with Mussolini and wangle a trip to Ethiopia. Government officials told him it would be absolutely impossible. No one had ever been allowed to visit the headquarters of Marshal Badoglio in Africa. Neither London or Washington knew either Il Duce's plans or the strength of the Italian forces. Which way might the Italian army strike from Ethiopia?

Calling on his friendship with Rossi, Donovan, traveling at his own expense, was able to arrange a meeting with Mussolini.

Arriving two days before Christmas, Donovan presented his letter of introduction from Rossi to Mussolini. His story was that he was an American businessman and wanted to understand the Italian situation because it was affecting his business at home. Told that Mussolini was too busy to see him, Donovan put on his act. He said

10

to tell Il Duce that he was just as busy and could not wait indefinitely. If Mussolini could not see him he wanted to know so he could return home immediately. He turned brusquely and left.

He was scarcely back at his hotel when the message arrived that Il Duce would indeed see him at three o'clock the next afternoon. An inveterate note taker, Donovan wrote in his diary, "I went to the Venetian palace at 2:50. At the door were two sentries, not particularly smart. Inside the corridor was a major domo, dressed like a Park Avenue doorman. I gave him my letter and he went to the telephone. A moment later a plain-clothesman arrived with a paper and compared it with the signature on my letter. I tried to get my letter back but they confiscated that. We climbed two flights of stairs, he pressed a button, a door opened and a footman in livery ushered me into a waiting room."

Promptly at three o'clock an attendant led him to what Donovan perceived to be the Council Room. Another door was opened and he entered a large room. At the far end Mussolini sat at a plain table. He rose, walked around the table and shook Donovan's hand. He asked Donovan how long he had been in France during the war. Donovan replied "nineteen months."

"Wounded?" was the next question.

"Three times," was the reply. Donovan made points when he added that he had received Italy's Croci di Guerra. Mussolini dropped his formality.

"And now you wish to go to Eritrea. Why?"

Striking at his vanity Donovan said he was interested in seeing the spirit of the Italian soldier. "I did not think much of the Italian troops in the World War—neither the discipline of the men or quality of the officers. After the war I saw your officers chased by crowds through the streets of Milan," he said.

Mussolini angrily retorted, "It is different now. You would see a vast change."

Donovan continued pressing his point concluding with the statement, "If Italy is to have a new Empire, she must have a new Tenth Legion."

He had hit pay dirt. Mussolini excitedly clapped his hands and replied, "Tenth Legion, that is right."

More discussion followed with Mussolini finally stating, "You will go to Africa. First to Libya, then to Abyssinia. You will see our colonization, you will see our soldiers and you will see for yourself that Italy has a new Tenth Legion."

Donovan visited Asmara, Adsum, and Benghazi where he stayed in a striped silk tent beside Marshal Badoglio's headquarters. He correctly analyzed the Marshal and was able to utilize that knowledge ten years later when OSS tried to break Italy away from the Axis.

Returning to America, Donovan tried to impress on American military authorities they were wrong about the quality of the new Italian fighting men. Their morale was excellent and they had improved artillery and planes. Donovan was alone in predicting a sweeping Italian victory.

A year later Donovan visited Spain to observe the civil war raging there. He carefully noted the weapons supplied the Loyalists by Russia and the weaponry given Franco's Fascists by the Germans and Italians. Of particular interest was the new German 88-mm gun that served as an anti-aircraft, anti-tank and anti-personnel weapon. Returning to America, Donovan discussed it with General Malin Craig, then Army Chief of Staff. No corrections were made in America's ordnance to counteract it and in 1942 that same gun almost defeated American forces in Africa. It inflicted frightful casualties.

Donovan and Chennault, each in his own way, made President Roosevelt and his Cabinet aware the war was not too far off. Stilwell in China and Eifler in the Hawaiian Islands also were preparing for the inevitable conflict.

2

In March, 1941, Eifler went to active status in the army. He was convinced Japan was about ready to strike. He remained with his Company K, 35th Infantry at Schofield Barracks, Honolulu.

A friendly competition developed between Co. K and Co. L, commanded by six-foot-five John Coughlin. His men were devoted to him. Seldom did Eifler hear him raise his voice. He would survey a problem area and calmly assess it, then pass on his orders almost like a request. Behind the shy grin, the lanky officer proved a man of strength. Eifler sensed something else in Coughlin. Here was a man who treated him as his equal while other company commanders did not—because Eifler was the only reserve officer commanding a company in the regiment.

Company L was rated tops in the regiment. Company K was at the bottom. Eifler posted these standings on his bulletin board and told his men they would remain there until they erased them. As his Company faced a challenge in the other men, Eifler found his own challenge in Coughlin. Cognizant of the difference in their military backgrounds, Eifler began studying every possible minute. He had to overcome the West Point barrier that kept him apart from his fellow officers. He pored through books on discipline, military tactics and strategy, maintenance, medical, sanitation, police, demolition, and physical combat publications. He was determined to pull himself up to what he considered the level of Coughlin.

Day by day his men took forced hikes, engaged in target practice, and fought each other hand to hand.

One weekend, Company K had the guard duty at the Red Hill Ammunition Depot. Eifler posted his sentries with customary orders. The man on the back gate was instructed that no one was to enter.

Several hours later two officers in a staff car drove up to the gate and asked the sentry to let them through. He refused. One officer leaned out the window. The three stars of a lieutenant general gleamed in the morning sunlight.

"Soldier, do you know who I am?" he asked.

"Yes, sir, you are General Short," the sentry grimly replied. "But my orders are no one is to enter this gate."

The general shifted. His aide looked pale. The general held up his hand and motioned the driver on. They drove off.

Eifler sat calmly in the orderly room that morning. He had processed some routine paperwork. His sergeant was working at his own desk. Suddenly the door burst open. He looked up and saw General Short and his aide striding purposefully into the room. Eifler stood and saluted.

"Are you the commanding officer, Captain?" he snapped.

"Yes, sir, I am," Eifler replied.

"Did you post one of your men at the rear gate with orders no one was to pass—not even the commanding general?" he continued.

By now Eifler had learned never to give ground or try to avoid a chewing if one was coming. He had no intention of trying to offer an excuse.

"Sir, those were my orders," he said.

The General stood for a minute, a smile crossing his face. He was remembering his early military career.

"Your man complied with your orders, Captain. He did his job. You are to be complimented." He turned and departed.

Eifler sat down to think it over.

In Burma, Chennault was thinking over his strategy to utilize his P-40's to the fullest extent. Suddenly his plan to bomb Japan surfaced. It was labeled JB PAPER 355.

On May 28, 1941, the formal proposal was made to give Chennault an initial force of 66 twin-engine Lockheed Hudsons and Douglas DB-7s, along with pilots, bombardiers and crew for the attack. More planes and crews would be made available as soon as possible. The B-17s which Chennault wanted were out of the question. They were too scarce and too valuable to be put at risk.

As the paper work for Chennault's project began building Eifler was looking at his own paperwork. It was now early June and he received notice he was to get a new man, an outstanding athlete, Sgt. Vincent L. Curl. Eifler immediately went to other company commanders and tried to swap him. The 35th Regiment was loaded with top athletes. Even though his Company K was at the bottom he still preferred a good soldier to a good athlete.

Curl was not swappable. On the day of his arrival Eifler sent a jeep to the harbor to pick him up.

Curl's memory of their first meeting remained vivid for many years after. "When the jeep picked me up I was on the last leg of a trip to a real 'home.' I knew I was wanted and could do a good job. I couldn't wait to meet the new captain. I entered the orderly room and

14

saluted. The captain was working on some papers. He continued working for at least five minutes. Finally he looked up."

"So you're Sergeant Curl," he half-grunted.

"Yes, sir."

"Well, for your information, Sergeant, I tried to get rid of you before you got here," he blurted.

Curl blanched. "May I ask why, sir?"

"Yes. This is not an athletic regiment and an athletic company, and I don't need any goddamn athletes. I need soldiers."

Curl braced himself. "For the Captain's information, I can soldier as well as being an athlete," he replied.

Eifler paused. "For your information, Sergeant, you can prove it," he replied. "Take over the duties of first sergeant."

Sergeant Curl was finally home.

Field assignments and problems were continually thrown on his company, as Eifler relentlessly fought them into a proud fighting unit. The picture of physical fitness, he encouraged them in all forms of body-building activities.

One afternoon he stood before his men who had just completed an assignment. "Hell, you guys aren't as tough as you think," he goaded. "Not one of you could even knock me down."

The men looked at each other, not sure of themselves.

"Tell you what—who wants to try? Come on...I'll let you hit me in the belly as hard as you want."

A burly corporal couldn't resist. A chance to prove he could deck the captain was too good to pass up. He approached Eifler, a little unsure he meant what he had said. Eifler clasped his hands behind his back, looked calmly at him, and said: "Go ahead and try, soldier."

The corporal did just that. He threw his whole body behind the punch and struck squarely into the solar plexus. Eifler's body moved back a few inches. He grinned, infuriatingly. The other men watched the corporal return to his position.

"Tell you what," shouted Eifler, "you can all try—one at a time. Come on."

Seventy-seven men, one after another, approached Eifler and took their hardest swing at him. When the last was through he still stood there, grinning. He had not even been moved one step.

"Maybe you better toughen up a little more," he said before dismissing them.

In later relating the incident, he did admit to having a sore belly that night. "Seventy-seven men all hit differently," he said. "But I never let them know it made me sore."

Sometime later Curl was on another assignment as Eifler now had

15

a permanent first sergeant. This man was admirably suited to the job and had thirty years in the service. To him Eifler must have seemed like a kid.

One day a young soldier entered the orderly room. He reported to the first sergeant, whose desk was only five feet from Eifler's.

"Permission requested to speak with the captain," he said.

"What do you want to talk to him about?" asked the sergeant.

"I want to make a complaint against you," he replied.

Eifler was looking out of the corner of his eye. The sergeant turned red, then granted permission.

The soldier approached Eifler and saluted.

"Yes, what is it?" Eifler asked.

"The first sergeant has given me company punishment, extra duty. Under the 104th Article of War only a captain can give company punishment," he said.

"Yes, soldier, that's right. Any punishment the first sergeant gave you is hereby rescinded," Eifler told him.

The sergeant stiffened and turned even more red. He was angry.

"However," Eifler continued, "now that it has come to my attention, what was the extra duty given for?"

The soldier recited some infraction of the rules.

"How many days did he give you?" Eifler pursued.

"Three days, Captain," was the reply.

Eifler pondered. "Well, soldier, you have your choice. Court-martial or company punishment."

Sensing victory, the soldier answered quickly. "Company punishment, Captain."

"Same punishment, seven days. I think the sergeant was very lenient with you," he said calmly.

The soldier sucked in his breath, turned, and departed.

Eifler, without saying it, had told his sergeant: "Good work, Sergeant, you run the company as you see fit."

There were no further complaints to the captain.

Convinced Hawaii would be invaded, the troops of the 35th Infantry established well-concealed posts. Caves and brush areas were utilized. Areas were crisscrossed with machine-gun nests where the enemy might swarm ashore. Troops moved to their positions in the dark to be familiar with trails, bluffs, and all natural obstacles that might be turned to their advantage.

During this time Company K steadily improved in morale and achievement. Eifler issued his famous challenge that he would not ask his men to do anything he would not do. The trouble was, this included anything. He became heartened to hear his men declare they were going to "beat the old man."

On July 23, 1941 President Roosevelt wryly remarked, "It might be a good idea for the Chinese to bomb Japan," and gave the go ahead for Chennault's plan.

The plan was to be operational within five months, by October 31, 1941. Japan was to be bombed in November. It was hoped the bombing would inhibit Japanese aggression against Singapore, the Dutch East Indies and the Philippines as well as providing American airmen with valuable combat experience.

America was supposed to be kept in the dark. The State Department issued fake passports. These were the same officials who revoked the passports of Americans who fought in Spain. The State Dept. as well as the U.S. Cabinet and the President were all in agreement on the conspiracy. The airmen were told to reveal nothing about their mission. But too much had leaked. The June 23, 1941, issue of Time magazine informed its readers that 100 P-41s had reached Burma and would be flown by "crack U.S. Army Air Corps pilots" who had been allowed to resign their commissions. "Tall, bronzed American airmen have been quietly slipping away from east and west-coast ports making their way to Asia," American readers were informed.

Delay after delay kept the planes from being shipped. On November 21st, 49 ground crewmen for the bombers had embarked from California on the long trip to China. They were still at sea on December 6th. And on that same day 18 Hudson bombers still awaited transportation from Burbank.

On Sunday morning, December 7th, Eifler was awakened at 0755 by the phone. It was Sgt. Curl. Eifler was due to go on 24 hour duty at 1100.

"Captain, you'd better get up here. All hell has broken loose," came the agitated voice.

"Sergeant, have you been drinking?" was a logical question.

"Yes, sir, but a bunch of red planes are bombing Wheeler Field."

"I'm on the way," Eifler replied, hanging up.

Even with the foreknowledge of Japan's plans it was still difficult to accept that this was really it. His mind sought for other explanations. "Red on the planes"—maybe it was the old red and blue maneuvers. Well, as Officer of the Day it only meant he had to go in a few hours early. He could imagine the grumbling of fellow officers who had to give up their whole day.

But his mind played back that excited voice. He wondered if this was really it.

It was now 0800. The rumble of heavy gunfire swept through the bedroom. His wife watched from her bed.

"It's just the navy practicing," she said. "They've been at it for weeks."

He continued dressing as the firing became heavier. An ominous feeling crept over him. He looked out the window toward the harbor. Overhead a B-17 flew lazily toward the scene of the noise. Eifler relaxed. Surely the pilot had a radio and if the attack was real he would not be heading into the fight in a bomber. The feeling crept back once more. Now he began rushing. He told his wife it just might be real.

As he reached the front door she called out to him: "Aren't you going to take the medals with you?"

He thought, then said: "I don't think so, honey. I won't be needing them now."

"Carl, that is foolish after all the work you put in getting them. It won't hurt to take them with you."

She was right, he thought. It wouldn't hurt. If it was a maneuver for the day only, he couldn't return for them on Monday. To instill zest in his men he had borrowed the medals from two friends, George Roberts in customs and Bob Aitken, a reserve officer. He also had a special pistol, a .22 caliber on a .45 frame. Eifler had borrowed it to give his men an edge, since no one else had such a gun yet. He went to the bedroom and returned with a box containing the medals and the gun.

As he backed his car out, a Japanese-American soldier from across the street came out and headed for the bus stop. Eifler asked where he was going.

He replied, "Schofield, sir."

Eifler waved him into the car. As he pulled away, his wife gaily called: "Call me when you get there and tell me about the war."

On the way to Honolulu there were small clusters of people looking toward the harbor. Everyone seemed confused and a little bit frightened. Driving through the main part of the town, Eifler saw that all was quiet and serene. It had to be maneuvers.

He drove the speed limit but not over. A car sped by with a naval officer who seemed to believe it was real. Behind him a police car followed with two policemen. Eifler wondered if they would accept it when he said it was a maneuver.

The policemen stopped in front of the penitentiary, and one began flagging traffic. Just beyond was a slight bend in the road. Beyond that bend was a large pillar of smoke, and it came from Pearl

18

Harbor. He had to assume a storage tank was on fire. At the next corner a policeman was waving traffic away from Pearl Harbor and into the hills. Eifler asked the reason, and he said he only knew something was wrong. Eifler turned away at his direction, but at the next intersection he made the only decision he could make—to put himself with his men, regardless. A policeman waved him over behind a long line of stopped cars. He swung to the left and passed him. He waved wildly for Eifler to stop. Then as suddenly he leaped aside and just as wildly waved him on when he saw the uniform. Driving on he approached Fort Shafter, headquarters of the Islands. He was startled to find it calm. No unusual activity prevailed. The sentry was pacing back and forth in front of the guardhouse. Several minutes later he lay dead from a strafing plane.

Beyond that point he entered the Manalani Gardens, a tropical beauty spot and favorite of camera clubs. The nature of the surroundings with its brown grass and mesquite seemed to say all was well. He topped the grade and saw Pearl Harbor below. A battleship was on fire. It was the *Arizona*. She was the torch issuing forth the long black column. Both the brilliant red flames and instinct told him her wounds were mortal. He felt a tremendous surge of pride as he watched. In her death throes she was magnificent with every gun trained upward and spitting fire. He watched bombs falling in the water but could see no planes. The thick haze obscured them. It seemed as if the day was now ending. Yet a thousand fireflies danced in mad disarray from the decks of the now listing ship. A scene straight out of Dante's *Inferno*, he thought.

He turned to the young soldier and asked if he had ever been in battle. His age confirmed his negative reply.

"Well, hang on, soldier. You're going into one."

The doubts were gone. It was war. He moved forward once more, headed for the barracks and his command. He thought about the fortifications already prepared. The plans for prevention of sabotage flashed through his mind.

As he swung alongside the road running beside Pearl Harbor, a bomb struck just in front of a hospital ship at anchor. Another landed just a hundred yards away from his speeding automobile. He was surprised the concussion and noise were so slight. The speedometer registered 70 m.p.h. Ahead of him the concrete began jumping in the air like drops of spilled water. Then he heard the combined cacophony of an airplane engine and machine gun fire. As the bullets hit the road in front of him he thought what a lousy duck hunter this pilot would be—he didn't know how to lead. Six enemy planes, one by one, tried their luck, but all missed. The bullets marched in paths before him, on either side and behind him. It was obvious he was to be spared to fight this war.

He moved into a small canyon, thankful for some protection. At the bottom, on a straight stretch, another flight began its attack. Again the bullets danced around him. He stopped at one point to wave a group of people out from under a railroad bridge. They had made the mistake of seeking refuge under a military target. Before he could reach them a plane came in low with guns blazing. He dug into the earth with his face and body. Bullet after bullet poured into the group. He looked up at one of the last planes and past the red markings Curl had mentioned. He saw the grinning face of its Japanese pilot. And he with only his .22 pistol!

When he reached the groups he was amazed. It was incredible that not one of them had been hit in spite of the withering fire poured into them. He told them to disperse—this was war. They promptly disappeared.

When he returned to the car the young soldier had disappeared. Eifler never saw him again.

Finally he arrived at the quadrangle of the 35th Infantry. Machine guns were everywhere. He took the reports of his first sergeant and the first lieutenant and was pleased with their action. He had the company assembled inside and told them their training was now to be put to the test. Whereas they had known company punishment for dereliction of duty before, now the enemy would be dishing it out— and it was now death.

The men moved swiftly to their defensive positions.

They were assigned to take over the guard of Fort Shafter. Eifler moved into the guardhouse. The mess sergeant set up his kitchen in the latrine. It was the only place with immediate water and waste-disposal facilities. He didn't like it but agreed it was fairly sanitary.

The men were jittery. Rumors flowed everywhere. One colonel told the men Japanese paratroopers had been dropped in green uniforms with an orange sun on their left breast. They were to be shot on sight.

"Thank God the men did not carry out the orders," Eifler later remarked. "We would have lost a hell of a lot of delivery men, garbage men, and some Boy Scouts."

The Japanese fleet was nowhere to be found, but that did not stop the persistent rumor that Hawaii would be invaded. Eifler set his men around the hospital in two perimeters. The outside group had rifles, the inner men shotguns. Darkness fell on Honolulu. All was quiet. Soon the soft drone of planes could be heard. It increased until suddenly the brilliant searchlights of Pearl Harbor pierced the sky.

20

They locked into the planes. Eifler was looking at some papers when one of his men called to him, "Planes are over Pearl, sir. They've been picked up by the lights." A few minutes later he further reported, "Parachutists descending, sir."

Eifler replied: "Are they within range?"

"Yes, sir," was the answer.

"Open fire," was the final command.

Rifles crackled through the night. Now "firecrackers" began dropping in the perimeter area. A soldier named Kennington was standing beside Eifler. The firing was getting hotter. Kennington stepped back. Eifler feared he was showing the white feather and ordered him back into firing position.

He replied: "I'm hit, Captain." A bullet had struck him, and he was sent to the hospital. A tree limb was sheared off and lay across the walk in front of the guardhouse. A number of the doctors' cars were hit by fragments as well as one of Eifler's trucks. Finally the planes were gone, the firing stopped, and the lights went out. All was quiet. Everyone wondered how many men were dropped and what lay in store for them in the morning.

The next day the truth came out. There was no Japanese attack. The planes were American from an aircraft carrier. They had come in without proper identification signals and had been fired on, several being hit. The parachutists were American pilots. Fearing the worst, Eifler inquired as to their fate. Happily, they were not hit during their descent and lived to fly other planes. The "battle of December 8th" would long be remembered by the citizens of Honolulu.

One post on the side of a hill continually fired down on Company K's positions. It turned out to be a nervous air corps group. The situation finally resolved itself when they shot their own cook as he returned to camp one night.

Eifler was called into army headquarters and ordered to tell his men they were to discontinue shooting the lights out of police cars.

"I will relay the orders, sir, but my men are shooting at every light they see. It might be wiser for the police to turn their lights off like all other cars are doing," he said.

The police complied, and that problem was solved.

Another captain and Eifler were ordered to stop the indiscriminate firing of the various outposts. Eifler laid out the positions on a map. Then he had a phone installed in each one. He told the men to leave the phone alone except for incoming calls. He would call them when a shot was fired, and they would tell him the direction it came from. He could then lay out the lines and figure which guard post had fired. The firing immediately lessened, and in two days it had ceased.

After he made the report on this, he slid to the floor and went to sleep. It was his first sleep since that Sunday morning, some ninety hours earlier.

On the morning of December 12, Eifler sat in his office. The provost marshal entered with a guard carrying a sawed-off shotgun.

"Captain Eifler, come with me," he said.

His manner was that of an officer making an arrest. Eifler remembered World War I when so many men had been arrested for simply having a German name.

"Shall I turn my company over to my lieutenant, or will I be returning soon?" he asked.

"Turn command over to your lieutenant," the provost marshal replied.

Outside Eifler entered a car, getting into the back seat. It was occupied by the chief of police of Honolulu. The provost marshal sat on the other side. They drove away, then pulled up and stopped at the police station. The chief got out. "See you later, Carl." he said. Eifler half-expected to be asked to go in for interrogation. He was perplexed.

The next stop was at the Federal Building, where they went to the office of collector of customs. Suddenly the light dawned. The army had about four hundred aliens on Sand Island. Prior to December 7, the FBI and army and navy intelligence had compiled a list of people whose loyalty might be questioned at the time of an enemy attack. Company L, commanded by Captain Coughlin, had practically disappeared. They were now guarding this camp with its detainees.

After a few words of explanation, Eifler said: "And I am then to command this concentration camp?"

He was reprimanded for using that term and was told it was a detention camp for aliens and those suspected of possible enemy activities. The only drawback was no one could spare men to serve in his company. It was to be designated the 111th Military Police Company.

The colonel he was with said the problem of manning the camp had him stumped. Eifler had an idea. "I would prefer to build my own company from scratch. Will you give me authority to go out and pick up men from the streets, from ROTC and wherever else I can find them? I ask only one man from my outfit, for first sergeant, Vince Curl."

The colonel agreed it had merit, secured signed authority from the local general, and Eifler was in business.

With three army trucks they proceeded. They stopped able-

22

bodied men on the streets and ordered them in the trucks. They visited the university and selected ROTC men. From the local Home Guard they selected more. When they were finished they had two hundred and forty men. They needed sixty.

Eifler stationed some sergeants around the men and started calisthenics. They continued until the men started dropping out and were then dismissed. When they were down to sixty men they stopped. Now to select the noncoms. He established a race course one quarter of a mile in length and had them race. He was at the finish line. As the first man crossed he said: "You are senior sergeant." Each succeeding man got a lesser post until he had his quota.

Then, with his men lined up, he asked who could fire a gun. No one. He divided them into squads and issued them sawed-off shotguns. At the edge of the camp he set up some boxes for targets. He taught the men how to load and fire. Ten minutes later his first squad was taken out and relieved the guard positions.

He saluted Captain Coughlin and told him he was relieving his men. As L Company rolled away, it struck him how odd it was that he had left his own well-trained company and relieved an even better-trained company—and now stood guard with sixty raw recruits. The inmates immediately started the rumor he was instructing his men on how to shoot them.

The sixty men went on duty immediately, later enlisting in the army. It was a point of interest that forty-seven out of the sixty went on to become commissioned officers.

Eifler's headquarters were approximately one hundred yards from the main compound. A large colonial-style home with approximately fourteen rooms was more than adequate. He selected a comfortable screened room upstairs and began operations.

One week later he was ordered to reactivate the 811th MP Company which was to be brought to full strength. Most of the men came from the 298th Infantry, a local National Guard regiment. He interviewed each man to determine his skills and background to better utilize his talents.

One young soldier gave his name which was the same as one of the detainees in the compound. Eifler asked if he was any relation.

"Yes, sir. He is my father," was the dutiful reply.

"Step out of line, soldier," Eifler replied.

Later in his office he told him: "Son, I have done many things, but never have I put a gun on a man's back to stand guard over his father. You will be going back to your regiment. Do you want to see your father first?"

He did. Eifler left them alone for a short period. When the young soldier left, Eifler visited the father. They were old friends. He was American but of German ancestry. Early in Hitler's stormy career, in a public conversation, this man had expressed his admiration of the Nazi leader. This meant nothing to Eifler, who considered the man extremely disputatious. He would always take the other side of any argument.

"Carl, you know darned well I am as good an American as you are," he said.

"Yes," Eifler agreed, "but we are in an unusual situation. You are a prisoner and I am camp commander. I can do nothing but keep you here. There is something you can do for me and for your country, though."

"You name it. I'll do it," he replied.

"Okay. The main worry of any commander is knowing what is going on inside. If anything is being hatched we need to know it at once. I want to know what is being discussed in the tents at night and especially any escape plans. Will you do this?"

"Yes, you can count on me," the man replied.

"Fine, I'll arrange with the lieutenant in charge that any time you give him the sign—say scratching your left ear—he will notify me. I will then call in a dozen prisoners for general interrogation, and you will be one of them. Then we can talk."

And that was the way it worked. Eifler was able to block several incidents that would have been embarrassing. There never was an escape attempt while he was commander.

Sergeant Curl came in one day to discuss a bet he had made with a lieutenant about the smuggling of items into the compound. Eifler had told the guards they had to be more concerned that he himself would smuggle things in than the enemy. If he ever succeeded in smuggling anything in they would have to answer to him. He was always thoroughly searched. Curl had told the lieutenant that, hell, he could put a machine gun in the center of the compound before the guards even knew it. Angrily the lieutenant bet him $20 he could not do it. Curl then told Eifler because he knew that if he succeeded the lieutenant would turn on him. Eifler told him to try it. The entire guard force knew of the bet. The day Curl decided to do it the guard on the gate asked if he had the gun on the truck. Curl said he did. The guard laughed and passed him, which was his mistake.

Curl set the gun up in the heart of the compound.

The lieutenant was furious. He came to Eifler and demanded that Curl be court-martialed. Eifler told him to go ahead and draw up the charges—but while he was at it to also draw up charges against himself.

24

"What for?" the lieutenant asked.

"Gambling with an enlisted man," he replied.

The lieutenant changed his mind. The close searching did continue, however, and with good results. A Filipino carpenter was caught with a hunting knife in his gas mask. When asked why, he said he wanted to kill one of those sons of bitches in detention.

One night the provost marshal called to say he was bringing in fifty women detainees. A separate building was constructed to house the women. Eifler requested his wife be matron. Permission was granted. He wanted someone he knew and could trust. At the time she was employed as a civil service employee for the quartermaster corps at Schofield barracks.

The day arrived. The cars pulled up, and the women began unloading. The bottom floor of the building was divided into a kitchen and mess hall. Upstairs was the barracks. Mrs. Eifler was standing in front of the women. They were about equally divided between Orientals and Caucasians. As Captain Eifler entered, he found them quietly seated around the mess hall tables. They ranged in education and social standing from prostitutes to a member of the royal family of Japan.

Eifler had already contacted headquarters earlier for a set of regulations to govern these people. He was told the last time the United States had conducted such a camp was during the Civil War. There were no regulations. He was on his own.

He addressed the women: "The Oriental women in this group will elect themselves a leader. The Caucasian women will do the same. Then the group as a whole will elect an overall leader. If a problem arises you will take it to your ethnic leader. If she cannot solve it she will take it to the overall leader. If it is still not solved she will take it to Mrs. Eifler. If she cannot solve it she will bring it to me. I am a soldier. All I know about handling problems is to handle them as a soldier would. I assure you if something is brought to me you will wish to God that it had not been." He turned and left. There were never any problems brought to him.

He also put into effect a basic rule he always had used with his troops. His men could eat all they wanted, but they could never throw anything out. A guard stood over the garbage pail, and if a man came up with food on his plate it was put in the refrigerator with his name on it. At the next meal the man ate the leftovers first before anything else. The detainees learned to live with it, and Eifler's food budget remained the lowest per person of any commander in the area.

The women became a source of delight to Eifler. He always

inspected their quarters in white uniform and gloves. He gave them a rating of 0 to 100. They never scored below 90. He would run his white gloves in the pots, over the range, and even over the garbage cans. Later on they got into the 98s and even 99s. One time he could find nothing on his gloves. He placed a chair in the center of their kitchen, ran his hand across a rafter, and came down with dust. They got a 99. When he eventually turned the command over to his executive officer, Lieutenant Springer, they received 100 for the first time. They were not overjoyed, however. Mrs. Eifler asked them why.

"Because the captain didn't give it to us," they replied.

The army had been holding the first Japanese prisoner of war. He was part of a two-man submarine crew. His partner was killed, either at time of capture or when the sub was sunk. When Eifler learned he was to have this man, he ordered a small building built to house only him. He did not want him held with the other detainees.

The man was a typical Japanese militarist—polite but aloof. He spoke no English. Eifler spoke a little Japanese. Soon they were able to communicate a little better.

Humiliated at his capture, the Japanese soldier begged for the opportunity to commit hara-kiri.

Eifler, in essence, told him to be his guest.

"Not in this filthy place," he answered.

"This place is as good as any," Eifler replied. "Go ahead and kill yourself."

"As an officer, Captain, I ask that you take me to your flagpole, give me a knife and leave me," was his reply.

Eifler had no intention of allowing him a ceremonial death. "Lieutenant, this is a clean hut. Why don't you just spill your guts on the floor right here, and it will all be over with," was his final offer.

The conversation ended and the Japanese remained a model prisoner.

Three weeks had passed since Eifler had been given the women to guard. He sat on his upstairs porch looking at their compound, then at the men's. There were many husbands and wives. He thought how he would feel if his wife was locked up just one hundred yards away and they couldn't even see each other. He could see no harm in letting them have a Sunday afternoon together. His wife agreed. That afternoon he announced that those men who had wives in the compound could visit with them the next Sunday afternoon.

Tension was high as the men entered the mess hall that day. The women were in the kitchen. Their reactions differed greatly. One woman launched herself over a three-foot counter, wrapping her arms around her husband's neck. Much more reserved was Dr.

Morrie, female, a member of the royal family of Japan. Her husband was also a doctor. He walked silently back toward the kitchen. His wife approached him. About three feet in front of him she stopped and bowed. He returned the bow, and she bowed again. This was repeated a third time. They then went to a table, sat down, and talked in low tones.

One afternoon the lady doctor questioned Mrs. Eifler.

"Do you hate the Japanese?" she asked.

"No," replied Mrs. Eifler. "Our countries are at war, but I don't really hate the Japanese people. Perhaps if they would kill my husband I would hate."

Dr. Morrie became excited. "Oh, but they will not hurt the captain. When they come I will tell them they are not to hurt the captain," she explained.

Sand Island had two boats: one small speedboat for personnel and a larger ferry-type boat that could carry more people.

One day as Eifler boarded the speedboat to return to camp, he observed Sergeant Curl waiting for the ferry. Under Curl's arm was a shoebox.

"Hop in, Sergeant. I'll give you a lift," he shouted.

Curl shifted his feet. "No thanks, Captain. I'll wait for the boat," he replied.

It seemed odd, but maybe he wanted to be alone, Eifler thought. The smaller, faster boat put Eifler ashore on the island before Curl got off his boat. Eifler got in his car and waited for Curl. He soon appeared.

"Come on, Curl, damn it. Get in."

The sergeant complied. They drove off. Eifler eyed the shoebox again. Curl stared straight ahead, obviously ill at ease.

"What do you have in that shoebox, Sergeant?" he asked.

"Captain, would you believe this is a sea gull?" was the earnest reply.

By now Eifler was approaching his headquarters. He swung into the driveway.

"Sergeant, what do you say you and I go inside and pull a couple of feathers out of that sea gull?" he said.

After several "feathers" had been removed, Eifler handed the bottle back to Curl. In so doing he had in fact given approval for him to take the bottle into the noncoms' quarters. If apprehended by another officer and brought to court-martial, Eifler's neck would be out a mile.

As he anticipated, however, the evidence was quickly depleted and disposed of. The sea gull never stooled on either.

A few days later Curl came in with a problem. There was no water. A freighter in the harbor had dropped anchor, rupturing the water line. Soon they were in real trouble. All the toilets were filled. There was no water for cooking or washing. He ordered his men to the harbor and told them to find the main water line. They did. A member of the harbor master's crew came along and asked if he had permission to tie into the line.

Eifler said he did not.

"You will have to disconnect," he was told.

Eifler pulled out his .45 automatic. "Now that I think of it, this is my authority," he replied. "You get to your bosses and tell them to get to my bosses and settle this thing. In the meantime I'll continue pumping water."

The man left. Eifler stationed a guard and told him no one was to stop the water. It took two weeks for repairs but in the meantime they had water.

Back in Washington people were scrambling in all directions. Rumors were rampant. The Pentagon was trying to fit the right men in the proper slots. China had one of the lowest priorities but still needed an American commander.

Stilwell was the logical choice even with his problems with Kai-shek. Stilwell made it clear he much preferred commanding an Infantry Division in combat but might consider going back to China only on condition he was Commander and not subject to any restrictions by Kai-shek.

T.V. Soong worked on Kai-shek and soon reported all was clear and Stilwell's wishes would be respected.

On January 23, 1942 he was officially appointed Commander in China and given the rank of a Lt. General which he would need to deal with the Chinese, British and French. Within three weeks he was on his way back to the Orient.

On February 17, 1942, a wire for Eifler came from Washington. It read: "Are you available for a Far East assignment?" It was signed "M.P. Goodfellow, Lt. Col., General Staff, G2."

Immediately Eifler thought of General Stilwell. In some way, the General had to be behind the inquiry.

The provost marshal suggested Eifler simply wire back saying "Not available."

Eifler said he had never turned down an order yet, nor did he want his record to so indicate. If it was to be turned down, it would have to be done by someone else.

The return wire bore the name of General Emmons, commander of the Hawaii Department. It said Eifler was not available unless the assignment was urgent.

Several days later a wire came back reading: "Glad you are joining this operation. Will have orders issued assigning you immediately to Coordinator of Information. Leave as quickly as possible for Washington. Wire how much travel money you will need. We will square travel and other expenses later." It again bore the name of Lieutenant Colonel Goodfellow.

Eifler was puzzled over the conflicting telegrams. He knew General Emmons had said he was not available. Yet the next wire from Washington said he was to be assigned at once to COI (Coordinator of Information).

The true story came out years later.

Colonel Goodfellow, prior to the war, was a newspaper publisher in the Midwest. One of his personal friends was Secretary of War Stimson. Stimson told him any time he needed to use his name, to do so. The one and only time he took Stimson's offer during the war was when he received General Emmons's wire refusing to transfer Eifler. He sat down and issued orders for Eifler to report to Washington at once. Then he signed the name of the Secretary of War.

Eifler's actual transfer, therefore, was effected by forgery.

The day his transfer came through, he called Curl into the office. "Sergeant Curl, this is where you and I part company," he said.

Curl was startled. "What do you mean, Captain?"

"I've been transferred to Washington and will be going back to the Far East," he explained.

"Take me along, Captain," he implored.

"Curl, don't be silly. Captains are a dime a dozen. Good sergeants are worth their weight in gold."

Curl thought for a few moments. "I'll take a bust," he said, finally.

Eifler was deeply moved and felt highly complimented. For a man with Curl's service and in his position to be willing to become a buck private and head into the unknown was a fine personal tribute. He stood up and shook his hand. "I'll do what I can," he promised.

On the afternoon of March 17, 1942, he bade a sad farewell to his wife and son, Sergeant Curl, and the rest of his officers and men. He wondered if he would ever see any of them again as the Pan American clipper took off for America.

3

In Washington, the need for a coordinated intelligence organization had been a subject of serious discussion through the first three months of 1941. Roosevelt recognized the need for a central organization responsible for gathering and coordinating intelligence information world-wide.

Politics, as always, played an important role, not only in the creation of such an all encompassing organization but in the choice of the man who would head it.

Among the candidates rumored to be on Roosevelt's list was William Donovan. Since travelling to Ethiopia during the Italian campaign and to Spain during the civil war, Donovan had frequently been used by Roosevelt as the eyes and ears of the White House. In 1940 he had made trips into the Balkans, even attempting to keep Yugoslavia and Greece from joining the Axis. His reports were carefully weighed by Roosevelt who clearly saw the course of events and knew where they were heading.

William Stephenson, known as "Intrepid," who had met Donovan while on a quiet recruiting trip in Canada and the U.S., advised British Intelligence that Donovan might be of help"..., perhaps a vital role, but it may not be consistent with orthodox diplomacy nor confined in its channels." Nothing could have better described Donovan's actions and his effectiveness.

Aware of Hitler's timetable for subjugating the Balkans, Churchill sought a way to sabotage or at least delay it. Who better to go but Donovan representing neutral America. The British invited Donovan and transported him to the beleaguered area to review their front line installations and the personnel manning them.

Although unsuccessful in his attempts to convince King Boris and the Bulgarian leaders to abandon their pro-German stance, he did cause them to hesitate before allowing German troops passage through Bulgaria to attack the British in Greece. Churchill sought a delay of twenty-four hours. Donovan's tactics gave Churchill eight days.

The Nazis were not unaware of Donovan's actions and termed his Bulgarian trip "an impudent act" by President Roosevelt. While he was in conference with King Boris, the Nazis stole Donovan's diplomatic passport. The Orient Express was held up twenty minutes while the American legation made it possible for him to cross into Yugoslavia where a duplicate passport awaited him. Dr. Goebbels in Berlin gave worldwide publicity to the incident stating the American State Department had ordered Donovan's immediate recall because he had dishonored his uniform and sullied his diplomatic status by getting himself into a state of complete drunkenness in a Sofia cabaret. They further added he was to be arraigned before a Special Court.

Finally Roosevelt put to rest the many rumors circulating about who would head the intelligence office by appointing yachting friend, Vincent Astor. Astor captained his own oceangoing yacht from time to time to gather bits of naval intelligence for the President. Roosevelt also seriously considered the appointment of New York City's Mayor, Fiorello "Little Flower" LaGuardia.

Though seeming to be sitting quietly on the sidelines Donovan was watching the dialogue. When Secretary of the Navy Knox asked him about what he had garnered on his forays into the European war he wrote a paper on the methods Britain used to gather its information in foreign countries. The paper, which included the full extent of the information and knowledge given Donovan by the leaders of British Intelligence, was later to become the genesis of American clandestine operations.

In his quest to establish one central intelligence agency, Donovan pointed out to the President that the U.S. had eight separate "fact-finding" agencies in the government: Army G-2, Navy ONI, the Federal Bureau of Investigation, the State Department's overseas attachés, the Department of Commerce's customs inspectors, the Secret Service, the Labor Department's Immigration Services and the Federal Communications Commission. All of their reports were either put on the President's desk or interpreted by each department busy looking out for its own interests.

In the report to Knox, Donovan wrote: "Intelligence operations should not be controlled by party exigencies. It is one of the most vital means of national defense. As such it should be headed by someone appointed by the President directly responsible to him and to no one else. It should have a fund solely for the purpose of foreign investigation and the expenditures under this fund should be kept secret and made solely at the discretion of the President."

Knox sent the report to Roosevelt but no action was taken for over a month while Roosevelt continued debating the creation of such a unit.

The British were pushing for Donovan's appointment with

everything they could conjure up. When Roosevelt asked Donovan for a report on the theory and practice of clandestine service William Stephenson, and Menzies, head of British Intelligence, supplied him with information to strengthen his hand. They made it very clear to the President that they favored Donovan's appointment.

Army and Navy Intelligence formed a solid opposition to the creation of such an organization. Into the fray came two major British intelligence figures. One was Chief of British Naval Intelligence, Admiral John Godfrey and his assistant, Lieutenant Commander Ian Fleming who later created the fictional James Bond. Their strong arguments in support of Donovan bore great weight.

What seemed to finally goad Roosevelt into action was the breakthrough of the German warships into the Atlantic. The German battleship *Bismarck* and the heavy cruiser *Prinz Eugen* were suddenly free and wreaking havoc. A single shell from the *Bismarck* sank the British battle cruiser *Hood*. In the same battle the British battleship *Prince of Wales* was badly damaged. Roosevelt feared the arrival of the German ships in the Caribbean.

On May 27, 1941, Roosevelt issued a proclamation "that an unlimited national emergency exists and requires the strengthening of our defenses to the extreme limit of our national power and authority." The stage now was set for the establishment of a permanent central intelligence organization and it was necessary to name the director.

At 12:30 p.m. on June 18, 1941, Roosevelt appointed Donovan Coordinator of Information, having agreed to the points outlined in Donovan's report which he had received from Knox. A lesser known provision was that Donovan was to receive no salary but would be entitled to actual necessary expenses. In a move designed to show that the government would not be overly generous, Donovan was forced to bear the expense for the telephone scramblers put into his residence.

Donovan resigned from his lucrative law firm. He was given the rank of Colonel.

One of Donovan's few intimates was Colonel G. Edward "Ned" Buxton. Donovan had known him as a battalion commander in World War I. Buxton had been Sgt. Alvin York's commanding officer and was responsible for transforming York from a conscientious objector to a national hero. Buxton was called to service by Donovan and served as the head of the Oral Intelligence Unit which interviewed and picked the brains of passengers arriving in America from Europe.

Another official of the fledgling organization was Preston Goodfellow, publisher of the Brooklyn Eagle. Goodfellow had been a critic of Roosevelt during the time Roosevelt had attempted to "pack" the U.S. Supreme Court. His editorials had been entirely opposed to Roosevelt's actions. Goodfellow was knowledgeable, had contacts and an analytical mind. He was to serve in an important upper level capacity for the balance of the war.

As Donovan reviewed the situation he noted few positive aspects of American preparedness. He was concerned not only with numbers of military personnel but the fighting spirit and innovative mood of his countrymen.

In 1940 the U.S. army totalled less than half a million men. In the fall of 1941 the new figure was 1,638,086. But the thinking of the military was still based on traditional or conventional warfare.

The weakness of that viewpoint was brought home both force-fully and humorously during military maneuvers that same fall. Both the Senior officers and 20,000 residents of Monroe, Louisiana, were witness to it.

In the midst of maneuvers in and around the little town people were enjoying the beautiful weather. Children played in the parks. Handsome young men flirted with the young girls while drinking nothing stronger than beer. They were admirable in their behavior and made themselves completely agreeable. But suddenly one evening the situation changed. The young men whipped out pistols, rifles and submachine guns. They commandeered buses and private vehicles. They entered the homes of civic officials and arrested them. They took over all public utilities. A Piper Cub circled the city dropping leaflets telling the people an invading army was on the way and resistance would be futile.

While the citizens tried to collect their wits the "army" did arrive in trucks with screaming sirens, smoke bombs and firecrackers. Machine guns, mortars and antitank guns were set up at strategic locations. Announcements were made in a local newspaper prohibit-ing church meetings and any kind of public gathering and proclaim-ing that food, automobiles and gasoline were now rationed. At the same time a group of Fifth Columnists, all local young men, began passing out pamphlets welcoming the invaders.

The crowning event was the appearance of "General Squarehead" who rode into town wearing a German World War I helmet, flanked by a squad of "storm troopers." General Squarehead was actually Cadet Ed Glusman of Louisiana State Universities Reserve Officer Training Corps. The eight hundred invaders and four hundred advance Fifth Columnists were also students from LSU.

In short order the citizens of Monroe began understanding the situation. After all, military maneuvers were going on all around them so the occupation had to be a part of those games. They entered into the spirit of their occupation.

The actual maneuvers consisted of Red and Blue armies. The City of Monroe was well within the Blue Army lines. Its commander, Colonel Dwight Eisenhower was astounded to hear of the Monroe occupation by "enemy forces." The Red Army could not possibly have moved that far north. Immediately a mechanized column was dispatched to recapture the city. The Red Army headquarters were equally baffled. Their commander wanted to find out who the fool was that moved that deep into Blue territory. All Red Army units were accounted for, none in that area.

Intelligence sources of both armies reported the city was still under military control. Both agreed to send umpires to find out just what was going on.

A military vehicle with a white flag flying from its antenna reached the outskirts of the city. The umpires, a lieutenant colonel and a captain were forced to walk with an escort of the guerillas. They walked down the silent main street where the citizens gathered to watch what seemed to be an old time "shoot-out." General Squarehead with his adjutant awaited them.

"We need to know which unit of the Blue Army you are," the Colonel demanded.

"Why?" was General Squarehead's reply.

"So we can keep our records straight."

With the revelation that the occupiers were ROTC students from LSU, the military command exploded. Colonel Eisenhower, receiving the news, turned beet red.

"College hijinks," he roared. "Send out an order we want no more ROTC units to be involved in the maneuvers."

Censured and unappreciated the students returned to their campus. The lesson, however, was not lost on General Dwight Eisenhower some time later as he put his agents and guerrilla forces behind the lines for the North Africa invasion. The lesson was also duly noted by Colonel William Donovan the new director of COI who was grateful these brash young men had made his point.

Even before the July 11th date creating the COI, Donovan's mind was searching out personnel of high and unusual caliber.

On July 10, 1941, he formulated R&A in his mind and went to Archibald MacLeish, Librarian of Congress for advice. MacLeish told him the COI could count on the Library to fully cooperate in any way possible.

On July 28, MacLeish called a meeting of his Library staff and representatives of the National Archives, the American Council of

34

Learned Societies, the Social Science Research Council and leading social scientists from many leading universities. Following this meeting MacLeish and his committee made recommendations which were almost completely followed. Dr. James P. Baxter III, President of Williams College accepted the post of Chief of R&A on July 31, 1941.

The work continued and by the end of October a most impressive group of men had been selected. All commanded respect in the 35 universities from which they had been recruited. They represented over 40 languages and dialects.

Other divisions were added and additional colleges lost top academicians as the COI brain trust began directing its intellectual assets into war channels.

Two months before Pearl Harbor the COI research staff had grown to nearly two hundred. It became the largest collection of top ranked educators and scholars ever gathered together in a single government agency. Top professors from the social science departments in all universities were brought aboard. In addition specialists in every area of intelligence were recruited. By war's end R & A had recruited over sixteen hundred social scientists from Washington alone. It was a national university of the highest quality. It had never been equalled before nor has it since.

Teams of behavioral scientists studied the German mind and psyche as well as the Italian, Japanese and Russian. How might the enemy react to a given situation? What then should be our response?

Unaware of how all these events eventually melded to produce the new methods of war into which America was now inexorably headed, Eifler flew east toward the mainland. He sat meditating on the plane, his huge stump-like fingers tousling his hair. The sunset over the Pacific was beautiful beyond description as the plane raced toward the West Coast, but was at complete odds with the inner conflicts that tormented him. His mind returned to the camp in Hawaii. The new commander would function well, he knew. What did trouble him was the possibility of the Islands being invaded. The Rising Sun had turned out a juggernaut that would continue rolling forward before ever being slowed down and reversed. The thought of his 35th Infantry fighting on the beaches and in the hills without him was particularly disturbing.

What really lay ahead? What in the hell was Coordinator of Information? A special Stilwell outfit? How much could he tell his wife?

On March 8, 1942, he landed in San Francisco. He cleared customs. As he identified himself at the Agricultural Department, a

Lieutenant Colonel Harris suddenly appeared and looked him over.

"Captain, are you going into town?" he asked.

Eifler said he was.

"Well, fine. Wait a few minutes and I'll drive you in."

Eifler knew this was a contact. To his trained mind it was far more than a coincidence. Some thirty minutes later, however, Eifler began to wonder if he had mistakenly read something into those few words. Again, his past training told him to wait.

Suddenly the officer appeared once more.

"Okay, Captain, let's go," he said. In the car he asked, "Have you decided on a hotel yet?"

Eifler shook his head.

"Fine. I think the Palace would be a good one for you."

The next few blocks were driven in silence. Eifler was not going to volunteer anything. It was up to the Colonel to make his move.

"Have you any idea what your assignment is to be?"

Eifler looked straight ahead. If this was really not his contact, then it was none of his damned business. If it was, he was testing Eifler to find out if he would tell his purpose, or at least what he felt his purpose was to be.

"No, sir, I haven't," he finally replied. "I think it may be connected with General Stilwell and an assignment to China."

The Colonel said nothing. The rest of the trip was made in silence. After checking into the Palace Hotel, the two men went into the dining room and ate. When finished, the officer asked Eifler to accompany him. They walked down the street a short distance and into a plain office. Here the colonel picked up the telephone. He did not dial but waited a few seconds and said: "Colonel Goodfellow, please."

Eifler knew Goodfellow was in Washington, and this had to be a direct line. He listened to one side of the conversation.

"Yes, sir, he is here... Yes, he evidently does... He mentioned General Stilwell and China... Yes, he will be on the plane tomorrow morning." He hung up the phone and turned to Eifler. From the desk drawer he removed an envelope. He handed it over.

"Captain, this is your plane ticket and your priority. Only a member of the White House can bump you off the plane. You leave at 1300 tomorrow. Good luck."

They shook hands, and Eifler returned to his room.

The next day he looked down on the city as the plane soared eastward. From the fringes of the war he now headed into the heart of his country's capital. The news was very bad.

The flight arrived on schedule in Washington, D.C. He got a ride into town and proceeded to the Army-Navy Club where reservations had been made for him. At every turn the name of Colonel Goodfellow appeared to be magic. He had not overlooked a single item. The following morning Eifler reported to the mysterious Q Building where the COI offices were quartered. He finally stood face to face with Colonel Goodfellow. They found themselves quite at ease as they discussed the flight and general conditions. Suddenly Colonel Goodfellow put it to Eifler straight.

"Captain, we are sending a group of saboteurs to China. We want you to command them. Will you accept?"

It was completely unexpected. "Saboteurs," he thought. His mind was not filled with intrigue or excitement. Quite the contrary. He saw a quick succession of the things saboteurs did—assassinations, forgery, robbery, and the like. His background of law enforcement rebelled—he totally rejected this sort of activity. His own opinion of saboteurs held that death was too good for them.

His military training prevailed over his own internal objections, however. He knew he had to do his duty regardless of danger or whether or not he liked it. He did not know how long he tumbled the thoughts over in his mind.

"I'd like to think about it for a while, sir," he finally replied. "Can I see you tomorrow with my answer?"

Goodfellow nodded his approval. Eifler rose and left the room. He walked the streets of Washington for a while. Then he had some drinks and finally ate dinner. He argued constantly with his own convictions and scorn for saboteurs.

In his room that evening he knew he must do what his country asked of him, regardless of his own feelings. He turned and suddenly found his own image in the mirror over the dresser. Unable to face himself, he reached for a whiskey bottle and threw it at the mirror, shattering it over the rug. Then he went to bed. The next morning he showered, dressed, and ate a light breakfast before returning to Goodfellow's office. He was ushered in and stood before the colonel, who said nothing. He awaited Eifler's decision.

"Yes, sir. I'll do it," he finally said.

The colonel smiled. "Good. Now what men do you want? Do you have any in mind?"

"Yes, sir. I want my first sergeant."

Goodfellow's smile dropped. "No, I don't mean that kind," he said firmly.

They discussed several other points. Eifler left to spend the rest of the day in thought about men and supplies. The next morning he returned to Colonel Goodfellow's office.

"Have you the men you want for your unit?" he was again asked.

"Yes, sir. My first sergeant," replied Eifler calmly.

"I said I didn't mean that type," the colonel replied a bit irritably.

Eifler had no other names, so they went into more detail about the area of operation and what was expected.

The next day Goodfellow again asked for the list.

"Sir, I would like my first sergeant," persisted Eifler.

"All right, you can have your goddamned sergeant," he exploded. "Now who else?"

It was the only time Eifler was ever to see him lose his temper. Eifler gave him more names. Captain John Coughlin; Captain Archie Chun Ming, a doctor from Hawaii; and Lieutenant Bob Aitken.

Goodfellow was relieved.

"That's better. See Colonel Williams, and he will get out the necessary orders."

Eifler was dubious about Chun Ming. He seriously doubted if even the powerful COI could get him. Colonel Williams dismissed his fears.

It was a matter of just a few days before the officers were in Washington. The first to arrive was Captain Coughlin. He greeted Eifler with his usual shy smile as he slid his lanky frame into a chair.

"John, I find myself in a very strange, unorthodox but powerful situation," Eifler began. "I need an executive officer. You are senior to me. I want you—but it is your decision. If you want it, okay. If not, I'll have you transferred anywhere you choose."

Coughlin didn't blink or hesitate. "I'm with you with both feet," he replied.

The following days were spent apprising Coughlin of what Eifler knew of the situation so far. Needless to say, Coughlin was not familiar with the China situation, let alone COI. He was not alone. Many of the COI personnel were not sure of what they were to do at this early stage. It was necessary to keep many sections in the dark about other sections. Those intended for the Balkans or France should not know about plans for the Orient and vice versa.

As the picture came into focus, it revealed that COI was formed to gather facts, statistics, and information both to aid the armed forces and also to manufacture propaganda for use in enemy-occupied countries. In addition, it was to plan and carry out sabotage and guerrilla operations. Anything that would hurt the enemy and aid the Allies was fair game. Later the propaganda division spun off into the OWI (Office of War Information), and COI became known by its OSS name.

And now the talents of a man dedicated to justice, fair play, and law enforcement turned 180 degrees. The skills developed in ferreting out the most clever smugglers were combined with those same illegal tactics to develop new ideas to harass and disrupt the enemy. For Eifler and for his compatriots, for the duration of the war there was no such thing as honesty, integrity, or even decency. The rules of warfare were to be abolished for this organization. The thin veneer of civilization was set aside, and the code of the troglodytes was reinstated.

It was to be the code of all COI agents. Top scientists, police, and respected Ivy League professors joined with criminals, gangsters and the nation's top crooks. Ideas that might have been suggested before but rejected as too foul were brought back for reexamination. Need to crack a safe, pick pockets, or forge documents? Who better to teach the COI recruits than those who spent their lives perfecting such talents? One forgery instructor was quite proficient. He would have you sign your name on a piece of paper. On two identical pieces of paper he would repeat your signature, then bet you $5 you could not pick your own. You couldn't.

Final graduation exercises for COI men included exercises such as breaking into America's war plants to steal plans or get statistics on production. No one else knew of these assignments, and all too often COI men were arrested by plant security police or FBI agents who were alerted by some suspicious citizens. While it was good training for the COI agents, it was not appreciated by the police or FBI, who complained their time was wasted in the apprehension of these "saboteurs." The COI theory was the opposite. It was good training for their men and also for the FBI. All too often the COI men proved they could come out with the goods.

The animosity of Hoover and the FBI spilled over into some incidents that upset the White House. Aware that COI was breaking into the Spanish Embassy at night to see what they might find, a domestic operation not within the scope of COI operations, the FBI reacted in an imaginative manner.

Waiting until the COI men were inside the Embassy the FBI brought two squad cars outside the facility, then turned on the sirens and red lights. The agents beat a hasty retreat from the building. The next day Donovan complained to the President. Hoover did the same pointing out the COI had no business within a foreign embassy. Roosevelt stifled a grin and told the two men their agencies must have better things to do with their energies and personnel. He suggested, however, that the COI refrain from domestic tactics that could be embarrassing to our government.

The COI area of operations was world wide with the exception of the United States, Central and South America which were to be handled by the FBI. Several months after the COI was formed Roosevelt felt the FBI should not be operating outside the continental limits of the U.S.A. He turned Central and South America over to the COI. Several of the FBI agents remained and became COI. The idea severely irritated Hoover who had his own way of handling such a situation. Rather than turn over the FBI files that would have helped the COI, he called for their destruction.

Derision for the upstart COI was not limited to the FBI. During one training exercise Colonel Donovan attended a formal Washington dinner. He bumped into an admiral who expressed his scorn for the fledgling COI organization. He referred to the outfit as a "Tinker Toy group spying on spies."

Donovan thought for a minute. Then he said: "I don't know, Admiral. I think that we could get your secret files and blow up your ammunition dump on the other side of the river before midnight."

"Ha," snorted the admiral.

Donovan went to a phone and called one of his men, Horace Schmahl.

Fifty minutes later an array of ranking navy officers arrived at the Navy building demanding to see the admiral. The sentry said he was not in and didn't know where he was.

The officers snapped that they would wait, then went to the admiral's office and disappeared inside. Once inside, one of the "officers," actually a safe cracker, opened the admiral's top-secret safe. They emptied it and left. The sentry smartly saluted, happy to be rid of them.

The officers took empty dynamite tubes and drove to the ammunition dump. They bawled out the officer of the day for not demanding their security clearances, then planted the phony dynamite. Before the dinner was over Donovan handed the admiral his top secret files and told him where to find the "explosives." There were red faces all around, and the next morning navy heads rolled. The COI men had gained new respect for themselves and their service.

Eifler found his area of authority expanding within COI operations. He was given command of the entire Far East: not only China but India, French Indochina, Siam, Malaya, Japan, and Korea. It was now his responsibility to plan operations into China expanding into Korea and thence into Japan.

While Eifler knew he must have been sent for by General Stilwell, it was a long time before he learned the full story. Shortly after the war started, Colonel Goodfellow had asked General Stilwell about sending over a group of agents to work with regular military units in China. Stilwell had said he liked the idea. A man was put in charge of the unit. Goodfellow had told Donovan of the conversation and that it looked like Stilwell was going to buy the idea completely. The next morning Donovan informed his staff that a unit was definitely going into China with Stilwell. That afternoon they got a turndown from Stilwell. Goodfellow went over to see Stilwell to find out the reason.

"General, I thought you liked the idea," he said.

"I still do, but I don't like the man you put in charge," was his reply.

"But we put a man in charge who had previously worked with you," persisted Goodfellow.

"Yeah, and that is the reason why. If you sent that man out to blow up a bridge, he would blow up a windmill and then come back and tell you why it was better to blow up a windmill," Stilwell retorted.

"Well, if that is the reason, then you pick the man, General."

Stilwell went to work. He listed twenty men he thought might fill the bill. Then he analyzed them individually and eliminated them one by one. Finally two names remained. One was a lieutenant colonel, a graduate of West Point. The other was Captain Carl Eifler.

He chose the lieutenant colonel. A few days later, Colonel Goodfellow made the trip to Texas to recruit Stilwell's choice. He arrived the day of the man's funeral.

A check was then initiated to locate Captain Eifler who was found in Honolulu, and suddenly the new unit had its leader.

Late one night Eifler and Coughlin sat in a barren office with a single manila folder. They had been asked to review its contents. It consisted of a general plan for sabotage in China. It bore a note of disapproval from a Far Eastern affairs expert. In addition, it bore the signature of a second Far Eastern affairs officer who also disapproved. A final endorsement, however, said: "It has merit. Send to Bill Donovan." The signature was that of President Roosevelt. The two men sat in silence, feeling awed and somewhat inadequate for such a responsibility.

Eifler always felt it crucial to establish the limits of his authority. He had been told it was unlimited.

"Can I have five million dollars?" he asked Goodfellow.

"If it is merited, yes," was the instant reply.

He had to put that answer to the test.

To satisfy himself that he was truly able to obtain a specified sum of money that would be given to him strictly at his request, with no complicated forms to complete, Eifler arranged to send Coughlin to recruit two men he had worked with earlier and who were now on the West Coast. One was Andrew Hulder, whom he had known while working on the Fire Patrol in Los Angeles. He had the highest respect for Hulder's ability and integrity. The other was Mel Hanks, whom he knew from their Border Patrol days. Hanks had been involved in the apprehension of smugglers and knew most of their tricks. Hanks was at this time the customs agent in charge in Seattle. Eifler realized he would soon be required to do considerable smuggling and wanted a man who could not only give advice but help in the training of other men.

"John," he said, "I am going to send you to California first, and then on up to Seattle on verbal orders to see and recruit two men whose names I will give you," he said casually. "And if I remember correctly, your wife will be arriving in San Francisco soon and you can see her," he concluded.

Coughlin showed concern. "Carl, a trip like that on verbal orders. I can't do that. I'd be court-martialed."

Eifler grinned. "John, you'll be court-martialed if you don't. That is an order."

Coughlin smiled his understanding.

Eifler picked up the phone to call Goodfellow's secretary, Miss Dockery. He requested she come down and give him $2,000 out of the safe, then arrange priorities for Coughlin's flight. There was no hesitation. She did so at once. Goodfellow was a reserve officer, and, when called to duty from his newspaper, it had been natural for him to bring Miss Dockery with him.

In an hour's time Coughlin was on the way to the airport with what cash he would need. Eifler returned the balance of the $2,000 when Coughlin returned from his assignment. As he wanted, he had obtained the proof that his authority was real.

Out of a list of over one hundred traits needed to ensure the success of the unit in the field, Eifler began matching the talents of the few men he now had to see how many were filled.

He needed the talents of an investigator; soldier; electrical engineer; lawyer; chemist; finance officer; medical doctor; radio technician; radio operator; demolition expert; craftsman; locksmith; someone with a knowledge of fine tools; mechanic; pilot; sound engineer; adjutant; supply officer; teacher; linguists in Japanese, Malaysian, Korean, Chinese, Hindustani, Burmese, German, French; business manager; railway construction engineer; and photographer.

How many would it take to fill these positions and make the

42

unit? Colonel Goodfellow thought perhaps only seven would be necessary. His assistant, Lt. Colonel Garland Williams thought they would need one hundred twenty-five. No one really knew.

The word was out now that a strange new outfit was looking for some talented and unusual men. COI wanted men who would come into the operation blindly. For openers the volunteers were told it was to be an important operation, full of danger. Further, they were told they would in all probability be signing their own death warrant if they chose to enter. After reading this opening statement, more men turned the idea down than accepted it. Those who gave the impression that they were out for glory or merely to raise a little hell were turned down.

At one point, Colonel Williams, was discussing several of the candidates with Eifler. They had been going over the records after the interview of an army man who had a record of petty theft and murder, although he had not been convicted on the latter. Williams, like Eifler, had been a former customs officer, though he had been stationed in Texas. Through the close association that is known to federal officers, he had heard of Eifler, and Eifler of him. Now, as the two former customs officers sat together Eifler said: "You know, I don't like that petty theft charge. As far as the possibility of murder, I can accept that."

Williams half-smiled. They both were thinking the same thing. As federal officers they wouldn't have paid any attention to a petty theft charge but certainly would have been interested in hunting a murderer.

In pondering this, Eifler realized how his thinking had turned 180 degrees. Now, a possible murderer was an acceptable recruit but pettiness was not to be tolerated. Indeed, had any applicant indicated he could not take the life of another human being, it would have counted against him. For other reasons, however, the man was not accepted.

Eifler was occasionally accused of recruiting some of his men in bars. This was not true, but anyone could be forgiven for making that assumption. He naturally desired the finest men he could obtain. When commanding officers were approached by other officers seeking some of their men to be transferred, it was all too often their policy to unload those men they deemed incompetent or misfits. It was considered a good time to "weed the garden," and they did just that. Like any pro sports team having to give up players for expansion teams, they naturally wanted to keep the best for themselves.

Eifler and Coughlin would go to the town near the military base they were interested in. Rather than going directly to the commanding officer, they would go into the bars and strike up conversations with those officers who were bending the elbow. This way it was easy for them to obtain the names of the men who were considered to be the best in any unit. Armed with these names, they would then set up their interview with the C.O. They would wait patiently while he extolled the virtues of his current crop of misfits, then request specifically those officers they really wanted. It proved to be a valuable means of recruiting some fine officers.

On one occasion, Eifler and Coughlin were invited to the home of Gen. M. B. Halsey of Fort Meade, Maryland. Again fate worked to help the struggling unit. Mrs. Halsey, later to be unofficially dubbed the "Mother of 101," showed a keen interest in the operation. She gave Eifler the names of several promising recruits. One was Lt. Floyd R. Frazee. He was needed because he had been a jeweler and was familiar with working with small tools, but he was not easily obtained. His commanding general refused to release him. Eifler, never known to dally, went to the colonel in the War Department who had issued orders for Frazee to report to COI.

"Colonel, what can be done to a general who refuses to obey War Department orders?" he asked.

The colonel replied: "Captain, what can be done to any officer who refuses War Department orders?"

That was all Eifler needed to hear. He went back to his office and picked up the phone. He called the colonel who had received the orders but had been stopped from executing them by the general.

"Colonel," he began, "you have War Department orders to transfer Lieutenant Frazee. I know the general has stalled them. It is now 1500. If Lieutenant Frazee has not left by midnight, I am going to prefer charges against the general. Will you please relay that?"

There was a silence. The colonel was trying to convince himself he had just heard a captain threaten to press charges against a general. He finally said he would so advise the general. Frazee reported immediately.

Another of Mrs. Halsey's recruits was Jack Pamplin, a young, civilian attorney. Pamplin learned of this unusual organization while sitting in a choir loft of a Presbyterian church. Some friends told him that this shadowy group needed a man with a law background who could also type. Pamplin fit the bill. He obtained the commander's name, called and arranged an interview. Jack Pamplin would never forget his first encounter with Captain Eifler.

"From behind the desk rose this mountain of a man. He walked around the desk and shook my hand, giving me the impression he intended breaking every bone. Then, with a smile that was alarming,

44

he put his hands behind his back and said, "Hit me in the stomach as hard as you can.'" Pamplin was dumbfounded.

"Do you mean it? In the stomach?" he queried.

"That's right. As hard as you can," Eifler persisted.

Pamplin drew back, and with all the power he could muster from his six-foot-three, 155 pound body struck Eifler squarely in the belly. Eifler neither flinched nor moved. He was quiet a minute, then turned and walked back to sit behind his desk. He completed the interview with Pamplin and dismissed him, after simply advising that he would be in touch with him.

Pamplin was a civilian and would have to be inducted. Eifler was disturbed that he might be joining to avoid the draft. He instructed Curl to proceed with induction, nevertheless. Pamplin failed the physical because of his teeth. Now Eifler would learn the truth. He told Pamplin that he would not now have to join up because he had failed the physical. Pamplin said he would have the dental work done and come in. He did this and was finally sworn into the army, then put on detached service to COI. Eifler long remained indebted to Mrs. Halsey for Frazee and Pamplin, whom he considered two of his finest men.

John Coughlin then recommended Capt. Ray Peers, a young officer he had known earlier in his career. Both Eifler and Coughlin were impressed with the manner in which Peers handled himself as well as with his obvious self-confidence. His initial interview with Eifler somewhat paralleled Pamplin's except he did not get to punch the new C.O. It was, however, quite unusual.

"To say I was in for a rude shock would be the understatement of a lifetime," he began.

"After an exchange of salutes, he offered his hand. I could see he was strong, and the way he grabbed my hand was proof. He proceeded to crack every joint, smiling all the time. Back of what he was doing was a message. Danger? The next thing, as if it were entirely habitual, he took a stiletto-type dagger and drove it a good two to three inches into the top of his desk. He looked pleased. I was confused. I had never had anything like this happen before, and all I could think was, 'What's next?'"

Peers further described his briefing as the most effective he had ever or would ever know. "Eifler used a standard wall map, and his strong hand moved along like a tank, covering nearly all of China and half of Siberia. By way of explaining what we were going to do in the Far East, he took me on a few verbal reconnaissance missions and ambuscades. We rode with the pirates on the Yangtze River, on Mongolian ponies with the warlords across the sands of the Gobi

Desert, operated with the Dacoits or robbers in the Mekong Valley. The impression was of parachutes, hit-and-run firefights, resistance movements, sabotage, of missions crisscrossed with danger. My role then, I thought, was shortly to become something I had never expected. I wondered why John had lured me into this. He looked at me pleasantly."

One evening Eifler sat talking with Mrs. Halsey in her home. The general was away that night, as he was much of the time. Eifler was concerned about her being home alone so often. He asked her if she had ever taken any self-defense courses. She said she had not.

An expert in jujitsu, Eifler decided to teach her a few simple defensive measures. One consisted of planting your foot firmly on that of the assailant, then striking a blow with the side of the hand to the windpipe. He softly demonstrated the move to her, stopping his hand gently on her throat. He asked her to try it on him to make sure she understood. She followed instructions perfectly, and the next thing he knew he was being revived on the floor. She had moved too quickly and caught him perfectly, knocking him unconscious. She was all apologies and alarmed over this man lying out cold on the floor. Eifler stood up, shook his head, and told her he felt she was an apt pupil. In all his years of dealing with violent individuals, he was never knocked unconscious except by a woman.

Recruiting was now begun in the Twelfth Division, dubbed "The President's Own." Here the bar-interview method was employed. Eifler and Coughlin picked up the names of two additional men. They were Lt. Phillip Huston and Sgt. Allan Richter, experts in communications. General Halsey gave three more names, all lieutenants—Bill Wilkinson, Frank Devlin, and Harry Little. The little group was beginning to expand.

Another man selected was a Eurasian, in his fifties. His health was such that he would not pass the military physical. He was needed because of personal acquaintance with many high-ranking Chinese officials in Japanese-occupied territory. Eifler felt this was a way to more quickly penetrate the customs and mystery with which Oriental leaders seemed to enjoy surrounding themselves. Eifler appealed directly to the surgeon general to make an exception based on two points. First, this man would most likely be killed, and that would take care of the situation. Second, should he survive his special mission, he would be well entitled to any pension or benefits due him because of what he would have performed.

Eifler won his point and was allowed to induct the man and attach him to the unit. To test the new recruit's resourcefulness (he had also been a smuggler), Eifler told him when the unit left for

China he would not go with them. Rather, he would have to get over on his own and report to Eifler when and where indicated. This also served a dual purpose. The balance of the unit was not even to know of his existence. He would be known only to Eifler and Coughlin and, when Peers took command, to him.

Selection of the men was naturally of gravest importance. It was, however, just part of the emerging program. Training was equally essential. It was a new ball game for America. Certainly it was not anything approved of in any part of America's past history. Most governmental leaders found it a bit barbaric to ' read other gentlemen's mail." But the British with their traditional rules of fair play had found it necessary for years to conduct espionage. What little information the United States had been able to glean was what had been gathered by ambassadors or relayed by friendly nations. There were no manuals to follow. No schools existed. The new spy organizations must simply make up their own courses, train their own instructors, and go up against the well-known and established organizations of the Nazis.

In a study of the diverse Western and Eastern philosophies, Eifler realized a great inability on the part of the United States to realize what it faced with the Japanese Empire. The Western logic was inflexible: it encompassed morality, religion, and thought patterns. The Japanese were dialecticians, holding that any existence was a contradiction. They practiced the concept of opposites and the means of harmonizing them. All manner of opposites could be united; therefore, a thing could be both good and bad at the same time.

The West had black-and-white concepts; the Japanese had vague distinctions. Western logic was described as a suitcase which was defined and limited. Eastern logic was like the *furoshiki*, the cloth Japanese carry for wrapping objects. According to need it could be large or small, and when not needed it could simply be folded up and put in a pocket.

Americans were deeply puzzled by the Japanese, who were seemingly completely unpredictable. They were barbaric and polite; hard workers and lazy; brave and cowardly all at the same time. The Japanese considered these not anomalies but one united whole, and they were puzzled that the Americans could not understand it. The Japanese considered a man with no contradictions could not be respected—he was too simple a person. The more contradictions in a man, the deeper he was. His existence became richer the more acutely he struggled with himself.

And how was this to help Eifler and his men? Not immediately in the guerrilla warfare, he realized, but one day it would be useful.

Until then, it would be filed in the memory banks, ready for instant use.

Eifler, Coughlin, and Peers made a list of the gadgets they would need and returned to further preparations for their trip. Word got out that COI was considering a mission into Korea. Eifler was besieged by Korean patriots and suspect-patriots. One thing was obvious—the Koreans loved letters. Eifler viewed letters from officials of all levels. One even brought a letter from Mrs. Eleanor Roosevelt.

One outstanding Korean was accepted who drew the code name "Alex." Alex came with a letter from Syngman Rhee. It was his desire to go with the first unit into China and serve as a link between the Korean government in exile and the U.S. and Chinese governments. He had degrees from three universities, including two master's degrees. He spoke and wrote six languages fluently. Still, Eifler was uneasy. Too many Orientals had been seeking a soft spot. Alex had to be questioned.

"Alex, are you sincere in your desire to serve your country or are you seeking a job you feel suitable to your education and position?" queried Eifler.

He said he was deeply sincere.

Eifler paused. "I have a position for you but not as a representative of your government. In fact, you would not be helping Korea but indirectly." Eifler paused to let this sink in.

Alex nodded.

"The job involves hard work and grave danger. And on top of that you would be doing it as a private in the U.S. Army."

There was no hesitation. Alex accepted. With his acceptance went Eifler's doubts as to his true intent.

His service took a unique turn when he was sent overseas to be returned as a "prisoner of war" to Camp McCoy in Wisconsin. There, among fellow Korean prisoners, he was to determine those of sufficient patriotism and intelligence, as well as hatred of the Japanese, who might become good agents. When he felt he had a candidate to be considered, he gave a prearranged signal to the camp commander who would then call in several men for infractions of the rules. Alex was always one of them. He would then give his report, and the commander would arrange for the candidate to be sent to a hospital unit. The commander was the only man in the camp who knew of Alex's true identity. An "escape" from the hospital was then arranged after the candidate had been approved by Eifler. From the hospital he would be taken to the Sherman Hotel in Chicago, and from there finally shipped to Catalina Island off California for final training.

The group of agents recruited in this fashion was to lead a

48

planned revolution in Korea, at which time specific units were to be put in Japan. This was the original plan for Eifler's group to penetrate Japan via Korea.

The time had now come for Eifler and seven of his men to proceed to a secret British espionage school. The remainder of the group was to be trained at a school being established in the United States by the first graduates of British schools. Even though all of the men could not take the full British schooling, a comparison of the two methods could prove to benefit the entire unit.

4

The school, located outside the United States, received the Eifler party of eight. All the men had to enter and be considered as privates in the British army. When they arrived, they were joined by another COI man known only as "Ben."

The school, known simply as Camp X, was one of the more closely guarded secrets of the war. It was located on the north shore of Lake Ontario, between the towns of Whitby and Oshawa. Today, a nondescript sign describes the area as "Intrepid Park." The park includes a gray concrete wall bearing four flagpoles and a bronze plaque. The plaque reads, not entirely correctly, "Camp X 1941-46. On this site British Security Co-ordination operated Special Training School No. 103 and Hydra. STS 103 trained allied agents in the techniques of secret warfare for the Special Operations Executive (SO,E) Branch of the British Intelligence Service. Hydra network communicated vital messages between Canada, the United States and Britain. This commemoration is dedicated to the service of the men and women who took part in these operations."

Had the people of Rochester and other American cities been able to look across the dark waters they would have wondered at the classes being held there and the students gathered from several nations. They were a mixture of obviously military types as well as non-military, young, middle aged and some in their fifties. All came to learn the rules of this grim and savage game and to get their first glimpse of the field upon which they had chosen to play.

The camp officially opened just two days after Pearl Harbor. Two years later it closed down after training some 500 students. Many were to become spies, secret agents or guerrillas. Included in its roster were men of the FBI, OSS, SO,E, SIS, BSC and the RCMP.

Forty six years after the camp's closing, information is still hard to come by. The British, known for secrecy, still hold the cards close to their chest. David Stafford in his book, "Camp X," has stated, "The obsession with secrecy is perhaps the true English disease," with the further statement, "the cult of secrecy is one of the rituals whereby powerful and informal elite groups exercise and protect their influence in British society."

With increased numbers of recruits from COI, then OSS needing training it became necessary to set up training camps around Washington, D.C. and bring in instructors. These included both British and the Americans who were graduates of Camp X. One of the English instructors was Captain William Ewart Fairbairn who was called both "Fearless Dan" and "The Shanghai Buster." Trained in the eastern art of self defense, jiujitsu, he revamped the Shanghai Police, of which he was a member, into a showcase. His Shanghai Riot Squad dealt with disorder in the city. He wrote a book on what could only be termed dirty fighting. One of his students said, "he had an honest dislike of anything that smacked of decency in fighting." The OSS loved him and brought him to one of their new camps, Camp B, just 60 miles outside Washington, D.C. Donovan brought President Roosevelt there to see his amazing demonstration of special weaponry and dirty tricks. Enthralled with Fairbairn, Roosevelt saw to it that he was assigned to OSS with the rank of Major.

One of the raw recruits who entered the training schools later described the change in philosophy forced on the students. "It turned our values upside down and we wondered about making a world fit for terrorists." Many found stimulation and new approaches to problems once they were able to put aside the barriers of fair play, honesty and ethics drummed into them from childhood. Others wondered how many future Frankenstein's were being created and what would happen to them when the war ended and they brought those skills back into a civilized society.

One of the more flamboyant Camp X students was a Canadian named Major d'Artois. He went on to serve SO,E in France in a slashing, destructive way. He devised a special telephone warning system to warn of German troop movements. He devised the tactic of kidnapping wealthy collaborators when he needed more money and holding them for ransom. Only after the war did he reveal that his response to the Germans when they executed wounded partisans had been tit for tat. The Germans preferred clubbing them to death with their rifle butts. "They killed fifty nine of my men. We retaliated by lining up fifty two of their soldiers and shooting them one by one," he said. It was interesting to note thirty of d'Artois group were women, all of whom adored their "Major d'Artois." At wars end d'Artois sought to remain in the British SO,E but he had gone too far past the barriers of civilization. He had become a true soldier of fortune, anxious to talk of his exploits and to continue in his wild and totally unorthodox fashion. He was not allowed to stay.

The first day of camp found the eight men (Eifler, Coughlin, Curl, Wilkinson, Devlin, Frazee, Chun Ming, and Ben) decked out in the uniform of British privates. While they stood at strict attention a

British officer, complete with swagger stick, gave close inspection. He then turned to face them and, directly to Eifler and Coughlin, said: "You look almost like soldiers."

They gritted their teeth, stared straight ahead, and said nothing. The had spent long hours practicing the British stance and salute until they were convinced they were letter perfect. Eifler made a mental note to repay this little favor at the earliest opportunity. His chance came several days later. By now the Americans had come to respect this British officer as a fine and dedicated man and one with a great sense of humor. For reasons of his own he had hung the nickname "Busty" on Eifler. Eifler had learned he was a Sandhurst man and that the worst insult you could offer one of them was to mistake them for a colonial.

On this particular morning Eifler was seated in a classroom and working with secret inks. The officer came in to observe the students at work. As he passed Eifler's desk, Eifler looked up at him. In a loud voice he asked: "Begging the Captain's pardon, sir. May I ask a question?"

Trapped, the captain could only give permission.

With full innocence registering on his face Eifler asked, "Sir, are you a colonial?"

The other students in the room kept their amused silence. The captain took it in stride, then leaned down to reply to Eifler: "Busty, you son of a bitch, we're even," and he walked on.

Eifler's unit was given a field assignment. They were to "ambush" a train and then return to blow up a "fort." A spot along the train track was indicated where the train was to be blown. The men were to sneak past sentries to the spot, plant a harmless charge to prove they made it, and return to the fort on top of a cliff to plant explosives. Eifler reasoned he and his men would be ambushed and captured as part of their training. He resolved to be neither captured nor ambushed. Putting himself in the instructors' positions, he tried to figure out just what they would do. Knowing where the "saboteurs" were going to hit the train gave the instructors a decided advantage. Eifler, therefore, moved his ambush up a hundred yards and used delayed fuses. This would confuse the defenders of the fort as to the time the returning enemy unit would be trying to blow them up. This part of their mission completed, the men started the trip back to the fort.

Actually the fort consisted of a tower right at the edge of a cliff. As they moved away from the train tracks, Eifler turned to Coughlin.

"John, they'll be setting up trip lights to catch us on our return. You take the men in the way we were told but delay for fifteen minutes. That will give me time to climb the cliff behind them and ambush the ambushers."

The timing was right. In fifteen minutes Eifler had scaled the cliff and was behind the British, who waited with ready weapons. He took a pound of gun cotton and put a primer in it. Then he shortened the fuse. He had crawled to within fifteen feet of them when one of his men hit a trip light and the flare went up. Jubilant, the British sprang to their feet with their weapons. Eifler lit the fuse and jumped up, throwing his explosive into their midst. "Jump, you bastards, jump," he shouted. They did just that as they dropped their weapons and ran. The explosion told his men he had outambushed them. Eifler lay on the ground roaring with laughter.

Ben, the other COI agent, came up with an idea that was to be used successfully against the Germans. It was called "the disappearing donkey." This caper utilized a new plastic explosive called "Composition C." A nondescript donkey would be loaded with seventy-five pounds of the explosive and a timing device. A small Arab boy would lead the beast into a German camp and tie it up just outside the tent of the highest-ranking German officers. He would then saunter off. At the right time, the donkey suddenly disappeared in a blinding flash along with surrounding tents and German officers and soldiers. "'Twas a far nobler thing" for the donkey to do.

Another phase of the training included discussion of something the men had never considered: the possibility that the Allies might lose the war. A British colonel said if this happened and their leaders told them to lay down their arms, they were to refuse. It was their responsibility to go underground and continue fighting until democracy was restored. He also said: "The politicians got us into this mess. Now it is up to the military to get us out of it." Then, grimly, he added: "When this is over, if ever these politicians get us into a similar mess, maybe we should turn our talents on them." Each man took a personal oath that should the time come and they lost, they would personally continue the fight. Then came the discussion of how to divide and conquer. For the first time the Americans saw how 40 million in the British Isles had ruled for so long.

Prior to their arrival at the British base, the men had made an agreement among themselves that no one was to be called "sir" or do anything to indicate any difference in rank. It was felt Curl would be the biggest offender, as he was the only enlisted man. Each time the rule was violated a fine of one dollar was to be levied. When the training was over, they would throw a party with the money. At end of the school Curl had never been fined; the big loser was Eifler.

Upon completion of their training, the eight men returned to

Washington to meet the balance of their group who had been trained in local camps. Upon return to the States, Goodfellow told Eifler he had put his name in for promotion to major.

"Colonel, I have a request to make," Eifler told him. "Coughlin has been senior to me and deserves the promotion also. I request you also include his name for promotion."

This was done, and both became majors on the same order a short time later.

Finally the day was at hand where the first COI unit was ready to go into the field. The need to get a full unit in operation was essential. The story of how close to failing COI came was to be revealed in later years. It had been opposed at the outset by the FBI and by both army and navy intelligence. A bill to abolish the infant organization actually lay on President Roosevelt's desk. No one had the courage to remove it, but someone did have presence of mind to continually move it to the bottom of the stack. This gave some valuable time to General Donovan and his colleagues, who finally convinced Roosevelt of the true need for the organization.

The completed unit now waited for final orders. They compared notes on what they had each learned in the two training areas. For relaxation there was a checkerboard, and soon the men were battling each other across the black-and-red squares. It was through this simple game that Pamplin noted an insight into Eifler's character.

"I had been winning more than my share of checker games," said Pamplin. "I was an average player but had spent some time as a boy working at the game. Eifler called me over and said he wanted to play checkers with me. I knew he had not been winning his share of the games with Coughlin, and this simply would not do with a person as intense as Eifler. So we sat down, and he had me make the first move. When I did so he said, 'Why that one?' I said someone had to make the first move and that one had no particular significance. After his first move I made my second. He immediately said, 'Why that one?' And again I gave an answer that I had to make some move as it was my turn. He wouldn't accept that and again asked why. With further moves and questions, he suddenly saw a pattern. I told him the strategy was to always cover one's flanks just like a military operation. With the game about half-finished, he suddenly stood up and said 'Game's over.' And it was. He went on to win after that."

Just prior to their scheduled departure date, Pamplin suffered an appendicitis attack and was taken to the hospital for surgery. In the meantime, the other twenty men were seeking transportation to China. Neither the army nor the navy could find anything, and it appeared the unit would die for desuetude.

Impatient with the bureaucratic delays, Eifler showed his true colors once more by seeking his own ship. When word of this attempt to charter a boat reached the authorities' ears, they suddenly found room and a sailing date was set. The men faced a hectic situation trying to get their gear aboard. Seemingly insurmountable obstacles were thrown in their path only to be overcome by tremendous effort. Eifler went to the hospital to get Pamplin released. The doctor said he could not go so recently after major surgery.

"Hell, he's going to die anyway," reasoned Eifler.

This logic failed to sway the doctor, a colonel. Eifler logically attacked this parochial attitude.

"He needs time to recover. That's what he can do aboard ship," he said. "We have our own doctor who can keep a check on him, and by the time we reach port he should be well."

He won his argument. Pamplin was carried aboard and made the trip with his fellow agents.

The first unit to leave for duty had no designation. One was obviously needed. Since it was the first, why not simply COI No. 1?

Somehow it didn't fit. Besides it would tell both the enemy and our own Allies it was our first. Finally, Colonel Williams came up with 101. Officially, then, the unit was to be tagged as Special Unit Detachment 101, later shortened to COI SU DET 101. Let everyone else wonder where in hell the other hundred units were.

One critical and puzzling problem was the alarming silence from General Stilwell's headquarters. He had made no inquiries as to the whereabouts of his COI unit, and had not replied to messages sent from Washington. It was determined he was hospitalized, but for what and how long was sheer speculation.

It was decided Eifler and Curl, now a lieutenant, would fly ahead to make sure all was in order. Further, it was agreed some of the COI toys should be brought along as an impressive demonstration of the new technical wizardry. They reasoned that some of the new plastic explosive, Composition C would make the impression they wanted. At least forty pounds of the stuff would be needed.

Eifler, with his customs background, knew the problem he faced in trying to take explosives on a plane without the permission of the country into which it was to be flown. It was just plain illegal.

"Do we have permission to fly the stuff through the various countries?" he asked.

"Major, we didn't even ask for it. It would take at least two years," was the reassuring reply.

Eifler looked out the window. "What do you suggest, then?"

"As I understand it, Major, you are an expert in smuggling.

Smuggle it."

Eifler left the briefing concerned about this next role. He would have to get the stuff on the plane at New York, and be reinspected at Miami, Brazil, Cairo, and Calcutta. Smuggling of many toys and explosives was a difficult and dangerous job. To do it five times in four countries, including his own, was something else. It took all the cunning and deceit he could now muster.

His first step was to get two identical suitcases, one for him and one for Curl. Curl's was to be packed with traditional gear. His first objective was to violate the U.S. laws about taking explosives from the country. To make his story, he stayed up all night drinking. Curl's instructions were to follow him and play it by ear. The next morning they walked into the customs office at New York, and Eifler asked where he could find another bottle. He was directed to a spot nearby. A short time later he and Curl returned. Eifler removed his "short snorter" bill from his pocket and looked it over. A short snorter was made up of foreign currency all taped together and bearing signatures of military personnel from all over the world. The more countries someone traveled to the greater the length of his short snorter.

Eifler spotted someone to pester, Brigadier General Melborne. Much to the dismay of the general, he began pestering him with his short snorter bill. The senior officer, very much a gentleman, ignored him. A young woman walked in carrying an infant. Questioning brought out the fact she was the wife of an army sergeant and traveling to meet him. Eifler put on a great show of admiring the child.

"Does he have a bank account?" he queried.

"No," answered the puzzled woman.

"Allow me to start one," pursued Eifler. With that he pulled a dollar out of his pocket and handed it to her. Curl immediately did likewise, making sure the general saw it. Now the general was drawn in and, with him, other officers. In a short time the lady had $24 for the child's bank account.

Convinced he had now proved he was both drunk and a fool, Eifler now made his move. He walked over to the counter and threw the bag with the explosives on it before the customs officer.

"Okay, what do you want to see first?" he shouted. Curl pressed close behind him waiting to see where he might be needed.

The customs man was only too aware of the condition of this man and was now anxious to get rid of him.

"Do you have any lighter fluid?" he asked.

"Lighter fluid? Naw, I don't even smoke." He grabbed his bags and moved on as if believing the examination was over.

56

The startled official decided he was just as well off with him gone and said nothing.

Eifler had not had to lie this first time. He truthfully answered that he had no lighter fluid. At the time he answered, however, his one hand was wrapped around ten dynamite caps in his pocket, and that plus the explosives in that suitcase would have taken the whole building out of the war effort. He and Curl relaxed aboard the plane under the unamused stare of the general.

The plane soon touched down in Miami. There would be no inspection here as they got off, but the same inspection would be repeated when they boarded to leave. They needed a new plan.

Eifler found a customs agent he had known named Williams and said: "Look, I have some important dispatches here I don't want to take into town with me. Can I leave them with Customs?"

The obliging Williams took them to the chief inspector, who agreed to lock them up. When they left the next morning Eifler had no difficulty getting them out of the safe, and they were naturally not inspected since the man in charge had taken them from his own safe.

In Brazil they easily employed the "identical-bag" switch. Eifler went through with Curl's bag. He came back through another door, switched bags, and Curl then went through with the same bag. The crucial problem arose in Cairo. They were all taken from the plane and put into what is called a lock-room situation. The only exit was through one door at which guards were stationed. All within the room were to open their bags at the same time. Eifler was forced to use another ruse. He now pulled from his pocket a diplomatic passport and said he could not be searched. The inspector looked it over, smiled, and handed it back.

"Yes, we can honor such a passport, but we do not always have to. This time we shall not because we have word an agent is trying to enter our country and we must inspect everybody," was his reply. In the same pocket to which he returned Eifler's passport was a photo of Eifler in a German officer's uniform. Discovery of the explosives would mean his arrest and personal search. That picture, taken at the British training camp, now loomed large in his mind. Suddenly Eifler straightened up, his face flushed with anger. "You have insulted me and my country," he roared. "I demand that you call the American Consulate—no, the American ambassador. Right now I demand it."

The unexpected bellow of rage accomplished what he hoped. The inspector lowered his voice and tried to say something. Eifler gave him no time to think or talk. He demanded and demanded. His theory came from his own background in customs. He knew customs inspectors were always in some hot water. So this man was bound to also be in some hot water. Eifler was going to throw more on him that he could handle.

The inspector backed down, and Eifler picked up the bag and stormed out of the room roaring and threatening. With Curl behind him, he hailed a taxi and made sure everyone heard him say: "Take me to the American Embassy."

Once in the cab the "rage" abated, and he was quite calm as he entered the Embassy to find the military attache.

"I have some important dispatches in this bag. I do not want to take them into my hotel. Will you hold them for me?" he asked.

The attache agreed, and the two men now went into the Shepphard Hotel to kill time for the next flight.

From a hotel room on the second floor of their hotel they relaxed and discussed the trip so far. They wondered how the other nineteen men were doing aboard ship. From a small piece of luggage Eifler produced a .22-caliber pistol. It was equipped with a silencer. This was one of the new secret weapons—one of the finest silencers ever produced, to be used by agents when the need arose. He felt the balance of the weapon as he strolled to the window. On the sidewalk below his window streamed the citizens of Cairo. Various Allied uniforms sprinkled the crowds. Just beyond the sidewalk was a small area in which grass and some flowers grew. Eifler felt it would be a good test for the weapon. Slowly he loaded the weapon and opened the window. People were walking on both sides of the area. He raised the pistol and fired into the dirt. The slight ping was barely audible in the room and not at all to those in the street. He smiled, raised the gun once more, and emptied it into the dirt. No one broke stride or looked up. The gun was all they said it was. It had passed its first real test. The next time would be for real.

The next day the two men picked up the "dispatches" from the Embassy safe. Returning to the airport, Eifler looked for the inspector he had intimidated, but he was either not on duty or hiding behind a counter or pillar. They boarded a British Overseas plane and headed for the final leg of the trip—India. All aboard were given a list of declarations to complete. It said to list all money. Eifler knew they wanted the sum of money each man was carrying. He decided to play the fool once more. Taking his short snorter from his pocket, he carefully listed each bill along with its serial number. It was a long and laborious process, but was to play a vital role in getting him through customs with no inspection. As soon as they landed, he sought out the chief inspector and began pestering him with foolish questions. "How long do you think we will be here? Do you want me to bring all my baggage up now? I'm worried about my short snorter.

Do you know what a short snorter is? I don't want anything to happen to my short snorter."

Then he picked up his tags and threw them on the counter. Over the top of them he placed the short snorter. He was told that wasn't necessary. Now he got indignant.

"It's not necessary you say—and I spent all that time filling out your papers. And now it wasn't necessary?"

His theory here was to take up as much time as possible and annoy them so badly they would be glad to get rid off him. The inspector finally asked if Eifler had an Indian bill on the short snorter.

When told no, he produced one to be added and waved Eifler and Curl on through to everyone's relief. They had crossed the last hurdle. The explosives were safely in India.

Plowing through the Atlantic, the transport bearing the balance of DET 101 men and supplies steamed to meet them. The official military designation of the unit was Task Force 5405-A. All task forces were commanded by generals. The 5405-A was the first and probably only one to be commanded by a major. Coughlin was often asked who was commanding this particular task force. He always replied: "Never mind who is the commander—I am the executive officer."

Task Force 5405-A was stenciled on all their supplies in the hold of the ship. The trip had been uneventful except for the past few days when they had encountered heavy seas and taken a slight beating. The ship now put in at the Gold Coast. Some of the men went ashore. Pamplin, slowly recovering, did not. Frazee was ill and in sick bay, and Pamplin went to talk with him.

"Jack," Frazee said, "why don't you go below and check our supplies? See if there was any damage in the storm."

Pamplin received permission from the captain and went below. He found a piece of chalk and put it in his pocket. Everything appeared to be in good shape, but he did notice quite a few containers with no designation on them. With his chalk he marked each of these containers with the "5405-A" designation. In later months he was to remark, "Normally I am quite a law-abiding citizen. I merely thought if something was unmarked it might be ours and, if not, we might be able to use it. I don't think we wound up missing anything and we might have had a few things over, but this was an act that resulted from the spirit Eifler instilled in the outfit."

At the same time as DET 101 was on its way to the Orient COI had set up important stations in both Berne, Switzerland and Istanbul. The Swiss post was headed by Allen Dulles.

Istanbul could be compared to a Marx brothers show of agents from Germany, Italy, Japan, Russia and of course the British SIS. COI agents were now added to this mix. All spent endless hours spying on each other.

As the war progressed, citizens of Istanbul regarded all foreigners as spies, with probable good cause. The city was host to Roberts College, one of the oldest American colleges outside of the U.S. The more affluent Turks sent their sons and daughters there. In the summer of 1942 there was a sudden influx of American lawyers and professors. The students nodded knowingly about the true purpose of these newly arrived Yankees. Among the students was Turhan Celik, a sophomore. One night in a night club he met one of the American "professors" who said he was gathering a bibliography on a less known Italian poet. They talked awhile about meaningless subjects and parted.

Several months later Celik was invited to the apartment of another of the Americans. His bibliographer acquaintance was also there. The question was put to him directly. How might he help the Allied cause. He had been checked out and his sympathies determined. But he said he was merely a student with no way to access enemy information or personnel. His first assignment was one that many men would relish, to get acquainted with a very beautiful young woman who claimed to be a Canadian.

"One of your friends, who is also working with us, knows her. He will arrange for the introduction. Find out if she intends to leave the country."

"How well should I get to know her?" he asked.

"That's up to you," was the broad reply. The bibliographer then thrust a copy of the *Divine Comedy* in Italian into his hands and asked him to translate it. He did so with no trouble. Celik followed up the translation with an alarming question.

"Are you from OSS?"

The two men looked at one another, then stammered.

"What do you know about OSS? Who else knows about OSS?"

Celik stated most of his colleagues had been talking about the sudden influx of Americans. They tried to figure out which of their teachers were spies. Each time a corpse was fished out of the Bosporous they tried to guess which of their "professors," acting in his OSS capacity, had done the job.

He was told to never mention OSS again.

A short time later he was introduced to the young lady as Ted

Andrews, a member of the American Embassy staff.

The meetings turned into an affair and a short time later as they lay in bed she questioned if he was really an American. He had explained his slight accent by saying he had been born in Europe and lived almost all of his life there.

Her suspicions were based solely on his sexual performance which she said was much more powerful than that of Americans. The lady obviously was both promiscuous and discerning. It would almost appear she had an international sexual score card.

In short order she asked her new lover if he might obtain a passport for her from his Embassy. She was all alone in Istanbul, her husband was away and she knew no one in the Canadian Embassy. Celik's OSS friends had no trouble in arranging for her visa to Canada. She would leave Istanbul, go through Syria and a few other countries, then on to Canada.

After her departure Celik asked who she really was. Though not really wanting to tell him, OSS felt he should know. His bed partner, the Austrian-Turkish beauty, was a German agent. She was responsible for the execution of several American pilots who had been downed in Austria. In Istanbul she acted as a Nazi counterspy infiltrating the resistance. OSS had been after her for a long time. In Turkey, which was neutral, they could not touch her. Outside Turkey she could be arrested and tried. In Damascus as she stepped off her bus she was arrested. Shortly thereafter she was executed as a Nazi spy. Celik got no extra credits for his special assignment.

DET 101 finally reached its destination as the ship proceeded around the Cape, and after a trip of nearly thirty days debarked in India. From here the men and equipment travelled by antiquated Indian train to New Delhi. Here they awaited further word from Eifler.

Eifler and Curl had been busy since their arrival in India. The task of getting to General Stilwell was more than they had bargained for. He had been hospitalized with yellow jaundice. The long trek out of Burma was still taking its toll. Getting over the Hump into China was a major effort. Because of the shortage of supplies and gasoline for the Fourteenth Air Force, anyone flying the Hump had to have permission of the general. Space was too valuable to waste on anyone unimportant to the war effort. Eifler's first request to fly to China was turned down. He was told: "He doesn't know you."

Eifler wouldn't buy that. He knew they had not even tried and demanded they "try" once more. This time permission was granted.

The flight was long, drafty, bumpy, and cold. Many hours later Eifler was ushered into the sparse headquarters of Stilwell. He saluted and they shook hands. After a few pleasantries, Stilwell became the general.

"Well, Eifler, what are you doing here?" he asked.

"Sir, I was under the impression you sent for me," Eifler replied.

"No, I didn't send for you, and I don't want you."

Eifler was puzzled. He explained the men of his unit were trained, had their own equipment and money. They were ready to go.

"Hell, Eifler, we can't use American agents in China," continued Stilwell.

He was more emphatic than Eifler wanted to believe. "General, we have twenty men waiting in India for this new phase of the war effort. "

Stilwell was silent for a minute, then looked up. "Tell you what—take a look around for thirty days—see what you can find and report back to me." The meeting was over.

Something was behind the scenes, Eifler realized. He also knew he had thirty days to find some way to get his unit into action.

Another smaller problem also faced him. As in the case of his dual passports, he had two sets of orders: one ordering him to report to General Stilwell and the other assigning him as military attache to the Embassy in Kunming. He was to use them as he saw fit. He knew there were two ambassadors who disliked undercover agents, one in Switzerland and the other in Kunming. Because a set of the Embassy orders were also in the hands of the ambassador, Eifler knew he must report. It was not too difficult to find out when the ambassador was out. At that time Eifler would report in, express his regrets at missing him, and state he would return later on. After several such visits the pressure began to be put on for him to call and set a time to report. At this time Eifler got Stilwell's headquarters to cancel the orders assigning him as military attaché, leaving only the orders attaching him to Stilwell.

Eifler found himself alone in a foreign land, not something entirely new to him. He realized COI was looking to his unit to get involved and prove to Congress and the War Department the value of this type of operation. Back in India his twenty men waited and wondered. It was fortunate the situation fell to a man with Eifler's imagination, boldness, and drive.

Prior to leaving Washington, Eifler had been introduced to and had lunch with a Chinese official of cabinet rank. This man was supposed to champion Eifler's cause. It was learned he had recently lost control of the roads. "Control" meant payoff and a sizable chunk of income. The Chinese official was distraught and seeking other sources of income. Eifler also had contacted Lt. Commander Milton Miles of naval intelligence. Sent to China to establish coast-watching stations, he had become closely associated with Gen. Tai Li, head of the efficient Chinese Secret Police. Eifler had great respect for Tai Li's organization. Its efficiency would be clearly demonstrated when an assassination attempt would be made on Miles in mid–1942. In a crowded railroad station Miles was suddenly aware of someone near him. At the same time, he felt a sharp pain in his back. He turned to confront his assailant and knocked him to the ground. He kicked him in the jaw. The downed man struck out once more with his knife, inflicting a long and deep gash on Miles's leg. Then he got up and dashed through the teeming crowd. A troop train bearing Indian soldiers pulled in and it carried a medic who was able to treat the stab wounds and stitch them up. Miles looked down and saw something on the ground. With a piece of gauze he picked up a grisly trophy of the attack. It was the assailant's tongue, which Miles's kick had severed. In describing the incident to Tai Li, he turned over the tongue. Tai Li nodded gravely. A few days later his organization picked up the would-be assassin. Justice was swift.

Eifler was not able to meet with Tai Li. Eifler did meet with the Chinese cabinet officer, however. He turned out to be one who did not believe in ceremony. At their initial meeting he stated: "We can dispense with the traditional greetings. Let's get right down to business."

He couldn't have said it to a better man. "All right," began Eifler, "I want to build a network for espionage and sabotage. I intend introducing units into Korea and eventually Japan. You have men, an organization, and contacts. We can work together."

The Chinese was pleased. "Who would command these men?" he asked softly.

"I don't give a damn who commands as long as I give the orders," Eifler replied.

The Chinese spoke to this. "I will command, and I will give the orders."

Eifler remembered this man was looking for additional income. He had no intention of lining the man's pockets for nothing. He knew the British had done exactly this. The money had been pocketed, and nothing had been done.

"You will give me the money and tell me what you want done. I will carry it out," continued his host.

Eifler phrased it another way. "Are you telling me I cannot come on Chinese soil to kill Japanese soldiers unless I give you money?" he asked.

"If you choose to put it that way, then that is correct," the calm Chinese replied.

"Well, I've got the money and I intend keeping it," Eifler said.

The meeting was over. No deal!

Eifler spent his entire thirty days in China making contacts and inquiries. At the end of his time he reported back to Stilwell.

"Has anything changed since I last talked to you, Eifler?"

"Yes, sir," Eifler replied. Then he employed every argument he had used originally. He had no luck. When he was finished Stilwell said: "No." From his voice Eifler knew he meant it. He knew a different approach was necessary. Eifler saluted and spoke.

"Well, sir, I must accept the fact that I have failed. And this is the first time I have failed. It's a little difficult to fail when you haven't had a chance to try." He did an about face and had just put his hand on the doorknob when Stilwell spoke.

"Eifler," he said.

"Yes, sir," replied Eifler, now turning back.

"Is Burma in your territory?"

"Yes, sir."

"How did the British take Burma?" he asked.

"By force of arms, sir."

"And how did the Japs take it?" he continued.

"By force of arms, sir," again replied Eifler.

"Then it should belong to anyone who can take it by force of arms, should it not?" finished the general.

"Yes, sir."

"All right, then I want you behind the Japanese lines. I want you to operate down there. Will you do this?"

"Yes, sir, I will. Could the general furnish some Chinese soldiers to work with me?" asked Eifler.

Stillwell looked over his glasses. "That's just like you. First you say you want to do a job, and then you ask me for the men to do it," he told him. He did give Eifler an okay to use Chinese troops and an order to go to Dibrugarh. Eifler never used either order. He had made up his mind he would find his own men at any cost and show the general. One final remark was made as Eifler again prepared to open the door.

"Eifler, I don't want you to feel too bad ninety days from now. Do you understand?" was his final question.

Eifler replied: "Yes, sir," turned, and left. He knew this gave him ninety days to prove himself. Ninety days to provide the "booms" Stilwell wanted to hear out of Burma.

64

During Eifler's absence the DET 101 men were hard pressed in the Imperial Hotel in New Delhi. Ranking officers could not figure out just what COI was and certainly not DET 101. Here was a select group of men with orders direct from the Secretary of War. They would tell nothing. One general wanted to grab the entire group and make MPs out of them. Another general called Eifler in immediately upon his return from China. He had his eye on him for provost marshal. Curl was also along. Eifler played it as dumb as he could. The exasperated general asked question after question, finding it hard to believe a man with the rank of major could really be that stupid. Finally he was convinced. In desperation he turned to Curl.

"Lieutenant, what do you know about any of this?" he asked.

Curl conjured up his blankest look. "Sir, I'm his assistant," he replied.

The general dismissed them, no doubt horrified these two men were on the Allies' side.

Calling the DET 101 men together, Eifler made the joyous announcement that they had a home—Burma. And what a home. The men poured over maps looking at the mighty rivers and thick jungles. The ranges of mountains were formidable. The people within those jungles were an unknown factor. Only one thing was known—the enemy lay behind that foliage, a clever and experienced jungle fighting enemy—the Japanese 18th Division with its main base at Myitkyina. Fifteen thousand seasoned troops, commanded by General Tanaka, were waiting. They had spearheaded the Japanese drive through Malaya, defeating some top British and Australian infantry and artillery units. DET 101's twenty-one men had a big job ahead.

They needed a base of operations. They agreed it should be near the Burmese border and as far north as possible to be close to China. Eifler, Coughlin, and Aitken set out. Through contacts, they made an appointment with a British colonel who had fought on the retreat to India. He was cooperative and suggested the man they should see was Sir Reginald Dorman-Smith, governor of Burma. He was in Simla in Nepal. Eifler proceeded to contact him. The initial interview was well remembered by Dorman-Smith.

"My aide came in to report a COI man waiting to see me. He suggested I clear my untidy desk of any unimportant papers. This I did and started to look busy by writing some harmless memo. In came the tough Yank. At that time I must have stood for all that he had disliked about us Limeys...an 'Imperialist' governor with a very British accent. Eifler was, to say the least, abrupt. He briefly described the goals of his Force 101 and said, quite rightly, that his mission could not succeed without a Burma officer who knew both the country and language."

"I want and am going to have your Stevenson," he roared.

"You may want him but you are not going to get him. He is not fit enough. I think that I have in Calcutta just the man who will suit you. The man, Wally Richmond, was on my personal staff all during the Jap invasion. He knows the country and speaks the language. What date do you want him to report and where?"

As Eifler paused a minute to digest this rapid turn of events, Dorman-Smith's mind went back to an amazing coincidence where he and Richmond had fought a common enemy together—without knowledge of each other. Dorman-Smith was commanding a company of the 15th Sikhs against the Afghans in 1919. Fighting in the remote mountain areas was difficult and demanding. Overhead flew a lone British plane observing the enemy. The plane was shot down by ground fire and the pilot, Richmond, captured. He was to be executed and had already been turned over to the women who performed the "death of a thousand cuts" ceremony when the British succeeded in ransoming him for a hundred thousand cartridge cases. The two men never knew of each other until they met in Burma over twenty-two years later.

"Eifler had little opportunity to speak," recalled Dorman-Smith later, "because at that moment one of the infamous Simla monkeys got through our window and Eifler left rather quickly."

Dorman-Smith continued: "Carl came to see me on the next day and showed me the pictures of my desk he had taken through a button-hole camera. What was my security like? I looked at the photos. They were right. I was starting a letter—'Dear Mum.' I think from that time on we did not appear as stupid as he had been led to believe. I ordered Richmond to meet Eifler in Assam."

Back in Dinjan, Assam, Coughlin and Eifler met Major Wally Richmond. He was warm and friendly and, fortunately, had a good sense of humor. This was a badly needed ingredient in such operations. From the way he conducted himself it was obvious he was sizing up this unorthodox outfit and the even more unusual Major Eifler. He did not have to stay if he chose not to. Fortunately, he took to it and added considerably to the story.

Dorman-Smith, while giving the appearance of a typical British official, actually was more of a rebel. True he carried the customary swagger stick, sported a well-trimmed mustache and British khaki walking shorts, but he was an Irishman and somewhat headstrong.

Appointed to the British cabinet as minister of agriculture by Neville Chamberlain in 1934, he remained steadfastly loyal to his "boss." Sent on a speaking tour through Australia and Canada in

66

1936, Dorman-Smith was brought to Washington, D.C., to meet with the vice-president. When the vice-president failed to appear and could not be reached, Dorman-Smith made a trip to the men's room where the missing vice-president was found—asleep in one of the stalls. "A bit too much of the bubbly at lunch," was the verdict.

Though Chamberlain was billed as the great appeaser, Dorman-Smith says this was not true. In closed meeting with certain cabinet officers, Chamberlain told them they were going to war but he was going to buy time for England. The cabinet was forced to ponder the problem that England faced with only a three-day supply of food available. Another member of that cabinet, Sir Winston Churchill, advocated something radical. He proposed every four-footed animal in England and Scotland be killed and the entire land be planted in wheat and corn to sustain the populace. All was quiet for a moment. Then Chamberlain turned to Dorman-Smith and said: "Well, Minister, how does that strike you?"

Never one to mince words, Dorman-Smith replied: "Do you really want me to answer that?"

"No, let's move along," was the prime minister's final remark.

A survey of England's equipment revealed only fifty operable farm tractors available. It was obvious a considerable number would be needed. In secret meetings with the Ford Company it was determined the number necessary—such number of tractors running the tidy sum of 4 million pounds. England did not want the Axis to realize they were preparing for war, and Dorman-Smith could hardly go to the floor of Parliament to justify this sum without the press picking it up. In a maneuver that would have made OSS proud, he went to the leader of the opposition and explained the situation. The leader agreed, then told Dorman-Smith to make his proposal the next morning. The opposition would not be present with the exception of the leader.

The next morning Dorman-Smith took his customary seat in Parliament. Across the house sat a lone figure representing the opposition. Sir Reginald rose to address the house, stating he wanted to request the sum of 4 million pounds for his department and for the good of England, but the reasons could not be given.

The leader rose from across the room and replied: "Well, that seems reasonable to me. I move it be granted and we move on," which was done.

The tractors were subsequently purchased and salted away in the farmlands for use at the proper time. Dorman-Smith had been able to find an additional 1 million acres of tillable farmland, and this plus the tractors enabled England to grow great amounts of food.

Though he was thrown together almost daily with Churchill, the two never got along, so outspoken were they both.

About the same time that Richmond joined Eifler and his unit a Kachin-speaking Baptist missionary was sent to help General Stilwell who requested he help Eifler. The missionary did not know that Richmond also spoke Kachin. Eifler had a sixth sense about this man and instructed Richmond not to show his knowledge of Kachin. The game had to be rough and tough. The backgrounds of the missionary and Eifler were as far apart as any two could be. Eifler told the missionary he wanted to hire natives to work as agents. He, Eifler, did not want to have to kill anyone, but anyone hired who did not work out would be executed. If a man had his training and could not fill the bill, he would be too dangerous to release. He could not jeopardize the program or other agents. Death was the only way out.

The missionary began his interviewing with Richmond sitting in. After quite a few men had been interviewed and none hired, Eifler called Richmond in.

"Now, what the hell is going on?" he asked.

Richmond spoke the one word that Eifler would immediately understand. "Sabotage, Major. Pure sabotage. He told the natives you were an agent of the devil and to have nothing to do with you."

Eifler instructed the missionary to report back to General Stilwell. He obviously would never fit the Procrustean bed.

General Frank Merrill, later asked Eifler who he thought he was to fire someone hired by General Stilwell.

"I didn't fire him," Eifler replied. "I simply told him I had no place for him in my organization."

A suitable headquarters was the next item on the agenda. Richmond suggested a small town called Nazira in Assam. It was the headquarters of a large tea company, on the edge of the Naga head-hunters' jungle. The manager was up in the hills in the unadministered Naga country. He might not be back for another day.

They waited. The landscape was beautiful. The hills in the background spread down to level out in the floor of the valley. Heavy clusters of tea bushes in neat rows were spread throughout the entire area. The tea pickers came to their work in long lines of dirty gray saris, many with naked babies riding on their hips. They chewed betel nut and evidenced it though wide red grins. They seemed never to be silent.

At night the cries of laughing hyenas chilled the air as they ranged in and out of the tea bushes.

The wait stretched into three days. Eifler immediately liked the place. He appreciated its privacy but also saw in the jungle areas a place to train his agents. He knew many of his agents would be city men who would need some jungle training in addition to that they had received when becoming agents.

They were referred to a company club where they might be more relaxed and get some spirits. In this case, the spirits consisted of warm beer. There were four men in the group at this particular point—Eifler, Richmond, Coughlin, and Aitken. They sat in the warm club looking out a large opened window. The view was down a sloping riverbank, lined with trees, to a small river. Among the branches of the trees were screeching monkeys who chased one another, scolded the young ones, and constantly scampered about.

Bored with the beer, Eifler went to his pack and brought out four bottles of Scotch he always carried for bargaining purposes. Scotch with beer was something new to Richmond. The men continued with the beer and interspersed it with Scotch. Soon a warm glow illuminated Richmond. He began wondering if Eifler was really the great shot he was reputed to be. He pointed to the monkeys, then to the .45 automatics with ammunition. These, too, were given to him.

Eifler did not really care to kill any of the monkeys. He did, however, shoot a few branches out from under them. Silence filled the room.

It was not clear later who challenged whom. Richmond claimed Eifler stated the British were not up to Americans in marksmanship. Richmond naturally disagreed. Richmond credited Eifler with the idea of shooting a soda bottle off his head, which "curiously enough I agreed to, with the stipulation I be given the same opportunity."

Both men agreed a small .38 would not do—it had to be a .45.

Moving outside, Richmond placed the bottle on his head.

"Shoot that off," he challenged.

Eifler did so.

"My turn," said Richmond. Eifler put a bottle on his head, and Richmond promptly blasted it off. Next he put a cigarette tin on his head, looked at Eifler, and said: "Now shoot that off."

Eifler easily did, then placed the tin on his head. Richmond removed it. His next target was a cigarette held tightly in his lips. He looked calmly at Eifler, turned his head, and said: "Shoot this off." Eifler fired, removing the cigarette a bare inch from his lips. Richmond spat the butt out, turned and said: "My turn."

Eifler clamped his cigarette tightly, turned and waited. A few seconds later it was snapped from his mouth. He felt the breeze of the .45 slug as it tore by.

Richmond was delighted. So far he had quite upheld the honor of the British forces. But he sought even a smaller target. Finally he had it. He ran inside and returned with the cork from a bottle of Scotch which had greatly inspired the match in the first place.

Triumphantly, he placed it on top of his head, looked directly at Eifler and said: "Take that off."

Eifler pondered that one. He raised his gun, then lowered it. He was confident he could do it, but he greatly feared "my turn." The shooting match was over but not its legend. It was told throughout the Orient and later became a favorite of Winston Churchill.

The final chapter was written many months later. At this point Eifler was a little tired of being called on to constantly perform. He had shot through the center of too many playing cards, coins out of the air, corks out of bottles, and even birds from the air. The end came at a press conference in a gloomy canvas tent. Old kerosene lanterns cast flickering rays into darkened corners. Down a table some twenty feet from Eifler sat a war correspondent. He put a glass on his head and called: "Hey, Eifler, shoot this one off."

Eifler was ready. Without leaving his seat, he picked up a lantern and held it in front of him with one hand. He whipped out his .45 and fired. The glass blew apart and fell to the ground. The correspondent left hurriedly, some of his peers say to change his shorts.

This ended the challenges, much to Eifler's relief.

While they awaited the manager's return other people now became curious as to who these four Americans were and what they were up to. They concocted a cover story designed to say little. The men were supposedly the advance unit of a field experimental group and needed headquarters. They already had a 5405-A designation, so they simply gave the designation Field Experimental Group, 5405-A. It said nothing else. The people at Nazira became most helpful and suggested different sites for smaller training camps. COI, Washington had trained its men in separate camps. Those destined for France or Germany should not see each other nor those from the Balkans. You could not identify any other agents if you did not know who they were. Eifler knew this same policy had to be followed in his training camps. Some groups would go into the jungles, some would work their way into central Burma, and some would go to the south. The less they knew of each other, the better. Eventually, twenty-six sites were selected for training. Upon the manager's return they reached an agreement with him allowing them the use of part of the property as a training camp.

DET 101 was now in its new home and ready for action. The officers moved into a large two-story English home with thatched roof. Nearby the enlisted men occupied a former tennis club building. Later, a cowdung basha was also built. Gurkha security guards

70

stood proudly and fiercely on duty at the gate.

The radio and cryptography rooms were located on the first floor of the large house. For additional personnel arriving in the future, a large tea-drying building was utilized. It boasted a corrugated metal roof. During the monsoons the men inside couldn't be heard talking, so loud was the banging of the rain.

Immediately after 101 was situated, a near-death blow struck. Colonel Goodfellow was promoted to deputy director of COI, and 101 became a forgotten unit. With a budget of $298,000 to start, Coughlin and Eifler each carried on them $10,000. They proceeded on the assumption money would be deposited into Lloyd's Bank and available to them. Captain Harry Little had been put in charge of the Calcutta headquarters to handle the vital supplies and incoming personnel. His post was of utmost importance for the survival of the Nazira camp and all operations. He handled depositing of money into the agents' account so they could have it as they came out of the jungle. Eifler now had to take a bold step. He withheld nothing from his men. He asked each to pay his own mess bill ahead for two or even three months. To a man they did. With this breathing room, Eifler went to Delhi to approach the Lloyd's Bank for $50,000. He was asked by the manager if he had authority to borrow this money in the name of the U.S. government. Eifler said he had such authority—that it went with his being an agent. Why, indeed, the U.S. government would be responsible; $50,000 was then deposited to the DET 101 account. Then he learned that Indian paper rupees were not acceptable in Burma, nor were Burmese rupees acceptable in India. His next trip was to Simla where he again visited with Sir Dorman-Smith. He put the plight directly to him. For reasons known only to Dorman-Smith, he also gave $50,000 in Burmese rupees to Eifler. This was to cause consternation with British intelligence, who also had sought funds from the governor's office without success. The "price" Eifler had paid, however, was a shooting demonstration before British officers. Dorman-Smith stated: "When the morning of the demonstration arrived, Eifler was in no condition to perform. He had a king-sized hangover. Since all the officers were assembled, I prevailed on him to take a revolver or two, which he did. It turned out to be one of the most amazing performances I have ever seen. He didn't miss a single shot."

A short time later Eifler reported to General Stilwell's headquarters. Stilwell was working at his desk as Eifler entered and saluted. He looked up as he became aware of Eifler's presence.

"Hello, Buffalo Bill, now what the hell do you want?"

"The General told me to report to him whenever I was in the

area," was the reply.

"All right, so you're in the area. You must want or need something."

Eifler did need something but he was not going to ask the general for money.

"No, sir, everything is going well," he said.

A general discussion ensued concerning progress, training camps, methods, and recruiting. Eifler carefully avoided the discussion of money. It remained for Stilwell to finally mention it.

"How are you fixed for funds, Eifler?"

"Fine, sir. No problems," replied Eifler.

"I think that's a lot of bull. You're scrounging funds from all over. Looks like your outfit is sucking hind tit."

Eifler paused a bit. He had hoped this would not get back to the salty old general. Now that it was out, he decided to face it straight on.

"When I came over I had adequate funds," he began. "Because of a change in Washington my funds were cut off. I have had to improvise."

A conflict entered the general's mind. The warmth that he felt for Eifler, like a son, versus that of a commanding general, responsible for one quarter of the world and facing a situation involving a man with an organization he never approved of to begin with. Finally he made his decision. He called in his chief of staff.

"Give Eifler $50,000 accountable to no one but me," he told him. Then, turning to Eifler he said: "Do you think that will hold you and your goddamned thugs for a while?"

Eifler nodded.

"Then will you give back to Dorman-Smith his money?"

"Yes, sir, as soon as I can," Eifler promised.

Stilwell then launched into a new subject. "Eifler, we have a bunch of Thais who want to operate in the area. Specifically, their homeland area. Can you use them?"

There was a hesitation on Eifler's part. Not that he could not figure a way to use them, but would he be expected to supply them out of his meager resources.

"I can use them, sir. I cannot supply them."

"I don't expect you to, Eifler. They have $50,000 with them. You'll have to figure how to get that money past the bandits."

Eifler said thoughtfully: "We can handle that, sir."

The meeting was over. Eifler received the $50,000 and left. The problem of getting Thai Group Commander Nicol-Smith and his group's money past the bandits was solved soon thereafter. Eifler and

Nicol-Smith decided to buy gold, convert it into buttons, and sew them on. Whenever they needed money, they could pull off a button. Complications soon arose, however. COI began its purchase of gold in south India, away from normal military units. In short order, British intelligence picked up these strange men purchasing gold who seemingly had vast amounts of money but could not account for it nor explain themselves. COI faced the task of calling the British off without explaining what was going on. The fact that COI was asking them to give up their investigation evidently convinced them they should comply, which they did.

The Thai group completed its final training, in the Nazira camps. Immediately after graduation, resplendent in their gold-buttoned clothes, they moved into action against the Japanese.

They were in a race with two teams of British and one Chinese group also attempting to enter the area. The primary goal of these groups, however, was not fighting the Japanese but trying to establish themselves as rulers of the country after the war was over. OSS had been warned not to get involved in the sticky political situation but could hardly refrain from being dragged in.

The British SO,E had formed a Siam country section of Force 136 at Calcutta that June. It was commanded by an executive of the Bombay-Burma Trading Corporation, a company that had held valuable shipping contracts and teak forest leases in prewar Thailand. They formed a second group from among Chinese Thai-speaking men who had been born in Bangkok. It turned out these men were all hostile to the British and were agents of Tai Li who had "helped" the British select them.

Then a new force surfaced. A mysterious telegram from Chungking announced the arrival of Pridi's envoy, Chamkad Balankura. Pridi was a former Thai Cabinet Minister and the "regent" to the child king. He was considered a strong leader of his people.

Before Smith could meet Balankura and arrange to fly him to Washington for consultation, Balankura mysteriously "fell ill" and "died of cancer." Tai Li had made his presence and intentions known.

Two other Thai representatives, Sanguan Tularai and Dengh Tilakh were held in Chinese custody. They had come out to make a special request—that Pridi and other anti-Japanese be smuggled from Bangkok to form an exile movement. The British were dead set against it. They refused to even meet with them.

OSS felt differently and by covert methods managed to get them out of Chinese hands and back to Washington before the "cancer" spread to them.

Lord Louis Mountbatten, supreme commander of the area had his own man—the son of an ex-Dane who had headed a street railway firm in Bangkok. The entire Thai group disliked him and the prince he represented. Later the groups met with Mountbatten and an attempt was made to join the OSS and SO,E groups. It did not work. The outcome was an agreement that there was room for two separate groups to work and each went its own way.

The political cauldron bubbled. In December, 1943, Donovan flew to Chungking to remove Miles from his OSS post. Miles had maintained a close alliance with Tai Li feeling he could work with him to defeat the Japanese in spite of his many shortcomings.

Back home the State Department was locked in diplomatic arguments with London and suggested a statement from them supporting "a free and independent Thailand after the war" and "that Great Britain has no territorial ambitions in Thailand."

The British response was, "the attainment by Siam of complete autonomy cannot be held to have justified itself in practice."

It went on to say Thailand should be placed under "some sort of tutelage" for a "period following upon the termination of the war."

The blatant expression of postwar imperialism stunned and angered the State Department.

And against the background of political maneuvering in London and Chungking the OSS group tried to keep its goal of infiltrating Thailand to bring the fight to the Japanese.

With a stroke of luck Nicol-Smith found a Swiss educated Chinese Catholic priest who knew the area and agreed to guide four of the Thai officers to the Thai border. The race to Bangkok was on.

In October the OSS Free Thais were at their receivers in China when they received their first transmissions from their colleagues. They had reached Bangkok. In short order massive intelligence was flowing from the country guiding Chennault's warplanes to targets and reporting on Japanese troop positions and strength.

The British, angered over the American success, attempted to downplay OSS achievements but were contradicted by the Thais. Donovan was committed to training and equipping the Thai forces regardless of political consequences.

The inevitable question was whether or not the British would openly object to OSS aiding Pridi's guerillas. The answer was that OSS would do it even in direct contravention of Mountbatten's directives. Happily a direct confrontation was avoided.

Later, when Germany's defeat seemed imminent, many OSS officers were transferred from that theatre into the CBI theatre. They were pleased with the unusual and mysterious culture of the Thais.

In turn the Thais liked the easy-going Americans who had no territorial claims on them. One of the most popular OSS men was a young officer who attempted an after dinner speech to some guerrilla leaders in his halting Thai.

"American officers hate Japanese, love Thai people. Otherwise they are no good, all the time drink whisky, shoot crap, fornicate, masturbate." His hastily taken language training course had failed him. The story of the officer's speech spread throughout the country like wildfire. The Thais loved it for it proved the Americans were indeed a different breed as they did not try to be superior or stand on dignity as the Japanese did.

5

Other graduates of Camp X carried out many strange and exotic missions. Along with Eifler, one of the first graduates was Ilia Tolstoy, grandson of the famous Russian novelist.

He was older than the great majority of his compatriots. In his forties, he had fought in the Russian Army during the first World War. He stoically bore the off hours craziness of his fellow students as they let off steam.

His mission born out of two reasons was to be one of the more unusual assignments of the war. First, in the Summer of 1942, with the Allies on the defensive, America and England had to consider the fact that the Japanese and Germans might somehow meet in the Middle East where the German army now was heading toward the Suez—What supply lines could the Allies use then? Looking at the map the answer seemed to lie on the ancient caravan route between India and China. The answer was Tibet.

The second reason lay in seeking support of the Dalai Lama, spiritual leader of the world's Buddhists, with an immense following. Countless numbers of Hindus, Jains and Buddhists had proclaimed that the navel of the earth and its axis lay somewhere in the kingdom of Tibet. Aware of the touchy problem with China, which laid claim to Tibet, OSS considered moving cautiously, then decided the war superseded political considerations.

Colonel Goodfellow became involved. To show good intentions and at the same time America's technology, President Roosevelt had a special watch created. It was a masterpiece showing not only the time but phases of the moon and the tides. Such a gift was bound to both impress the Dalai Lama and hopefully win him to the Allied side.

In July, 1942, Tolstoy and fellow OSS officer Lt. Brooke Dolan left on their mission with a hearty send-off by Donovan himself. Dolan was an accomplished explorer of the Far East in addition to being an adventurer. Fellow OSS officers were less awed by the magnitude of the task taken on by these two men. They named the two "Mud" and "Slug."

They stopped in New Delhi to confer with General Stilwell and await arrangements being made by the British who sadly shook their heads. Finally the lengthy and dangerous journey began.

Following narrow trails the OSS caravan moved slowly up and into the towering Himalayas in September. "Scientific instruments" and nearly three hundred pounds of camera equipment accompanied them. The spectacular scenery was additionally brightened by colorful caravans coming down the same narrow trails bringing grain, wool and hides.

They received courtesies by virtue of the Red Arrow letter that had come from the Dalai Lama. It was about two feet long and sixteen inches wide. It fluttered from a standard and was to tell village headmen to care for them and provide transport at reasonable rates. At one point Dolan fell ill. Pneumonia delayed the mission but in a manner that eventually was to prove beneficial.

While he recovered, Tolstoy gathered some Tibetans and played polo and led them in cavalry drills. In Tolstoy's opinion his familiarity with horses and expertise in handling animals eliminated many barriers that otherwise would have stood between the Westerners and the horse-loving Tibetans.

It took another month for Dolan to recover before "Mud" and "Slug" and their small caravan could move on. At 14,000 feet they had trouble breathing. Tolstoy was later to write a *National Geographic* article in 1946 wherein he stated, "we sometimes felt the effect of the altitude and would wake up in the night gasping for breath. We found that propping ourselves in a semi-sitting position was best for sleep."

Tibet had its own untouchables—the Porus. In visiting their village Tolstoy remembered these were the buriers of the dead. Actually, while they are called buriers their practice differs. They cut the cadavers into small pieces and put them out for the vultures. In this manner they make their living.

While Tolstoy would have preferred hunting some of the game that they came across he did not because the Dalai Lama had forbidden the killing of wild animals. Many photographs were taken not only of the game but strategic spots that might later be sabotaged should the Japanese occupy Tibet.

They came upon the well known Samden Gompa monastery. It was headed by a five year old abbess called the "Diamond Sow." Here Dolan's scholarly skills came into play in discussing the origins of the Diamond Sow. In 1717 the monastery was then a nunnery. The Mongols besieged it. After a lengthy time the abbess was forced to open the gates. At the same time she turned all her nuns into sows. The Mongols beat a hasty retreat after witnessing this miracle.

Tolstoy and Dolan were given magic seeds wrapped in prayer-covered Tibetan papers. Aware of the Asian propensity for gift-giving, the two men had numerous gifts to likewise dispense. In their luggage were dress uniforms that they donned when meeting local dignitaries.

New experiences continued daily as they wound their way upward, finally reaching the Mystery City of Lhasa. At a roadside park they were taken into a tent. Before them was a table bearing dried fruit and candy. Large copper teapots provided hot buttered tea. After appeasing the spirits by throwing rice over their shoulders the men were presented letters of welcome and ceremonial scarves from the various levels of functionaries of the Tibetan court.

Later they inspected a detachment of the Trapchi regiment which served the Dalai Lama as his bodyguard. After this they entered their temporary home, the house of the British Political Officer for Sikkim, Bhutan and Tibet. They waited for the Court Astrologer to consult the stars and determine the most auspicious time for their meeting with the Dalai Lama.

The time was finally decided—December 20, 1942 at 9:20 a.m. High above the town the Potala Palace stood perched on a huge rock. Precisely at 9:20 a.m. that day the two OSS officers went first to the roof of the palace, then to a small room used for official receptions. For a short time they stood before a heavy curtain with rows of monks seated before it. Finally the curtain was drawn and they entered the throne room.

Seated cross legged on his square throne of teakwood inlaid with gold the ten year old Dalai Lama wore a peaked yellow hat. On a lower throne to his right sat the regent who exercised all civil and ecclesiastical powers until the Dalai Lama was of age.

The Dalai Lama received the visitors and the gifts they bore. According to the customs of the country the gifts were first laid on a scarf, then presented. They included a photograph of President Franklin Roosevelt in a silver frame, a presidential letter in a cylindrical casket and the gold wristwatch. A small model galleon in silver was added as a personal gift by "Mud" and "Slug." Tea drinking and rice-throwing ceremonies followed, after which the Dalai Lama saw other pilgrims seeking his blessing.

In return for his gifts the Dalai Lama sent President Roosevelt Tibetan stamps, some rare coins, four pieces of gold and a presentation scarf.

OSS had outlined the goals of this particular mission as "to observe the attitudes of the peoples of Tibet; to seek allies and discover enemies, locate strategic targets and survey the territory as a possible field for future activities."

OSS was satisfied that "Mud" and "Slug" achieved most of these goals.

The government of China, however, was most displeased with the mission. Chiang Kai-shek and General Tai Li expressed their displeasure with what they considered meddling in China's territory. They were even more upset with a request made by the Tibetan government. It was for a radio transmitter.

The request did not seem complicated and was duly relayed to OSS. In short order the arrangements were made. State Department officials, however, learned of the request and promptly tried to quash it saying it would be, "politically embarrassing and cause irritation and offense to the Chinese," who had territorial claims in Tibet. Chiang Kai-shek "would not welcome the introduction of such a potent facility as a radio transmitter," since they would not "have any control over the transmitter or the material broadcasted." Very strongly the State Department recommended that OSS forget it.

Before leaving Lhasa for the five month journey to China, Tolstoy had strongly recommended the transmitter pointing out they had been well received and treated and that he felt a bond had been reached with the Tibetans.

In November, 1943, the transmitter reached Tibet. The action angered the Chinese government who sought to block all further OSS expansion into China.

An interesting problem arose when the caravan disbanded in China and the two men proceeded to Chungking. Inflation was rampant and upon selling the animals and equipment there turned out to be a surplus. They asked OSS-Washington how to handle it.

Colonel Preston Goodfellow recalled, "It threw the officials into a quandary. They had never had a profit. There were no forms to complete or way to explain why some money was due to be turned back. Our officials told us they didn't want to hear any more about it, it was an OSS problem. We finally solved it by putting it back in the general OSS fund."

It was grinding salt into a sore when months later Brooke Dolan surfaced as an OSS representative to the Chinese Communists up north.

Both "Mud" and "Slug" received the Legion of Merit for their unusual and hazardous journey.

Eifler had further discussions with Dorman-Smith whom he began to regard with fondness It seemed the governor was rather a maverick himself. Stilwell never did like the governor and had on occasion referred to him as "Sir Doormat." Eifler, however, realized that this Englishman was more intelligence-minded than most politicians.

From May, 1939, when he had assumed the governorship of Burma, Dorman-Smith felt Japan would invade Burma. His own intelligence units said they would not. He summed it up himself rather succinctly: "I based all my actions on the assumption Burma would be invaded. This was just a hunch on my part. Such was our odd setup in Burma that I had no say in military affairs, apart from bitterly complaining to London that our forces stationed in Burma were incapable of offering any effective resistance to a serious invasion. Politely I was told to keep my big mouth shut!"

Neither COI nor its British equivalent, SOE, were popular with the High Commands. There was a suspicion of private armies, assassinations, and such. Dorman-Smith felt this changed somewhat after Dunkirk. He was a proponent of "left behind" parties, small guerrilla bands that were typical of COI operations. When the invasion did come, he contacted a British officer who had shown success battling Chinese infiltrators into the Shan states and asked him to organize some "left behinds" to make life a bit more uncomfortable for the Japanese. Here was a politician who thought along Eifler's own lines.

Dorman-Smith had infuriated many of his peers by associating with "dark faces." In governing Burma, he had many Burmese officials and dealt with them as equals. While not general British policy, it was effective and brought much information to the governor he would not ordinarily have enjoyed. A few short days after Japanese forces had invaded south Burma, one of the Burmese ministers addressed himself to Dorman-Smith.

"Your excellency, we will show you the secret trail the Japanese will use to enter north Burma."

As governor, Dorman-Smith was well aware there was some secret trail the Burmese smugglers had used for many years. The British had never found it. Delighted to be offered this aid, he took down full particulars and immediately dispatched it to British General Sir Alexander. General Alexander and his staff ridiculed the whole idea and took no steps to defend the rugged area where a patrol might have held off several battalions. The Japanese invaded exactly as the Burmese minister had predicted, and all of Burma fell.

At Nazira, Eifler sat on the veranda of the large house now occupied by his men. With him was the British manager of the tea plantation. A native ran up with a chit. The manager read it, turned to Eifler and said: "Would you like to get a python? There is one down at the corner of the plantation."

Eifler replied by jumping to his feet, running inside, seizing a shotgun, and saying: "Let's go."

They followed the native through the rows of tea bushes to a spot where a cluster of the workers stood in fear, looking on the ground. Pushing them aside, Eifler saw something rare even in the Orient. There were two king cobras, not pythons, and they were copulating. Eifler fired and cut one in two. The second slithered off into the brush. "Grab a stick, pin him down," roared Eifler. The natives made no move to get near the dreaded snake. They knew not even the white man could survive the touch of the king cobra. It was now almost out of sight. Eifler lunged forward and grabbed it by the tail, pulling it back. "Get me a stick or something to pin it," he yelled.

One of the natives came out of his trance long enough to hand him a dah, a large curved knife. Eifler now knew he had death by the tail. He would give a quick upward yank, which would cause the head to snap back toward him. At that point he would attempt to behead the snake. If he missed—the snake would win. The natives drew farther back, realizing what was now going to happen. The giant American locked in a death struggle with a ten-foot cobra was tense but confident. He made his play, and the snake's head came into view as it turned to attack its tormenter. In that split second the dah flashed, and with perfect timing the cobra's head was severed. Eifler went back to try to find the other half of the first one he had shot. A third cobra now put in its appearance. It was evidently a younger one for it measured only five feet. It was quickly dispatched. The natives refused to touch even the skins of the dead snakes.

The next morning Eifler was sleeping soundly when the manager awakened him. "Carl, you've got to get up," he said.

"What for?" asked the sleepy Eifler.

"The natives won't go back to work until they see you. They think you're dead," he informed him.

"Why the hell would I be dead?"

"Their legend is that no one can touch a king cobra and live. Some say you were seen alive last night. Just let them see you."

Eifler arose, put on his uniform, and casually walked out onto the open veranda. Across the front yard, spilling out through the gate and down the little road were hundreds of Indians. A low murmur arose. Excited conversation filled the air. Slowly they rose from their haunches, turned, and strolled back to work. The legend had been defied. Sahib Major was indeed alive.

The Nazira training camps were now in full operation. Men and boys of all nationalities were receiving instruction in radio, cryptography, demolitions, parachuting, assassinations, and every necessary phase of operations. But they needed actual practice in the jungles. Just to the north of Nazira lay the Naga lands. Heavy jungle growth hid the fierce Naga headhunters. Eifler said this was to be the final training grounds for his agents. He did fear, however, that the Nagas might not cooperate. He did not want his trained agents winding up as grisly trophies on some village pole. Especially he did not want his men to have to fight the Nagas and get a full uprising underway. One morning Eifler went to one of his native instructors and said: "We're going up into the hills today to see the Nagas. We leave now."

Each man carried a sidearm. They walked past the buzzing tea fields where the workers seemed as numerous as the bushes. Soon the neatly trimmed rows gave way to ragged underbrush. They began climbing and entered the large black jungle. The trail was clearly marked. The growth was extremely heavy. They could not see more than five feet on either side of the trail. Several miles farther they ran into three young Naga girls. The girls threw their baskets aside and ran up the trail. The instructor turned to Eifler.

"The fact those women ran could mean the Nagas are on the warpath. Nagas are trained to protect their women. Their men are often decorated for going into another village and capturing their women. The women will now report our presence."

With this bit of cheerful information, Eifler moved forward. The instructor reluctantly followed. From the heavy foliage came ominous silence. They knew they were being watched. Soon a noise was heard just ahead. Eifler stopped. "Call out and say we are friends," he said.

"I don't speak their language," was the comforting reply.

"Well, damn it, say it in any language you can, then," Eifler said.

In Hindustani and Burmese the instructor relayed the message. Eifler added it in Japanese. Silence. They moved forward. They broke into a small clearing where three Naga men sat on their haunches. They were naked and staring unconcernedly into a small fire. Eifler tried sign language. He seemed to be getting nowhere. It was apparent one of the men was the most important, so Eifler made attempts to communicate with him. A standoff. Finally the Naga reached over to a small knapsack lying on the ground. He removed a tin can. From it he removed a smaller can. From that still a smaller can, and so on until five cans in graduated sizes lay beside his dirt encrusted feet. From the final one he pulled a folded piece of paper and handed it to Eifler.

Eifler read it and stifled an urge to burst into laughter.

The note was written in English, obviously by someone in the

82

local village. It stated the bearer of the note and his people wished to work for the U.S. Army. Even the jungle savages knew American personnel were in the area.

The Naga chief and his tribe were hired on the spot. Eifler moved them to O Camp where they simply lay around for a month. There really was nothing for them to do but with them on the payroll, the native agents would be safe. To give them something to work on, Eifler ordered a dugout made from a tree. Several weeks later he checked to see if it was done. It had not even been started yet. He asked why. The answer was simple—he had failed to provide them with the log.

Eifler made it a habit to visit the camps to see how his boys were doing. As they came through the obstacle courses, he would pull his .45 and put a few slugs several inches in front of them. He wanted to see how they would react under fire. Fortunately, his uncanny accuracy held true, and none of the agents became statistics in the camps. One case of misjudgment, however, did result in an injury to one of the original DET 101 men. Maj. Archie Chun Ming did not react as Eifler anticipated when he threw a Naga spear. It passed entirely through his foot and on into the earth. It was quickly withdrawn, and Chun Ming rushed to a nearby hospital for treatment.

"Archie never blew the whistle on me," said Eifler. "If I hadn't told what happened no one but the two of us would have ever known." Later Chun Ming fell ill and required surgery. With no doctor available, Eifler performed the surgery himself under Chun Ming's directions. The Doctor described it as a "very professional job."

Eifler found it necessary to visit Calcutta once more for several reasons. One of them was to check over the DET 101 branch being run by Capt. Harry Little. This vital link made certain that supplies as well as personnel reached their destinations in Nazira. All was well with the Calcutta headquarters, and Eifler set out to see about a counterintelligence unit to work against the very strong Japanese ring established there.

As was common with police operations everywhere a working relationship with the local prostitutes was established. It was always amazing how much information the local ladies of the night could provide. The most famous prostitute was a striking redhead named Margot. She was so well known that the Calcutta DSM was known to stand for "Did Sleep with Margot." Later those who did not make the grade equally claimed it as a "Didn't Sleep with Margot" notation, so all who reached Calcutta could now claim the designation.

Shortly after Eifler's return to Calcutta and subsequent visit to solicit help from the ladies, a lavish military party was held in Delhi. Many of the British officers had their wives with them. None of the American officers had their wives. One American officer decided it might be a good idea to bring Margot. After all, she was a beautiful woman and would attract much attention. He swept into the dinner hall with her on his arm. She was the picture of charm. She smiled radiantly and, to their horror, began addressing many of the assembled officers by name. Wives began asking their ashen-faced husbands who she was. Several officers suddenly remembered important duties that called them away from the party. The American officer had brought as much action to that party as a stray cat entering a dog show. Eifler always denied that he was the one responsible.

Several weeks earlier Eifler had met a British colonel who had stayed behind in Burma to harass the enemy. He was now in Calcutta, and a small party was held for him and his wife. He then disappeared, evidently on another assignment. This was not at all unusual, and no one questioned it. On one of Eifler's visits to the red light district he ran into the colonel's wife. They both acted as if they had never met, and he never mentioned it.

There were two streets in the district—the upper and the lower. The more desirable and higher-priced women occupied the upper. When Father Time put his unmistakable mark on the women, or they acquired V.D., they were moved to the lower street. Some information of value was gathered from these contacts.

In Nazira it was agreed a cover name and identity was needed for the DET 101 men. The earlier designation of 5405-A was resurrected and combined with the questionable name of Field Experimental Station 5405-A, which told absolutely nothing. Surely the presence of sentries, the arrival and departure of all kinds of soldiers, and the transmission of radio messages that rode on the soft summer nights told some of the story.

The Naga payroll arrangement soon bore additional fruit. The natives reported seeing parachutists coming down in the mountains just above Nazira. The plane bore a red circle. It hadn't taken the Japanese long to find out where the COI headquarters were located. A bonus was offered for the heads of these men. Grinning, the Nagas departed, happy to serve in their normal fashion. About six days later several of them ventured into camp with a large bamboo basket. It contained the heads of the parachutists. Their arrival coincided with the afternoon mess. The basket was put on the table where the men were eating. Those with squeamish stomachs hurried from the room to lose their lunch. They never heard the end of it. The Nagas were compensated and left with all parties well pleased—with the natural

84

exception of those in the basket.

To try to make life a bit more bearable for the enlisted men, a small toilet facility was constructed which included a shower and an actual flush toilet made out of cement. It was cold but did serve the purpose. Late one evening one of the men was utilizing the stool. To his horror, he heard Eifler outside conducting one of the English wives on a tour of the facility. They came in the shower side where Eifler pointed out how the cement had been used, the drainage, the crude but effective plumbing, etc. Eifler then walked into the toilet where the man sat. He continued describing this additional room and did not beat a hasty retreat as the embarrassed occupant anticipated. The unsuspecting Englishwoman followed from the shower area until she realized there were now three people. Her face turned bright red as she looked away. The man looked pitifully at Eifler who calmly remarked: "That's okay, soldier, don't get up," and marched on out the door. The man claimed a four-day case of locked bowels.

The unit was not without other problems. In one case one of the enlisted men was sent to Calcutta with classified material in a dispatch case. He was armed with the usual Colt .45 automatic. As the train began its long and arduous trip, the sergeant began nipping at a bottle. Slowly the level of the bottle dropped until he was finally well lubricated. Also in the same car were two British soldiers. There were many cases of hard feelings between the Americans and the British. The sergeant felt this had to be one of them. He began by throwing a few remarks at them about the general poor character of all British subjects. They wisely ignored him. Then he began getting specific about these two in particular. He questioned their ancestry and said how sad it was their parents had obviously never married. At this point he got their attention, and now they returned a few bon mots about Americans. The sergeant by now had used his most choice adjectives and four-letter words. He reworded some of his best phrases and, for emphasis, drew his .45. Realizing the debate was about to be lost, the two British soldiers beat a strategic withdrawal to the head. Sensing total victory now, the sergeant leaped to his feet and ran down the aisle after them. His dispatch case was completely forgotten and he had lost all concern about it. He raised his .45 and fired several shots through the door. Fortunately, he did not hit them. As calmer heads intervened to break up this little disagreement, a scuffle ensued. The sergeant managed not only to lose his dispatch case but also to fall from the train. It was assumed he had some assistance on the latter.

When the report reached Eifler, the sergeant was locked up in Calcutta by army authorities. His list of violations was lengthy. Eifler was furious. His bellows echoed from the Naga Hills and back again. "Goddamn, I want that son of a bitch brought back here and now."

It was pointed out he was in the custody of the army, who would bring charges.

"He is my man. I will not have someone else court-martialing one of my men. Curl, you and Aitken bring him back. And I mean bring him back."

The two men knew better than to point out the difficulty of getting him released. They thought of breaking him out but decided against that. Relations between the army, the air corps, and the highly secret COI operations were not the best. Arriving in Calcutta, they proceeded to file considerable delays and other legal maneuverings. Finally he was released to their authority and returned to Nazira. Eifler was in rare voice as he finally faced the thoroughly saddened sergeant. After the chewing, he was reduced to a private and returned to his duties. He was never able to be commissioned because of this blot on his record.

Later Gen. Frank Merrill asked Eifler what he had done to the erring sergeant.

"I took his stripes, General," he promptly replied.

"For how long?" was the next question.

Eifler paused. "Oh, do you think a month is long enough?"

The salty old general called him a son of a bitch, and that closed the conversation.

There was never any doubt as to who commanded DET 101. Eifler was always decisive and vocal. He did not make all of his decisions on his own. He realized the talent of other officers, and they often thoroughly discussed various plans before a decision was reached. He in particular conferred with Coughlin and Peers. He remarked that Peers was one of the most difficult men he had ever had to manage. Most certainly Peers would have returned the compliment. In spite of this, a genuine respect existed between the two men. Eifler's flair for boldness, imagination, and innovation could not be matched. Peers was equally adept at organizing and managing.

On one occasion Eifler sent Peers to Karachi with one-way orders and replaced him with a second lieutenant. Peers later sent word he had "learned his lesson" and asked to return. He was returned.

The CBI (China-Burma-India) theater was in chaos a good deal of the time. General Stilwell fought a continual and losing battle for more men, equipment, and priority for his command. He fought a constant battle against Chiang Kai-shek, whom he always referred to as "The Peanut." During 1942 the CBI theater had a priority listing below that of the Caribbean. Stilwell felt Chiang Kai-shek was in a contradictory position. Obviously, Chiang wanted a defeat of Japan but one with no effort on China's part. China wanted to coast into the winner's circle. Chiang, he felt, had an insidious reason for demanding more and more arms, even though he refused to turn the Chinese troops against the enemy. The more help diverted to the Orient and Pacific, the more it would relieve the pressure on Germany. In so doing it might help Germany to defeat Russia. China greatly preferred a Nazi victory to a strong Russia on her border. Stilwell likened Chiang's government to that of the Nazis. "Same type of government, same outlook, same gangsterism," he wrote home to his wife.

In the many training camps of DET 101 the need for additional personnel was felt more acutely than ever. Eifler continued inquiries of top personnel from the increasing numbers of U.S. troops arriving. One in particular was a young, fresh-shaven lieutenant. Eifler liked his style. After a brief conversation, Eifler applied for his transfer, and a few weeks later he became a part of DET 101, probably with little idea of what he had really joined.

On his first routine assignment he disappeared. He was found, quite drunk, sitting in a yard with some natives. He was brought back to an irate Eifler.

"Lieutenant, get your drunk butt in bed. When you've slept it off, report back to me," he shouted.

"I'm not drunk and I won't go to bed," he replied.

Eifler walked over, slapped him soundly and repeated the order. This time it was obeyed.

The next morning he reported, freshly shaved. He saluted. "Sir, I request permission to speak to the inspector general," he said.

"On what subject, Lieutenant?"

"A superior officer is forbidden to strike a junior officer. You hit me yesterday. I want to report it," was the clipped reply.

"Permission denied, and if I ever hear you speak of it again I'll cut your goddamned throat," was the terse reply. Eifler went back to work. The lieutenant went back to drinking.

Coughlin then reported he had found the lieutenant drunk in a British club. Eifler had forbidden him to drink. Court-martial was out of the question, however, because an officer cannot forbid a fellow officer to drink. Eifler called him in and told him he was giving him an unsatisfactory rating and transferring him to another command.

"I don't understand your action, Major. I am a damn good officer."

Eifler nodded. "You are a damn good officer when you're sober, but that isn't often enough. I'll tell you something else, Lieutenant.

You can do a good job under the new C.O. and make me look like an ass, but you won't. You'll get drunk before you get through Calcutta, and the MPs will pick you up." He then dismissed him.

The transfer went through. COI operatives in Calcutta later reported that he had been picked up, drunk, in Calcutta and shipped back to the United States for discharge.

In the training camps around Nazira, the instructors relentlessly worked the would-be agents in hand-to-hand combat, forgery, lock picking, picking pockets, map reading, Morse code, cryptography, silent ways of killing sentries, and working on special equipment. A radio was desperately needed that would feed back across the miles. The Burma mountains stood in between. The communications section was under command of Lt. Phillip S. "Gob" Huston. In particular Sgt. Alan Richter was hard at work on this project. His instructions were to make a receiver and transmitter small enough to be carried but powerful enough to do the job. Also at work with him were Sgts. Don Eng and Fima Haimson. The sets were built from scratch and hunger. The commercial sets they had brought with them from America didn't work. The monsoons flooded them out. Also, they all operated on a.c. current which was unavailable in the jungle.

Fortunately, among the supplies, were many components such as resistors and capacitors and a lot of wire. To get the transmitters working the men had to take the transformers apart and rewire them. Eifler's instructions indicated the transmitter and receiver had to be both small and not in excess of forty pounds complete with batteries. The men scrounged around trying to find the components. Nothing would work.

The military had some bulky equipment—some of their hand generators were considered, but were too big. After three or four weeks of improving on the design, they came up with a transmitter that had a single tube. It had a "home brew" receiver that contained three tubes. They couldn't standardize on the transmitter or receiver because when they ran out of one type of tube they would have to use another. In Calcutta they found enough commercial parts to set up a small assembly line. The equipment they started with was built on aluminum chassis that were actually the belly skins of C-47s that had crashed at Dinjan Airport. They fabricated their own variable tuning capacitors out of C-ration cans. The resistors proved to be a real problem. Finally they took some flashlight cells and removed the carbon rods to make their own resistors.

When the first set was completed, it was taken one hundred miles away to be tested. It worked fine. The transmitter and receiver weighed eight to ten pounds apiece. The battery pack took up the rest, but it was all within the forty-pound limit. Before taking it into Burma, one final test was made. Don Eng went into lower India, a distance of about two thousand miles. From Mysore a regular schedule was maintained. Eifler's request had become a reality. Eventually there were seventy-two of these sets working all over Burma. They were crystal controlled, and the men had to find calibration crystals to get day and night operations out of them. They got them from old signal corps equipment. The crystal was on 3,500 kc., and daytime doubled the frequency. The antenna was a piece of insulated wire thrown over the limbs of a tree or bush. The lower the aerial, the better the distance.

One thing the ingenious men could not make themselves was the gasoline necessary to run the main camp generators. Visitors to the camps often felt themselves in great demand as the hardworking radio men insisted they stay "just a little while longer." What the guests did not know was that one of the group was busily siphoning some of the gas from his vehicle to insure a steady supply. The men never knowingly caused someone to run out of gas on the return trip. After making the radio units, many of the men went into the field with their stepchild. Richter moved south in Burma to Sumprabum to set up the first field base. Later on the Japanese moved farther north, forcing the evacuation of that base.

It is a fact no one radio operator can fool another in sending and receiving. A certain touch or feeling is developed by training and living together. The British knew this when they captured a German agent in London and asked him to send false information to his base in Germany. They prevailed on him to do so with the promise of knighthood. He did his job and in a secret ceremony was knighted. No such honors or glory awaited 101's operators. They did become involved with something else, however—telepathy. Many times Huston, Eng, and Richter picked up each other on either seldom-used frequencies or at times when normal operations were over. For an unknown reason they would turn on their equipment and hear the other calling with a desperate message. Often it solved a critical problem of some mission. There was a feeling of a higher power intervening to give DET 101 an unexpected assist. They were always grateful.

Behind the well guarded walls of OSS headquarters in Washington was the research and development division. From within its corridors came all types of exotic weapons and poisons.

Heading it was Dr. Stanley Lovell, a noted chemist and holder of over 70 U.S. and foreign patents. He was credited with the invention of many of the new weapons used by OSS. He was termed "Professor Moriarty" by Donovan who hired him for his "devious mind."

His answer to the question of what would be the one weapon he would want were he to land in the dead of night on an enemy coast where he would encounter German patrols and dogs was a masterpiece.

After searching his imagination he said, "I want a completely silent, flashless gun—a Colt automatic or a submachine gun—or both. I can pick off the first sentry with no sound or flash to explain his collapse, so the next sentry will come to him instead of sounding the alarm. Then, one by one, I'll pick them off."

After being told he was the man for OSS he went home to look up all references made about Professor Moriarty by Arthur Conan Doyle in his well known Sherlock Holmes stories.

"Famous scientific criminal...the greatest schemer of all time...the organizer of every deviltry!"

Lovell typed out the words and kept the paper under the blotter on his desk. His work began in earnest—as well as deviltry.

Contemplating the sudden switch in ethics Lovell went to Donovan to tell him of a concern—that the American public would not condone dirty tricks. Donovan's reply was to the point.

"Don't be so goddamn naive, Lovell. The American public may profess to think as you say they do, but the one thing they expect of their leaders is that we will be smart. Don't kid yourself. P.T. Barnum is still a basic hero because he fooled so many people. They will applaud someone who can outfox the Nazis and the Japs. Never forget that the Connecticut nutmegs were made of hardwood. Outside the orthodox warfare system is a great area of schemes, weapons and plans which no one who knows America really expects us to originate because they are so un-American, but once it's done, an American will vicariously glory in it. That is your area, Lovell, and if you think America won't rise in applause to what is so easily called un-American, you're not my man."

Lovell did see the point and summed it up saying it would be his job to enlist other scientists to "throw all your normal law abiding concepts out the window. There's a chance to raise merry hell. Come, help me raise it."

The silent, flashless gun was developed. It was a Colt action hi-standard with clips of a special .22 bullet. Donovan was so impressed he took it into the Oval office and while the President dictated a letter to his secretary Donovan fired a full clip into a sandbag he had brought along. When Roosevelt finished his dictation Donovan handed the hot weapon to him and said, "Mr. President I've just fired ten live bullets into that sandbag over there in the corner. Take the gun by the grip and look out for the muzzle as it's still hot."

So impressed was Roosevelt with the weapon he asked for his very own, then said, "Bill, you're the only black Republican I'll ever allow in my office with a weapon like this!"

Realizing the vast importance of such a potent weapon the OSS kept close tabs on who received it and its final disposition. In spite of the tightest records some of the weapons were reported as "destroyed" or "missing in combat." After the war the guns surfaced in the hands of the Haganah, the Jewish underground in Palestine. They were used with terrible effect. Anyone in a British uniform was a target for this unseen weapon. It was felt one reason Britain surrendered her mandate was the terrible sniping that could not be traced.

Lovell knew one of the main things his agents would need was faked documents, even counterfeited currency of various nations. This presented a tremendous problem because the Germans and Japanese both employed special fibers, invisible inks, trick watermarks and special chemicals incorporated into the paper so a forged document could be recognized immediately. He sought approval of the U.S. Treasury and Secret Service, either of which might be upset at such an operation. A short time later Lovell met with Secretary of the Treasury Morgenthau. Morgenthau had agreed to ask President Roosevelt if OSS might proceed. He told Lovell, "You come over here at eleven o'clock tomorrow. If I say, 'the President has a cold and I was unable to see him on your problem,' that means he allows you to go ahead at full speed. If I say, 'I took that matter up with the President and he refused authorization,' that means exactly what I say."

The next day Lovell entered the office to find at least twelve other men gathered around his conference table. As Lovell entered Morgenthau turned to them and said, "Excuse me, gentlemen; this is Dr. Lovell of OSS" He then turned to face Lovell and said, "Now, on that matter you asked me about, I was unable to see the President for approval because he has a cold. Do you understand that, Dr. Lovell?"

Lovell replied, "Yes, I do, Mr. Secretary. Thank you."

Although elated at the top level approval Lovell suddenly realized another terrible truth. He was all alone. If there was any breach of security, if anyone discovered the forgeries and duplicates and the press brought it to the public who then screamed about such "un-American" acts, Morgenthau had at least a dozen witnesses who could say they had heard the problem had not been taken to the President. Lovell was in it alone.

From that moment on OSS received the full cooperation and backing of the Treasury and Bureau of Engraving departments.

Work continued on other unusual items. Exploding candles were designed for European women to put on the night stand of their German conquerors. It would burn perfectly until the flame reached the high explosive composing the lower two-thirds of the candle. The wick then extended into a detonator which was embedded in the explosive.

Teams of behavioral scientists delved into the minds and psyche of the Germans and Japanese.

A device was invented that would blow the wheels off of a train. By use of a photo-electric device it was designed to activate when it went suddenly from light to dark as in entering a tunnel. The idea was to not only block the tunnel but to likewise have the device on the rescue train that would come from the other end of the tunnel. Knowing the thoroughness of the German character, but also the lack of imagination since they were trained only to follow orders, OSS put a label on the device stating, "This is a traffic control device of the Third Reich and is not to be tampered with by order of der Fuehrer. Heil Hitler." The OSS thinking was right, the Germans never questioned the strange device.

Americans who had been captured by the Germans reported they were never searched in their fob pocket. This was a small pocket that sat over the appendix and was used by Americans for carrying a pocket watch. Examining this for some possible device to help a captured agent the R&D laboratories came up with a single shot weapon. It measured 3 inches by a half inch and somewhat resembled a golfers stub pencil. It could not be reloaded. It was cocked by lifting an outer integument of the tube with the fingernail and holding the tiny gun in the palm of the hand. It fired when the operator squeezed the little raised lever down into place again.

Its use in one case was vivid and dramatic. An OSS agent had been picked up by the Gestapo. Though not sure who or what he was the German officer felt something was not right. After frisking him and finding no weapon they put him in the back seat of a command car and headed towards the German headquarters for further questioning. The officer had the car stop in a small village and got out to phone ahead to be sure a certain interrogator would be available. In the car the agent sat with only the military chauffeur in the front seat. Removing the "stinger" the agent put it at the base of the driver's skull and fired. Pushing the body to one side he took off in the car and drove back to the American lines. The weapon not only saved the agent's life but allowed allied planes to destroy the German headquarters where the agent was being taken. By telling the driver what route to take the German had given the OSS man vital information. Though not all uses of the weapon were so dramatic, many other agents also owed their lives to it.

Many devices were created because agents in the field said they would be useful. One who had nearly been trapped in the Adlon Hotel in Berlin said he would have given anything if he could have created a panic in the lobby. As it was the Germans picked up someone else.

Lovell's answer to that problem was "Hedy." It was a simple firecracker device. When a small wire loop was pulled it simulated the screeching effect of a falling Nazi bomb, then ended in a deafening roar. It was totally harmless. By activating the "Hedy" the agent had a chance to escape in the turmoil he had created. It was named after actress Hedy Lamarr.

On August 28, 1943, Lovell and Donovan were giving a talk to the Joint Chiefs of Staff. Lovell was demonstrating some of the more simple devices. As he spoke he activated a "Hedy" and tossed it in a wastebasket. A few seconds later the shrieking and howling began, concluding with a loud roar. Lovell and Donovan were surprised to see two and three star generals all fighting to exit the room via its single door. The demonstration was most successful but the two OSS men were never invited back.

At OSS staff meetings Lovell continually pointed out the advantages of democracy over dictatorships. In the latter there is chaos if the top man is lost, whereas America is the classical example of a smooth transition when our Presidents die or are assassinated.

"Lop off the head and the body falls," Lovell said. He then began plotting, how to get after the Axis leaders.

One day he saw a chance. A report came in stating that Hitler and Mussolini were going to have a war conference in the Brenner Pass.

At a meeting one of the S.O. (Subversive Operations) group said, "Let's parachute a cadre of our toughest men into the area and shoot up the bastards! Sure, it'll be a suicide operation, but that's what we're organized to carry out."

Donovan turned to Lovell and asked, "How would Professor Moriarty capitalize on this situation?"

Lovell said, "I propose an attack which they cannot anticipate. They'll meet in a conference room of an inn or a hotel. If we can have one operator for five minutes or less in that room, just before they gather, that is all we'll need."

Others in the room muttered under their breath. Heads were shaking in skepticism.

"Gentlemen, hear Professor Moriarty, if you please. Now what do you propose to have your man do in this conference room?"

"I suggest that he bring in a vase filled with cut flowers in water, and that he place it on the conference table or nearby."

A general on the OSS staff said, "So what."

As a West Pointer he had not been taught the fine art of dirty tricks.

"In this janitor's hand is a capsule containing liquid nitrogen-mustard gas. It's a new chemical derivative which has no odor whatever, is colorless and floats on water. I have it available in my laboratory," Lovell answered.

Now he had everyone's attention as he continued.

"As our man places the big bouquet on the conference table, he crushes the capsule and drops it in between the flowers. An invisible, oily film spreads over the water in the dish and starts vaporizing. Our man is safely out and I think he should disappear into Switzerland if possible."

"Forget the agent. What happens in the conference room?" the general pressed.

"Well, if they are in that room for twenty minutes, the invisible gas will have the peculiar property of affecting their bodies through their naked eyeballs. Everyone in that room will be permanently blinded. The optic nerve will be atrophied and never function again. A blind leader can't continue the war—at least I don't believe he can."

Several people started talking at once.

Lovell interrupted saying, "There's a big pay-off possible, if it is done."

"What's that, professor?" was the next question.

"Let's be completely bold in capitalizing on the event. If the Pope in Rome would issue a Papal Bull or whatever is appropriate it might say, 'My children, God in his infinite wisdom has stricken your leaders blind. His sixth Commandment is "Thou Shalt Not Kill." This blindness of your leader is a warning that you should lay down your arms and return to the ways of peace.'"

Donovan was quiet for a minute weighing the merit of the scheme. He turned to Lovell and said, "I'll see my friend about that idea, Professor Moriarty." He mentioned the name of a high church official. Then he turned to the staff and said, "You see why we have so depraved an idea man as Professor Moriarty on the staff. If he had been born a German I wouldn't give ten cents for Franklin Roosevelt's life."

Lovell couldn't resist saying, "but General, I was born a Cape Cod Republican."

With all preparations made for the Brenner meeting it was

changed at the last minute. German security, possibly with its own Professor Moriarty, recognized that the Allies would have a golden opportunity to get their leaders at one fell swoop. The meeting place and date were changed. They met in Hitler's private railway car with a tight ring of SS troops surrounding it.

Though the idea was not carried out it was nevertheless an introduction into a new method of warfare for America. Certainly the game of war is over much quicker if you can checkmate the King and ignore the pawns. They will surrender when told to do so.

Continuing to research possibilities of neutralizing leaders, Lovell read a report on Hitler by the person assigned to study him. He discussed with America's top diagnosticians and gland experts the fact that Hitler was definitely close to the male/female line. His gender was almost in question. His poor emotional control, his violent passions, his choice of companions all led Lovell to feel that a gentle nudge to the female side might work miracles. The German people might feel less inclined to follow *der Fuehrer* should he turn out to review his troops in a purple formal with silver shoes.

Further study showed Hitler was a vegetarian, his vegetables coming from his Berchtesgaden garden. A plan to get an OSS man or an anti-Nazi "gardener" to put female sex hormones, a carbamate or other quietus medication into Hitler's garden was approved. The fact that Hitler did not turn gay led Lovell to wonder if it was really tried or if the "gardener" threw away the syringes and medication.

A new idea with a deadly twist came about during a visit to Lovell by Admiral Milton "Mary" Miles who flew in from his China base. He was accompanied by Naval Captain Dr. Cecil Coggins who was to return to China and teach in the Chinese School of Assassination and Sabotage under the tutelage of General Tai Li.

Miles and Coggins had in mind a special poison that could be used against the high ranking Japanese officers who visited the Chinese prostitutes in Peking Shanghai and other cities. The poison needed to be so cleverly designed or packaged that the women could easily conceal it, the nature of their work not leaving them many places to hide the deadly dose.

Lovell decided on a botulinus toxin, the inert poison developed by botulinis bacterium. It was chosen because it is a natural toxin often found in vegetables, sausages or other similar foods not properly cooked. The poison was so deadly that housewives tasting string beans put up by a cold pack method had been instantly killed by eating a single bean. The botulism would therefore most likely divert suspicion from the Chinese hostesses.

The lethal dose was packaged in a gelatin capsule, so small it was about the size of a pinhead. The ladies were to be told to moisten and stick it behind their ear or in their hair. At the proper time insert it in the food or drink and it was *sayonara* time.

A coded message later arrived in Washington to the effect that the poison did not work. Lovell assumed it had somehow lost its potency.

Such was not the case, however. In reading the directions and looking at the tiny capsules, the Naval detail in Chungking felt they were totally incapable of killing anything. To test their theory they tried several of them on a hapless donkey wandering around the courtyard. When nothing happened they decided the toxin was really harmless and tossed the shipment in a drawer. Had they told Dr. Lovell what had transpired he would have told them that donkeys are one of the few living creatures immune to botulism. Many Japanese officers owe their lives to that simple beast.

Not all devices from Lovell's laboratories were ones of death and destruction. One was designed solely for psychological purposes. It was to give a lift to the people of China, long suffering under a brutal Japanese occupation. The Japanese soldier had a phobia about his toilet habits. He would not defecate anywhere near his companions but would take elaborate precautions to go off by himself. OSS came up with a chemical that produced the vile smell of a loose stool. It was put into a small toothpaste like tube. The tubes were then given to Chinese children who could sneak up behind a Japanese soldier, give a quick application to the seat of his pants and run. The soldier, smelling as if he had just had a revolting accident, would run from the village in humiliation to the delight and ridicule of the Chinese. Another plus of the product was that when the offending clothes were washed the substance infected any other clothes in the same batch. Appropriately it was named, "Who? Me?"

It won no battles but was definitely a morale booster.

An area of disagreement between Lovell and Donovan lay in the field of bacteriological warfare. President Roosevelt was totally opposed to it. Donovan would have no part of it. Warfare was fought by men, real men, shooting and bayoneting one another. Lovell thought exposing a soldier to a lethal or incapacitating organism was far less barbarous than putting a bayonet in his stomach, twisting it and leaving him to die from infection or loss of blood.

One day Lovell was invited to the Academy of Science building and introduced to Dr. George Merck, President of Merck and Company, Dr. Edwin B. Fred, later President of the University of Wisconsin, Admiral Rollo Eyer and John P. Marquand, the great novelist.

From there he was introduced into the inner circle of bacteriological warfare.

John P. Marquand was a scholarly bacteriologist and virologist. He named the laboratories where virulent organisms were cultured, "The Death Farm." In numerous discussions with Marquand the two men discussed pestilence and pandemic organisms.

Operation TORCH, the invasion of North Africa, took Lovell's mind from the subject as he watched the British in action knowing the Americans were about to land.

The tides of battle moved west, then east as the British battled the Italians. With the defeat of the Italians the Germans assigned one of their greatest generals to take over. It was Rommel. In short order he won back all the land the Italians had lost and was applying serious pressure against the Allies. The Americans had landed at Casablanca, Oran and Algiers. Their supply line was a single rail line that wound its way from Casablanca through the foothills of the Atlas mountains to Oran, Algiers and Tunis.

The battle at Kasserine Pass was a disaster. When it was over the sands were barely distinguishable from the bodies of American soldiers who died. Mismatched and improperly commanded they were caught in a massive German trap. Five thousand Americans were killed, wounded or missing by the time it was all over. A pall hung over the army who wondered when, if ever, Americans could match Rommel's veterans .

Adding to the horror of the battle was the performance of the Air Corps. Two or three squadrons of Flying Fortresses, ordered into battle to drop bombs on the Germans, missed their target by one hundred miles. They bombed the town of Souk el Arba, killing and wounding many Arabs.

On top of this came the boast of Herman Goering promising greater defeats on these Americans than Dunkirk. To paint even a worse picture OSS agents in Tangier and Melilla in Morocco suddenly sent in reports that large numbers of German troops were concentrating there. It was unexpected. OSS feared that they were engineers whose job was to destroy the single rail line that supplied the Allies.

Lovell was called in to the Pentagon. With the gloomy picture before them it now looked as if Franco might bring Spain into the war on the side of the Axis. Lovell was ordered to take whatever steps he might contrive to "eliminate Spanish Morocco." He replied it was clearly "out of channels." In positive terms he was told the matter was not to be discussed or disclosed to Donovan or anyone else.

Lovell knew the reason for secrecy. "Whatever steps" meant any and every means possible to destroy the enemy.

Working with Doctors Murray and Reed, Lovell manufactured a simulated goat dung. Goat dung was common in Spanish Morocco as it seemed there were more goats than people. But this particular goat dung was very special. It contained an attractant for house flies so powerful it would call them out of hibernation. It also carried an assortment of bacteria from tularemia and psittacosis to all the pests known to the Fourth Horseman of the Apocalypse. Flies were everywhere in Spanish Morocco at this summer season.

A fly has a nasty habit—he regurgitates whatever he has eaten if more attractive food happens along. So the Moroccan house fly was to be the culprit to incapacitate all of Spanish Morocco. Nothing was said of the civilian population who would likewise suffer severely. It would not be possible to kill only the Germans. The fact had to be accepted that civilians were to be sacrificed to stop the Axis threat.

It was decided to airdrop the goat dung on the flat roofs of the natives houses. While some might question how the stuff got on the roof it was not felt to be a problem as not too many people were inspecting roofs. Also they probably wouldn't be around too long anyway.

The operation, dubbed "Capri-cious" was well along when our agents radioed that the Germans were leaving *en masse*. Hitler was throwing them into the Battle of Stalingrad. It was a greatly relieved Dr. Lovell along with Doctors Murray and Reed who were able to close the books on this operation.

Donovan, had he known of it, would have likewise agreed. It was one of the rare times Lovell ever took on a project without letting Donovan know what was happening.

In a separate instance a milder form of bacteriological action was used to accomplish an important mission. It was directed at Franz von Papen. During World War I he had been sent as Military Attache to America and Mexico. After that war he said the philosophy of the Weimar Constitution was "detestable" because it held "all power derives from the people." As an aristocrat he felt the Hohenzollerns would one day be restored to power.

He became Chancellor of Germany for a period. But feeling that the rising Nazi Party under Hitler must be represented in the government, he turned the government over to the Nazis. In turn he was placed under house arrest but convinced Hitler he was more valuable establishing ties with Austria. He wound up as Ambassador to that country. This was to be the pattern of the clever man who always seemed to land on his feet. He shifted allegiance to whatever side he felt would win the war.

His dossier showed an eight month gap, however. It was between August 5, 1944 and April 9, 1945. During this time he was in American custody. Even then he was praising "gallant Goering" and saying, "You can trust Adolph Hitler's immaculate word of honor."

OSS, however, recognized this devout Catholic layman as a stark realist and ruthless and clever opportunist. OSS had first made its move in 1943. Donovan was in the near east where he met one of his agents from Ankara, Turkey. Known only as "Mac," he exchanged information with enemy agents. One of his contacts was most important. It was von Papen. To get some special information to von Papen and have time to let it solidify it was necessary for Mac and von Papen to spend some time together. Mac would give him some vital intelligence but it would be so timed that by the time Berlin received it it would be too late to apply countermeasures. That would convince von Papen we could be trusted and Berlin that von Papen was still working in their interests.

The problem of arranging a way for them to spend time together was solved with an application of bacteriological "medication." A staphylococcus aureus in crushable glass ampules was provided. It was non-lethal. Mac was told to put it in von Papen's food as well as his own. While it would make them both deathly sick it would not kill them.

During a fine dinner in the German Embassy in Ankara Mac was able to introduce the yellow powder into their food. After the meal the two men sat in the study. Mac then proceeded to give his valuable but too late information to von Papen. A short time later they were both seized with violent stomach cramps. They went immediately to bed. The German doctor put the blame on the custard.

They were toilet bound for days. Sharing the same discomfort they talked on a different level than they ever would have before. The general discussion was never known but the results told the story. The man who had switched his loyalty from the Kaiser to the Weimar Republic to von Hindenburg to Hitler had made yet another switch. He had evidently been convinced by Mac that the Germans would not win the war.

von Papen was one of only two Nazi leaders exonerated at the Nuremberg war trials. Unnoticed was the fact he had been in his castle in Bavaria after the breakthrough at the Remagen bridge. Since he was in Ankara just the day before, only the U.S. Air Force could have made it possible for him to return that quickly. It would appear that Mac was able to promise immunity to von Papen from any trial if he would switch to the Allied cause. Both sides kept their bargain.

For all the brilliance of Donovan and President Roosevelt they shared almost a total naivete concerning the Russians. Lovell discovered Russian spying when they attempted to get a top secret film of a new navigational aid made by Donald Fink. It was promptly reported to Donovan who told Roosevelt. Roosevelt's reply was, "Bill, you must treat the Russians with the same trust you do the British. They're killing Germans every day, you know."

In a staff meeting shortly thereafter Donovan told Lovell, "I saw the President yesterday. He again said to treat the Russians as we would treat the British. A delegation of Russians is coming soon to inspect Professor Moriarty's bag of tricks." For a second time Lovell failed to obey. He manufactured a "Vodka" out of pure ethyl alcohol and water which he served his Russian guests. The devices demonstrated were only the simplest ones such as booby traps, limpet mines and a plastic explosive they already had. They asked to see the silent flashless gun. It was so altered that when fired in a darkened room it was not only deafening but blinding. The Russians left mumbling some Russian words probably dealing with Lovell's ancestry. All they took with them was the ersatz Vodka.

Other exotic weaponry, or in OSS terms, "toys," were to include small incendiary bombs to fit under bats' wings for release over Japan. They would then fly under the eaves of the wood and paper houses and burn cities to the ground. It never worked out. The same idea had been considered but with rats that might run into buildings. Lovell determined a rat could carry a payload of 75 grams attached to its tail. The Russians trained explosive-laden dogs to run under German tanks. Lt. Shaheen of OSS suggested if a bomb was dropped on an enemy ship it might be guided to that ship if a cat was attached underneath. The theory was that the cat, hating to get its feet wet and always landing on its feet, would guide the bomb to the ship. The idea died along with the cat on its first trial.

Another idea revolved around disabling German equipment. The Poles first mentioned the long German supply lines going through their country as the Germans fought in Russia. It was noted that slave labor served these tanks and trucks as they put in oil and gas. This gave them access to the vehicles for whatever device might be employed. OSS went to work. The first device was the use of 1 percent phosphorous oxychloride in the oil in the crankcase. After running several hours the bearings were destroyed. After numerous experiments and full cooperation of American industry a final combination was agreed upon. Now it must be packaged small enough that the laborer could easily hide it until he slipped it into the engine. The final package was the "Turtle Egg" that, dropped into the oil filter,

100

not only disabled but destroyed the engine. It was used with great effect by those servicing the German machines.

Sleeve guns with silencers, submersible motor boats and rafts, pocket incendiaries, limpet mines to sink enemy ships, exploding coal, miniature radios, electronic bugs, exploding briefcases and time delay explosive devices all tumbled from the OSS laboratories, each effective in its own way.

Eifler was soon to approach Lovell with a request for a special, deadly item that could have changed history.

6

In June, 1942, a message from Washington to Nazira informed DET 101 that COI was abolished and the new name was Office of Strategic Services, OSS, for short. Now the unit was OSS DET 101 The old COI name was dropped in Washington's trash receptacles. The shifting of gears was smooth as the new organization leaped into high.

Early in September, 1942, a U.S. Air Corps colonel crashed in Burma. Eifler, alerted to the incident, made his way to the air corps headquarters in Calcutta. He had been asked to rescue this officer. He immediately decided to drop in a native Kachin to lead him out. Studying the area he stood in the map room, an air corps officer reading him the coordinates.

Suddenly another officer appeared with an even more urgent task. A plane from the Tenth Air Force had crashed in the open sea just off Rangoon. It was estimated to be twelve miles from the shore and had ten men aboard. It was urgent that every effort be made to rescue these men. Apart from the humanitarian aspect, with the loss of this plane, every one of that squadron had been lost to enemy action. Not only was it regarded as a jinx squadron, but the loss of the men was bound to lower morale. None of the other flyers had been rescued.

Those gathered around looked hopelessly at the message. Eifler, they knew, was a man of imagination. But his men were guerrillas and agents. This involved the open sea and, obviously, the Navy.

It was for just such an eventuality, and for the added advantage of putting agents ashore on enemy-held territory, that Eifler had made a special request several months earlier. He had petitioned Washington for an air-sea rescue-type boat. Just the day before he had been informed by Harry Little that the boat lay crated in Calcutta harbor. He was anxious to get it uncrated, afloat, and ready for action. General Davidson, commanding general of the Tenth Air Force, came out.

"Eifler, is there anything you can do or suggest to rescue these men?" he asked.

Eifler never hesitated. "General, we'll go get them," he said. He put in a call for his men to meet him at the Calcutta dock. All speed

102

and priority were given to unloading the crate containing the boat. Inside was a 63-foot speedboat powered by two Hall Scott engines. Hurriedly the crating was ripped off and the boat was lowered into the water.

The DET 101 men scurried to the various bases, all British, to obtain needed gasoline and supplies. The tanks were not nearly large enough to carry sufficient fuel for the estimated nine-hundred mile round trip. Drums of gas would have to be carried aboard. The British had rules against carrying a volatile fuel on deck. Happily, this was an American boat, and the drums were rolled aboard to the wagging of British heads.

There was no armament aboard. Several tommy-guns were put on for possible emergency. Late that afternoon the Tenth Air Force said they could abort—the British Air-Rescue was going out. Eifler said he would go anyway, just as insurance.

At 0700 the next morning the boat rolled down the Hooghly River. Aboard was Eifler; Comdr. Hal Williams; Comdr. Jim Luce, a doctor; a British officer who knew the Burmese coast; photographers mate Harry R. Martin, an air force navigator; and a DET 101 man with his radio set, and the crew. They moved swiftly down the river, avoiding the bodies of Hindus that floated like so many logs on their way to the open sea. At the end of the river, just before entering the bay they stopped to ask at the pilot boat if the men had been rescued. The answer was negative.

Commander Williams said: "Carl, this whole entire idea is insane. We have a new boat, never tested. We don't know these waters. In the name of sense, let's abort the damned trip."

Eifler looked at him. "You can get off here if you want. I'm going on," he said.

"But the whole idea is absolutely crazy," Williams persisted.

Eifler paused. "Yes, crazy enough that if I don't make it I can be court-martialed, and if I do make it I'll be decorated. There are ten Americans down out there."

Williams said nothing more—he remained aboard. The motors roared as the DET 101 "navy" headed for its first mission. This was to be the shakedown cruise, and there was no possibility of considering it anything else but a desperate gamble. For the entire day they ran southeastward at full throttle. The water was normal. Logs and bodies floated by occasionally.

Dusk came and with it the hazard of striking something increased. Finally darkness engulfed the little boat. Suddenly the boat shuddered as it struck something in the dark. It paused momentarily, then roared off again into the darkness. All men were instantly alert.

Was there any hull damage? They listened for any signs that might tell them the engine was faltering because of propeller damage. They checked for signs of seepage, but all was well. Whatever they had struck had caused no damage.

Dawn crept over the Bay of Bengal. The men began searching the sky for a PBY. They had been told it would circle over the downed men to help the rescue craft locate it. They knew they were now in the area, and it should be in sight. Unknown to them, the plane had been delayed when it dropped down to check a ship that proved to be Japanese. They had exchanged shots, but neither was damaged. A few minutes later Eifler and his crew spotted the PBY circling. The men in the raft were so near the Japanese ship that they had been lying low while the plane attacked it. Now with the enemy ship gone the men stood as the small boat, with American flag flying, hove into view. The PBY watched as the two craft came together.

Eagerly but tenderly the 101 men helped the injured and wounded aboard. There were only nine men. One had gone down with the plane. Luce immediately gave first aid to the wounded. At this point, the last drum of gasoline had been dumped into the tank. Only what was in the tank remained to get them back to their base. They estimated that they did not have sufficient fuel to make it all the way to Chittagong and decided to try for Akyab instead. They had to gamble that the Japanese would not have a plane up to spot them.

Through the day they moved northwest. A storm came up and buffeted them considerably. At last, darkness covered them once again and gave them protection from enemy aircraft. During the night it was reported to Eifler that the British officer kept pulling the boat out. Eifler tried to figure just how far he took the boat off course and compensate.

Finally, daylight returned and with it the cheerful estimate of the navigator that they were one thousand miles from where they should be. Eifler checked the map and said they would hit Akyab by 1030. At 0945 they spotted land. A plane came out and circled. The ship had no recognition signals. As they came to shore they realized a strange but wonderful thing—they were actually at Chittagong. They entered the mouth of the river—and ran out of gas. They also saw something else—a British rescue craft headed downriver to rescue the downed crew. They were told to abort—all men were safe.

Washington needed no further selling by Eifler of its need for speedboats or Eifler's ability to put them to use in a life-saving and dramatic fashion. The airmen were returned to duty after treatment. Eifler's prediction was correct—he was decorated for the mission, receiving the Legion of Merit as well as warm letters of praise from the Tenth Air Force.

Eifler recognized the need for a light plane, able to flit in and out of secret jungle landing strips. It would facilitate putting agents in and getting injured or sick men out along with captured supplies and prisoners. Word reached him of a plane which the British were going to sell in south India.

He summoned Capt. John Raiss, a former Wall Street broker.

"Captain, how would you like to become a major?" queried Eifler.

"Very much, sir," he replied.

"Good. There is an airplane for sale down south. You go down and buy it for me. I understand they are asking $90,000."

Raiss knew of the DET 101's shaky financial condition. He thought it over and asked: "What about money?"

"Never mind about money," was the rejoinder. "Just go down and get it for me. When you've bought it, tell me and the money will be forthcoming," was the confident reply.

Raiss left to look over the plane and found it in good condition. It was indeed for sale, and the asking price $90,000. In addition to the money which he knew Eifler did not have, he found he would need the approval of British Air Vice Marshal Peirse. He flew to New Delhi to confer with the Marshal. "Eifler doesn't want that kind of plane," declared the Marshal after hearing Raiss' story.

Raiss gave a patient explanation that Eifler did very much want that kind of plane. After he had exhausted every argument he could, he added: "I have a chance to make major if I consummate this. Eifler doesn't pay off for anything but results."

Peirse thought that over, then made his decision. "Captain, if you will go to General Merrill and get his permission, I'll give Eifler a plane that will meet his needs."

Raiss thought that fair and stood to leave. Peirse added: "By the way, if you have any chance of picking up some packs of Lucky Strikes, I'd sure appreciate it."

Raiss said he would see what he could find. He then proceeded to a meeting with General Merrill and gave him all the details. Merrill immediately saw the ploy.

"No soap, Captain. If I ask that guy for a DeHaviland Moth he'll ask me for a DC-3. No way will I do that."

Raiss saw the elusive gold leaf fly slowly out the window. Nevertheless, he returned to see Marshal Peirse. Before going in, he rounded up what he could of the Lucky Strike cigarettes. It amounted to only six packages. He entered Peirse's office, saluted, and dropped the six packages of cigarettes on his desk.

"Sir, I flopped," he began. "I don't get my gold leaf."

"Why?" asked Peirse.

"Merrill said if he asked you for a Moth you'd ask him for a DC-3."

There was silence for a minute or two as Peirse thought that one over. "I'll tell you what, Captain," he began. "If you will be at the Dum Dum Airport in just five days at 0800, the Moth will be there. Just possibly the British officers on duty won't know what it is there for or whose it is. Just walk up and say, 'That's my airplane.'"

Raiss grinned, saluted, and departed. He immediately phoned Eifler to tell him of this development.

"Captain, do exactly as he said," said Eifler. "I'll be down to pick it up."

On the given day and at the right time Raiss walked down the side of the Dum Dum Airport. There stood the Moth and beside it a perplexed British officer with a clipboard. He was looking at the plane's identification numbers and back at his papers. Raiss approached him.

"That's my plane," he said.

A look of relief flooded the Tommy's face.

"Oh, thank God," he said. "I'm glad of that, 'cause I have no record of the plane and was wondering what to do with it."

Raiss had the plane pulled to one side and he did not leave it until Eifler arrived and flew it away. It was a fortunate transaction for six packs of cigarettes.

Back in India, Eifler realized the unit needed a native—both intelligent and strong—to deal with native employees. He was to be a majordomo. Again fortune smiled, as the right man came along. His name was such that no one could ever remember it, let alone pronounce it. Eifler simplified that—he was named Pete. He was large for an Indian, a Hindu with a large mustache. That plus his turban and fierce eyes would have made him a casting director's delight. He was hired at the rate of 45 rupees per month. He was immensely proud to be serving the C.O. At night he would sleep across the threshold of Eifler's room so no one could enter without disturbing him. Eifler gave him the responsibility of handling all tips. No records were kept. It was felt Pete was honest, according to his standards. He simply told Eifler when he needed more money and how much. Naturally, other men asked Pete for advice and chores which he could perform after he had done Eifler's work. More tips found their way into his pockets. Soon additional servants were hired. Cooks, sweepers, launderers, cobblers, tailors, and the ever-present water boy. Pete commanded them like an army general. He invented the "tradition" that all officers were to give him a tip when they became promoted. By listening, he would always know who was on the list before they did. Prior to signing on, he demanded 30 days' leave a year and religiously held Eifler to it. On one occasion he demanded Eifler give him 200 rupees.

"What the hell for?" asked Eifler.

"My daughter getting married. You promise me that much money when she get married, so now you pay me."

Eifler recalled no such incident. "Was I drunk when I said it?"

"Yes, but you say so. Now you pay," was the earnest reply.

Eifler paid. Pete left for the wedding.

He was an institution all through the war and well worth his pay.

In October the training camps continued to flourish with increasing numbers of native agents added daily. It was in November that Eifler decided it was time to make a trip into the dense Burmese jungles to get "the feel" of it. He swiftly arranged a small party of some 101 personnel, including his bearer, Pete. They flew to Fort Hertz, jeeped a short distance down the road, and got out. Pete was unaccustomed to shoes. He was pleased, however, with the pair of boots provided him by Eifler. He wore them proudly around his neck. Eifler had instructed Pete to put the boots on this time. From others who had been down these trails, he knew danger existed for bare feet. Many refugees and soldiers had died and their bodies left to decompose along the trail. Their bones had been trod into the muddy pathways and were now splintering. The splinters were sharp enough to sometimes even cut through leather. The monsoons had left a soggy mess of corpses in various stages of decay. Eifler had not told Pete where they were. Several miles down the trail he turned to the stern faced Hindu.

"Pete, do you know we are in Burma?"

There was no change of expression. Pete looked casually around. He said: "I cook you a Jap for breakfast."

Farther down the trail they came upon small bands of Chinese soldiers, lying pathetically, awaiting death. They were too sick to go on or care for themselves. Death by starvation waited them—or at the fangs of the man-eating tigers that roamed the trails at dusk. They pleaded for water. Many were near death from dehydration. One man held up his canteen to Eifler and painfully begged for water.

Eifler, having none himself, walked on by.

A little farther on, one soldier raised his rifle toward Eifler's back. Eifler did not see it, but Pete, following, did. Quickly he pulled out his large knife, raised it over his head, and kicked the rifle aside. The soldier looked up at the face bristling with rage and the large upraised knife. Pete said: "I cut your head in two pieces." Then he

107

paused, put the knife in its sheath, and walked on, leaving the man to a slower death.

A while later they came on the sound of running water. By now they were thirsty and needed to refill their canteens. They walked to one of the small crystal streams that flow out of the Burmese mountains. Eifler knelt to drink. He looked directly into the face of a dead Chinese soldier, just below the surface. He moved a few feet upstream and looked into another dead face. When this was repeated a third time, he simply said "the hell with it" and drank, oblivious to the dead eyes. Two thousand Chinese had died along this small stretch of trail. It would have been more merciful had the Japanese continued northward and executed the men quickly. A short distance farther they turned back. They had seen the first of many trails that would carry 101 agents deep into enemy territory. In many cases, the jungles were to prove a more dangerous enemy than the Japanese forces.

Operations were forming at Nazira. Some of the men stood ready for first penetrations. It was December, 1942. The Pearl Harbor attack was just a year old. U.S. forces had fought well, but the Japanese seemed to go wherever they willed. As the people of America were now united in a war they just might lose, every possible method of fighting the Axis was being utilized. From its badly shattered fleet to its expanding ground forces and growing air force, America knew there would be no quarter given or asked. And in a small tea plantation, in the map room, the DET 101 forces prepared to move. Gear was checked out; uniforms of the British forces were secured; and, under the cover of being British soldiers, Eifler, Coughlin, Richter, and two civilian members of 101 left Nazira for the Chabua Airport on December 27, 1942. Their plan was twofold. First, they would establish a forward base at Sumprabum, Burma. It would consist of a supply depot, a radio listening post, and a forward training area. Second, they would complete final training in the face of the enemy and decide on the plan of action for 101's first operations.

They left the Chabua Airport in two DC-3s with four fighters as escort. Arriving at Fort Hertz the morning of the 28th, they were greeted as Americans and told they were expected. This was a shock, to say the least. Their cover story was that they were actually reinforcements for the Kachin Levies. The plan had been carefully coordinated through the British SO,E and British Fourth Corps Headquarters. Eifler had personally contacted and received permission from the commanding officer of the Kachin Levies, Lieutenant Colonel Gamble, as well as Lieutenant General Scones, commanding the British Fourth Corps. The 101 men were very much British,

108

according to their uniforms. It seemed even the coolies were well informed and waiting to see the first U.S. soldiers arrive. Eifler, furious, asked a British captain who blew the cover.

"Colonel Gamble, sir," was the clipped reply. "He told us a month ago an American radio group from the Tenth Air Force was going to open a station either here or in Sumprabum, and we assumed you to be that group."

Eifler stomped away. Since the Kachin Levies cover was blown, he decided to adopt the new cover. They switched back to American uniforms. Prior to leaving for Burma, Eifler had made arrangements with Colonel Gamble for animal transportation. There was none available. The British captain said Gamble had left orders that the Americans were to be given priority, but no one knew just when they would be coming. Eifler had given Gamble the exact date of arrival.

Final arrangements included rounding up of sufficient coolies and fourteen elephants. On December 30, the last supplies were out of Fort Hertz and on the road to Sumprabum. On January 6, 1943, they entered Sumprabum. They reported to the political officer's headquarters, where they met a Mr. McGuiness. He was the assistant political officer of the Myitkyina area. When told the Americans were there to take over the building Colonel Gamble had arranged for them, he looked puzzled. No such arrangements had been made, he told them. He stated the only vacant buildings in the area were those of the Baptist Mission, about half a mile below the town. The bewildered 101 men looked at each other and shrugged. Something or someone was obviously drastically wrong. They went to inspect the buildings. Inspection revealed three or four houses in medium state of repair one small church a school building, and a building that could be used either as a schoolroom or warehouse. At the entrance of the path leading to the church was a broken-down Chevrolet with a dead Chinese in the front seat.

They all agreed this place would be acceptable with a little repair and modification. It was assigned to them on request. A little while later two additional British officers put in their appearance. They offered their services. One was Captain Reid, an MEW (British Organization Ministry of Economic Warfare) man whom Eifler had met once before. The other, a captain, was acting commanding officer of the Levies in Colonel Gamble's absence. He reported Gamble had gone forward to inspect the troops. The "troops" were not soldiers in the known or accepted sense. They had had no kind of military training whatsoever. Their weapons consisted of everything from muzzle-loading flintlocks to more modern muzzle-loading percussion caps. They also had some shotguns, some modern Enfield rifles, and

Bren guns. Their mission was to guard the roads and trails leading out of Japanese-held territory. They were to ambush and harass the enemy if he tried any forward movements.

The Kachin Hills had always been a restricted area. Civilization had only slightly touched them. Prior to the outbreak of the war, no one could enter the hills without a permit from the political officer (district commissioner). As late as 1923 the Kachins fiercely resisted British control by ambushing British officials. Because the terrain encompassed rugged mountains and heavy jungles, the British had to be satisfied with small outposts. The general geographical area of the Kachins is that area north of the town of Myitkyina, east of the Chin Hills and west of the China border. There are other tracts and areas where the Kachins do dominate.

The term "Kachin" denotes not only the tribe known as Chingpaw but other allied tribes such as Maru, Lashi, Atsi, and Kanung. The language was simple. As used locally and idiomatically, it made the Chingpaw a distinct individualist. Life in the hills made the native resourceful and very independent, as he had to constantly outwit nature and his enemies. In his religion the Chingpaw worshipped the Nats, or evil spirits. Special places of honor were kept for the Nats in each modest shack. Here only they could sit. Special offerings of food were placed on the outside for the Nats to eat. No one dared offend these invisible creatures.

The Chingpaw's theology was unique. They believed that early in the history of man all the tribes and people of Burma were called by God to south Burma to receive gifts. When all assembled, each tribe was given a book with the printed "word" and instructions. Then they returned home. The Burmese, living in south Burma, were already in their own backyards. The Shans and Karens, who lived in central Burma, had a bit farther to go, and the Chingpaw, or Kachin, had the longest trek—clear into northern Burma. Before they reached their homes they were so hungry they ate their book. A short time later they were called again to south Burma. The Kachins started the long walk. They took nothing with them. The other people, however, read their book and saw they were to receive jewels and money, so they prepared and took great baskets. The bulk of the wealth therefore went to them, and the Kachins took back only what they could carry in their hands. A third call was now given, and the tribes prepared to return to the south. This time the Kachins were ready. They made enormous bamboo baskets and marched the winding trails into the central plains and on south to the meeting place. The other people read their book and saw they were to receive Nats, or evil spirits this time. They went empty-handed. Now in reverse, the

110

Kachins returned home with by far the greatest share of the evil spirits in their great baskets. Weary from the long journey, they swayed on the trail, causing their baskets to dip and spill out the evil spirits along the trail. From then on no Kachin would be willing to be on the trail at dusk, and special offering places were set up to appease the Nats. To the simple Kachin mind, this explained why they were poor and beset with misery, poverty, and ignorance.

The Kachin made the home his unit of civilization. His laws were communistic in application. The custom of feuds between families had modified his life and character in many ways. He learned to be careful and crafty and indirect in his approach to strangers. The Kachins respected the opinions of their elders, loved children, and considered women almost as beasts of burden. Only through the male line could the traditions and indebtedness to their ancestors be passed on. The Kachin loved intrigue. It was a part of his survival. These unique people were estimated to number around 2 million. It was fitting such a unique and distinct type people were to be thrown together with an equally unusual group of Americans. The Nats must have laughed till their evil sides ached at the thought of these two different peoples joining forces. The Japanese, however, were not to find it too funny.

At the end of December, Eifler received a message telling him he was now a lieutenant colonel.

On January 7 a runner arrived to report advancing Japanese. They were reported to be moving north from Myitkyina. The Kachin Levies had ambushed them just north of Nsopzup, forty-five miles above Myitkyina. The 101 men began moving to the front. Eifler felt the reported one thousand enemy troops to be exaggerated.

Borrowing a jeep that had been reconstructed from parts of abandoned vehicles, they arrived that evening at the scene of the battle. Colonel Gamble was there, and Eifler met him for the first time. He appeared indecisive and a little bewildered. He was proper in his uniform and spoke with customary British accent. He reported the enemy force was actually a strong patrol of some four hundred men.

The Kachins had carefully prepared the ambush site in advance. They had planted *punjis* (fire-hardened bamboo spears) on the other side of some fallen logs which would give cover to anyone being fired on. These logs were on the lower side of the road. This site was selected because the terrain ascended at a sharp angle on one side of the road and descended at a more gentle angle on the other side. When the Japanese advanced to this point, the Kachins opened fire. The enemy immediately jumped over the logs and onto the punjis.

111

The Kachins then broke the engagement. It was reported that the Japanese could be heard screaming for well over an hour.

First enemy casualties were estimated at twenty-four, then fifty. Only one body was recovered. His uniform and equipment were sent back. One of the problems that was to plague the 101 men was the fact that the Kachins had no idea of numbers. Conflicting reports might range from ten to one hundred enemy troops holding an outpost.

Eifler had a chance to discuss his goals directly with Colonel Gamble. He told of the 101 desire to penetrate the Pedaung Forest and send a group to Myitkyina with a radio. It was all too easy. Gamble would give them anything they wanted. Both Coughlin and Eifler were tremendously heartened.

Upon his return to his headquarters, however, Gamble did a complete turnabout. Now, nothing was possible. Plans which he had laid out several days earlier were not only impossible but silly. One particular plan which he had suggested and Eifler had outlined to his two leaders was ridiculed by Gamble. In the presence of all the 101 personnel, he said: "You can do that if you are tired of them, if you want to get rid of them, if you want to get them killed."

During this time Eifler and Coughlin noted Gamble was having all the road mines removed. His junior officer, Leach, had mined this road in accordance with the mission of the Kachin Levies. Gamble did not need the explosives. He simply and suddenly decided that the Japs could not come up that road anyway and that to have it mined was a defeatist attitude. This was not sound military tactics. Gamble stated his mission was a defensive one, to just ambush and run. The next minute he would state that should the Japs advance, he would "lick them." Eifler asked permission to cache certain supplies in the immediate jungles. He explained that when the 101 men began operations against the Japanese, the Levies would no doubt be blamed. This would result in a Japanese attack overrunning their area. Gamble shook his head wildly. Permission was refused. It was impossible for the enemy to advance northward.

Next, Gamble approached Eifler and Coughlin with a request for switches, booby traps, and all manner of such items of sabotage. Eifler was more than generous and said he would even be willing to train his men in their use. Eventually he gave Gamble over six hundred pounds of toys, flares, incendiaries, and gasoline so that he could booby-trap all trails leading up from the enemy positions. This was, of course, completely inconsistent with Gamble's statement the Japanese could not advance anyway.

Shortly after two of the 101 men began training Gamble's men in the use of the supplies, and long before the British were proficient in their understanding, Gamble informed Eifler he need no longer instruct the men. He said he learned a number of the men in the Levies were sufficiently familiar with the items of destruction. Eifler withdrew his instructors.

That night Eifler and Coughlin sat analyzing what was now an impossible situation. They agreed they must break away from Gamble but yet retain his good will.

The following morning Eifler told Gamble they were going to try something different. He asked for the use of a jeep which would save four days of walking. Gamble refused: gasoline was too short.

"I have my own gasoline," Eifler pointed out.

"But it was brought in on my transport," retorted Gamble.

Actually, the gasoline was packed in on the backs of the coolies which were furnished by the political officer's office, not by the army. Eifler realized it was useless to push the matter anymore and dropped it.

Eifler was extremely concerned. He realized he was not dealing with a rational man. Coughlin concurred.

The billets that had been assigned to Eifler and Coughlin were taken back less than two weeks later. They had to move into lesser headquarters. They requested to be moved back to their original billets. Permission was refused—Gamble declared that the buildings were not fit to live in.

The decision was made to leave the listening post in the hills but not let Gamble know they intended to continue with their original plans. Eifler then told Gamble he considered the plan impractical and wanted to withdraw the unit. In the event future conditions changed, a captain and four men would be sent in. Eifler asked if Gamble could furnish a guide. Gamble said he could and instructed his intelligence officer to bring in a certain man. Eifler examined the man from a security standpoint. What he learned was a little shattering. The man was a suspected Japanese agent. He was under arrest and being taken back to India. This was the man Gamble was willing to let guide Eifler. In a fit of self-preservation, Eifler passed.

On January 18, the unit left Sumprabum, leaving behind Richter, a native operator, a civilian, and a radio. Five days later Eifler and Coughlin met Political Officer Leyden of the Myitkyina area near Fort Hertz. He expressed surprise when informed the 101 unit was pulling out of Burma. He had been in India requesting just such a unit. The governor of Burma had requested he give 101 every possible assistance.

Eifler informed him it was impossible to work with Gamble. A pause followed. "You might as well know," Leyden began, "I objected in the first place when they assigned Colonel Gamble to north Burma. For many years he has been known as 'Mad Gamble.'"

This was no news to Eifler. They were both reluctant to go into more detail. The man was, after all, a colonel in the British army, and Eifler had no desire to embarrass the other British officials. Leyden, however, did ask for an opinion from the medical officer assigned to Gamble's unit. The report confirmed it all. The medical officer stated that, in his opinion, Gamble was not sane. He had actually ordered Gamble out of Burma several months earlier and did not know why he had been returned.

Messages received from Sumprabum indicated continual harassment by Gamble. He would one day declare certain buildings as unfit and demand the 101 men move. Then, after the move, they would be told to return even though nothing had been done to the buildings. Since a large aerial was involved, it was an extreme hardship on the men.

The decision was then made to send in Captain Wilkinson with his unit. He bore specific orders from British Fourth Headquarters to Gamble that 101 men were not under his command and he was to render them all possible assistance. The Wilkinson unit passed through the area and moved into the area above Myitkyina.

The Japanese were well aware something was going on to their north. As Eifler had predicted, they began a heavy movement toward Sumprabum. At this point Gamble changed his mind once more. He decided he could use some of the 101 men. He sent one of his officers to the 101 headquarters with the request of borrowing four "101 toughs." The fact he had previously stated his men needed no more instruction, but now did, in no way was embarrassing to him. Eifler instructed his men to give all possible aid, and the "toughs" were assigned. They did a splendid job of booby-trapping the trails. On a sudden impulse, Gamble ordered all civilian personnel out of the area. Knowing the terrain, Eifler said that the Japanese couldn't possibly move their troops that quickly. Gamble, however, was the one in command. Planes flew in to bring out evacuees. One C-47 carrying all of Wilkinson's coolies crashed in Chaukan Pass, and all aboard were killed.

Wilkinson's group was not removed. It moved into its pre-established position with its two radios. They were in a direct line for the U.S. planes flying the Hump with precious cargo for Stilwell and Chennault. They were intended to render aid and rescue the crews of planes that crashed, whether shot down by enemy fighters or as a result of mechanical problems. When the radio set was estab-

114

lished at Sumprabum, a British communications problem developed. Relay from the British Fourth Headquarters to the American Tenth Air Force was taking too long. Now the 101 station was able to relay the same information to Nazira, which sent it to the air force immediately. This speeded up the information on enemy targets by two to three days and often made the difference between a successful bombing run and one that struck positions evacuated a day or two earlier. Finally, the presence of the few 101 units in the field was being felt by the enemy.

The next step was to put yet another group in even closer to the Myitkyina base. An airdrop was decided as the best method. On February 6, 1943, Eifler, Coughlin, a Captain Barnard, and a rating of the Burmese navy, a radio operator, made a reconnaissance flight over that area to select the drop site. The next day, after examining the photos, Barnard and the Burmese radio operator dropped into the Koukkwe Valley to make sure it would be safe to put the rest of the group in.

There were many problems. The group to jump was well aware of the fact they were to use British parachutes which were known for a high percentage of failures. The jump area had tiny clearings. To miss it could mean severe injuries or being hung up in a tree a hundred feet from the ground. In addition, the area teemed with man-eating tigers. In spite of this, it was felt the mission would succeed.

The men made a perfect drop and signaled they were okay. Two containers with supplies were dropped—one failed to open. When the men failed to come on the air later, it was hoped it was because the radio had been destroyed in the ruined container. The following day the same plane and crew left, with the deletion of Eifler and addition of Peers. Arriving over the zone, they saw panels indicating the radio had indeed been destroyed. Everything else was okay. Ten men were dropped, along with more supplies. Three of the four Kachins who, prior to four days before, had never seen a plane at close range, jumped with no hesitation. The fourth balked at the door for a split second. Coughlin knocked one hand down, Peers the other. Captain Oliver (Oscar) Milton, who was leading the group in that day, applied a well-aimed kick to the proper area, and the recalcitrant flew out the door. Milton was right behind him.

The group all landed successfully, took what supplies they could carry, and hid the rest. They checked their maps and moved into position to carry the war to the enemy. There were no delays. They were able to report to Nazira that they had ambushed enemy patrols, placed booby traps and blown bridges. It was during the demolition of one of these bridges that one of the first 101 agents, a native named Pat, was killed when his charge went off prematurely. A nearby enemy patrol chased the rest of the team. Agent Bunny drew their fire as they pursued him into the heavy jungle. He later rejoined the group safely. Milton began a daily routine of collecting and relaying information and causing whatever damage he could to the Japanese forces.

Back in Nazira, Eifler put another of his plans into operation. The mission he had in mind was actually not intended to start for several more months, but groundwork had to be laid. He weighed many factors, then decided to put his plan into action. He called in Curl. He detailed a request from Stilwell for certain information about the Ledo Road area. Pausing to let it sink in, Eifler concluded: "It can't be done, but Stilwell thinks it can. I want you to try, and when you fail I can tell him why it can't be done."

Curl thought that one over. Eifler watched as he took the bait. He raised one eyebrow and looked at Eifler. "You think it can't be done?"

"That is right," Eifler reiterated.

Curl grinned. "That's all I want to know. Can I pick my own men?"

Eifler said he could.

For several days Curl made his plans. He selected his unit, drew the necessary provisions, and moved into the field to start operations. Eifler waited for ninety days, then recalled him. The meeting was held in the special operations office in the tea planter's home.

In a relaxed atmosphere a bottle of Scotch was produced. Each man had a drink. Also present was Frazee. The friendly brother-in-arms spirit prevailed. Finally the time came for the report, and Eifler became the tough, unyielding C.O. He banged his huge fist down on the desk.

"Okay, Lieutenant, your report," he demanded.

Curl made a detailed report of all pertinent details. He included what was attempted, what was wrong with certain decisions, the performance of equipment and key individuals, and summed up the total operation. There was a long silence. It was broken by Eifler.

"In other words Lieutenant, you failed."

Never one to excuse himself, Curl said: "Yes, I did."

Eifler turned to Frazee. "Pull Lieutenant Curl's name from the promotion list," he said. Both Curl and Frazee had just been submitted for promotion to captain. Frazee was visibly upset with this callous treatment of a friend and fellow officer.

"That isn't fair," he blurted out. "You said yourself it couldn't be done."

Eifler was calm. "We pay off for success. not failure."

Frazee, now flirting with a court-martial. drew himself up and said: "Sir, I request permission to pull my own name from the promotion list until you see fit to promote Lieutenant Curl."

"Permission denied," said Eifler. "Curl, take ten days' leave and report back. That is all." Eifler picked up a file and began reading it. The two lieutenants looked at each other, stood, and walked from the room. Further discussion was useless, they knew. Eifler did know the mission was impossible. He wanted Curl to fail but for a specific reason. He wanted Curl so mad at him that when he was sent on the real mission he would exert superhuman effort to succeed and really show Eifler the stuff he was made of. Frazee approached Eifler from time to time, puzzled over his seemingly unfair attitude. Eifler gave him only one answer. "Ask Curl. He knows I don't pay off for failures."

Reports trickled in from various locations that Curl was on a giant bender. It did not distress Eifler. He felt if anyone ever had a drunk coming it was Curl. At the end of ten days he was still drunk and muttering over and over: "That old son of a bitch." Eifler ordered him sobered up and brought in. A disheartened Curl now stood before him. With no reference to the past, Eifler told him he was going in on a similar mission but he would now have to do it Eifler's way.

Curl jumped at the chance. "Can I take the same men?" he asked.

"Anyone you want to," he was told.

He left with spirits uplifted. He was going back in and would be able to prove his worth.

The unit needed a code name. During his military career Curl had played in many baseball games. In one he dropped a fly ball and drew a rebuke from one of his teammates that included the unflattering term "Knothead." Amid much hilarity it was decided his group should be known as Knothead, and it was so logged.

A few days later the Knothead group flew to Fort Hertz and began infiltrating the Japanese lines. Detailed reports began flowing in. The group was picking up additional Kachin soldiers who had been scattered in the original fighting. Pamplin was operating as cryptographer, among his other duties, and Haimson was radio operator. One day a message from Nazira was received and decoded. It was simple and to the point. It read: "Captain Curl, congratulations." It was signed: "The old son of a bitch."

Two other agents made up the balance of the Knothead group. They were both Burmese and bore the names Skittles and Hefty.

Skittles was invaluable, not only for his knowledge of the terrain which he had been over many times before as an engineer, but for his linguistic abilities. The hill tribes scattered throughout central and north Burma spoke a great many dialects. Skittles could speak seven of them. He also spoke perfect English, Burmese, Chinese, Siamese, Kachin, Hindi, and Urdu. He was to prove one of the most valuable of the non-American agents.

As the Knothead group moved through the outer Kachin villages, they heard of a Kachin leader by the name of Zing Htung Naw. This man had refused to have anything to do with the Japanese and had retreated into some of the most remote mountains just out of their reach. Those who followed him helped him with his sporadic raids against the Japanese. He was ill-equipped, but there was no doubting his fighting spirit. A graduate of the University of Bhamo, he also had his wife with him. It was natural for this man, a governor of his area, to come in contact with Curl. The joining of the two made Knothead into even a more formidable force. It was obvious that what was to be a sabotage and espionage unit with hit-and-run ambushes would not turn into a guerrilla army. The people now rallied around Naw, and Curl advised Nazira of the fortunate incident. The Kachin weapons were something out of the past; muzzle-loaders and flintlocks formed their firepower. Curl demonstrated the carbine, shotgun, and tommy-gun. Naw's enthusiasm was boundless when he thought of his men being equipped with such weapons and with other necessary equipment for the first time. Curl radioed for, and got, airdrops to equip other Kachin soldiers who now came from their scattered hideouts. The narrow trails were becoming busy arteries as the jubilant natives saw a chance to strike back against the hated Japanese.

One of the most unusual men to serve with an OSS unit now joined the fast growing group. He was Father James Stuart, an Irish priest. Another priest, a Scotsman named Father MacAllindon, also was to serve on the DET 101 roster. Father Stuart had a reputation that preceded him. His wit was charming but could also be devastating. He used his intellect to appear so naive the Japanese could not believe he knew anything. He had remained behind with his people as the Japanese advanced. He was a Dominican, an order headquartered in Omaha, Nebraska. For several years he had labored among the Kachins, and he spoke their language perfectly. He had a limited background in medicine and meager supplies but had made a tremendous impression already on the xenophobic Kachins.

When the news came that the Japanese forces had arrived just outside the village where he lived with over a hundred refugees, Father Stuart made his decision. He would not melt into the jungle and abandon his people. He had preached of God's love and help in time of trouble. Now he would show them how to live those words.

He told his people to remain where they were at the outskirts of the village. He walked out onto the lonely dirt road and waited for approaching Japanese cavalry headed toward him. He knew how the sheriff of a small western town must have felt waiting for the bad guys and the inevitable showdown. The Kachins had all disappeared. The monkeys continued their din from the trees, and a few birds were in evidence. Then Father Stuart heard the clip-clop of the Japanese horses bearing the imperial forces and his destiny. At the head of the column rode a major, his Samurai sword swaying from the rhythm of his mount. Behind him were the junior officers and enlisted men looking straight ahead as they prepared to pass through yet another dusty village. The major was incredulous to see a white man, unarmed, directly in his path. Obviously, he was not going to move.

The column approached the white man. He stood, hands on hips, refusing to budge. At the last minute he raised his hand to halt the column. From his horse the Japanese officer looked defiantly at this apparition. The priest looked equally defiantly at him. Slowly the major dismounted, unhooked his holster, and walked up to Father Stuart. Assuming his most disarming smile now, Father Stuart spoke in English and innocence.

"Are you Chinese?" he asked.

The major was beyond belief. He turned and spit on the ground. "No," he blurted. "We are Japanese. Are you English?"

Father Stuart copied him completely to the direction in which he now spat. "No, I am Irish," he replied.

The major walked from side to side, trying to figure him out. He drew his sword from the sheath and drew an arc at Father Stuart's feet. He pointed to the lower portion of it and said: "This is England." Then, pointing to the upper portion, he said: "And this is Ireland. Where are you from?"

Without hesitation, Father Stuart pointed his toe to Ireland. He followed that with the information he knew would be asked. He was a priest and was traveling with war refugees. He wanted to tell his people that the Japanese would not harm them and asked if the soldiers might have some food for them. The major's eyes burned into those of this foolish priest. He seemed harmless enough, but he was a white man. He could be what he said he was—or he could be British. He looked back at his column of cavalry who watched impassively. Turning abruptly to Father Stuart, he said: "We have no food to give you. You may remain with your refugees but do not get in our way. You will be watched."

He swung astride his horse, motioned his column forward, and they moved down the road. All but one young officer looked contemptuously at the priest. Their eyes met, and Father Stuart saw a face with compassion.

He returned to his refugees and gave them spiritual and medical aid. He scrounged food from all possible sources. As often as possible he visited the Japanese camp to ask for supplies. Several of the Japanese officers took a liking to him and in turn visited his shack. One of them was the young officer whose look of compassion had touched the priest's heart. He confessed to Father Stuart that he was a Christian and that there were other Christians in the Japanese outpost. He also said that there was a continuing discussion whether to kill him or not.

Continuing the role of a dupe, Father Stuart pulled the Japanese leg outrageously. One day a U.S. fighter swept low over the area, its white star clearly visible. Later he excitedly told one of the higher Japanese officers of having watched a Japanese plane swoop over the village. It was patiently explained to him that it was not Japanese but American. Father Stuart persisted. "I clearly saw your star on it."

"The Japanese star, when used, is red. The white star is American," replied the officer, amazed at this naivete. He was certainly not aware the wide innocent eyes were carefully cataloging his rank, the size of the outpost, caliber of their weapons, quality of the commanding officers, and what other information he could glean concerning the name of the unit, its past campaigns, and where it intended to go. For amusement there was another Jap officer who considered himself the Nelson Eddy of the imperial forces. Father Stuart implored him constantly to sing his "favorite," the old chestnut "Rosalie." He held his amusement behind the wide, innocent stare as the man employed his three-note range and extolled the virtues of "Rosarie, my darring."

Late one night the young Christian officer came to his hut. He told Father Stuart the decision had been made to kill him. The men were on the way. Realizing his death would in no way help the refugees, Father Stuart thanked the officer and disappeared into the jungle. He was never to hear of this officer again but often mentioned him in his prayers.

On joining OSS, he quickly changed into a military-type uniform. It consisted of the basic U.S. khaki slacks and shirt, an Aussie hat, an Indian knife, tennis shoes, and a .45 automatic. He was a master strategist and militarist. He could well have been a soldier. He claimed he was headed for this profession but made the mistake, along with his brother, of practicing it in the illegal Irish Republican Army. The British, he claims, gave him the choice of jail or going on into the priesthood, which he had also considered. He explained his religious military dichotomy simply: "My mission is to help my people. The best thing for them right now is to get the Japanese out. Then we can go back to what we were doing before."

Only once was he known to have lost his temper—something the Irish are noted for. In the early days of the war his false teeth were stolen by a Chinese soldier. He is purported to have mentioned this in an evening prayer: "O Lord, you have told us to love all people. Can't you just this one time reclassify this person?"

Surely, there was at least a grin in heaven.

Additional personnel were now rolling into DET 101. Two young lieutenants, Jim Tilly and Gerald Larsen, were immediately sent on to the field. Larsen joined Wilkinson at Forward. Tilly reported to Knothead. Both were highly successful in leading the small but wiry Kachin guerrillas.

Tilly and Eifler never did see eye to eye. The difference in rank, however, kept it from ever becoming an issue. Tilly said: "My first impression of Eifler was through a murky photograph handed to me in Washington. It showed a bearded giant dressed either in khaki or a canvas tent, crouching in a jungle clearing, one hand all but concealing a tommy-gun. Whether he intended using it for a back scratcher or to throw at the enemy was not clear. Since the photo had obviously been taken in the midst of combat, I felt it regrettable the angle had not been sufficient to show a regiment of the enemy in flight— what a grand recruiting poster."

Tilly was of the opinion that he should include a large Old Glory in his request list just to make sure this particular commander should know where his allegiance lay. The first meeting of the two was typical of a young officer reporting to his new C.O. As a pink-cheeked shavetail, Tilly saluted and started the normal reporting procedure.

"Cut that crap. Just tell me the story of your life," Eifler snarled.

During the discourse, Tilly mentioned a brief bit of flying experience: "Eifler immediately appointed me as pilot for the organization, notwithstanding the fact I was color-blind and not qualified by the army to fly." While the assignment was alarming, the responsibility was more acceptable when Tilly learned there were no planes.

Tilly had been at Nazira for forty-eight hours when it was decided to ready the DET 101 airstrip. While his engineering talent was as scarce as his flying ability, Eifler nevertheless demanded a commitment as to completion date of a suitable landing strip. A 1,500-

foot runway was needed. There was no mechanical contrivances, only hundreds of coolies. For lack of anything better, Tilly gave a three-week estimate. Eifler contemplated this figure, said he'd give him three days, and stalked off. Tilly nearly did it. A short time later Eifler went on a trip. His last instructions to Tilly were to continue extending the strip. When he returned, he summoned Tilly. Tilly recalled the discussion.

"Lieutenant, how are you doing on the strip—how long is it now?" Eifler asked.

"About a half-mile, sir," was the reply.

"What in the hell are you extending it for? Isn't half a mile long enough?"

"Your last instructions were to keep extending it," he replied.

"Well if that isn't the silliest thing I ever heard of. What if I had been gone another year? What would you have done then?"

"I'd have built it clear across Assam, sir," was the final reply.

One never dropped Eifler's orders by the wayside.

While Eifler, on occasion, gave some of his men some king-sized problems, he was generally on the receiving end of frustrations with both the British and Washington.

In an attempt to coordinate his operations with British units, Eifler and a British officer tried to see the chief of British intelligence in New Delhi. They went from one post to another, all manned by Indian troops, getting passes and the runaround. Each time they would progress just so far up the line when the day would end, and they would have to start again the next day. One night Eifler said to his British friend: "I'm getting damned tired of this runaround."

His partner thoroughly agreed. Eifler went on: "If you are willing to stick your neck out, I'll show you how to see this guy."

The Limey, well aware of Eifler's flamboyant and aggressive nature, thought that one over a minute. Finally the frustration of previous attempts took over. "I'm with you," he said.

Eifler wrote out a note saying: "I am an enemy agent and I am going to blow this goddamned building to hell." Then he got a blue seal and red ribbon and finished it up. The next morning both men went from guard to guard flashing it. In ten minutes they were in the chief's office. Eifler threw the note on his desk and said: "There's what your goddamned security is worth." The meeting then proceeded.

The next time Eifler went in all the Indian guards were relieved and British troops stood sentry duty. Eifler had once again shown his prowess in cutting the Gordian knot.

A classic example of problems with Washington arose out of

Eifler's request for shotguns. The simple Kachins were not really sure of the tommy-gun, but did understand and like the shotgun. It was apparent they were far more apt to stand up to the skilled Jap troops with the shotgun. Accordingly, Eifler wired Washington for five hundred of the weapons.

"As usual, there was some idiot in Washington who always has to question everything rather than assume the commander in the field knows what he is doing," Eifler said. "They said it was an unusual request and could I justify it?"

Eifler was angry at being questioned and especially at being asked to justify anything. Compulsively, he wired back: "Yes, I prefer muzzle-loaders. The natives can make their own black powder and use the nuts and bolts from wrecked vehicles for ammunition." News of that answer to Washington was well known to all 101 personnel who anxiously awaited the reply to this sarcasm.

Amazingly enough, this request was not questioned. Instead they sent out to find muzzle-loaders. In a warehouse, covered with dust, someone found five hundred brand-new Springfield muzzle-loaders that were never used in the Civil War. The weapons were immediately sent over. Anger turned to pleasure when it was discovered the natives considered this one of the finest weapons they had ever seen. Curl used them as awards for his best soldiers. One of war's incongruities was the battle sound where the bark of carbines and the rattle of tommy-guns was punctuated by the full-throated roar of muzzle-loaders. The guns intended to help General Sherman with his march through the south now roared their belated message in Burma.

Other units were finding their pre-planned bases to the north, east, and south of Knothead. An English major, Red Maddox, commanded a small operation known as Tramp. It was described simply as a hide-and-seek group. They were to see, hear, and transmit only for a planned movement of Chinese troops later on. They were not to fight at all except in self-defense. Their operations were to prove of inestimable value in future months.

As Eifler received general instructions to harass the enemy but was left to his own devices, so were the various units in the field. They alone decided on how to carry out their missions. In retrospect some would now be condemned, others praised.

One American agent, who shall remain unnamed, showed a direct approach to his problem. He and a native agent stopped two men along the trail for interrogation. The two men said they knew nothing. The questioning was pursued, a bit more forcefully this time. They looked at one another but again repeated they knew nothing. This time the interrogator pulled out his .45 and said he would repeat the question just once more. Then he made a decision as to which was the weaker of the two. He put the gun against the other man's stomach. He repeated the question. Silence. The gun roared, and the man fell dead on the trail. He now put the gun in the other man's stomach. Not only did he come up with the answer, he joined the unit.

This was not standard 101 recruiting procedure, but behind enemy lines certain problems called for special solutions. One day a British officer, separated in battle from Gen. Orde Wingate's forces, stumbled into the 101 camp. He was relieved to find sanctuary, a safe place to rest, and something to eat. He spent a comfortable night. The next morning his host asked him if he would accompany him on a task he had to perform. He was more than willing. There was much rumor and speculation as to what the 101 agents were actually up to, and he was anxious to see and learn all he could. The two men approached a native, standing with hands tied behind his back. The British officer was informed this man was an enemy agent. To his horror, he also noticed the man stood before an open grave. The American said: "You know the penalty for being caught," then drew a dah and beheaded him with one stroke. The head and corpse fell into the grave. The American looked casually down, crossed himself, and said to his guest: "May the Lord have mercy on his soul...you know, I never know what to say at a time like this. Let's go eat breakfast."

The proper British soldier promptly threw up and said he had suddenly lost his appetite.

Now with booms regularly being heard from behind Japanese lines, Eifler found himself more and more involved with battling red tape just to stay alive. He remarked he spent over 90 percent of his time fighting Washington and top brass; 10 percent the enemy. If this was actually the case, the enemy forces could be well pleased. His truncated reports to Stilwell's headquarters were designed to merely inform him of essentials and successes. He knew the acid-tongued theater commander hated unnecessary and detailed reports as badly as Eifler did himself. Eifler also was well aware of an oft-repeated phrase that when the nuisance value of OSS surpassed its military and espionage value, it would go. Eifler had developed the habit of being present, when possible, as the general's plane came into his area. The plane, dubbed *Uncle Joe's Chariot*, would land, and the general, with several members of his staff, would then sweep into the local headquarters for interviews and reports. Eifler would make himself known but say nothing. Stilwell could never miss his bulk and would more often than not call out: "Hi, Buffalo Bill. Come on."

124

Eifler would then join him to report and tell of his thoughts and answer any questions. Many times Eifler was introduced to senior officers as the army's number one "thug."

During his frequent absences from Nazira, along with Coughlin, Peers filled in as active C.O. His selection proved to be valuable to a greater degree than anyone could have hoped or predicted. Handsome and with craggy features, he would listen to suggestions and was capable of evaluating quickly and moving quickly once his decision was made. He was well respected by all the 101 personnel.

DET 101 was not without its problems, however. A Group was facing lots of Japanese pressure. Slowly the Japanese forced them northward until they were on the border of China. They radioed Nazira for help in the form of Chinese currency and passports. The efficient OSS organization had them ready promptly, and they were dropped to them at the border. They then crossed into China to regroup and plan their early return to Burma and the war.

The war in China was not moving at all. Chiang Kai-shek still found reasons not to move his armies against Japan. Stilwell faced problems that were incredible. He was the only one with sufficient courage to tell the generalissimo the truth, and it was not appreciated. He found some allies in a surprising quarter. Madame Chiang Kai-shek sympathized with the general as did her sister, Madame K'ung. "Ella" and "May" (as Stilwell called Ei-ling and Mei-ling) told him of their concern for China due to the lack of any military action. There held meetings that could only be described as conspiracies. Stilwell felt that they must have been influenced in their support for him by their brother, T. V. Soong, the Chinese ambassador to America. Quite the contrary, Soong was pressing for Stilwell's recall, and in between the two men of power stood the two sisters. The sisters were both Christian and they told Stilwell they were holding prayer meetings for guidance. Stilwell summed this phase up with a brief note to his wife in Carmel: "Isn't this a hell of a way to fight a war?"

The loose alliance of warlords that Chiang tried to hold together by playing one against the other proved him to be a master juggler. If he had only used his cleverness and corruptive devices against the foe, the Japanese would have been driven out before Pearl Harbor.

Corrupt warlords and officials ruled as minor despots throughout the country. In one region the local authority was a man named Lung Yun. He ordered all two-wheeled carts to be equipped with rubber tires. As they were by far the most common vehicle, his order affected many people. It just so happened that he had several warehouses full of these rubber tires which he had confiscated during the earlier days of the war when the traffic came heavily over the Burma Road. After the peasants purchased and installed the rubber tires, he passed a new law levying taxes on all carts with rubber tires.

In January, 1943, the poker playing by China's top men and America's military leaders nearly reached a standoff. The Chinese were demanding a billion-dollar loan. They stated they had some very attractive offers from Japan to drop out. The Americans offered their viewpoint. After conferring with General Marshall and Stimson, General Somervell said the United States was now ready to "get tough." In a meeting on January 20, with Secretary Morgenthau, Somervell stated America was going to stop building the Chinese airfields for the B-29 bombers and hit Japan from "another direction." He offered a few more aces to fill out his hand. The United States could "break" Chiang by withholding all future aid. Or they could buy out one of his competitors for $100 million, and "there are lots of candidates." Gen. Lucius Clay suggested diverting Lend-Lease to some of the provincial generals or else moving out of China at a slow pace.

Nothing came from it except an American realization that Chiang could not be depended on either to fight the Japanese or to keep his word. Small wonder Stilwell identified with Eifler, who could exercise complete control over his disparate personnel. The strength of the DET 101 men lay in a sense of unity. Officers and enlisted men worked together with a singleness of purpose. Hard-core militarists would have been astonished at the thought of officers and enlisted men from all branches of the service, along with civilians and people from other nations functioning in a unit without bickering or animosity. The designated commander functioned as such whether or not he had officers of equal or even superior rank with him.

In early 1943, British Lieutenant General Irwin summoned Eifler to his Delhi headquarters. He furrowed his brow over a map of Burma as if to accentuate a specific problem. His finger reached out and touched an area on Burma's east coast, touching on the Bay of Bengal. Eifler followed his direction. He was pointing to Akyab.

"Eifler," he began, "the Japanese have a most efficient fighting force in this area. It is there ostensibly to protect the coast from invasion. But it also is positioned to be able to move north or south or even east to reinforce Mandalay. It has a weak point, however, supplies." He moved his finger down a small, thin line designating the road south to Sandoway and toward the port of Rangoon. "If we can cut this road, we can give them some problems and somewhat cut their mobility."

Eifler was ahead of him. He noted where the road crossed over the Taungap Pass. "General, we can cut that road. That's what my men are trained for. If you will supply the boats to get us there, you can count on us."

They shook hands.

Key men were selected from those already in the OSS training camps. Others were recruited who came from that area and in particular those who knew the coast. They were transferred to a camp of their own where they trained for several weeks. They were dubbed W Group. All selected were Burmese and Anglo-Burmese. They were proud to be returning to their native land to strike a blow against the invaders.

Eifler breathed a sigh of relief as he saw the group being readied. It was one of the least of his worries. He had full confidence in his instructors and in the caliber of agents selected. He did not have the same comfortable feeling for the position of his OSS unit and its relation to the CBI theater. He knew Stilwell was backing him as far as he felt he could.

The problem Stilwell faced in China with the OSS desire to work there and Miles's jealous guarding of the theater as his own soon posed a serious question of authority. On February 16, 1943, Eifler sent a ten-page report on the status of OSS SU DET 101 to Donovan. It reported that at the last conference with Goodfellow and Williams a decision was made to avoid any further jurisdictional dispute by relieving DET 101 from its OSS ties and assigning it to Chungking, under Stilwell.

Shortly after the message was received in Washington, Eifler was told he was relieved as the Far Eastern representative of OSS and Captain Miles was so appointed. No official order, however, was ever issued. There was no T/O (Table of Organization), and Eifler found his unit was neither fish nor fowl. He could not promote men as they earned such promotions. He pointed out it was imperative that he be given some definite guidelines and that his unit be a T/O, either from OSS or in the CBI area under Stilwell. He further reported the unit sadly in lack of personnel, which was hampering expansion. He further pointed out that more and more of his men were kept occupied by the overwhelming burden of normal administrative detail rather than the training of new agents. Even though some of the groups were now trained and ready for action, they still required a high degree of supervision for morale purposes. He stated that on numerous occasions he had found it necessary to order officers and enlisted men to leave their work after midnight and go to bed.

He also pointed out the problem arising from verbal orders. In cases of utmost secrecy it was academic. Security was constantly violated because it became necessary to explain his orders to everyone he came in contact with. The average army officer found it hard to believe OSS men were operating on some missions at such a high level with no written orders. In some instances OSS men were given verbal authority to draw on supplies from army depots, but the officers in charge of those depots knew nothing about it and demanded written orders.

Included in the report was a chart showing the requested T/O.

Realizing the value of the success of their first field unit and backing a man like Eifler, OSS worked to solve the problems that he presented. Recruiting was begun in earnest. The T/O was approved, and soon new blood began pouring into the dried arteries.

Many of the problems were brought to Eifler's attention through other channels. Stilwell did not discuss his weighty problems with anyone, nor did Eifler. Both men were alike in the handling of their own problems. They neither asked nor gave any quarter. Both men wore the same field-type hat with the large round brim and peak top. It was said by the men of the theater that you had never been really chewed out unless one of the two men in the field hats got ahold of you. Stilwell no doubt held the edge for the razor-tongued comments, while there was no question Eifler held the edge in volume.

Soon, Eifler informed British headquarters that Group W was nearing completion of its training. General Loyd, commander of the British 14th Division, promised the necessary boats. A certain type of craft was selected, but a more careful review of the charts indicated it was unsuitable, so a different type was chosen. Shortly thereafter, Eifler, Richmond, Curl, and the entire W Group left for Chittagong, to the north of the target area. Upon arrival, they were told communications were out between their area and Calcutta. It was vital for them to be in contact with Calcutta, so Richmond left to reopen the lines using the OSS radios which had now proved to be superior to any others in the theater, either British or American. He left in the afternoon. That night the Chittagong air alarms wailed, and overhead Japanese Betty bombers made their appearance known. Their target happened to be Assam where they managed to destroy some of the badly needed U.S. planes.

Pending Richmond's return, Eifler and his British hosts went over the plans and charts for the tenth time. They studied the weather reports, tides, and currents to make sure they were not overlooking the smallest detail.

A further nautical switch was made after Eifler and the British assessed the number of men in W Group plus the required crews. Now the Royal Indian Navy was put in charge of the job. The ship was selected that was best suited to the operation. A great storm swept over the Bay of Bengal, delaying their departure.

While they were waiting Eifler was asked to give a demonstration of instinctive firing with a tommy-gun. He wanted to show the assembled British and Indian officers how to use the weapon for effective marksmanship while under fire. Curl joined the group and was pressed into the actual demonstration. Eifler stood in front of a large target with the weapon. Curl stood off to the side holding a .45 automatic. His job was to fire the .45 into the target, just inches from Eifler's face, while Eifler fired the tommy-gun at right angles. The demonstration began. As Eifler fired short bursts, he felt the breeze of the slugs from Curl's gun. This was closer than he intended. From the corner of his eye, he noticed Curl was also instinctively firing. He jumped back.

"Aim those bullets, you fool," he shouted.

Curl straightened up, smiling. "I'll feel much better doing that sir," he replied. The demonstration continued, with three hundred officers seeing something entirely new in the handling of weapons, not to mention the superb marksmanship. Curl, no slouch himself in that field, emptied a clip of seven bullets, putting them all into one enlarged hole. The British had previously exhibited little willingness to employ the tommy-gun. They had never been instructed in using it for short bursts; rather, they had been accustomed to emptying the entire clip and then having to stop to reload. From Eifler's demonstration they learned a new respect for the weapon.

Several days later the storm abated. It was time to put the group to sea and ashore below Akyab. A small, sparsely populated island just south of Akyab had been selected as the landing site. Again, a more detailed study of the area showed they still did not have the right type of craft. The waters where they were to put ashore were very dangerous. The high turbulence called for rubber reconnaissance boats. They secured five from a small stock located in a British warehouse. They were put aboard the larger ship.

The agents, meanwhile, had packed their gear into forty-pound waterproof packs. They had a total of fifteen hundred pounds to move ashore and into the jungle for safekeeping. Once ashore, they would leave the equipment they could not carry and come back to it as they needed new supplies. The plan was for four of the rubber boats to carry equipment and the fifth to carry agent Slim. He was to go in first to test the water and make sure the boats would not be caught in treacherous currents.

On May 6, 1943, three launches of the Indian navy, commanded by a British officer, departed from Chittagong. Early the next morning they passed from British waters into Japanese waters. A sharp lookout was kept for hostile planes and for native craft. Should an unfortunate native craft sight them, they would have to sink the boat and take those aboard prisoner for fear they might report it to the Japanese. Timing was essential because of the tide. A shallow reef lay ahead and could be crossed only at a specific time. They reached the spot right on time, and all watched carefully as the launches crossed the troublesome spot. After this came the area where mud volcanoes caused the murky waters to bubble in ominous gurgles. The last known survey of these mud volcanoes had been made in 1898. All of the men on board were becoming apprehensive by now. They watched the sky for Japanese planes, the horizon for Japanese or native boats, and the water around them, which was even more threatening. As darkness engulfed the small group of boats, the danger of being spotted lessened, but the danger from the unknown waters increased. A short time later Richmond approached Eifler.

"Look, Carl," he began, "I am your liaison officer and as such must bring a message from the skipper. He was told he could turn back if it appeared too dangerous to continue. He does not like the look of things and wants to abort the mission."

Eifler looked grimly into the churning waters. He had feared something like this. "Wally," he began through clenched teeth, "he is the captain and in command. Tell him I cannot counteract any decision he makes, but if he is asking my opinion, I say we continue."

Richmond waited for a minute, evidently thinking of how to report Eifler's words back to the captain. He turned and headed back. He did not return for some time, but Eifler was well aware with each passing minute that the ships were not changing course. A short time later he reappeared and stood silently beside Eifler. Then he told him: "Okay, we will go on. The commander said he'd sink all three of his boats before he'd let any damn Yankee colonel say the British are yellow."

To coincide with the tide, the boats maintained a 12-knot speed. They were moving through the uncharted shoals, and mud volcanoes still disturbed the waters. Their boat shuddered as it struck something, but quickly moved on with no apparent damage. They became aware of the shoreline when someone spotted a light. It turned out to be a fire. Richmond assumed it to be some farmer clearing the land prior to planting. After the fire had consumed itself, the farmer would then turn the ashes under for fertilizer. The agent on board who knew the area where they were to land did not recognize any landmarks. One thing was quite obvious: the rocks were large and

numerous, and the current was extremely treacherous. Finally at
0130 the launches stopped their engines and anchored. The rubber
boats were lowered over the side and immediately swamped. Everybody prayed the men had done a good job in waterproofing their
gear. Slim went ahead in his boat. A few minutes later he returned.

"Jap patrol boats," he reported, gesturing toward the shore. Eifler
motioned a second agent into the boat and told them to return to see
if they could sneak through. As they rowed away, Eifler decided to go
also and followed in his own boat. He felt it might possibly have
been a case of jitters and seeing something that really wasn't there. A
few hundred feet away he reached their stopped boat and peered into
the dark. Slim was not mistaken; the patrol boats were there. In
addition, there were shacks along the beach where there should have
been jungle. That would mean patrols and dogs. The three boats
returned to the launches, and they moved south once more. About an
hour later they again stopped. They had just one hour to land the
rubber boats, unload them, and start the return trip. It was past that
now. Eifler reasoned that if they did not find the right spot to land
soon, he would go in right where the fire was seen near the shacks.
The sentries along the beach would least suspect enemy agents to
land in such an obvious place.

Slim had gone ahead in his boat once more. He reported the rocks
were too thick to allow passage of even the small boats. Eifler then
ordered him to swim in. There was a moment of silence, and it
became apparent Slim was not going to do it. It was not a question of
bravery—it simply was a matter of swamped boats treacherous
waters and enemy sentries. He was emotionally and physically
exhausted.

Eifler unbuckled his gun belt, took the rope from Slim's waist,
and tied it around himself. He slipped over the side and worked his
way through the rocks and rushing waters to find a spot large enough
to pull the boats through. He was battered time and again against the
huge boulders and realized he was being hurt. His feet found the
bottom, and he began walking. Suddenly he dropped into deeper
waters; he had been on a reef. He swam and walked, then swam some
more as he went over several reefs. Finally he reached shore. He
looked quickly in all directions for any sign of life. He realized that
his only weapon was a knife. Fortunately, he was alone. He began
pulling on the small rope around his waist. It soon brought in a larger
rope, and with sheer brutal strength he now pulled the rubber boats
in, one tied behind the other. The men excitedly leaped ashore, and
all began unloading the fifteen hundred pounds of supplies. In fifteen
minutes it was accomplished. Eifler solemnly warned them to carry

everything into the jungle, off of the beach, before repacking. Then he shook hands with each man, warned them never to be taken alive, and jumped into the lead boat accompanied by the three British officers who had also come in to help.

The return trip was a nightmare.

Trying to tie the emptied bobbing boats to the dinghy with hands numbed by cold was exasperating. Two of them broke loose and thrashed around on the rocks. If discovered, their presence would clearly indicate a landing party. They had to be taken back. Eifler leaped back into the water and retrieved them. They were finally secured to the dinghy. At that point a large wave struck them, throwing the dinghy high and dry onto a large rock. Over the side went Eifler again, now dazed and bleeding. When the next wave came in, he pushed the dinghy free and jumped aboard. Once more it was thrown back onto a rock, and the process of Eifler going over the side and pushing it back with the next outgoing wave was repeated. Finally the dinghy with its tag-along cargo reached the open waters. They rowed to the launches only to find they were gone. Everyone had an idea as to the next move. Eifler ended the discussion.

"Gentlemen, I am the senior officer. We will keep together, and you will follow me."

He struck directly away from the shore line. They continued rowing and listened for any sounds that would indicate where the launches had gone. A short time later they heard the sound of anchor chains. They called out and heard the reassuring reply of their comrades. Willing hands pulled them aboard. The decks were slippery with the blood of a British officer who had been injured while the boats were being launched.

Richmond told Eifler they had been forced to move to deeper water when the tide went out, as they were in danger of being trapped within the rocks. In addition, they had heard gunfire from the shore and assumed those in the landing party were killed or captured. When three hours had passed and with daylight only an hour away, the commander had ordered the boats to return. Richmond had pleaded for the boats to stay while there was still a chance. The commander had told him: "How do you think I feel to have to log one Yankee colonel and three British officers left behind? I have these boats and men to think of and must be out of sight by daylight."

Richmond finally talked him into another half-hour. At the end of that time, he ordered the anchor raised for the return trip. The sound of the anchor chains the returning men had heard indicated just how close it had been.

132

Now the strain was over. Eifler slipped, exhausted, to the deck. Then he passed out. When he came to, his head hurt terribly and he was completely deaf in one ear. Loud, ringing noises plagued him. Richmond gave him some temporary pain-relief pills. The boats, with open throttles, roared up the coast and on the morning of the 9th reached Mandaw.

An ominous silence cast itself over the area now. Days passed with no radio contact. Was the entire ordeal for nothing? The radio operators switched frequencies and strained for the faintest sound. They spent continual shifts at their receivers. Nothing. Some time later the final facts were learned. The agents had either disobeyed instructions and repacked on the beach, or in some manner a single flashlight battery had fallen from its container and remained behind on the beach. The next day a local fisherman picked it up. Suspicious, or perhaps to gain favor with his Japanese masters, he turned it over to them.

Quickly the Japanese sealed the area and sent out patrols. In a matter of time the group was apprehended. Witnesses said they were cut down in a hail of bullets, their mud-streaked faces shouting defiance to the very end. Group W was scratched from the list.

Eifler went from bad to worse. The pain increased, and the ringing in his ears persisted. He downed bottles of pain-killer pills and bourbon in a desperate effort to fight back. Tremendous in spirit and physical strength, he was powerless to defeat this tormenting adversary.

For three long pain-ridden months Eifler clung to his command, overseeing the actions of his men in the field. He became forgetful, sinking into short periods of amnesia. A young attorney from Donovan's law firm came over to inspect the DET 101 operation. He returned to report the extent of Eifler's injuries and that, in his opinion, they were keeping him from full effectiveness. Such an effect on Eifler was therefore harmful to the entire 101 unit. He suggested that Eifler should either be hospitalized or removed from command.

Eifler realized he was getting worse. He agreed he should be hospitalized, and in August, 1943, checked into the 20th General Hospital in Ledo. Wanting to keep in communication with his men, he brought along communications Sgt. Sam Schreiner, who had recently arrived in the theater. Schreiner had been in the OSS Washington message center and had transferred to DET 101, anxious for some action. Those in the hospital and unaware of the nature of Eifler's injuries certainly felt something was drastically wrong with a man who would bring his own radio operator when he could utilize the hospital's message center. Had they seen any of the normal 101 messages, they might well have understood why regular military channels of communications could not be employed. Aside from security, there were messages sometimes requesting permission to assassinate a certain native official who was being uncooperative. The messages from the field were quite often spiced with colorful language, not standard in regular message centers.

It was several days before Eifler realized he was hospitalized for other than physical reasons. He tried to leave, without success. A problem had arisen in the field, and he needed to see General H. L. Boatner, chief of staff for the Chinese army at Ramgarh. He also requested permission to leave to see General Stilwell. Permission was denied. Eifler said he was going to go anyway. The doctor in charge said if he did, he would mark Eifler as "incompetent." This would have ended Eifler's service career, so he dropped that approach. He did finally get permission to visit with General Boatner, who was a few miles away. Here he explained his predicament. Boatner listened gravely and said Stilwell was on his way by plane. Eifler waited for him.

Stilwell landed and promptly went into mess. Eifler went in, saluted, and sat down to talk with him.

"Why are you in the hospital, Eifler?" the general asked.

Eifler replied: "I'm not sure, sir, but I think they think I'm crazy."

Stilwell snorted. "Hell, they didn't have to hospitalize you for that. I could have told them you were crazy."

Eifler explained his situation. Stilwell agreed to come to the hospital the next morning to determine "if the generals are running things or the goddamn doctors."

Prior to the officers' arrival the next morning, an encephalogram was performed on Eifler. When Stilwell and Boatner arrived he was lying back in excruciating pain.

The three talked for a few minutes. Then the generals left.

Eifler noted with satisfaction the looks on the faces of the doctors and nurses who felt his request to talk with them was akin to that of a dog barking at the moon. He was doubly pleased when he overheard one of them remark: "Talk about the mountain coming to Mohammed."

An hour later the executive officer of the hospital came in to tell Eifler he could leave any time he wanted to. He added: "I suggest you stay in bed three more days in view of your operation."

Eifler wasn't feeling too much pain, having been used to it for so long anyway. He elected to leave right then. He sat up in his bed, swung his legs over the side, and promptly lay back down. He remained in bed for three more days. He said later that he felt they knew he was in utter pain those three days but refused to give him anything for relief. In return, Eifler noted every possible violation he saw and made a full report to the authorities when released. It was, he later said, the only time he ever "ratted" on anyone.

Upon his return to Nazira he sat down to review the overall Burma situation and how his agents were functioning. Knothead was doing well under the command of Curl. South of this group, and under the Knothead command, was Skittles, who was doing a superb job. The chances he took in the execution of his duties gave considerable alarm to everyone. He was too valuable to be lost in some minor skirmish.

Further south and to the east was Operation Pat. It was headed by two young Anglo-Burmese, former officers of the Burmese army, Patrick Quinn and Dennis Francis. Their camp lay within twenty miles of the Japanese bastion in Myitkyina. Their unit at this time consisted of some fifty to sixty guerrillas. It was later to grow to over four hundred fighting men. Still farther south and east of Pat was Drown. Captain George Drown, a British officer who came from the Kachin Levies, commanded his men in missions as far away as forty miles from his base camp. Drown was as proper as any Englishmen could be. Though living in the dense and humid jungles, he still availed himself of English properness. He shaved twice daily, had his own personal valet who handed him his shaving gear in proper sequence without a word. Tally-ho and all that. His operation was quite smashing. Wilkinson continued with his Forward unit to the north.

All groups were turning in valuable information to the air corps and receiving splendid cooperation from fighters and bombers who roared out immediately to strike hidden ammunition dumps and supply areas. The Japanese were aware who was giving out the information but found it almost impossible to strike the evanescent OSS men. The highly touted 18th Division that had rolled over the poorly commanded Chinese troops at Nanking were being picked off slowly but surely by a polyglot guerrilla force that never let up. Surprisingly, the native agents got along beautifully despite the many different tribes and nationalities they represented. Two years earlier they had willingly ambushed one another. Kachins, Karens, Shans, Burmese, Chinese, Anglos, and Indians put aside all differences and quickly absorbed the OSS spirit of one goal and one only—destruction of the Japanese.

One day an exciting message came to Nazira. A Japanese pilot had been captured. Any kind of a Jap prisoner was a rarity, but one of their pilots was something special. He had been shot down by a U.S. fighter and parachuted to a spot just two miles south of N Sop Sop, a Japanese stronghold. He requested the natives lead him to the nearest Japanese base. They led him, instead, into the hills. He still had his sidearm and began getting suspicious when he felt the terrain was not what it should be. Before he could pull his weapon, they jumped him. He was well skilled in hand-to-hand combat and gave an excellent account of himself before the natives finally overpowered him by sheer weight of numbers and tied him up. Everyone was well covered with bumps and bruises. He was taken to Pat's headquarters. Pat wired in to ask if he should make an attempt to smuggle him back or just bump him off.

"Hold him, we'll get him out," was the reply.

This fighter pilot was of unusual importance because of a special problem the air corps was having. They could not determine where the Jap Zeros were coming from that regularly attacked and destroyed U. S. cargo planes flying supplies to China. Repeated bombings of all known Jap airfields had failed to diminish their strength. The planes had to be operating from some hidden bases well concealed from the natives. At Air Corps request, all 101 men had carefully searched for these enemy air units. The phantom planes simply could not be located even with the help of the many agents and native sympathizers in the area. Could this prisoner solve the riddle?

The first problem was how to get him out. It would have to be by air. The nearest camp with a possible airstrip was Knothead, nearly one hundred miles away. Eifler made the decision to have him taken to Knothead. Even though the strip was not ready, it would have to be by the time the prisoner arrived. Tools were dropped at the partial strip, and Curl put the men to work getting it ready. The Piper Cub was about to perform its most important task.

Eifler was sure the pilot, a Samurai, would attempt suicide by trying to crash the plane. He was disgraced by his capture, and this would be a glorious way to die for his emperor. Eifler asked Chun Ming what he could get to knock the man out for the trip. The army hospital at Chabua provided the answer in the form of a syringe and special medication. To make doubly sure Eifler got the directions straight, they were written down.

The next morning another message was received. A Japanese infantry officer had been captured near Forward. Could an interpreter be flown in?

Eifler had a better idea. He would fly in and bring him out. This would be a test case for the plane. The trip was shorter. In addition, the man, being an infantry officer, would not be as valuable for intelligence purposes as the pilot. If he could be tied sufficiently to prevent his wrecking the plane, it would be that much easier in working with the pilot. Eifler planned to fly from India to Fort Hertz, refuel, then fly to Forward. There he would pick up the officer, refuel, and head for Knothead. He would pick up the pilot, refuel, and return. Some day's work!

At Knothead things began to happen. Curl put out the call for natives to come work on the airstrip. Of prime importance was the safe return of the pilot to NawBum in time to meet Eifler. Pamplin was put in charge of the journey, which involved six days each way over the treacherous Chinglaptu Pass. The area was fairly well secured from enemy patrols but not necessarily the wild animals that on occasion gave the 101 men considerable problems. Pamplin took sixteen men who would act as guards so there would be no chance of the prisoner escaping. Along the way Pamplin noted specific spots where the narrow trail dropped over six thousand feet, excellent spots for the returning pilot to attempt suicide. He pointed them out to his men so they would be alert to them.

The small party arrived at Pat, glad to be over the first leg of their trip. There was no time to rest, unfortunately. The prisoner looked like a caged animal, ready to take advantage of the smallest error on his captors' part. He was lying on a bamboo stretcher, tied hand and foot. Pamplin reasoned this would be the best way to return him. Even on foot with ropes held in front and behind, he still might leap hard enough to go over the edge and take some natives with him. The party started back. The sixteen men took turns with the stretcher. Pamplin couldn't help being amused at the incongruity of the whole thing. Eight months earlier he had been a civilian and singing in a choir. He came into a strange outfit to do its legal work. Now he was bringing out one of the first Japanese prisoners of the war. Prisoners were so rare the British had a standing offer of a fortnight's leave to any Tommy bringing one in. The Japanese made sure none were captured on the battlefield; those wounded that could not be returned were killed by their comrades.

Each narrow spot was carefully passed with the stretcher being tilted away from it to lessen the chances of a sudden weight shift catapulting the prisoner and some of the natives to certain death. It proved a safe return journey. Pamplin arrived at NawBum to find the field prepared. Eifler had dropped extra gasoline for the return trip and carefully laid out his time of departure from India and arrival to pick up the pilot. He had made sure it would give him sufficient daylight should he be delayed.

The day before Pamplin's return, Eifler had left Nazira for Fort Hertz where he was to refuel for the Forward camp and the first prisoner. He was told there was ample fuel at the fort. When he arrived he found that was correct, but it was all 100-octane, too powerful for his plane. He rechecked his fuel and decided he had enough to make it. In flying down the river and gaining altitude, he wondered if he would have enough to make it back. Upon touch-down at the camp, he decided he did not. Over in the bushes lay the wreckage of the ill-fated OSS No. 1 which had crashed there earlier. The men were able to salvage some fuel from it and put it in the tank. Satisfied he could now make it, he prepared to load the prisoner and leave. He made sure the prisoner was bound securely and had him loaded aboard. They took off.

Half an hour later the prisoner began complaining. His bonds had stopped the circulation. Soon he was screaming in pain. Eifler had some morphine and considered turning to jab it into his legs. He was surprised at hearing a Japanese scream from pain. By the time the plane landed twenty minutes later at Fort Hertz, he had been scream-ing continuously. He was taken off, grateful to have his bonds re-leased, and led away for interrogation.

The next day Eifler took off for NawBum. He was glad to see the Knothead strip and flew low over it to check it out as well as let the camp know he had arrived. It also gave the natives time to clear the bamboo huts from the field that were placed to make it look like a village from the air. The strip both dipped and twisted. Landing required a cutting of the engines as the plane dropped in over the high trees. The Jap pilot watched impassively. He had not yet showed any emotion. There could certainly be no question in his mind as to what that plane meant.

The little plane came in to a perfect landing. Eifler jumped out with his little medical kit ready. Curl, Pamplin, and Haimson rushed out to greet him. There was no time for visiting. He was led to the prisoner. Their eyes met. There was no visible sign of hatred between the two, merely a matter of trying to sum each other up. Both were highly trained officers, and both were dedicated to their country's war effort. Eifler undid the kit, taking out the syringe and inserting the needle and the new wonder drug, pentothal. He put in 20 cc's, enough to keep the pilot out until the plane was safely back in India. He placed the tourniquet to find the vein, instructed Pamplin to keep time, and plunged the needle into the exposed vein. To his horror, he saw a bubble form. He knew air bubbles in the bloodstream could cause death, but it was there and he had to follow through. Slowly he pushed the plunger down, forcing the fluid in. Then he told the pilot, in broken Japanese, to count after him. He counted to ten. The pilot did likewise. Nothing happened. He was still as alert as before. Eifler's eyes lit on the problem—the tourniquet had not been released. It was immediately undone, and the pilot went out like a light. No bonds were around him, but a noose was fashioned around his neck with the end passed through the fuselage and into Eifler's lap. Should he come to and cause trouble, he would simply be strangled. The Kachins seemed amused at the elaborate precautions but could not realize that in the air it would be possible for him to bring down the plane and die gloriously.

Eifler was sitting on the pilot's feet as he warmed up the refueled plane. He roared downhill on the short slope, went to the very end, and barely cleared the trees. The men on the ground breathed a sigh of relief. About halfway back, at nine thousand feet, he ran into a rainstorm.

"I could not describe the situation of flying in a blinding rainstorm with no instruments other than compass, altimeter, and a tachometer with mountains on both sides ranging up to fourteen thousand feet, and an enemy pilot so closely wrapped about my back he could lean forward and bump me with his head," he later said.

Either the cramped position or the weight of Eifler on his feet might have started bringing the pilot out of it in less than two hours. He moaned and whimpered, but again Eifler could do nothing. He was sure the pilot would still be unconscious when they landed. Soon he saw the welcome sight of the Chabua field, and the plane rolled in safely. The small reception committee included an ambulance and a doctor.

The doctor commented that, although the pilot had awakened, the drug had kept his mind and body from functioning together. Eifler was anxious for the interrogation. While the pilot was recovering, Eifler got some food and freshened up a bit. Later, with Chang acting as interpreter, the interrogation began. That day it produced nothing. The pilot answered very little to the interpreter and said nothing of value. It was obvious he would be a tough nut to crack. The next day Eifler decided to try a new approach. He based it on two points. First, he felt the pilot actually understood English, although he would not admit it. Second, Eifler prided himself on a fair-to-good understanding of Oriental psychology. In particular, he knew the seriousness of dishonor to a Japanese warrior. He keyed his approach to this point.

Within the small room were several chairs and the customary wooden table. Eifler was standing. The pilot, Chang, and two other Intelligence officers were sitting. Eifler had not confided to the others his plan.

"Chang, to begin the questioning today, ask where he flew from," Eifler began.

The question was asked and repeated. Silence.

"Ask him the name of his unit and commanding officer."

Again repeated—more silence.

Now Eifler put his plan into effect. He opened the door and called in a doctor. The doctor said nothing but quietly went to the table and slowly unrolled his equipment, being careful to put in front of the pilot a 20 cc syringe, a large needle, and a vial of "truth serum." He assembled the syringe and began filling it from the vial.

Eifler started the next phase of his act. He walked rapidly back and forth, seemingly in great distress. He spoke out loud but apparently to himself. "I just don't want to do this to this man. He is an honorable soldier of the Japanese Empire, and this drug is a terrible disgrace. He is too honorable to do this to." He walked to a small window and looked out. There was no question about the fact he was very much torn over his next move. He turned to Chang and said, almost pleadingly: "Chang, see if he won't tell us anything." Chang tried again, but still had no success.

More dramatics ensued, as Eifler played his role to perfection. He addressed Chang: "You know how I hate to do this and dishonor a fellow officer, don't you? He has his duty and carried it out. I have mine and must also carry it out. We might have killed one another in combat, but we didn't. I would rather have killed him than do this now and dishonor him. Chang, try again, so we can spare him."

He could not tell if a flicker crossed the stoic Japanese face but did know Chang's questions still remained unanswered. The cat-and-mouse game was repeated several more times—each time with the words "honorable Japanese officer" and the word "dishonor" being clearly used.

Finally, Eifler played his trump card. Completely "distraught" over what he must do, he turned to the doctor and said, "well, you see I have no other choice. Go ahead, Doctor." He turned to leave the room, so he would not have to witness the degrading scene.

As he reached the door, the pilot spoke in a loud voice: "Wait. I'll talk."

Eifler did one more bit of acting in turning and appearing to be astonished that the man understood and spoke English. He could not let him know he had been tricked.

Evidently the dishonor of the drug was greater than the dishonor of talking—or so Eifler had led him to believe.

His base, he revealed, was at Meiktila, just south of Mandalay. He was told he lied because aerial photos of that area revealed nothing.

Now the big secret came out. The Japanese aircraft were pushed into revetments and covered with sod. But they were there, at the edge of the forest. The air corps checked its maps once more. Sure enough there were the tell-tale shadows of deep gashes that had been ignored before.

The next day American bombers roared out of Assam to destroy the planes. The pressure on the cargo planes greatly decreased. Eifler returned to Nazira. He was pleased.

7

The Nazira headquarters was constantly buzzing with something new, something bizarre. Mail from relatives asked all too often just what was going on. Naturally, only limited information could be given which only heightened Stateside interest.

In August, 1943, twelve enlisted men arrived. They came in response to Eifler's desperate request for communications personnel. They were greeted by a partially grown bear that gave them cause to wonder what other exotic pets might be around. The bear had been given to Eifler by an officer at Chabua whose colleagues decided it was time for the little cub to go. Eifler brought it back and thoroughly enjoyed his few moments of relaxation with it. It soon grew to about seventy-five pounds and began making known its tremendous strength in spite of its size. In addition, its claws and teeth were quite strong. It enjoyed roughhousing and soon proved to be too much for most of the men. Eifler alone was able to handle it, the two of them rolling over and over on the lawn. Many debates raged over just who was doing all of the snarling and growling. After a while, the men were sure to check carefully before entering the yard to make sure the 101 pet was not out. If the bear was out, a footrace ensued with the man trying to make it to the building and get inside, safe for a while longer. On more than one occasion someone was forced to climb a tree and wait to be rescued. The bear seemed to lose interest if he had to climb a tree after his playmate. Eifler returned from one of his frequent trips and was told the bear had disappeared. He believed someone had it shot but never knew for certain.

In one of the training camps was a group comprised of five Anglo-Burmese. It was dubbed the Hate group. Earlier they had gone into the field but had been recalled for an unusual reason. They had been put into the Salween River Valley area, bordering on China. Because of the terrain they were forced over the border from time to time. To reach their designated camp, they found it necessary to move through one considerable stretch of Chinese territory. They were stopped by the Chinese warlord controlling that area. He demanded money for their "protection." It was paid. A few miles farther a new warlord appeared and demanded money. The demands increased to the point it was simply impossible to meet them, and the unit was brought out.

As a result they were spoiling for action, and 101 was equally anxious to put them into another area. Many weeks after they were recalled, it was decided to put them into their original intended area of Lashio via another route. Two parachuted in first and sent back reports that all was well. The other three soon joined them, and the unit functioned well. They met their schedules on time and sent a steady flow of vital information. Of particular importance was their accurate reporting of enemy troop movements. Both the army and air corps waited regularly for the messages to see if there was any concentration of troops that might foretell a Japanese push. Suddenly their radio went dead. Nazira monitored it continually, but they never came on again.

Another OSS unit later reported that all five men had been captured. Since they had been living in five separate villages, it was apparent one had been forced to reveal the whereabouts of the others. The men had been moved from jail to jail by the Japanese and were lodged now in the Lashio jail. It was also reported they were being subjected to terrible torture.

Their suffering was ended one day when three American bombers swooped low over the jail and, with precision bombing, leveled the structure along with all its occupants. A special place remains in OSS annals for such gallant agents.

Another blow to DET 101 was dealt by a fire that leveled an army *godown* (supply shed) in Chabua. Stored in that structure was considerable communications equipment and black powder, not to mention 101's only jeep in the area.

In September, Hal Williams sent a letter to Eifler and Coughlin advising of some new top-secret equipment he was securing for 101. From the navy had come an item known as "Rebecca-Eureka." It was a radar device that went into an airplane to provide range and bearing. It had three scales which, to use Williams' words, "would put you right over a gnat's ass and no fooling." Effective up to nine miles and at twenty thousand feet, it was to be a tool that would help 101 in finding its men with more ease when airdrops were critically needed or additional personnel were to be parachuted in. A second item was a supersonic device. Each of the men in a patrol unit could secretly and silently communicate with the leader through a small pocket device. Another device was called "Mad" and was installed on planes to locate hidden ammunition dumps. Williams also made mention of paper parachutes for supplies. The 101 needed chutes capable of dropping 100 pounds at 16 feet per second at a speed of 150 mph. A supply of these chutes was ordered, when available, for the Nazira headquarters to test. They would be not only less expensive but also more easily disposed of. A final item he mentioned was a combination cook-stove and battery charger. It would operate on any type of fuel, including wood, and at the same time recharge flashlight batteries.

Eifler came up with a simple device for use in occupied areas. The Japanese officers were, like soldiers everywhere, inclined to tip the bottle. The morning after they would take aspirin, handed to them by their native houseboys. The Eifler aspirin tablet looked like any other tablet except his had an added ingredient in the center—cyanide. Sayonara!

Adaptability and ingenuity were two key OSS words. In Washington, Lovell received a request from Europe for an explosive that might be worked into lumps of coal used for the boilers of locomotives. It was produced as requested. Because different coal was used according to the country where it was mined, OSS had to make the "coal" in different sizes and colors. The engines in Burma, however, burned logs. The next step was logical. Logs were carefully stripped of their bark, hollowed out, and filled with explosives. The bark was replaced, and the innocent-looking log put back in the stack with its non-OSS companions. When later thrown into the boiler, it did its job. Happy Fourth of July.

The OSS training program included the "principle of three." It was to be used when an agent felt he was close to discovery and knew who was on his trail. If the agent was in France and realized a certain person was making too many inquiries, he would write an anonymous letter to the Gestapo concerning the activities of that person. First he would tell two easily checked truths. His third statement was a lie accusing the target of an offense of such gravity that the Gestapo, accustomed to receiving valid information from him, would take care of his problem permanently. The normal pattern was for the methodical Gestapo to check out the accusations in order. After finding the first two to be true, they seldom bothered to check out the third statement. The agent could eliminate his problem without risk of uncovering his own activities. A tip of the hat to the efficient Gestapo service.

This principle did provide an amusing incident in 1943. A class of agents had completed their training and were given a leave prior to going overseas. They were given false identity papers and told to assemble in the lobby of a certain Philadelphia hotel on a specific night. At 7 P.M. their contact would walk into the lobby, purchase a cigar, bite off the end, and walk out without lighting it. They were all to follow him.

To test the theory one of the men wrote an anonymous letter to the FBI. He gave them three statements. (1) A group of enemy agents would be assembled in the lobby of a certain hotel in Philadelphia on a certain night. (2) Their leader would come in and buy a cigar at 7 P.M., bite off the end, and leave without lighting it. They would all follow him. (3) They would then proceed to the Philadelphia Navy Yard and blow up the battleship *Iowa*. The fateful night arrived. Our hero sat apart from his comrades reading a newspaper. From behind pillars, high-backed chairs, and palm fronds peered strange faces. Promptly at 7 P.M. the leader entered, walked over to the tobacco counter, and bought a cigar. He looked at no one, peeled off the cigar wrapper, bit off the end, and walked out the door. All the agents, save our tipster, arose and sauntered out the door. Immediately the net closed, and they were all arrested.

They had been instructed not to reveal their identities if they were arrested. They didn't. Quickly the FBI discovered all their papers were fake. It is rumored that it took the efforts of Donovan himself to calm an angry FBI. The fate of the unidentified agent was not known. At least he should have been convinced of the possibilities that lay in using the principle of three.

This was not a tactic that could be used very well in Burma, since Americans could not pass as anything but Caucasians. The basic principle, however, could and was. OSS 101 men utilized it in their black propaganda efforts. They published "Japanese papers" which professed to make certain claims and promises by Japanese officers. Using a Japanese format and occasionally a Japanese plane, the papers were sometimes dropped over native and Burmese towns and villages. The papers made rash promises that could never be carried out and caused the Japanese to lose considerable face when the promises failed to materialize. If the Japanese told them the Americans were responsible the natives in all honesty could report they saw the Japanese planes dropping the papers.

Another use of the deceit principle was the faking of an offer to work with the Allies and signing a known Japanese name. It would conveniently fall into the wrong hands, and soon thereafter there would be one less enemy to contend with. On many occasions the Japanese soldiers were found with surrender passes and orders allegedly issued by their superiors which were confusing or would tend to make the soldier lose confidence.

The Japanese had been more clever in their handling of the people of Burma than in many other countries. Rather than the customary "currency" ground out by army presses, they issued notes stating: "The Japanese Government promises to pay to the bearer on demand the sum of...." Impressed by this seemingly kind treatment, the acceptance of the Japanese claim of Asia for the Asians and a hatred of the British, the Burmese returned more good will than the Allies cared for. The solution? OSS had a sample of the money picked up with an air hook, flown to Washington, and counterfeited by the hundreds of thousands. The operation was deemed so important that OSS purchased a paper mill to make sure they got the right paper. The enemy never discovered it was counterfeit. Eifler also had a small supply counterfeited in Calcutta, but the work was such that it was easily detected by local experts. He was afraid to use it for fear it would give his agents away. It was later utilized but in a different way. When a collaborator was found, a large amount of the Calcutta money would find its way into his hands. In a matter of time the Japanese would discover who had the bad money and take care of the collaborator, thus helping the Allied cause. It was then given to thousands of natives who soon wrecked the economy in selected areas. Shortly afterward the Japanese army presses ground out the normal currency, and the Japanese were forced to take off the velvet gloves.

Eifler faced continuing and increasing pain. He was taking painkillers constantly. In spite of the pain, he remained in the thick of the growing 101 battle. He instructed Richter to get contact established with Chungking. He wanted closer ties with General Stilwell's headquarters. The order was more easily given than carried out.

Richter had monitored the New Delhi transmissions as well as those from Chabua. He had little to help him. OSS had no call letters of its own. Rather than point this out to Eifler, who would simply have said he didn't give a damn about the technicalities, Richter decided to establish his own. This proved to be quite confusing to the established radio bases because they had no idea where the call came from or who these strange people were. To further confuse the situation, both ham procedures and a military procedures were used and even some OSS procedures. Nazira would simply crank up energy and break in on a transmission. Naturally they were asked who they were and would have to reply: "We can't tell you but here is the message." The messages were accepted.

At one point a message was received from the chief signal officer in Washington, D.C. asking by whose authority OSS had been given some of its weird signs. Richter chose to ignore it, since he could not answer it. Thirty days later a follow up message came through. By this time the chief signal officer of the CBI theater had been transferred back to the States. Richter then advised that the officer, a Colonel Monahan, had assigned the signs. Shortly thereafter official call signs were given, and the Nazira transmissions became legitimized. The Eifler spirit had again carried the day.

Eifler had a visitor one day. He was an officer attached to General Stilwell's staff. He stated that Stilwell would like to see Eifler. While not an unusual request Eifler felt he had an idea of what Stilwell wanted to discuss with him. He said he would report to Stilwell as soon as possible. A short time later he reported to the General's headquarters in New Delhi.

The two wasted little time on small talk. It was obvious to Eifler that Stilwell had a major problem on his hand. Soon it came out.

Stilwell pointed out to Eifler that if the U.S. was to further the war in a logical way it would be necessary to get Chiang Kai-shek out of the way. The big question was: would Eifler agree to do it and could he do it without getting caught or involved?

Eifler was neither surprised nor overwhelmed with such a request. He nodded his head and said he could figure out the way to do it. Stilwell stressed the point that it would have to be done in such a way it could not come back on Eifler or his men. Eifler rose, saluted and shook hands and departed.

On the way back his mind immediately searched out various plans. First was the direct approach of a sniper s bullet. Either Eifler or one of his men would pull the trigger. But there was no assurance the sniper would not be caught. No, it required a more delicate approach.

Eifler realized he had not been given license to do the job. He was to research the job, figure it out and take it back for approval. Stilwell had not indicated he wanted it done immediately. After more thought Eifler decided it would have to be a poison that would leave no trace. An autopsy could not reveal anything. It would be necessary to discuss this with R & A in Washington, D.C. He did not know when he would have that opportunity.

Upon his return to Nazira he had the basic plan formulated. It was to involve only three other men besides himself. They would each not know who else was to be involved. Individually he called them into his office. He did not tell them what was to be done. "I will need you on a mission that cannot even have a name," he began. "I will think of it as a no-name mission. I cannot ever tell you what it is until we start. At that point I will need your absolute confidence and willingness to do whatever I say.

"It is highly dangerous and will be distasteful—but it needs to be done. If you want to say 'no,' then do it now and no hard feelings."

Each man immediately said he was with him all the way. They returned to their duties to await the call.

There was to be no further action on the plan for nearly two months.

In early October, Eifler felt it necessary to fly to Forward and talk with Wilkinson. Rather than pilot the plane himself he took as pilot a Captain Majors, from the China National Airways. The takeoff and flight went smoothly. The arrival at the strip revealed a problem. The landing strip sloped downward, then up. Past the strip were some tall trees. Many had been removed. Majors commented it would be rough taking off. It was to prove an understatement. The plane rolled to as smooth a stop as could be expected on the jungle strip. Hurriedly, it was pushed out of sight and covered with vines and leaves. Eifler and Wilkinson shook hands and walked back to his shack. They talked for a time about Wilkinson's operation, future plans, needs of the unit, and the overall operation of 101 in Burma. Outside the native soldiers waited and speculated. *Laku*, a native rice wine, was kept in supply. It was made and stored in hollow bamboo. The process was never revealed in detail to the white man, but it was enough that it did exist in the dreary, insect-infested terrain. It was offered as a greeting to the white *duwas* who entered Kachin areas and it was considered an affront to decline. Many teetotalers found themselves reeling after sipping but a portion of their filled cups. It was not a light drink.

Several hours later, their talk concluded, Eifler and Wilkinson left the shack and walked with Majors to the airstrip. The natives wheeled the plane to the end of the strip, and the two men climbed in. Majors started the engine, listened to it carefully as it warmed up, then signaled Eifler he was going to start. For added speed, several natives ran behind pushing on the tail until they were outdistanced. The little plane used every foot of the runway, and at the very last moment the plane took off. The weight was too much. It nosed forward and crashed head-on into the ground. It was damaged heavily, but Eifler felt might later be repaired. Fortunately, injuries were minor. Eifler had a cut leg and swollen mouth where he had struck the back of Majors' seat. The natives pushed the wreckage a few feet farther into the brush to immediately conceal it. Eifler and Majors stood sadly by looking it over. Eifler instructed a cover be built for its protection in case it might later be salvaged. They started the walk back to the camp where they would spend the night.

The next morning they prepared to walk out. Majors wore only a pair of low-cut oxfords. Fortunately, Wilkinson had in his supplies a new pair of GI shoes in his size. Majors decided he could break them in on the trail. Eifler felt it not too good an idea. A few miles down the trail he was proved right, as the blisters formed.

148

"Colonel Eifler, you've got to have the damnedest outfit I ever saw. Imagine being fitted for a new pair of shoes way behind enemy lines," he began. "A good thing, too. Those shoes of mine never would have lasted."

Eifler grinned. "The new ones will, but will you? We've got over a hundred miles to go, and the trails aren't going to be easy."

Majors ruefully rubbed his sore feet. "You know, Colonel, the only walking I have ever done is across a hotel lobby and maybe up a flight of stairs, but I wouldn't even do that if I could take an elevator."

The brief rest concluded, Majors wrapped dampened leaves around the sore spots and hobbled on. That first day they made only ten miles and stopped at another Wilkinson outpost. To avoid the dense swarms of mosquitoes, they wrapped their heads in silk maps and stuck their hands in their pockets. That night Majors went right to bed. Eifler stayed up to discuss conditions with Wilkinson, who had accompanied them, and Father MacAlindon, who had joined them.

Like Father Stuart, Father MacAlindon had remained behind with his parish when the Japanese neared their area. He was the unofficial headman of the Triangle area. This area had not yielded to the British authority until 1935. Prior to this the people there had practiced slavery and paid no taxes. This was reversed with the introduction of British troops. The priests found themselves trying to bring Christianity to a people for whom of law and order was a new concept. Blood feuds still ran rampant, and black magic added to the missionaries' problems.

During one of the existing feuds two distant cousins of a man killed by a Kachin policeman attacked that policeman's distant cousin. They sliced his stomach open with a dah. To help him along, they poured a large bottle of iodine into the gaping wound. Somehow he managed to get away and staggered into Father Stuart's area. Father Stuart attempted to save his life, taking the man back to his own shack. The attackers now returned to ransack the belongings of their victim, as was the custom. They arrived only to find him still alive, though barely, with Father Stuart in attendance. There were thirty of them, all armed. Father Stuart headed out the window while the natives proceeded inside to finish off their victim. Arriving at Father MacAlindon's place several miles away, Father Stuart related the story. Father MacAlindon should have been a fighter instead of a priest, so great was his love of a good fight. Being senior to Father Stuart, he first criticized him that he, a priest, would run from thirty armed men. He then grabbed a shotgun, returned to the scene, and promptly ran the thirty men off into the jungles. It was too late to help the victim, who by now was in several pieces.

Early in the Japanese occupation the fighting priest was warned his area would probably be occupied. He picked up a box of grenades left behind by the retreating British and kept them beside his bed. He put a loaded shotgun at each window. His raw courage united the Kachins. The Japanese never reached his village of Kajitu. He was subsequently ordered from the area, along with Father Stuart, by the British. He too ran into some of the 101 men, was recruited, and returned to Forward to continue working with his people. He was invaluable for his knowledge of the people, their language, customs, and the terrain. Even beyond these rare talents he would have been of value to 101 because of his courage, adaptability, and resourcefulness. He had little trouble adding sabotage and espionage to his repertoire.

Eifler sat studying Father MacAlindon as the firelight flickered and danced on his face. The room was filling. The jungle grapevine had relayed word that the great colonel *duwa* was in the area. Headmen came from all over to pay their respects. Through the priest they relayed their gratitude for arms and food. To Eifler it was a scene from another time. He sat cross-legged on the floor with the natives. The fire, before him, cast its smoke through the thatched roof. Wild dogs sat at the door peering in, hoping for a handout. Under the raised floor pigs rooted and grunted. The *laku* flowed, and chickens and eggs were presented. Slowly the Kachins left after paying their respects. Finally the men turned in for the night.

Wilkinson had sent a man ahead to a Chinese major who had a mule. He asked for the use of that mule for two to three weeks. The major was not pleased but was sufficiently indebted to Wilkinson that he agreed.

The next morning Eifler and Majors bade Wilkinson and MacAlindon good-bye and started the next leg of their trip. That afternoon their guide took them into the area of the Chinese major, who had loaned them the mule. Majors' foot was somewhat better, and Eifler's leg was considerably better.

That night they found an abandoned shack on the edge of a native village. The view was spectacular. It looked across a valley to Mali Hka, which was occupied by Japanese troops. Eifler stood on the small porch with its bamboo railing. The mountain fell away sharply from under the shack. Suddenly the porch gave way, dropping Eifler down the side of the mountain. His plunging fall was broken by some bushes loaded with thorns. Majors, unaware of what had happened, was astounded when a bruised and bleeding Eifler

150

made his way back to the shack. When he realized Eifler was not hurt badly, he burst into laughter.

The men ate from their rations and prepared to turn in for the night. Outside the shack the native guide slept by the mule. He indicated through sign language that the mule might get loose. Eifler checked the tether and, satisfied, turned in.

During the night Eifler was awakened by Majors shouting: "Eifler, there is someone in the room. I've got him covered."

Automatically Eifler crouched, his .45 ready. There was no sound except for Majors' excited breathing. Convinced they were alone, Eifler went over to where Majors sat, his carbine in his hand. He was burning with fever.

"Bad dream, Majors," Eifler said.

Angrily, he denied it. "It was no dream. Someone started to open the door, I shouted and he ran," Majors retorted.

Eifler went outside to check. He retied the mule, using knots that would be nearly impossible to untie. The native looked up but indicated nothing amiss. Eifler returned, got Majors back on his pad, and the two went back to sleep.

The next morning the mule was gone. The guide indicated it had gotten loose. Eifler refused to accept it.

Returning to a now awakened Majors, Eifler found him with a higher fever—it was malaria. A few quinine tablets remained in a small medical packet. Eifler gave him the tablets to hold down the fever. He slipped into a troubled sleep. It would now be impossible to move. Eifler knew it would be several days before the fever broke. He left Majors to his troubled sleep and went outside.

Maybe Majors was right about the visitor, he thought. There was no question in his mind that the Chinese major had reclaimed his mule. He made a note to radio Wilkinson as soon as possible to cross the Chinese from his list of cooperatives.

Eifler's tremendous amount of energy could not be bottled up. He practiced knife throwing. He attempted to teach the natives how to identify planes by their various markings.

Finally he could stand the inaction no longer. There remained two horses, and he loaded the delirious Majors on one and started out. They covered twenty miles that day, arriving at a headman's house in the evening. Eifler studied the house. It was about seventy-five feet long and thirty feet wide. It was constructed of split bamboo with a thatched roof and stood about eight feet off the ground. The long building was divided into many compartments, each housing a complete family unit.

The Kachins are great spirit worshipers. Some years back they had practiced human sacrifices. Now they used chickens, goats, buffaloes, and pigs. The head of a sacrificed buffalo was kept inside the house as a permanent reminder to the spirits. This headman was obviously wealthy by native standards, for many buffalo heads adorned the thatched walls. Interspersed with the heads were spears, bow guns, and a muzzle-loader. At the center of the building the roof was approximately twenty feet high. It sloped down to a height of about four feet where it joined the walls. In the middle of the room was a box, about four by four, filled with dirt. At its center blazed the traditional fire. The smoke rose and disappeared through the thatched roof.

A small compartment at the end of the building was assigned to the two Americans. They stored their gear and returned to the main central section. As they were seated before the fire, the Kachin elders began arriving to pay their respects. They did not say a word but silently sat facing Eifler and Majors. A few minutes later, offerings of food appeared—a delicious meal of fried chicken, eggs, jungle vegetables, and some unidentified meat. While they ate, another native produced two quarts of native beer. Eifler handed one back, indicating they were to drink also. They quickly produced bamboo cups and proceeded to indulge. Before drinking, each poured a few drops beside the fire as their offering to the Nats. Eifler followed suit to their great pleasure. In silence they watched one another eat. Two different periods of time—two different nationalities watched the flames dance as they temporarily became one.

Eifler broke the silence, ordering his guide to bring out a musette bag and distributed its opium to the visiting dignitaries. There were murmurs of approval as the natives gratefully received it. In the background Eifler was watching the children who were gathered to look at the great white *duwa*. He found some chocolate D-rations and ordered them broken and distributed to them. Delighted, the children disappeared, leaving the men in silence again. Conversation was stilted. About an hour later the old men silently excused themselves. Only Eifler, Majors and some children remained. It was time to go to bed.

Returning to their assigned rooms they lay down on the plain bamboo floor. Eifler used his musette bag as a pillow and positioned himself so that he could look down the long hall through the door. He saw many of the old men returning to lie around the fire, smoking their opium. He went to sleep with the smell of opium in his nostrils.

The next morning he awoke to find three children and an old man sitting beside him, silently watching. When it was announced the *duwa* was awake, breakfast was immediately produced. Eifler noticed a soreness in his head. There was a hard lump inside his musette bag. He checked it out and found his "pillow" did indeed have a lump in it . . . blasting caps. He grinned, repacked them, and after breakfast they started out once more.

Majors was steadily improving but still very weak from malaria. The two men left that morning after thanking their hosts. With new provisions they disappeared down the narrow, winding jungle trail. News of their arrival always preceded them, and their reception was similar at succeeding Kachin villages. It took thirteen more days on the trail to reach the base camp at Chabua. The trip was never dull. As they rode into one village, they saw it filled with fluttering pennants. This was a Japanese custom, and both men reacted promptly. Majors threw a shell into his carbine, and Eifler whipped out his .45. The natives realized their guests' concern and quickly reassured them it was but a local celebration of some sort. To add to the trip's wide assortment of incidents, there were crumbling banks that several times threatened to throw them into raging rivers as well as one collapsing native bamboo bridge.

As they reached the forward base at Chabua, Majors thanked Eifler for the interesting time he had been shown and reported back to his unit. Eifler learned that General Stilwell was at this particular base with some State Department officials. Eifler knew he had been told of the plane crash and of the long walkout it prompted. He decided to report to Stilwell then and there, regardless of the fact he had not shaved for over two weeks nor changed clothes, had lost his shoes, and wore only the remnants of a khaki uniform.

To those State Department men gathered in a primitive hut near the Burmese border, it must have been a thrill just to realize their proximity to enemy territory and talk with the famous Stilwell. To see first hand one of the deadliest OSS men walk in filthy dirty, barefooted and bearded, and know he was fresh from a two-week trek through enemy lines could only be an addendum to tell their grandchildren.

He was ushered into the presence of the assembled men. He saluted Stilwell and reported his return to duty. Stilwell, always the general in others' presence, acknowledged the salute and took his report. Eifler then turned to leave.

"Eifler," said Stilwell, "have you eaten?"

Eifler turned back. "No, sir," he said.

"Well, I'll have a place set for you, and you can eat with us," was Stilwell's reply. He then had a place set at the table beside him. Eifler was ravenous for some decent food and no doubt showed this as he devoured the meal. Stilwell steered the conversation away from

Eifler. He was most anxious to convince Washington of the problems he faced through Chiang Kai-shek's conniving.

Having now finished eating, Eifler asked permission to be excused. It was granted. As he walked out the door, Stilwell accompanied him. The door shut behind them, and immediately Stilwell put his arm around the huge shoulders.

"Eifler, you've got to quit taking these damn fool chances," he stated.

"Sir, I told you this was no Boy Scout game," replied Eifler.

"I know, I know. But at least know the capabilities of your planes, Eifler, will you?"

The two unorthodox soldiers silently clasped hands, then turned and went their respective ways.

Eifler was warmly greeted by his men back at Nazira. It was midnight and he went immediately to bed. The next morning his men awakened him with "congratulations." He asked: "What for? I've walked out before and I'll walk out again."

The congratulations, however, were for his appointment to a full colonel. It had come in early October while he was walking out.

He read messages from his men with growing satisfaction. They were really giving the Japanese army fits.

He made notes of new areas to be covered. In the reports from his greatly increased units, he looked for a pattern that might be developing that would not be visible to an individual unit. It was a giant chess game, with the 101 units being positioned to harass or check those enemy units being masterminded by the Japanese general. If one 101 unit reported a convoy passing through and the next unit did not report it, out went the request to see what they were up to. Where did it stop and why? Was a new outpost being established?

He was concerned over the Chinese troops moving into Kachin territory and the possibility the two forces would clash. He was even more aware of continuing bad relations in China between Stilwell and the generalissimo. Stilwell had told him of the Blueshirts, the equivalent of the Hitler Brownshirts and Italian Blackshirts. Stilwell felt Chiang needed these thugs for his protection. There had been no election in China since 1935. Stilwell asked Eifler one time: "Do you know what that schoolboy wants now?" He went on without waiting for an answer; "Twelve B-29 bombers. They're not even off the drawing board, and he wants twelve of those goddamned B-29's."

Eifler felt that probably no general in American history had ever faced such an impossible command. He was greatly moved for the man he so deeply respected. He was powerless to help in any way but one, but knew he would not dare to take such authority on

154

himself.

He listened to the sounds from below where new messages came in from Burma. He reached for the next batch of reports and started through them.

Major Aitken was busy with his daily log at Fort Hertz. The various 101 men and units that came through were dutifully logged as to their date of arrival and departure. The impersonal listings barely scratched the surface of actual events. On November 11, he logged: "Arr. Comdr. Luce and 16 men fr. Base; Pvt. DeWeese from base; Brig. Bowerman, Major Cairns and Colonel Breakey from La Awng Ga. Dptd. Pvt. DeWeese and 8 recruits to Assam."

The rapid return of DeWeese with eight recruits was self explanatory. Eight new natives had been recruited and sent to Fort Hertz where they were picked up and taken to Nazira for Training. The other officers from the native village were British, reporting back to their base. The brief log notation "Commander Luce and 16 men" could have been made into a multi-page report. Jim Luce was indeed a navy commander and a fine doctor. He was assigned to Forward, and he and his group of men now began the first leg of their long journey. They were to have picked up sufficient coolies and guides at Fort Hertz for the trip. The coolies were not ready as promised. On November 14, the log revealed: "Dptd. Comdr. Luce Major Aitken and Lieutenant Pittard to La Awng Ga."

On November 15: "Arr. Comdr. Luce Major Aitken and Lieutenant Pittard from La Awng Ga."

Finally, on November 19: "Commander Luce and party south."

What the log did not include was the reasons for the delay and ensuing frustration.

On November 6, fully five days before their arrival, Eifler had advised Fort Hertz that Luce and his party were on the way and would require coolies. When they did arrive, British Colonel Breakey confirmed with his Brigadier Bowerman that all transport was engaged until November 16 for transporting supplies and equipment to the south for a company of troops. After their release from that assignment, five elephants would be returned.

Three days later Luce and Aitken went down to La Awng Ga and completed arrangements for coolies for the trip south from that point. The Fort Hertz coolies could be sent only as far south as that particular village. From there the La Awng Ga coolies would move to Tinghnang, where they would in turn be relieved. On November 17, Colonel Breakey disclosed that the *mahouts* had been given leave until November 22. He apologized for the error and agreed to recall as many as possible. Later on Breakey said he could have three elephants ready for the morning of November 19 at about 0900. The men began repacking their equipment so they could take the essential and leave the balance to be air-dropped. The next day Breakey found it would be possible to assign twenty political prisoners and agreed to have them at the compound at 0800 on November 19.

On the morning of the 19th, the twenty prisoner-coolies arrived. Shortly afterward one elephant appeared. After Luce twice interviewed Breakey, another elephant arrived. Later there was another meeting of the two men, and five boys arrived to act as coolies. Aitken supplied two additional porters from the local guard. All were loaded and started south.

Arrangements had been made by radio with Major Coffey in La Awng Ga to have the coolies from that station proceed north to meet and relieve the Fort Hertz coolies at an intermediate point. At midafternoon the five boys recruited by Colonel Breakey returned at the last minute. They were refusing to work. Their loads and Luce were taken south that evening by Lieutenant Pittard, the air corps officer temporarily quartered with Aitken.

The bungling by the British had caused over a full week's delay. Aitken hoped the problem had stirred up sufficient interest on the part of the brigadier to forestall future similar problems. This delay fortunately did not prove to be a bad omen for the group. It did take them nearly a month to reach their destination, the small village of Ngumla just above Myitkyina. Luce had with him Sergeant Ed Scharf and two other enlisted men. As they went through the villages, Luce gave medical aid to those in need. All information on Japanese movements was dutifully reported back to Nazira. Luce became ill with malaria and had to be carried for three days. Scharf took command and through the interpreter continued relaying news back to 101 headquarters.

They soon heard one chilling bit of news. Japanese troops were moving through the same villages, just one day ahead. Fortunately, they never stayed over a day, and the two units did not come together.

Luce was to prove valuable far beyond his medical knowledge. He turned out to be a master strategist and commander of his men. He won great respect for 101 with his compassion for the natives. One day while awaiting an airdrop of supplies and six new men, they watched three C-47s begin circling the drop zone. From out of the sun, six Japanese Zeros screamed in, guns chattering. The three planes were all shot down. All of the men in two planes were killed. The third plane had two survivors. After they were treated and rested up, they returned by foot to their base at Chabua. It was a sad day for

156

101 for the loss of their men and the fine air corpsmen who exposed themselves to danger daily to supply the various OSS camps.

Shortly after that, an American cargo plane crashed while trying to fly the Hump to China. The natives found two men dead but the captain and two enlisted men alive. They could not walk. The Japanese immediately appeared, but the natives hid the men in a cave. Unable to get any information, the Japanese left. The men were then taken into Forward where Luce treated them, and eventually they were able to return to their own unit. Forward would have been a success if it only rescued those downed U.S. airmen. That, combined with espionage, sabotage, and its guerrilla activities made it a unit of inestimable value.

The twenty-second man of the original unit was still working as an undercover operative in Calcutta. His presence was still not known except to Eifler, Peers, Coughlin, and Harry Little. To date, his activities had not been a success. A well-oiled Japanese espionage machine existed in Calcutta. It was so efficient it could broadcast activities of various American officers on the same day from its various radio stations. The evening broadcast would offer: "Today was a busy day for Major Clark of the Tenth Air Force and Captain Watkins who shopped in New Market, had lunch at Firpo's, and attended the afternoon cinema before going back to their base," then fill in with details of new arrivals of men, their equipment, and often names of their wives back home.

Calcutta was a vital port for the Allies. The Japanese launched sporadic air raids against the city, some of them all too effective. Mountains of supplies were arriving to be flown on to China. DET 101 was too occupied with its Burma operations to effectively take on the task of counterespionage in Calcutta. It was left to the army and British agents to counter the widespread enemy informers. The Indians were quite anti-British, and the benevolent promises of "Asia for the Asians" did not fall on deaf ears. Many of the first Americans to arrive in India were surprised to see the mild-mannered Indians silently give them the finger as they went by in trains or trucks. This "flipping of the bone," as it became known, was often exaggerated by the Indians' grasping their arm just above the elbow and using an upraised forearm to make sure the Americans got their meaning. The Americans cheerfully returned the greeting but wondered what the Indians had against them. One grizzled British sergeant said to think nothing of it—they were not used to the Americans and assumed they were British. The Americans, always quick with a quip, soon learned derogatory statements in the native language, much to the chagrin of their superiors, who tried to quash the exchanges for fear of more drastic native action.

A major air raid was feared in Calcutta. Counterespionage forces in Calcutta seemed unable to get at the top men. OSS in Washington decided to try its hand. They sent over Major George White, originally recruited from the Bureau of Narcotics. He had helped them when they were experimenting with truth drugs. He was briefly and correctly described as dedicated and deadly. He appeared roly-poly, with an angelic smile that would disarm anyone. He was sent with instructions to find the head of the Japanese spy ring.

Tokyo Rose did not pick up his arrival. He was unobtrusive and silently studied all reports to date by various counterintelligence agents. He listened intently to all evening Japanese broadcasts, looking for a pattern. He walked the streets of Calcutta, observed unloading of ships, and sat silently in bars listening to conversations of Allied officers, watching to see who might be eavesdropping. For several weeks he appeared to be doing nothing. He reported to no one and made no comments on any of his observations. When it came time to act, he would do so in unmistakable terms.

One day he made his decision. He left his room and began his quiet walks through the streets. On a crowded side street he paused as he observed an elderly Chinese man, leaning on a large staff, hobbling along. He was softly singing to himself. As he approached White, there was sudden action. White lunged forward, ripped off the "old man's" wig, tore off the upper part of his clothes, and shot him dead. As quickly as he had moved, he now disappeared. With the report of this assassination by an American officer, a yelp of British rage was heard. The tradition of justice had been violated by the brutal murder of an Oriental. The yelp soon faded when it was proved conclusively the dead man had indeed been the key figure sought, and the air raids diminished only to nuisance bombings.

White met with Eifler in Calcutta. He had been in the secret training camp in the class ahead of Eifler and his group. The men had known each other in earlier days. A Washington official had asked White to tell Eifler they wanted him to discontinue his use of narcotics. It was an odd situation for Eifler, who had spent a good portion of his life fighting the narcotics traffic. The Japanese had refused to allow opium in the area. Eifler had allowed its use for two reasons. One was its importance in paying for services of guerrilla soldiers and informers. Money was of no value in the jungle. Only salt and opium had sufficient value to warrant the risk of one's life. Secondly, he realized it was nonaddictive to the natives, who either ate or smoked it. OSS had told its various groups in training that they were to observe the customs, including food and drink, of the countries they would inhabit. Eifler believed in this philosophy, and on several occasions in north Burma had joined the natives in the eating of opium. He listened to the request relayed by White and saw no reason to discontinue his operations. They were too successful, and he felt in no way immoral or egregious.

This action in no way nullified the continued efforts of Japanese spies, as this author learned, firsthand. A simple party thrown by enlisted OSS men at our Tollygunge headquarters just outside Calcutta dramatized continued enemy probing. Approximately ten of us OSS men had as our guests ten Anglo-Burmese and Anglo-Indian girls and some Burmese agents on leave from Burma action. Dancing, refreshments, and carefully guarded small talk filled the air.

Most of the girls had brothers or cousins with OSS in Burma and were aware of the nature of the organization. One of the Anglo-Indian girls, named Joyce, had no such relatives. She was one of the more attractive girls, and I was pleased with her as my date. She asked questions that might have been expected of a young girl who was vaguely aware of who these men were. Those questions that touched a bit too deeply were dismissed with traditional American kidding and nonsense. When she asked what a certain man did, who just happened to be an undercover agent in Calcutta, I said he was a pencil sharpener or a janitor. The party was a success, and the men took their dates home in taxis or military vehicles. I took Joyce home, but was not invited inside, to my dismay, though I was promised future evenings of enjoyment with her.

The next day I was asked to report to the British intelligence headquarters. Joyce, it appeared, was all too well known to them. She was living with a Japanese sympathizer. He was known to be part of the Japanese network of spies. He and Joyce were free only because they were being watched with hopes of catching higher-ups. British blood pressure had risen considerably when it was reported she was taken to an OSS party at OSS headquarters.

"Sergeant, just what did you talk about—more important—what did she ask?"

My pride considerably wounded, I thought over the events of the night before. "Captain," I began, "it was just a general fun-type party. No one got drunk. There was absolutely no discussion of any military or OSS operations. The party was in the recreation room of our living quarters. There was no access to any papers or other items that would have been of interest."

The captain leaned forward intently. "Did she ask where you had been, what you did in the organization?"

"No, she did not."

"Then," he continued, "did she ask about any other men and what they did?"

"Yes, she did ask about several," I said.

"Who were they and where do they operate?" was the reply.

I quickly named four men. As I spoke the last name, a sinking feeling hit me, for I saw a pattern. Of the sixteen men in the room that night, those four were the only Calcutta agents. I finished my statement with that fact.

Quite calmly the captain wrote down the facts. Then he looked up pleasantly. "Sergeant, what did you tell her about those four men?"

"Nothing at all, Captain. I gave them all crazy duties like pencil sharpening or emptying waste baskets and told her two were coolies," I replied.

Now I began to burn. My male ego was hurt, and on top of that my professional ability had been challenged.

"Captain, let me continue seeing her. Let me see how much I can find out. She would have no idea I am on to her." I sought both a chance for service and to make up for what I considered incompetence.

The captain toyed with his cigarette. "Sergeant, you did no damage. You had no cause to suspect her, and your training kept you from giving her any information. Anyway, it is obvious she knows who these four men are. Within three hours she will know you have been here, so your cover would be blown. I am going to ask that you not see her again. Will you agree?"

I attempted to think of some argument that might keep me on the case. From the face of the captain and his tone of voice, I knew it was futile.

"All right, Captain, I agree."

We both stood. The captain offered his hand, and we shook.

"War can be a bloody mess, I'm afraid," the captain said, grinning. With a forced smile, I agreed, turned, and left—sad but wiser. Good-bye, fair Joyce.

To the north new events were shaping up. One of the war's great characters, British General Orde Wingate, had been sent to Burma to organize British guerrilla operations. His men were named Chindits after the lion-headed dragons standing guard outside all Burmese pagodas. This Chindit, actually spelled Chinthe, is the only thing in the Buddhist religion that is permitted to use force to guard the sacred pagodas. Winston Churchill had taken Wingate to the Quebec Conference. Here the operations in Burma were discussed. Churchill

160

summed it up with the statement: "I consider Wingate should command the army against Burma. He is a man of genius and audacity and has been quite discerned by all eyes as a figure quite above the ordinary level."

Wingate's force consisted of twenty-four battalions. He was to be given three more, consisting of American infantrymen, which never materialized.

Wingate decided to make his mark negatively. Whatever was the traditional or accepted approach, he would take the opposite side. He returned politeness with rudeness. If you liked the Arab, he favored the Jew. He delighted in receiving visitors to his camp in the nude. The higher their rank or position, the more he delighted in their uneasiness as he would lie naked on his cot. On some occasions he was known to scrub his private parts with his toothbrush as he calmly discussed the war and his philosophy. He was known to shun the use of a wristwatch for an alarm clock he wore around his waist on a rope. Early in his operations he received great press acclaim for entering Burma and severing the Japanese rail line in two places. It was never reported that OSS agents had already cut the line in over fifteen places with no loss of life. Wingate's losses had been heavy.

Actually, the cutting of those rail lines caused a problem at staff headquarters in New Delhi. Eifler was discussing the fact that his men were nearly to the lines below Myitkyina. The British major general of intelligence asked questions, and Eifler gave full cooperation. The next day Eifler was asked to meet General Stilwell at his plane prior to his departure from New Delhi. With him was a British brigadier general. Stilwell was, as usual, brief and to the point.

"Eifler, do you have men cutting the Myitkyina-Bhamo rail line?"

"Yes, sir, I do," he said. The major general had been quick to get to Stilwell.

"Did I or did I not tell you to stay north of that point?" pursued the general.

If he had so told him—and Eifler had to assume he had or thought he had—Eifler did not remember it. In no way did he remember being given a definite point he could not proceed beyond. But, Eifler's philosophy had always been never to embarrass his boss, even though he might be wrong.

"Yes, you did," he quickly said.

"Under whose orders did you change my orders?"

There was no answer. There had been no emendation of any Stilwell orders. Still Eifler felt his course clear.

"Under my own, sir."

"Can you change them?"

161

"Yes, sir."

"Change them."

Eifler looked straight at him. "Yes, sir."

The British general now spoke up: "You see, we have men operating in that area. They're liable to kill your men."

Eifler turned to him and laughed. "Kill my men . . . why, my men are trained to operate in enemy-held territory and kill Japanese. Do you think they're going to be killed by British going in there—British going in in military force?"

"Colonel, the possibility also exists our men could get to the area your men have already mined and get killed," the flustered brigadier said.

"Yes, that is perfectly true," said Eifler. Still looking at the brigadier, Eifler continued: "I was under the impression that this was a two-way street. We were to tell each other of our operations." Turning to Stilwell, Eifler continued: "I have had no word that this organization operating there was from the British. Neither they nor you told me they were out there. I'll take responsibility for this, though. None of my men are going to get killed, and the British are not going to get killed either. My neck is on the block."

Stilwell looked at him. "Your neck is already on the block," he said comfortingly. The discussion ended, and Eifler left.

Had the conversation ended at the point Stilwell told Eifler to change his orders, Eifler would immediately have done everything in his power to stop his men. He felt, however, that the British had not been fair and were seeking some unearned publicity. He therefore made sure that his men did actually reach the line first and cut it before the British did.

The incident that eventually brought Eifler and an angry Wingate together arose out of an Eifler action in Burma. Some Allied troops had been taken prisoner in a native village. Eifler sent word in that the men were to be treated kindly and not turned over to the Japanese. He would send in someone to lead them out. In the event they disobeyed, he would "burn them out." To emphasize his point, he told them just when he would hit them and how. The natives foolishly chose to disobey and turned the men over to the Japanese. True to his word, Eifler had those involved "dispatched with extreme prejudice."

The story was reported to Wingate, who was undoubtedly smarting over the activities of this unorthodox American organization. He asked Eifler to visit his headquarters so that they might talk. Eifler was prepared for Wingate's appearance having heard a story of a prior visit to his headquarters from a visiting British officer. True to

162

form, Wingate appeared naked except for his hat. He motioned Eifler into a canvas chair and sat in another one beside him. It was teatime, and a bearer stood by with a kettle of boiling water. Wingate leaned forward to emphasize a point with Eifler, using the infuser for emphasis. He paused to let it sink in. Casually he dropped the infuser and scratched his testicles. Then he filled Eifler's cup and said: "Care for some tea?"

Eifler shook his head.

Wingate smiled. "Oh, weak stomach, eh?" He proceeded with his own, obviously enjoying the discomfort he had caused.

With Eifler he quickly he got to the point. He discussed the incident in the village and asked if it was true that Eifler had ordered natives executed.

"Yes, sir, I did," was the firm reply.

The ensuing discussion showed Wingate that Eifler would not back down from his point—that he would do anything to protect his men and end the war. There were no rules to be observed. Wingate's theory was that the natives should obey the "law." The law consisted of following the rules of those in military command.

Eifler reasoned that if he controlled the area, then the natives must obey him. He made his difference of opinion with Wingate quite clear: "I am the law—my orders will be obeyed. If they choose to disobey or ignore them, then they must bear the punishment." If future executions were called for, in Eifler's opinion, he would order them or do them himself. Wingate realized he faced a man of iron whose authority was absolute, and he could do nothing about it.

"I would rather see my own men die than execute natives," he said. To show how strongly he felt, he put it in writing. Eifler later made this letter and Wingate's interview known to the U.S. chiefs of staff:

Wingate % Central Command Agra 7th October, 1943 .

Colonel F. Eifler A.P.O. 629 (U.S. Army, Nazira, Assam.)

My dear Colonel,

I was very glad to have the pleasure of meeting you, although your dramatic appearance in the middle of the night did not find me at my intellectual best, I am afraid. I have long heard of your daring and courageous work on the Railway, and did hope to have been able to co-operate with you last time. However, next time we will do equally well. I will keep in touch, and we will see how things pan out.

I remember your mentioning the execution of a traitor, who was responsible for the death of some of my men. While the execution of traitors is justifiable when their treachery is proved, it is a matter that requires proof, especially in the case of the Burmese. I have had many accusations of treachery made to me against Burmese, by my own men, but have never established one, and in several cases, have succeeded in proving that the man accused was quite innocent. There is a danger in bumping off without proof, apart from the fact that it is, of course, a crime. From the military point of view, it tends to create distrust in the minds of these very timid people, and they logically argue that the only safe thing is to have nothing whatever to do with either side. I would rather risk loss of men through treachery, and enjoy co-operation, than isolate myself completely by action designed to frighten possible traitors.

As regards the treachery, there again, a man is not necessarily a traitor because he reveals the presence of British troops to the Japanese. We may regard him as a traitor, and deal with him as such, if he has any kind of contract, or has entered into any kind of engagement with us, but if he is simply the head man of a village, whether the occupying power is British, Japanese, or Hottentot, he cannot be blamed for carrying out what the occupying power tells him are his duties, the infringement of which, the occupying power will immediately punish in the most ruthless and final way.

Forgive my giving you what may appear to be something in the nature of a lecture, as I am certainly not in a position to do so, but as I know you would hate as much as I would, to take life unjustifiably, I feel that I ought to give you the fruit of my own experience in Burma.

Hope we meet again soon.

Orde Wingate

Personnel recruited in Washington began arriving in larger numbers at Nazira. A large metal-roofed tea-drying building down the small dirt road from the main headquarters was utilized for the enlisted men. The message center expanded to fifteen cryptographers and radio operators by November, 1943. Infantry and communications personnel arrived, took brief training periods, and infiltrated through or parachuted behind enemy lines to get in their first licks against the Japanese. The high skills of saboteurs and spies were not required of many of them. They would primarily conduct fighting operations. During the time they did spend with the early DET 101 men, however, they all did learn some of the tricks of the trade. The men first went into combat as members of a patrol. Soon they would command their own patrol, then platoon, and eventually company. Always they listened to their Kachin scouts, who had an uncanny knack of sensing enemy ambushes.

In November some additional 101 personnel arrived in Calcutta. Small groups of enlisted men, lieutenants, and captains were common and routinely checked into and through the 101 headquarters. This particular group, however, happened to be navy men and consisted of photographers under the command of Captain John Ford, well known for his Oscar-winning films.

Several days after he was due to report to Nazira, Ford found himself still tied up in Calcutta. He was waiting for some tailored uniforms. He put in a call to Eifler to report his presence in India and explain his delay in reporting. Eifler, taking the call from a Captain Ford, assumed it to be an army man and was extremely angry that he was late in reporting.

"You son of a bitch. Who the hell do you think you are to be telling me you'll get here as soon as you can?" he used for openers.

Ford was not known for his sweet disposition or soft tongue. One could well imagine how he received this blast. Before he could reply, Eifler went on.

"You'd damn well better be here within twelve hours or I'll court-martial your ass," he concluded.

By now, Ford had his second wind. "Why you old bastard…who the hell do you think you are talking to?" he retorted.

"I am not concerned one goddamned bit who I'm talking to. You are overdue, and unless you want to cool your butt in a cell for a couple of weeks you move your ass—and I mean fast."

The phone clicked. Ford looked at the phone, then slammed it down so hard those near him jumped.

"Screw that old bastard," he muttered. "Let's go."

After they had picked up their uniforms, Ford and his crew set out for Nazira. Those at Nazira who knew of the explosion held their breath as the two men met.

"Hello, John, how the hell are you?" growled Eifler, his huge hand extended.

"Great, Carl. Good to be here with you," replied Ford.

The threatened civil war had failed to materialize. Eifler had been aware of the Ford disposition—one that rebelled at attending meetings he considered useless. He was known for refusing to attend top-level OSS meetings in Washington, and the rumor was that Washington was glad to ship him off to the battle lines where he might rub against the enemy and do some damage to them.

Early in the war Ford had put together a crew of the top Hollywood cameramen. He and his crew had filmed the war for America. Their work at the battle of Midway was a classic. In North Africa they had been in actual combat; in some cases, they holed up on farms while German tanks rolled all around them. Ford, regardless of danger, took his men where the best camera work was to be done. Many area commanders, not anxious to have these men killed in their area, breathed a sigh of relief as they moved on.

Rumors flew as to their reason for being at the 101 area. Early in 1943, Donovan had asked Eifler if he would like to have these men arrive to film 101 operations. Eifler felt their presence would not interfere with his operations and that it might be nice to have his men recorded on film. He said he would accept them when they could report. Many people felt that their presence at Nazira was really politically motivated. From the early days of the war when Congress authorized Donovan to establish COI and gave him $35 million, there were questions as to just what was going on. Continued sums poured into OSS coffers, and congressmen were asking questions. A film of OSS in action could be made and shown to Congress, hopefully satisfying them the money was not being squandered. It would give a view of their operations that would be impossible to give in a report on paper.

Immediately the cameramen went to various camps, and the cameras went into action. From Dibrugarh and Chabua the C-47 planes dropping supplies into Burma were accustomed to seeing the last-minute arrival of a jeep and watch as one of Ford's men ran toward the plane, his camera in one hand and a bottle of beer in the other.

Other men went into actual operations, walking the trails with Kachins and American combat men.

In one of their deepest penetrations, CWO (Chief Warrant Officer) Bob Rhea joined Sergeant Mel Rackett, a radio operator; Burmese agent Rex King; and this author, acting as cryptographer, in a parachute jump into Knothead in mid-December, 1943. Two C-47s carried the four of us and supplies to the small landing strip where, just a month earlier, Eifler and Majors had landed. A third C-47 also carried supplies and in addition Ford himself and one of his cameramen, Jack Swain. The two men filmed the first few passes over the strip while the planes dropped containers with supplies that required parachutes, then free-dropped bags of rice and salt. Some of the

166

supply chutes failed to open, plunging the wicker containers into the ground and destroying their contents. Ford and Swain wondered what this might do to our morale as we prepared to jump on the last pass.

The planes flew at an 800-foot height to stay hidden from view in the little valley as much as possible and also to keep us in the air the shortest time possible should a nearby enemy patrol open fire on us. To record the jump, Rhea strapped a camera to his ankle, the lens pointing down. As the jump master gave him the signal to go, he reached down, turned on the camera, and jumped, closely followed by Rackett. The landing area was so small that another pass had to be made for King and me. We went out the door a split second apart. King landed on the strip where the first two had come down. I was carried into the jungle and unceremoniously dropped through some large trees onto the jungle floor.

Dazed, I found myself on my feet surrounded by thick jungle vegetation and a small circle of Kachin guerrillas. They were not approaching me. Then I realized I had pulled my .45. Sheepishly, I returned it to its holster as Pamplin and Father Stuart broke through and rushed to greet me with outstretched hands. However, their hands did not grasp mine, but, rather, they circled around behind me, grabbed my parachute pack, and expertly removed the D-rations. The concentrated chocolate, I soon learned, was a delicacy. Their robbery concluded, we finally shook hands.

All of us were quickly assimilated into the operation. Rhea filmed various activities within the camp, then went out with patrols to film actual combat. The pictures Rhea and his comrades shot all through Burma became a fine picture diary of 101's exploits.

A smile crossed Eifler's face as he read a request from British intelligence. When OSS was new to Burma, Eifler had requested their help in introducing OSS agents into the field. The British had expressed their regrets, saying they would like to help but it might jeopardize their own men now behind the lines. It didn't take long to realize that they had no such agents and that this was a clever way to not have to admit it. Now, a year later, they were ready to put their own operatives in but felt the need of OSS help. Since the situations were the same, Eifler decided their own words would be adequate and in exact language expressed his regret at being unable to help.

The tremendous growth of 101 was evidenced in a December 1, 1943, report from communications officer Huston. It reported a total of twenty-nine field stations in operation, an increase of fourteen over October. One key radio was put in the hands of a man attached to Pat. He was to be stationed just above the airfield at Myitkyina and report all activity to the U.S. 51st Fighter Group. In addition, he reported the weather three times daily. This was especially valuable in that it eliminated the need for the air corps to run a test flight over the area to be attacked.

Operations at Nazira had grown to such a heavy volume it became necessary to split operations and handle part of them at the training location of Gelekey. Messages increased 100 percent over the previous month. There were sixty-three students in training in ten different camps, of which fifty-eight were being trained strictly as radio operators. In addition, these agents were also trained in cryptography.

Eifler made a quick calculation. There were 188 students and agents at camp or in the field out of 303 on the payroll. He had never liked the ratio of men in noncombat duties to those in combat—a figure the army and navy used to check their own efficiency. When he added to it the number of Americans in the field, it pleased him to realize the greatest percentage by far of his men were in active operations. While he realized a certain percentage of men in supply and support roles were necessary, he also realized the greatest damage was to be done in direct contact with the enemy. Here again, he and Stilwell had in common the dislike of paperwork compared with actual combat.

Another paper contained the report of certain information sent through Chungking to the Korean government in exile in Washington, D.C. Information had been gleaned through the bugging of confessional booths in China. Eifler had set up a system whereby information vital to the Koreans was reported through this Catholic church and relayed to America. It was the only link the Koreans had between their government in exile and themselves in China. In Washington, Syngman Rhee carefully read the messages and relayed words of encouragement to his people. Eifler was greatly satisfied that he had established this communication.

Eifler and Peers spent several hours going over the 101 operation. They discussed future projects, personnel, and promotions. Eifler had always felt he must keep one grade in rank above Peers. He considered Peers hard enough to handle as it was. They got into a discussion of this. Peers was speaking of his capabilities. He told Eifler he considered himself a better officer than he. Eifler pondered this. "Ray, that is your right to think, of course. Do you also consider yourself a better officer than John Coughlin?"

Peers spoke with confidence. "Yes, Carl, I do. If you would start the three of us equally, I would come out on top every time."

There was no doubt in Eifler's mind that Peers was an exceptionally fine officer. It would have been impossible to compare all three men equally, so divergent were their backgrounds and talents. There was no question of their dedication and devotion. Even with differences in opinion, all three always held the highest respect for each other. When Eifler was away on his frequent missions, either Peers or Coughlin assumed the command smoothly, and the efficient 101 machine continued without a hitch.

Eifler received a representative of OSS, Washington. He was a Navy commander and in charge of worldwide OSS operations. His method of talking and questioning was more authoritative than inquiring. Finally Eifler felt he had determined something the commander was trying to get across without saying.

"Just a minute, Commander," he began, "are you telling me that you are my boss?"

There was a moment's hesitation.

"No more than I am boss of all operations anywhere in the world," he replied.

"Well, let me tell you something, Commander. You get your ass back to Washington, and when you get some more rank you come and see me."

All meaningful dialogue had just been terminated, and the commander did go back to Washington. He made his report to Donovan.

Giving no advance notice of his intention, Donovan suddenly appeared at the Chabua airstrip. Eifler immediately flew over to pick him up in the Moth. Donovan was most anxious to see the unit and its men. He arrived on December 7, 1943.

His trip to Nazira was unusual even by OSS standards. He was given a personally conducted tour by Eifler. There was mutual respect as he shook hands with those just returned from active duty or just about to go in. Those meeting him knew him to be one of America's bravest fighting men, holder of their nation's highest awards. His face was almost cherubic, his smile disarming. It was obvious he longed to be in the thick of the battle once again. Those days he had inspired and led his brave Fighting 69th in France left a certain mark on him that was evidenced by his step and the lift of his chin. He looked longingly at the situation maps, questioning the makeup and responsibilities of individual units. He showed his remarkable memory by asking about key men whose names he had learned through the messages sent back. He asked about morale, personnel still required, supplies, and all manner of items that would concern a dedicated commander.

That night the two men sat in the DET 101 war room. They had enjoyed a hearty meal and told some good stories.

Eifler drew the curtains away from seven different war maps.

"General Stilwell told me he might want to approach Burma in seven different ways," he explained. "I was supposed to organize each one of them, and I did."

Donovan cast a cursory glance at the maps and remained seated. "That's what I mean about you, Carl. You are too goddamned ambiguous about organizing. What do you mean by organizing?"

Until then Eifler was not aware that he had a problem, but suddenly he knew he did. From the tone of his voice and his question, it was quite evident that Donovan had come out to put Eifler down. There was no question but that he had been motivated to this by Eifler's final instructions to the navy commander, the chief of OSS operations worldwide. Eifler quickly turned the situation over in his mind, and came up with what he thought was the right solution.

"Would the General like to go behind the lines and see for himself?" It was a gut challenge—a daring thing to do with a man of Donovan's character. He was equal to it.

"When do we leave?" he asked.

"First thing in the morning, sir," replied Eifler, smiling for the first time.

The next morning they approached the plane. John Ford and Nicol-Smith were there with other officers to take pictures of Donovan and Eifler preparing for their flight.

Eifler had selected the Knothead camp for the visit. He already knew the landing strip, poor as it was. Also, he knew it to be one of the best DET 101 units, both in size and in effectiveness. The camp was 150 miles behind enemy lines and nearly 275 miles from Nazira. It was well beyond the round-trip capacity of the little plane. Immediately an order went out for the air corps to drop drums of fuel for the return flight. A series of code messages were encoded and sent to Knothead that could be flashed to advise when the plane left Nazira and for Nazira to be notified when the plane landed safely and when it took off. Eifler picked up his parachute and strapped it on. He had a second one handed to Donovan. Donovan shook his head and waved it away.

"Carl, I'll not be wearing one this trip," he said.

No need to ask why. Eifler knew what his boss was thinking. He must never be taken alive, and, should the plane crash, he would go with it.

"General, if we land within fifteen feet of a Jap, I will bring you back. Please put on your chute," replied Eifler.

Donovan weighed this statement for a few seconds. No doubt he was thinking of Eifler's survival and walkout from several previous plane crashes. He reached for the chute and several hands helped buckle it on. The two climbed into the little plane.

One of the men present groaned as if he was carrying their weight himself. Eifler at 250 pounds and Donovan at 240 certainly gave the plane a test of durability.

"That damned plane will have a double hernia if it gets off the ground," one of the mechanics said.

The plane was equal to the challenge. It lifted over the bushes and trees, was silhouetted briefly against the Naga Hills, and headed east into Burma. The first message was now flashed, alerting Naw-Bum and the Knothead group that their guests were on the way.

It was impossible to talk in the plane above the roar of the motor. Donovan could clearly see that Eifler was following the course of a river for a while. He also noticed Eifler scanning the sky for enemy planes. The jungle below him was the heaviest he had ever seen. In about an hour he knew they were now over enemy lines. Eifler was reading his map and watching his compass carefully.

In another two hours Eifler pointed down, and Donovan looked on a small native village clearing with high jungle foliage on both sides. He watched as the village seemed to disappear, and a crude landing strip became evident in its place. Eifler made his approach, came in just clearing the tall trees at the end of the strip, and made a perfect landing. Before the plane stopped rolling, the houses were already being moved back to reestablish the camouflage. The plane was taxied into the side foliage and covered with branches. The two men climbed out to shake hands with Curl, Pamplin, Father Stuart, Haimson, and Zing Htung Naw. Immediately NawBum camp sent the message to alert Nazira that the men had landed safely.

Donovan was introduced to the wiry Kachin soldiers, whose exploits he had read again and again in the Nazira messages. He noted some of them were scarcely taller than the American rifles they carried. He was particularly pleased to meet Father Stuart, by now a legend in Burma. The two Irishmen found a common bond in their ancestry as well as in their aggressive spirits.

While Donovan talked with the Knothead men, Eifler walked up and down the landing strip. He knew the takeoff would be a close thing with the weight the little plane had to carry. He paused at a spot approximately 80 percent down the crooked strip. This would be the last possible moment on the ground. If the plane was not airborne at this point, it would not clear the trees. Having already crashed, he certainly wanted to avoid another, particularly with Donovan.

His mind, trained to always seek a backup plan, now looked for a second plan should the plane not be off the ground at that spot. To the right was a break in the trees. He reasoned he could bank the plane sharply, wings vertical to the ground, pull through the opening over the hill, and dive toward the riverbed. It would be his only chance.

He walked back to where the Kachins were refueling the plane from the gasoline dropped by the Tenth Air Force. He checked his watch and knew it was time to go.

The two men boarded the plane. Eifler had the natives hold it back while he revved it up to its full power. Then he signaled for them to release it and push. They did, and it began its trip over the bumpy, dog-legged strip. He gave it everything he could to get up speed. He then saw his space running out, and, at the spot he had selected earlier, he pulled back on the stick to get off the ground. The plane didn't respond, and he was nearly 90 percent of the way through that precious ground space. He would have to go with his other plan. By then he knew he could get off the ground but could not possibly clear the trees ahead. He pulled back, banked to his right, and vertically went through the open spot in the trees as he had planned. Once over the hill, he dived rapidly toward the river, leveling off about five feet from its surface. He flew along the river, gaining altitude. Then he flew back over the hill, buzzed the strip to show all was okay, and the trip back began. It was 1435. The plane stopped at a small strip where Stilwell's forward camp was located. Stilwell was not there and they knew it, but they did need more fuel. As they stretched their legs, Donovan said calmly: "You didn't think you were going to make it, did you?"

Eifler grinned. "General, I knew we'd make it. But now you see I need more horsepower on the nose for these operations."

Donovan nodded.

At 1700 NawBum received the message that the two men had arrived safely in Nazira. Everyone relaxed.

In the long list of events that made up the colorful life of General Donovan, his family later told Eifler that this trip was one of the highlights. He frequently remarked that it was one of the greatest thrills he had ever known. In addition, it satisfied a need, for he was the only head of a major espionage service who had not been behind enemy lines. Now he had.

The trip also satisfied Donovan as to the necessity of light planes for DET 101. He had seen numerous requests from Eifler for such aircraft. He was unaware they had all been ignored. Some strongly worded messages went back to Washington. DET 101 was to get its planes as well as other badly needed supplies. He approved ten L-1 planes, which were eventually delivered and used to great advantage during the 1944-45 campaigns . They became widely known as the "Burma Butterflies."

Before departing Nazira, Donovan had a final conference with Eifler.

"Carl, I think it is time for you to return to America. I am issuing orders for you to return immediately."

Eifler was stunned. It was the last thing he wanted. "Sir, I have a job to do here. I have just got things rolling. I need to stay and build my organization."

Donovan was ready. He knew the order would strike Eifler this way. "Carl, you have a job to do in Burma. I have a job to do world-wide. We need you for morale purposes in America. The war needs to be fought there. Besides, I'll have your wife brought over from Honolulu, and you can see her." That clinched the entire argument. Eifler confirmed he was not being relieved of 101 permanently and agreed to return.

On December 9, 1943, Eifler received a secret order from General Donovan. It directed Eifler to proceed from Nazira to headquarters, Office of Strategic Services, Washington, D.C., for temporary duty. Upon completion of temporary duty at Washington, D.C., he was to proceed to London, England, Italy, North Africa, and Cairo, Egypt for the purpose of performing temporary duty at each place. After completing such temporary duty, he was to return to his proper station in Nazira.

Much speculation followed this strange order. Eifler only reported he was to return to Washington, D.C. Many of his men assumed it to be because of his injuries and a report sent back by a Donovan aide that he was physically unable to carry out his duties because of the head injury. It was heightened by the fact Donovan had been gone less than forty-eight hours and had personally seen Eifler in operation.

Donovan had told Eifler the OSS headquarters in Washington awaited his reports like a best seller. Immersed in paperwork and deluged in a sea of security systems and rationing, he felt it would be good for morale if Eifler would return and personally talk to the OSS staff as well as to personnel in other theaters. Eifler knew there was to be much more than this, but his job was to obey not to question.

He turned command over to John Coughlin and two days later left Nazira for Washington, D.C.

8

Once again a plane carried Eifler away from his men and back to Washington, D.C. This time he had tasted warfare of the OSS variety, and his men had been bloodied. They had already piled an impressive record against seasoned Japanese jungle troops. He looked forward to seeing his family once more and, beyond that, going back into action against the foe. He went over his orders again, wondering just what lay in store for him.

The orders were precise and impersonal: "On or about 9 December 1943 you will proceed from Nazira to Headquarters Office of Strategic Services Washington, D.C. for temporary duty at that place. Upon completion of temporary duty at Washington, D.C. you will proceed to London, England; Italy; North Africa and Cairo, Egypt, for the purpose of performing temporary duty at each place. After having completed temporary duty at all of the places named, you will return to proper station, Nazira Assam, India."

Donovan had told Eifler of the morale problem in Washington, D.C. So he understood what was wanted of him there, but he did not know what to expect at the other OSS posts in Europe and North Africa. He did not spend a great deal of time speculating, however. Whatever his orders were, he would carry them out.

He was anxious to talk to the OSS men and women in Washington who worked long hours supporting the agents in the field and saw only messages to tell of their efforts. On occasion an agent might be brought in for a new assignment, and they would get a chance to see what he looked like and maybe talk with him over lunch or a cup of coffee.

One man in particular Eifler wanted to see was the young attorney on Donovan's staff who had, on an earlier inspection, reported back to OSS Washington that Eifler was unable to effectively carry out his command due to the head injury and subsequent amnesia. It had not taken long for that information to get back to Eifler.

As his plane touched down in Washington, D.C., Eifler picked up his gear and disembarked. He was warmly greeted by Buxton and ushered into a staff car. During the drive to Eifler's quarters they talked of his flight over, but not much else. There would be ample time to go over many details in staff meetings. Besides, Eifler would

174

need a little time to recuperate, adjust to the new time zone, and get his thoughts in order. He was to report to headquarters the following day. After a relaxing shower, Eifler went to bed early.

The next morning he put on his freshest uniform and proceeded to his "temporary duty." He was amazed to see the tremendous increase in staff since he was last there. The security arrangements were as strict as any he had ever encountered—so much so that it angered him a bit. A buzz of excitement spread through the various departments as the man who was by now a legend made his lumbering appearance. If they were looking for something unusual, it was not long in coming. Eifler spotted the attorney who had reported him as "unable to carry out his duties." He strode over, grabbed him by his lapels, and propelled him against the wall. He lifted him several inches off the floor and shouted: "Listen, you son of a bitch, if you ever interfere in my activities again, I'll kill you."

He then released him and went on into his first interview. The attorney, visibly shaken, said nothing but was seen heading for the men's room. There was silence throughout the rest of the room.

Eifler personally delivered several lengthy reports to operations. He discussed the various problems his men experienced and spoke about how he felt Washington might better serve them. He asked to read the daily messages from his unit so that he might be informed constantly as to their progress and problems. He was given an idea of the number of addresses he would make to the people in OSS headquarters and, in addition, told he was to make certain information available to the chiefs of staff of the armed forces. In his interview with the senior aides of the Joint Chiefs of Staff, Eifler made a strong plea for Stilwell.

"Gentlemen, he is one of our rare fighting generals." said Eifler. "If you men will give him one squad, just one squad of American fighting men, then, by God, see what he will do."

He went on to point out that Stilwell was immersed in paperwork and Chinese politics, none of which he wanted. He pointed out the fact that Wingate had a great number of troops and he was ready with one item—the letter from Gen. Orde Wingate which Eifler hoped would suffice to get command of the U.S. troops back in American hands.

Stilwell had heard the American GIs would serve under Wingate's direction. While Stilwell was impressed with long-range penetration tactics, he was not paying enough attention to the fact that Wingate's losses had been heavy and he had abandoned his wounded to the enemy. "After a long struggle we get a handful of U.S. troops, and by God they tell us they are going to operate under

Wingate! We don't know how to handle them, but that exhibitionist does! He has done nothing but make an abortive jaunt to Katha cutting some railroad lines that our people had already cut, got caught east of the Irawaddy and come out with heavy losses. Now he's the expert. That is enough to discourage Christ," was Stilwell's not unexpected response. What finally changed the U.S. decision to put the troops under an American general was not known, but the letter Eifler showed had to be of some value.

Wingate also proved himself adept at expressing himself. When he was told of the American decision to put the troops under an American general, he said: "You can tell General Stilwell he can take his Americans and stick them up his ass."

Eifler had a number of films that Captain John Ford's cameramen had made available. Several days later, the interviews concluded, he began his talks to the assembled OSS personnel. In casual tones he spoke of daily intrigue. He described indifferently how a decision might be made to assassinate a noncooperative native, how the Kachins "questioned" captured agents. He told why some requests for supplies, seemingly quite ordinary, were sometimes put through as emergency requests. He knew these messages were sometimes received in Washington with raised eyebrows. Busy as they were, it must seem to them that the emergency coding was used routinely.

He cited one specific example of an emergency requisition for cough medicine. Why should such a routine item command priority handling? One of the units in Burma had put a census group on a particular well-traveled road just outside Myitkyina. This group was to count all trucks and troops moving in or out. They reported to Nazira daily, and in turn Nazira dispatched their information to general headquarters of both the army and air corps. Many of the men had bad colds. They worked so close to the Japanese, a cough could give them away. If they were pulled away for even a few days, they would lose count of troops and equipment within that Japanese bastion. The cough medicine was important, therefore, in order to keep accurate information on that area.

In the films he showed them the Nazira headquarters and various training sites. They watched native agents who had never been more than twenty miles from their birthplace as they flew in from Fort Hertz and took training as radio operators, learned to use modern weapons and hand-to-hand fighting methods. They went on ambushes, forded swirling rivers, saw opened wounds where men burned blood-sucking leeches from their bodies. They felt a thrill as they saw the faces that belonged to the many names they knew—Peers, Coughlin, Aitken, Frazee, Little, Curl, Wilkinson, Luce, Tilly,

Larsen, and others. They watched the natives, known only by their code names, Hefty, Marty, Skittles, Betty, Burma Sam, and many others as they went about their deadly business in a calm, efficient manner. Some laughed as they saw Americans in the native dress, a long skirt wrapped around the waist, and large knives strapped to their sides. Some of the Americans in the film wore turbans. Some were in British shirts or Chinese, depending on what they could get if an airdrop was overdue. The jungle, they soon learned, was hard on equipment.

They watched in silence as Ford's photographers filmed actual ambushes, and they could see first hand how Japanese troops marched unknowingly into the muzzles of the concealed 101 men and native soldiers. In some cases the leader of the column, a native, was spared because he was a 101 agent himself. They learned how the jungle grapevine could often relay news faster than the OSS radio. And they came to know the loyalty and devotion of the Kachin soldiers as well as of the native agents of all nationalities.

After the films, Eifler answered questions. He enjoyed the talks because he felt it more closely knit the main headquarters to the men in the field.

Intensely loyal to his men, Eifler made it a point to have relatives of the men in Burma over to his hotel room. Here he would again show the films so those relatives might see their husbands, sons, and brothers. In one such showing, Hiram Pamplin exhibited intense interest in what his brother Jack was doing. He asked if he might be transferred into DET 101, saying, "If it's good enough for Jack, it's good enough for me." Eifler said he would look into it.

As it was casual conversation, Pamplin doubted that anything would come of it. Two weeks later, however, he received orders transferring him from his unit to active duty with 101. He was later to serve in combat beside Jack in central Burma. He learned from the very beginning that what Eifler said would be done, would be.

Eifler, having personally selected all of his original 20 men was curious about how other OSS personnel might be recruited. The only way he knew was to personally go after those men whom he felt could well serve their country in the capacities that would be required.

DET 101 was now nearly two hundred strong in terms of its agency force not counting native guerrillas. Most of the men had been selected and trained in Washington and sent over. Some had been excellent, some misfits. Now that he was in Washington he asked some questions about recruiting at a briefing. There was no set pattern, he found. Many were selected on the basis of their linguistic ability, others for scientific backgrounds, still others who had lived overseas in those areas OSS intended infiltrating where they could give practical advice. Military men were recruited for ambushes and the brief fighting that might occur, and demolition experts and friends of foreign politicians that might be influential were also called upon to join.

Criticisms had been leveled at the number of society names and academics that had been hired. OSS was often charged with being elitist. But then when a person who had traveled extensively and could speak several languages was needed, where else could they be found?

Not all recruiting was done in Washington. OSS chiefs had authority to hire natives on the spot if they fit a particular need. OSS Cairo chief Colonel John Tuhlman was hampered by the fact only a few Americans spoke any of the Arabic dialects OSS needed to know. He had been told there was a group of merchants with ties in Turkey and Palestine who were suspected of being enemy agents. The problem was they spoke in dialects completely unknown to OSS operatives. Tuhlman was invited to a dinner at the home of Britain's Air Force Chief, Air Marshal Arthur Tedder. During the dinner conversation he picked up a statement by Mrs. Tedder that her twelve year old son had learned many dialects during the Tedder's years of service in the Middle East.

After dinner Tuhlman asked the Tedder's if he might "borrow" their sons talents. "He might be able to pick up the information we want."

Calming their fears Tuhlman said all he wanted the boy to do was play in the lobby of a hotel where the merchants stayed and listen to their conversation. Mrs. Tedder could be in the lobby having a cup of tea.

The boy carried out his role to perfection. At play in the lobby he overheard the merchants discussing a sabotage project they were planning. The enemy agent status was confirmed. The men were arrested and a German ring broken up.

What was the youngest counterspy ever "hired" by OSS paid for his services? Offered anything he wanted by Tuhlman, he asked only for a stamp album. Washington quickly flew the eight dollar item over by priority air freight.

It was true many misfits found their way through OSS doors and did nothing of value except travel on high priority classifications and travel to secret bases for no real purpose.

A high level of intelligence was not the sole criteria OSS looked for in an agent. Many intelligent people lacked common sense. They could be totally inflexible, a serious flaw for a successful agent who might have to alter plans at any minute to fit a developing situation.

Many children of wealthy families served in OSS. Andrew Mellon's son, Paul, was administrative officer of the SO Branch in London. Paul Mellon's sister, Ailsa (at the time the world's wealthiest woman), was married to her brother's commanding officer, the chief of OSS-London. Other Mellons and Mellon in-laws held espionage posts in Madrid, Geneva and Paris. The two sons of J.P. Morgan served in OSS-London. A Vanderbilt was executive officer of the SO Branch in Washington. A DuPont directed French espionage projects in Washington.

Though it was true OSS was riddled with communists it also had some anti-Bolshevik Russian emigres, some having descended from fallen nobility. The names of Smolianinoff, Ledla-Mocarski, Yarrow and Tolstoy were on the roster. The last OSS commander in London was a Romanov, a relative of Czar Nicholas.

Russian "Prince" Serge Ubolensky headed OG groups working with the French Maquis at the time of the Normandy invasion. He had been a former officer of the Imperial Russian Army and traveled to America after the revolution. He supported Franco and the fascist victory in Spain. He was sad over the betrayal of Yugoslavs delivered into the hands of Tito and the communists. Even so he worked willingly and bravely with the French Maquis, many of whom were communists. He was embarrassed to be honored in a ceremony by the "Bolsheviks" of the Maquis.

Labor attorney Arthur Goldberg, Arthur Schlesinger, Julia Child, Stewart Alsop, Walt Rostow, Allen Dulles, John Birch, Herbert Marcuse, actor Sterling Hayden, John Ringling of circus fame, ex-governor of Rhode Island, William Vanderbilt, were also on the roles.

An aspect of this modern world conflict that America was totally unprepared for was psychological warfare. When Donovan was on his tour of Europe in 1940 he noted how the Germans made the fullest use of threats and promises of subversion and sabotage against politicians in Europe. They sowed dissension, confusion and despair among their victims and belittled any faith or hope they might display. Donovan reported to Roosevelt that America was not prepared to handle this type of attack, nor was England. Donovan added he considered it was as essential as military preparedness.

The British, however, were ahead in their psychological screening. At an executive staff meeting in October, 1943, the idea of creating a psychological-psychiatric department was proposed. Colonels John A. Hoag and Henson L. Robinson of the Schools and Training Branch were very interested. Their training programs had caught considerable heat for poor recruiting. They had no way of determining how a man in the field might react. Some who were high-strung simply cracked in the field. They might go months without seeing an American or even a white face. If they lived in China for an extended period and ate nothing but local food while under extreme pressure they might not make it. Indeed eight men had already been recalled who should never have been sent in.

Interesting stress tests designed to measure the psychological fitness of recruits were designed and given to candidates at Camp S. The recruits including women, civilians and military personnel from buck privates to colonels arrived in civilian clothing. None were allowed to reveal their true identities. They were given problems to solve.

Four would be taken to a remote area and dropped off with materials to construct a small shed. They were told they were to have it done by five o'clock when the truck would return for them. The one put in charge (actually the candidate being evaluated) would immediately organize the men, lay out the materials, look at the plans and start work. Unknown to him was the fact two of his "colleagues" were actually OSS staffers whose job was to sabotage the whole thing. They ridiculed the whole idea, the OSS in concept, the other men in their group and questioned the leadership ability of the man left in charge. They either refused to do anything or did it in such sloppy fashion it had to be redone. The frustration mounted as the day wore on and the man in charge realized he was not going to get the job done. Usually he would finally attempt to do it himself or with the help of the one other willing to help while the two "saboteurs" did nothing but harass the whole project. The shed was never put up by any group but much was learned about the stress capability of those left in charge.

Other tests included the problem of moving a group of men and a hundred pound rock over a small stream without anyone getting wet. The recruits were given wooden planks that were too short to span the creek. As they attempted to find a solution they, too, were subjected to extreme verbal harassment by members of the assessment staff.

The sophisticated training procedures called for filling out numerous papers in which the recruits made value judgments about different events, their colleagues and manufactured situations. The new OSS Psychological Staff set standards and attempted to find those who "could get along with other people," those who had "freedom from disturbing prejudices" and finally to weed out those who had "feelings of national superiority or racial intolerance."

180

Eifler could only wonder if he would have passed these batteries of tests. He was a man of action with an unusual mind. To evaluate him would have been a near impossibility. To determine his capabilities would have been absolutely impossible.

Following this there was yet another staff meeting of top OSS personnel in Washington. Donovan, at that time, said: "I consider Colonel Eifler as the outstanding agent developed by the United States in this war."

What Eifler had already shown in daring, imagination, ingenuity, and organizing earned him this spectacular tribute by Donovan. What lay ahead, and the true reason for his temporary recall, was now laid out for him.

In a top-secret meeting a new, bizarre plan was proposed to Eifler. Present at the meeting were General Donovan, Colonel Buxton, and J. M. Scribner, deputy director of Strategic Services Operations.

Donovan led off. "Carl, this new operation will not even be given a code name. It is one of the biggest items of the war to date. We cannot even tell you much about the men you will be working with."

Eifler waited for the discussion to continue.

"There is one thing I can tell you, however, and that is that you will be the smallest one in the project."

The remark was obviously referring to his rank in the operation, not to his physical size.

"What can you tell me of my new assignment?" queried Eifler.

There followed a briefing on something new in warfare—atomic power. Escaped slave workers had informed OSS agents in France of the importation of heavy water from Norway. The report, dutifully forwarded to Washington, D.C., had caused considerable alarm when its potential was realized. Further investigation showed the German scientists had been hard at work in this field for some time. It was known that the German atom-splitting activities had been secretly moved from the Kaiser Wilhelm Institute in Berlin. A Swiss physicist who was in touch with the German physicists provided the general location from letters written to him postmarked from a small cluster of German towns. He also was able to give them the name of the top physicist whose loss to Germany would be disastrous insofar as this project was concerned. Eifler began to see the picture. He immediately saw a small band of infiltrators, quick assassination, and it was all over. No particular problem.

"Colonel Eifler, do you think you can kidnap this man and bring him out to us?" was the unexpected question.

Immediately his mind switched to the new proposal. To get to their top man would be problem enough. To then kidnap him and bring him out of the country would be quite a task even for Eifler. In his mind, however, there was nothing that was impossible.

"Yes, I can do it. When do I start?" was his simple reply. One of the men banged on the table.

"By God, that's the most refreshing thing I've heard in this whole damned war," he said. "Everyone else has said it is impossible."

Eifler was thinking well ahead. "Can I select my own men?" he asked.

"Of course you may," he was told.

"I'll need a few days to think of my plan and personnel, sir. May I meet with you in three days?" Permission was granted.

Sitting quietly in his room Eifler poured a drink and slowly sipped it as he mentally went through the logistics of his new mission. He had not been told that he was not the first OSS officer to become involved with this particular German scientist. Whereas Eifler's education was quite limited the other agent, Moe Berg, held degrees from Princeton, Columbia and the Sorbonne. He was a successful lawyer and businessman. He spoke twelve languages including Latin and Sanskrit and was an internationally renowned linguistic scholar. In addition he was a marvelous athlete. As a Chicago White Sox catcher he reached his peak in 1929. He batted .287 and received votes for Most Valuable Player. He was injured in 1930 and came to the sad conclusion he could never reach the standards he had set for himself.

He had a special talent for dialects. He could identify a speaker's hometown by listening to him speak. He identified people from Marseilles, France and Coffeyville, Kansas.

His phenomenal mind soon became legendary. He was asked to appear on a popular radio show, "Information Please," on which panelists were asked to answer esoteric questions. The public response to his appearance was so great that he was invited back. In an attempt to stump him a panel of reporters prepared the questions.

He was asked to identify the Seven Sleepers, the Seven Masters, the Seven Wise Men, the Seven Wonders of the World and the Seven Stars. Not only did he do so but he added it was impossible to know the true number of stars in the Seven Stars since the Pleiades in the constellation Taurus were bunched too closely together for anyone to count them. For a finale he was asked to identify the Black Napoleon, the modern Hannibal, Poppea Sabina and Calamity Jane. He answered them all correctly, without hesitation. In 1934 he visited Japan, this time as part of a team of all-stars that included Babe Ruth and Lou Gehrig. Berg was the only one carrying a letter of introduction from Secretary of State, Cordell Hull.

Berg's teammates did not know he was engaged in undercover work for his government. He skipped an exhibition game to "visit an American mother who had just given birth in Tokyo." Instead, he actually took carefully selected pictures of Tokyo from the top of that hospital, one of the tallest buildings in the city. His photos were later used by General Jimmy Doolittle's pilots in planning their 1942 attack on that city.

While in Japan, Berg made an extraordinary broadcast to the Japanese people in flawless Japanese. He pleaded for them to avoid a war they could not win. The next day President Roosevelt called to thank him, which gives an idea of how closely the White House was following his actions. Shortly after that the Japanese government banned baseball calling it a decadent American sport.

Was it more than coincidence that Berg and Eifler were both involved in spying on Japan in 1934 and later became the two to whom OSS turned for action against this German scientist?

When the war broke OSS recruited Berg. He first dropped into Yugoslavia to speak to the forces under Tito, then to the Serbian camp to talk to Mihalovich's people. He prophetically told the U.S. that the people supported Tito.

His next mission involved the German scientist. Donovan sent Berg to determine Germany's progress in developing an atomic bomb. He first went to Norway where he reported a plant producing heavy water. It was bombed heavily. In Italy he learned of another German atomic center in Duisburg. This one was also devastated in bombing raids.

Donovan next assigned him to determine the extent to which Germany was planning and developing radiational warfare. He followed the trail to scientists in France and Switzerland. Utilizing his fantastic mind he became an expert on the fine technical aspects of atomic energy and radioactivity. He became expert enough to discuss these subjects with the world's top specialists.

His most dangerous mission involved finding and making contact with Germany's number one atomic scientist, Werner Heisenberg. He would be the only man who would know if Germany was nearly ready to produce the bomb. Berg was even prepared to "eliminate" Heisenberg if need be.

Employing an elaborate scheme Berg lured the scientist to Switzerland to give a lecture on quantum theory. He evaluated the lecture, then managed to attend the dinner party afterward. Due to his polished German no one knew Berg was an American agent.

Berg reported that Heisenberg stated he did not believe Germany would win the war. Both President Roosevelt and Winston Churchill as well as the scientists working on the Manhattan Project were filled in on Berg's amazing reports. Collectively they agreed to leave Heisenberg alone but continue monitoring his progress.

For eighteen months OSS and the Manhattan Project closely watched Heisenberg's progress. Intelligence reports indicated there might be more progress in the German laboratories than we realized. It was time to check up again in a slashing, dramatic way. Donovan selected Carl Eifler.

Eifler requested all available information on intelligence within Germany. Preparing to infiltrate the Nazi police state at the height of a major war and bring out their number one atom scientist was certainly one of the more hazardous missions OSS and the Manhattan Project might dream up.

Eifler learned no penetration had been achieved. The Gestapo was thorough and brutal. The British felt no penetration of the Reich was possible, especially by the "inexperienced" Americans, and directed little effort in that direction. They felt any such attempt was impossible without a fairly strong local resistance organization.

With no safe house or contacts within Germany, Eifler was to abduct his man under the noses of the tight security forces and in some manner smuggle him out of the country for return to the United States. They wanted his brain, not his death.

Again the Eifler computer went into gear. He had to develop a logical story that would satisfy the Allies and not arouse the Axis. He needed enough men but not too many. What would their functions be? What talents would be required? He worked out various plans on paper. He studied the map of Europe, in particular of Switzerland. Two days later he had the plan laid out and ready to implement. He returned to his appointment.

"Well, Eifler, have you selected a plan?" Buxton asked.

"Yes, sir, I have."

They motioned for him to continue.

"I will go in through Switzerland. To get acquainted with the area I will be known simply as an officer concerned with OSS bases in that area, I will need orders taking me there to demonstrate our toys and to lecture OSS personnel. I will need to go to our bases in London, Italy, and Cairo."

Buxton saw the beginning of the cover but wanted to pursue it further. "What is your reason for going to Switzerland?" he asked.

With a trace of humor in his voice, but a straight face, Eifler answered: "Colonel, we are interested in how customs is handled between a neutral country, such as Switzerland, and a belligerent such as Germany. With my background in customs, I would be the logical man to go there and make such a report for the government. It would give me the opportunity to observe their border stations and figure out how to violate them. I can get into Switzerland. And I can get him into Switzerland."

"How about getting him out?" pursued Buxton.

"I have that figured out, too. Once he is in, I will take him to a certain airport where you will fly him out."

Eifler knew no light planes could be employed. The terrain and length of any such flight would be too much for the L-1s or Piper Cubs he had used so successfully in Burma.

"It would have to be a big plane," he added.

"It would be one of our larger planes," was the reply.

Eifler thought back to a statement he had heard before going to India. He had been told then that there were two American ambassadors who would have nothing to do with covert plans. One was in China; the other in Switzerland. It was just his luck to be faced with running into the other after his experience with the first.

"What about our ambassador and the violation of Swiss neutrality if we fly a military plane in?" was Eifler's next question.

"The ambassador knows nothing of it and would not help in any way if he did. It is better he be left out entirely until it is over. The violation of their neutrality may cause them to have to break off diplomatic relations with us to save face, but that is a gamble we will have to take."

Eifler pondered this for a minute. "Does the plane fly him to England?"

"No, we do not want him in English hands. It would do us no good. We not only want him out of the war, we want to pick his brain."

"Where will he be flown, then?" pursued Eifler.

"The plane can fly him directly over the Atlantic. Once clear of the European coast, you and the scientist will be dropped to one of our submarines who will take you aboard for return to the United States."

The plan was bizarre and so dramatic it was absurd. Buxton loved it. He continued his questions. "If the timing of the plane and submarine are off, or the submarine is being chased by German subs, or a hurricane is blowing when they get ready to ditch, what of these possibilities?"

There was a smile from all the officers. "Eifler, you are the last person in the world to be talking about risks."

He realized the truth of their statement. But he did have one final question: "All right, I have kidnapped this man and smuggled him safely back into Switzerland. Now suddenly I am surrounded by Swiss police and cannot get him to the airfield. What are my orders?"

"Very simple, Colonel. You are to deny Germany the use of his brain."

That he understood. "Okay, so I bump him and am arrested for murder. Now what?"

The answer was simple and chilling. "Then, we will deny you."

It was the expected answer, but Eifler wanted them to say it. "I'll start selecting my men immediately. I will need to go to the West Coast to pick up two former customs men who will fit in with my plans," he concluded.

They shook hands all around. Eifler walked from the room preparatory to his flight to San Francisco. The newest and most secret OSS operation was now being launched.

There remained one highly important piece of unfinished business for Eifler, however. This had to do with the Stilwell request that Chiang Kai-shek be eliminated. Still feeling poison was the only way, Eifler visited Stanley Lovell in the R&D laboratories.

They discussed the possibility of using the botulinus toxin that had been developed for the prostitutes in China to give the Japanese troops. This had the unique quality of paralyzing the lungs so they could not function. After death there would be nothing that an autopsy could reveal. If, however, a doctor was present during the victim's final death throes, he would be able to recognize that the victim had died due to the lungs' inability to function.

Eifler's decision was definitely made. Upon return to India he would inform Stilwell that he was ready to use the poison and how he intended getting it to Chiang Kai-shek .

The trip from the nation's capital ended on a rain-soaked San Francisco runway. Eifler was able to see his wife and son for the first time in over two years. He really had no leave, so vital was the project, but he did manage to spend time with them around his duties. His former Customs friend, George Roberts, was still with Customs in Hawaii. His other man, Lee Echols, was in the navy and stationed right in the bay area. Both men leaped at the opportunity to join OSS, hazardous as it was. Roberts left a well-paying position to join OSS. Eifler had told him he would have to come in as an enlisted man. It made no difference.

Upon arriving at his hotel in Washington, D.C., Roberts checked in as a civilian. He reported to Eifler and was then inducted and outfitted. The next day he checked at the desk for his mail in the uniform of a private. Eifler had the paperwork in the mill, and that afternoon he was promoted to master sergeant. The next morning he approached the same clerk with the six stripes plainly showing. The clerk looked apprehensive but said nothing to him. Later that day Eifler came through and was called aside by the puzzled clerk. He described the rapidly changing status and rank of the new guest and summed it up with: "What the hell goes on here?" Had Roberts remained at the hotel another five and a half months, the clerk would have seen him in the uniform of a second lieutenant. It was just as well he was on duty elsewhere.

Prior to leaving Washington, D.C., Eifler had called in a young lieutenant concerning the ten L-1 planes Donovan had okayed for DET 101. He told the lieutenant that the planes were crated and on the dock in San Pedro. The lieutenant was to put Eifler's name on every crate to make sure they actually reached 101. He was all too familiar with cargo being diverted by other areas of command. The lieutenant left to carry out his orders.

A short time later Eifler was at OSS headquarters in San Francisco displaying the catalog of toys and demonstrating the various weapons and gadgets. He had ordered the young lieutenant to report to him there to make sure he had put Eifler's name on all the crates. The lieutenant gave a brief explanation of shipping procedures. Only units and numbers could be listed; no names were ever put on crates or other cargo, he reported.

Eifler halted him impatiently. "Lieutenant, I am not interested in learning about shipping requirements. I said I wanted my name painted on those crates."

"Sir, I'd be court-martialed if I did that," protested the officer.

"Lieutenant, you'll sure as hell be court-martialed if you don't," pursued Eifler. "Now get your butt down there and do just what I said." He turned from the officer, who suddenly aged five years. He later was informed that all planes had arrived at their destination with his name prominently displayed on each crate. To no one's surprise, the lieutenant never put in a request for transfer to 101.

With the interviews and recruiting completed, Eifler flew back to Washington, D.C. Echols and Roberts would shortly follow and be briefed during Eifler's absence. Actually, the "briefing" was to be a full training of a total of ten men, including Echols and Roberts. With addition of Richmond and Curl, it would give a complement of twelve men plus Eifler. The training program was to be arranged in conjunction with a Captain Allison, Stanley Lovell, and Colonel Robinson. Captain Allison was to follow through for Eifler, making sure the program was fully implemented during Eifler's absence.

Lovell proposed that some personnel specifically trained in electronics be attached to the team. He could foresee the possible need of such talents. Considering the fantastic devices and schemes already credited to him, it would have been foolish not to heed his advice.

Much thought had to be given to the delicacy of Eifler's actual mission. He would be traveling to OSS units with their own commanders. He could not give them full details of his actual mission. In fact, he could tell them nothing. Yet he must have authority to do those things he considered essential to the success of his actual mission.

A special memorandum dated March 8, 1944, was sent to the various OSS commanders in Europe and North Africa. In part it stated: "...Colonel Eifler may be requested directly from Washington to undertake particular special operations. In the event he is, he will be advised by General Donovan's office directly, and owing to the nature of certain of the operations which may develop, it may be the General's wish that he proceed with their implementation completely on his own initiative. Obviously, these undertakings may not be engaged in without Theater Commander approval but the manner in which this is to obtained, the method of execution, and the security of the operations are left completely to Colonel Eifler's discretion as he may be instructed by the Director's Office at the time he is directed to undertake the mission. It is appreciated here that this arrangement raises a delicate problem in relationships, but General Donovan has requested me to advise you that he is completely conscious of this problem and that he expects it to be made to work by you and Colonel Eifler together."

The final paragraph of the two-page memorandum concluded: "I will add that the Director considers Eifler's mission one of highest priority and importance, and that the possibility of difficulty is thoroughly realized here, but 109 (Donovan) has instructed me to advise you that the Eifler mission 'must be made to work.'" It was signed "J. M. Scribner, Deputy Director, SSO," and bore the P.S.: "General Donovan has seen and approved this letter."

With the communication went a two-and-a-half-page summation of the March 7 meeting with Donovan, Bigelow, Scribner, and Eifler in which the mission had been discussed. It pointed out that Eifler would be directly charged as the special representative of the director of OSS and that neither he nor his personnel would be under the jurisdiction of the Strategic Services Officers in the theaters to which they would be assigned. Paragraph 5 gave Eifler his cover story, to acquaint the various army commanders with the special OSS toys and devices. Subparagraphs of 5 stated Eifler had requested transfer of Lieutenant Colonel Richmond and Captain Curl of DET 101 to his new mission. This had been approved by Donovan. In addition, it advised that Eifler would spend most of his time in the field, moving from theater to theater, personally implementing the overall plan. In probably one of the most sweeping directives issued during the war, the orders included: "The movement of Colonel Eifler's personnel between Theaters is specially exempted from the provisions of General Order No. 16, Supplement No. 2, which requires permission from Washington for the movement of personnel between Theaters. The Director has granted permission to Colonel Eifler to move his personnel between Theaters at will."

Here was a sweeping authority given to few men, certainly no other one bearing merely a colonel's rank.

The final paragraph stated: "Communication between Colonel Eifler and his personnel, either by cable or pouch, shall not be subject to inspection by the Theater Officer as provided in General Order No. 9, Supplement No. 31."

Donovan had said he would give Eifler his own "little OSS" and with this order he delivered it. Such was his confidence in what Eifler had demonstrated he could do and what he was capable of doing to meet this greatest of all challenges.

About this time, Eifler received a long distance phone call from the headmaster of the Palo Alto Military Academy. His young son was now attending school there. An unusual problem had arisen that needed Eifler's attention. The son had been relating fabulous stories of sexual prowess, complete with the most intimate details. He was twelve years old, and his classmates found him to be an unbelievable man of the world for his tender age.

Somewhat hesitatingly, the schoolmaster stated the tales were indeed authentic, not just wild imaginations. In fact, it appeared the young boy had outlined a few things even the schoolmaster had not tried. He was obviously at a loss as to what he could do next.

As he talked, Eifler already knew the problem. The boy had been thrown together with soldiers right after Pearl Harbor. With Mrs. Eifler busy as a nurses' aide and Eifler commanding the troops and a POW camp, the boy had had soldiers as his only companions. Every day Curl would trot the boy before Eifler with some "infraction" which would then get him KP duty and keep him occupied. In his spare time, however, he listened in the background as the men talked of their various successes with the opposite sex. It was evident now that he had a fantastic memory and a convincing delivery on top of that. Eifler suppressed a grin.

"Is the boy there with you now?" he asked.

"Yes, he is," was the reply.

"Put him on, please."

Eifler knew he had to stop his son from telling such stories but he did not want to humiliate him. He had decided his approach.

A weak voice came on the phone: "Hi, Dad."

"Hello, son," he began. "You know the war separated us, and I have not been able to be with you as I would like. But, son, somewhere in your upbringing I must have failed to teach you something." He paused to add effect to his next words. "A gentleman never tells," he concluded.

A slight pause, then he heard a feeble, "Yes, sir."

"Remember that and that I love you very much."

There were no further stories, he was later told. The boy had not had to lose face to his father.

It was to be a few more days before Eifler left for Europe. He spent as much time as possible going over details of his new mission. He also found time to read the messages coming from 101, still officially under his command.

A ticklish situation had arisen involving another breach of Chinese security. Some time earlier the United States had broken the Japanese code. It had to be one of the best-kept secrets of the war. The knowledge it gave America resulted in some grave defeats for Japan. Through this source of information, it was revealed the Japanese had in turn broken the Chinese code. Such a message could not be transmitted to China. If it were, the Japanese would learn that their own code had been broken. China was pushing for equal footing with the combined chiefs. The British were adamant because it was known information leaked through their circles like a sieve anyway. General Marshall undertook the problem. He called in the Chinese ambassador, T. V. Soong, and swore him to secrecy with upraised hand. He instructed him to personally fly to Chungking to relay the news and change the code. He also told him that if he violated his oath and sent the information by radio, the United States would easily find out and that would be the end of him. He obeyed explicitly.

In early April Eifler left on his new mission.

His introduction to OSS–London brought him into another world. Violence and destruction were everywhere evident in the smouldering ruins of the many buildings leveled by the savage Luftwaffe bombings. It was warfare on a wholesale scale.

190

He had heard of the heroic efforts of the Londoners who fought the fires in the streets even while the bombs fell. Now he was able to see them firsthand. The loss of civilian lives was greater than he had ever witnessed.

The purpose of his mission, so secret it bore no name, was constantly in the back of his mind. But he always kept his cover story up and played his role to perfection.

His head injury inflicted constant pain. He was reminded of it, not just by the headaches, but by the little pills that jiggled in their case in his pocket and to which he was tied in order to get through each day.

The London base of COI/OSS was established before Pearl Harbor. Donovan first arranged for the office to be set up in August, 1941. It was actually established three months later, in November. The basic agreements between the U.S. and London had considerable effect of OSS operations in Europe, Africa, and the Middle East.

Other Branches, SI, SO and R&A followed shortly. One year later the personnel numbered over 100. In 1944, R&D and Medical Services were added. By then the authorized personnel numbered over 2,000. A total of 14 branches were in operation.

Britain, struggling with military reverses and inadequate forces, welcomed the intelligence operations of COI/OSS and cooperated fully. MI-6 and SO,E were anxious to keep tabs on the operations of their Yankee cousins. In fact, they exerted so much influence, it verged on control.

Eventual negotiations resulted in each nation having its own designated area of operations. Such operations were to be only under the control of the agency under whose jurisdiction it was authorized.

Before the many small areas of conflict were ultimately resolved, Donovan had to go to the Joint Chiefs of Staff. While the border lines were fairly well designated, both sides grumbled and continued to violate each other's orders.

The OSS operations, originally housed in the U.S. Embassy soon outgrew its welcome, both because of space requirements and the degree of secrecy its operations demanded. At one point the Embassy demanded and was denied access to OSS messages.

OSS established training camps outside of London, as they had outside Washington and as Eifler had in India. Similar classes in sabotage, cryptography, radio, silent killing, arson and demolition were conducted in some very stately mansions.

One thing Eifler had never had to consider before was the creation of fake identities, supporting documents and the acquisition of authentic clothing for his agents. In the Orient an American spy was simply an American and could never pass for an Indian, Burman, Chinese, Malaysian or any other Oriental. While most Europeans might physically be able to pass as the citizen of another country, assuming their necessary language skills were good enough, other criteria had to be considered before someone was recruited.

First, was the matter of loyalty. Did the individual presenting himself or herself really hate the Germans enough to kill? Did he or she have the courage and nerve enough to play the very dangerous, and often fatal game? An abiding hatred and a desire for vengeance had to be carefully considered. In fact, such attributes would often be cause for rejection. The individual who had a consuming passion might well be too intent on satisfying personal vengeance to the detriment of the mission and the lives of other agents. This was dealt with in the OSS recruiting manual. It said, "a man should not have too many ideals, should work with his intelligence rather than his heart."

OSS sought stable, flexible, cunning and devious individuals. As one agent summed it up, "a burglar with morals."

A large number of technicians were required to support the agents going into Europe. The BACH section was created to provide cover stories and see that its trained agents went in with proper papers and clothing. Going into a country where there was a tobacco shortage? If the agent was a smoker with nicotine stained fingers they would have to be cleansed with a pumice stone. The Germans wouldn't miss that.

Americans faced the hazards of being Americans when going up against the Gestapo. Lapsing subconsciously into American habits might betray a man and his entire mission. Americans turn cake or pie with the point towards them, not so the Europeans. Americans cut their food first and then transfer the fork to the other hand. The Europeans do not switch hands. The angle a cigarette is held can betray an American pretending to be a French laborer or war worker. If the agent had dental fillings or bridgework it would have to have the workmanship and materials of the country he was claiming as his own. His glasses must be ground in Europe and have frames of European origin.

The recruiting game eventually got into German prisoner of war camps. Those claiming that they were willing to go back into the Fatherland to work against Hitler had to be carefully screened. The ones most valued were people who had knowledge of the structure of German society and its communication lines.

Once selected they were checked by X-2. Could OSS be in danger of dealing with a counterspy?

192

Eifler marveled at the extensive files and reams of paper the BACH section employed. There was an alphabetical listing of German towns that included the color of the street cars. The Gestapo had a habit of asking that question. The fake identities of those claiming to be orphans required a burial place for their parents. The obituaries of German cities were read and a ready catalogue of names was prepared and made available to be supplied to agents.

One BACH member, with a casual manner, talked at length with German prisoners. When they were last home how was the food? Any change in ration stamps? What streets had they observed that had been bombed out? What addresses? These were important for establishing home addresses of agents because they could not be checked out.

Of course, some of the shrewder POW's realized why they were being asked these questions, but most were lonely and anxious to talk to someone other than their comrades.

Female agents did not require the meticulous attention that their male counterparts did. It was easier to make up their cover stories. They could move about more easily and were able to utilize natural feminine wiles to throw interrogators off the track.

Even with this thorough preparation, Germany proved to be a difficult bastion to penetrate. The highly trained and suspicious secret police were everywhere. In addition, the citizens had been intimidated into reporting anything that was at all suspicious. As each German had to carry many different kinds of identification papers the counterfeiting of those documents presented special problems.

But the Nazi war machine also had a flaw in its armor. Germany had imported over three million people to work in its factories. Three million foreigners taxed even the most efficient police system. The easiest cover for an OSS agent was that of a foreign worker. It would give him an excuse for speaking only broken German or with an accent. He could show great confusion trying to understand what the Germans were asking or telling him. He was not eligible for the draft. He could work his way into the most highly secret war factories.

An agent might even go first class and claim to be a member of the Gestapo. Due to the large size of that organization and the fact that its members dressed as civilians and blended into the populace, the claim might not even be challenged. Besides, few German officials had the desire or bad judgement to tangle with the Gestapo.

What of the many documents the agent would be asked to show the Gestapo? Food Stamps, ration cards, work permits, paybooks; all were expected to be available for inspection on demand. A counterfeiting operation was necessary. Its products could enable an operative to pass the scrutiny of the enemy—or could result in his capture and probable death.

Just behind the Grosvenor Street headquarters was a large home that had originally belonged to Christopher Wren. A wealthy Englishman bought the residence, had it dismantled and moved from its original location and then reassembled in London. This became the home of the OSS printing plant that counterfeited the documents used by its agents in Europe.

To staff such an operation OSS looked to men with printing and photoengraving backgrounds. Willis Reddick had a prosperous printing business in Springfield, Illinois. He had a degree in journalism.

As a reserve officer, Reddick hoped to obtain command of an infantry company, but was surprised to wind up in an empty basement which belonged to OSS. Here he learned his fate. His orders were direct but puzzling. He was to recruit men, then equip and direct a printshop for forging documents. He would need forgers and counterfeiters. The problem, however, was that he could not reveal the purpose of his actions and he had no funds. He analyzed the problem, decided it was hopeless, then asked for a transfer out of OSS. OSS, recognizing it needed his talents, refused the transfer and hauled him back to finish the job.

He teamed up with an equally frustrated OSS agent, Henry Morgan, grandson of J. Pierpont Morgan, and the two became an inseparable team. Morgan was frustrated over his inability to obtain false passports. The State Department was horrified. OSS then advised that if they could not get them legally they would have to print their own. The State Department relented.

As a team they raided the personnel of the Federal Bureau of Engraving and Printing and major commercial printers. They held one simple argument in their favor to the employers who did not want to lose these men. If they don't join OSS then they will be drafted.

After a short time it was evident the operation needed to be closer to the area of operations. In April, 1944, Reddick came to London to rebuild his counterfeit operation. His cloak was still "Research and Development."

The necessary equipment never arrived from America. It was evident the plant would have to be equipped in wartime England, no small chore. An offset press was loaned to them by one British firm. Then they got a photoengraving camera. But they desperately needed a lithographic press.

194

A new member of the team, Second Lieutenant Carl Strahle arrived from Washington. He was well versed in printing. Shortly after arriving he was sent to Birmingham where one of England's largest printing operations was centered. His mission was critical and obvious.

He was warmly received and invited to address a Rotary luncheon. He spoke warmly of American-British kinship. The Briton who had befriended him took him to the printing plant manager. He explained Strahle badly needed a lithographic press but he could not say why. The press would be returned at war's end. The bonds of Rotary were never stronger. The press was rented to OSS for a dollar a year. To put the final touch on the incident it was delivered on July 4, 1944.

Now the operation began in full force. The Rotary-acquired press turned out forgeries and all kinds of counterfeiting. While such actions violated all four principles of Rotary such transgressions could be forgiven for the duration. In the large old house the engraving operation was established in the kitchen. The heavy presses were set on the concrete floor of the garage. A total staff of eighteen, including engravers, offset cameramen, retouchers and artists plied their trade amid carved moldings and ancient leaded windows.

Added to the personnel were commercial artists and photoengravers from *Life* magazine, the *Saturday Evening Post* and advertising agencies.

The problems of watermarks and fluorescent papers used by the Germans were eventually overcome. The next problem surfaced with the completed documents—their "aging." It would not do to produce new, fresh documents. They had to be battered, wrinkled, sweat stained. They were treated with potassium permanganate or stained with coffee and baked in an oven. If the weather was hot and humid then the aging was done by carrying the documents under the armpit.

There was an uneasiness among Strahle and Reddick as they saw some of the side benefits their engravers were enjoying. Counterfeited cigarette and ration stamps kept the men well stocked in those hard to obtain items. Some of them had been looking longingly at British currency—but that was obviously not a permitted target for their skills.

With proper documentation an agent would need a believable cover story. This was under a different division headed by a well educated Russian Jew named Dr. Lazare Teper. An economist, he had studied at the Sorbonne and Johns Hopkins, then became an officer of the International Ladies Garment Workers Union in New York City. When the draft board reached for him OSS beat them to the punch.

Sent to London to create believable stories for the agents, he spent his time seeing every spy movie available and studying life inside Germany. Newspapers from Germany brought a wealth of information on new regulations, changes in curfew hours or ration allowances.

Teper had been inducted as a private and remained so. His operation was assigned offices in a building that bore the code name "Milwaukee." For the code name of his operation he selected BACH, the name of his favorite composer. Dealing with higher ranking British officers Private Teper found it expedient to dress in civilian clothes. Presumed to be of a higher rank, Teper usually sat beside the commanding officer at various functions. It was at such a function that a major complained to Teper about the prodding he was receiving from another officer concerning his progress on an assignment. He said, "I do not intend to have my work checked by any damned Captain." Private Teper nodded understandingly.

A new department was needed for the next step. The Division of Intelligence Procurement (DIP) was established to further perfect the skills of the clandestine agents in passing for what they were not. George Pratt, who had been the chief of the Labor Division was put in charge. He was extremely well acquainted with the exiled European labor leaders in London. He was not as knowledgeable about putting agents into Europe. He requested additional help and he was assigned Hans Tofte, a Danish-American whose speech was laced with the accent of his homeland. His thinning blonde hair was often tousled as if he had been running.

Tofte had journeyed to Peking at the age of 19 where he had studied Chinese. He came to America in 1940 as the Nazis moved into Denmark. William Stephenson picked him up for his knowledge of Oriental languages and culture and sent him to Singapore. With the fall of that bastion he returned to the U.S. and entered the army as a private. From there OSS picked him up. Even in the free-wheeling OSS, his free spirit was, to some, a source of aggravation.

Tofte successfully ran weapons into Yugoslavia from Italy. He and his partner, Capt. Robert E. S. Thompson, were awarded Yugoslavia's highest military decoration for their daring gun running.

Another member of their team was a new man, Sterling Hayden. Described as an emotional 28 year old lieutenant , he had entered OSS due to a friendship with Donovan's son. He was a tall handsome ex-merchant seaman who had achieved instant fame in motion pictures.

The team utilized a fleet of fourteen schooners that were pro-

196

vided by a Wrigley's Chewing Gum executive who commanded an OSS maritime unit in Cairo. Hayden became enamored of the tough partisans who fought so bravely and under the most severe conditions. It was easy to become enamored of these leftist partisans of Tito's if only for their dedication and bravery.

After that venture Tofte went to the DIP taking his colleague, Thompson with him.

Tofte's story book career and talents took him into CIA service at war's end. Several years later, as a director of covert operations in Korea in 1951 he set up "boom and bang" operations when truce talks began. These were designed to keep the communists off balance. He infiltrated six agents into the Russian base at Vladivostok to monitor possible Russian intervention. In addition he cut the telephone cable under the Yellow Sea. This was used by Chinese officers in Manchuria to communicate with their superiors in Peking. The loss of this link forced the Chinese to use radio communications which the CIA could monitor.

His most spectacular action was actually one of piracy, pure and simple. The Chinese were losing thousands of their troops in North Korea due to an epidemic. They desperately needed medical supplies. Indian Prime Minister Jawaharlal Nehru sent these supplies, including three field hospitals, on a freighter. Washington' s orders were brief and blunt. The supplies must not reach their destination. The big problem was they were being transported on a Norwegian ship with a Norwegian crew so attacking the ships at sea was out of the question. Tofte's plan was to sabotage the ship when it put in to Hong Kong. The ship, however, did not stop there. Now extremely bold action was required.

Arrangements were quickly made with the Nationalist Chinese. The Norwegian ship was stopped on the high seas by unmarked but armed ships. The crew was held at gunpoint while the hijackers unloaded the entire cargo. Having accomplished their purpose the attackers let the ship and crew proceed with the belief they had been hijacked by Chinese pirates.

Tofte served the CIA in other countries before being dismissed in 1966 when he was charged with keeping CIA classified documents in his home.

Through the European nationality desks various recruits were obtained. Donovan was concerned over the makeup of these people and turned to psychologists for help.

Dr. Henry Murray was appointed as the Chief of Psychology. He told Donovan, "The whole nature of the functions of OSS was particularly inviting to psychopathic characters; it involved sensation, intrigue, the idea of being a mysterious man with secret knowledge."

Eifler saw the entire assembly line. Recruits were obtained through the national desks of DIP, while BACH concocted their cover stories and Reddick's people fitted them with authentic clothing and false documents. Then operations provided air transport to their destination.

The magnitude of the London-Europe operation was rather overwhelming to Eifler and he was pleased with the simplicity of his DET 101 operation.

Many times in packed rooms he demonstrated the use of new OSS "toys." The admiring group of assembled officers from many nations pressed closely to see what he was doing. They made many notes and asked countless questions as they viewed some of the tiny devices that were dangerous and deadly.

In addition Eifler threw in a few simple magic tricks he had learned while on the Mexican border in the early 1930's.

His timetable called for him to move on.

9

Although the German air force had been badly mauled, Luftwaffe pilots still made their presence known. As Eifler departed London every precaution was taken to be sure his plane would not run into German fighters. A heavy fog over the channel was welcome.

The Germans were more concerned with monitoring activity in England, as they sensed a pending invasion. Single unarmed aircraft were not high on their priority list. Almost on schedule the plane touched down at a remote base on Corsica. Eifler was well aware of the history of that small island and felt it fitting OSS had a small base there. He conferred with its personnel, discussed problems facing them that he might be able to address and left the following day for his next destination, Bizerte in the northern-most point of Tunisia.

Eifler knew there were some problems in Bizerte that were unique. The amount of OSS personnel and their supplies were meager. They faced German-occupied Tunisia on the east and a hostile Spanish Morocco on the west. It was truly a British show. The Germans were concentrated around Tunis and Bizerte. The northern flank of the Allies was held by SO,E alone. It was extremely unusual to use highly trained intelligence agents as infantry. It then developed that the OSS men were to be used in reconnaissance patrolling and, in one case, holding a small sector of the front. The British lines contained a few French junior officers and were also manned by anti-fascist French and Spanish recruits from concentration camps, the Corps Franc d'Afrique and elsewhere.

Recruiting Arabs to work with the British and OSS was next to impossible. This was due to the problems between the French and Arabs. The Americans were associated with the French and treated the same. No bribes of any kind seemed to work.

What did work was a hostage system. When a village was entered where loyalty was wavering the eldest son of the most important man in the village was taken captive and held in the nearby lighthouse pending his father's arrival. The father arrived with gifts demanding his son's release. He was sent to get good information on the German and Italian positions. When he returned, if the information was satisfactory, the son was released. This had become the chief source of intelligence in the Bizerte area.

Morale was low, men were sick and the situation precarious. Eifler's mission was primarily psychological, to let them know they were important and necessary to the war effort. He did what he could and was glad to fly out two days later.

Skimming low over the water the plane landed near the Anzio beachhead. Artillery fire was quite audible. Several time German aircraft strafed nearby targets. All around was the debris of war.

The OSS officer who greeted Eifler told him all his men were behind the enemy lines gathering intelligence on troop movements and in many cases fighting alongside the partisans.

By now Eifler's demonstration of the "toys" was almost routine. He lectured on methods and demonstrated new explosives and ways to sabotage enemy equipment. The men in attendance were always fascinated with the new gadgetry and asked many questions about his operations in Burma.

A General Officer of G-3 in the Fifth army requested a private audience with Eifler. He asked Eifler if OSS could silence some large guns that were battering American positions. The guns were in a cave and came out only to fire, then returned making it impossible to bomb them. It had to be done by some type of sabotage. Eifler gave it some thought, then discussed it with OSS Colonel Carter and left the action to be taken in his hands.

Though not on his agenda he was asked to go to Cassino and speak before the men fighting there. He did so, and, in the process, got an extremely close view of the fighting going on in the hills.

His next flight was over Italy where he landed at a secret airbase in Brindisi, Italy. It was just outside Bari, headquarters of the Fifteenth Air Force which serviced many OSS missions into the Balkans.

The base at Brindisi was under the tightest security. Here OSS men operated loading the special cargo for airdrops into Yugoslavia. In addition, agents to be dropped, both British and American, boarded at Brindisi. The aircraft from that facility also serviced secret operations in the Balkans, northern Italy and Central European points, including Poland.

It was not a large sprawling operation. Facilities were spartan. Most of the OSS men wore khaki uniforms with little if any insignia designating their rank. A few had designed their own insignia for self satisfaction but it was strictly unofficial. The brass would have frowned on it but not too many of them came in contact with OSS personnel. When they did they chalked it up to the peculiar people within that organization and said nothing.

As the passengers debarked from the plane Eifler didn't even

200

bother to look around. He had been in many of these secret bases and could practically describe them before arriving.

That day, a few hundred yards away, Edward Hymoff was busy loading a plane for a mission to Yugoslavia. Technically his rank, frozen when he entered OSS, was Private First Class. But rank meant little here which was one of the benefits of being in this clandestine outfit. Some of the other OSS personnel wore paratrooper uniforms of the units where they had originally been serving.

Their new organization was called, SBS, Strategic Balkan Services. Some wore a small American flag on their right shoulder, and a black strip with faded yellow letters on the left shoulder reading "U.S. Contingent."

Asked by the pilot if he would like to go along Hymoff said he'd go "anywhere, any time, any place."

Asked if he didn't need permission he said he did not. He had no boss, no one to report to. When the plane left he was on board for a trip into German held territory.

There was a greater divisiveness between anti-Nazi forces in Yugoslavia than almost any other theater OSS operatives found themselves. The split was between the Partisans, Tito's forces, and the Chetniks, Mihalovich's people. Both were fierce in their hatred of the German occupation forces. It was a pattern OSS had seen before when its communist agents (Tito's men) were at odds with the Monarchists (Mihalovich's men). So important was the need for order in Yugoslavia that the Germans had put in fifteen Reichswehr divisions and over 100,000 heavily armed occupation troops.

The Allied command, facing twenty six German divisions in Italy, found it essential to bottle up those German forces in Yugoslavia. The Allied forces were having enough trouble in Italy with the Germans as it was and a sixty percent increase was unthinkable.

To make sure the German forces remained where they were both the British SO,E and OSS planned their strategy. American officers, recruited in Washington and Cairo, were dispatched to act as military liaison with the Partisans and Chetniks.

On August 18, 1943, the first Americans were flown from Cairo and jumped into the headquarters of Mihalovich. Four days later, on August 22nd, the next group of Americans left that same airport and were parachuted into territory controlled by Tito. At the latter's headquarters they found a surprise.

The Partisans already had their officers, many of them Communist. Obviously they were not disposed to working with the Americans. What they wanted was American weapons and supplies but no

Americans to oversee their operations.

Another problem arose with the British. Two different British groups, SO and SO,E had signed an agreement giving SO,E the right to coordinate SO activity. On top of that the British in Cairo controlled air transportation making OSS beholden to them for any favors.

The big problem was communications. The Americans were under British command and had to stay at base if they were to wire messages through British radio. Many messages of military intelligence were delayed so long they became useless.

In November, 1943, Donovan traveled to Cairo and established the right of U.S. agents in the Balkans to their own radio networks.

On December 26, 1943, the first two American teams, designated ALUM and AMAZON were sent into Slovenia by SI. These teams carried their own radios.

Incorrect navigation caused three of the seven men to be dropped directly into a camp of White Guards. These were pro-Axis troops. Either the White Guards were confused and took the landing to be part of an Allied invasion or they chose to conveniently look the other way and leave the area. In either case the teams were able to escape. Later, at considerable risk to their own lives, they returned to retrieve their secret code books. The ALUM team reports on military targets were excellent. Its leader, a Yugoslav, was an all out advocate of Tito. The ALUM reports contained the locations of anti-aircraft and interceptor fields, battery sites, gun calibres even to their serial numbers. They managed to get from a captured German the complete AA and locator system of southwestern Austria. From this they were able to work out two safe flight paths, one northeast and the other northwest toward Munich. The group expanded to fourteen men. A fifteenth died when his parachute failed to open. In June, 1944, a unit consisting of two Partisans and one American actually crossed over the border of the Greater Reich. On the side of a hill overlooking the main railroad line from Zidani Most to Ljubljana they built a bunker out of logs they cut themselves. They buried their transmitter, battery and pedal generators under this bunker and camouflaged it so well it was all but invisible. For forty four days they poured intelligence into OSS headquarters. Natives, instructed to do so by the Partisans, left food baskets in nearby pickup areas twice a day.

A railroad guard stumbled upon their bunker and they were forced to leave. For several days they transmitted additional rail intelligence. Their last transmission was August 5. After that they were never heard from again.

The OSS and the Partisans were bringing in downed U.S. fliers thanks to escape routes established by OSS. In nearby fields the Partisans housed and cared for the fliers. On an irregular basis OSS worked out an evacuation plan for these fliers. By VE day the Air Crew Rescue Unit of the Fifteenth Air Force had brought out about 1,600 fliers. The morale of air crews flying over the area was considerably enhanced with the establishment of "safe area" maps. These showed the Partisan controlled areas. During their first four months in use they helped in the recovery of 467 airmen.

American representatives with the Partisans received MO propaganda pamphlets for distribution. They were designed to frighten collaborationists and encourage surrender of both German troops and satellite troops. The results were not what had been intended. The Partisans reported they were deluged by deserters from both groups. The Partisans were not equipped to guard them, feed and clothe them or even house them. In addition they were filled with hatred for them. Lacking both feelings for and logistics to handle them they could do only one thing—they shot them. Agents in Yugoslavia asked OSS to refrain from using this particular approach.

OSS headquarters were confused by reports from OSS officers with Tito and Mihalovich. Each reported favorably on the leader with whom they were serving. Finally the decision was made in early 1944 to go with Tito. All American and British representatives were withdrawn from the Mihalovich encampments. It did not lessen the need for intelligence from all sections of Yugoslavia and especially to bring out Allied airmen who still had to bail out in the Mihalovich areas.

On August 3, the HALYARD team jumped into Pranjane, some fifty miles south of Belgrade. Here Mihalovich had picked up, housed and fed over 250 U.S. fliers. The three member HALYARD team used 300 laborers and sixty ox-carts to construct an airstrip six hundred yards long. On August 9 and 10, all 250 airmen were evacuated. By the time HALYARD left three months later over 400 airmen had been rescued and evacuated.

The Russians presented their customary problem. Seeking to take credit for American supplies they attempted to bully their way into OSS operations in Bari. They wanted desperately to supply Tito and make sure he would be there at war's end to carry out the Communist philosophy. They attempted to land planes with supplies (and the red star) but the area they had selected was under heavy weather. Snow storms completely shut down the field. Finally American ingenuity solved the problem. Gliders with skis were employed and the gliders bearing American and Russian representatives as well as supplies landed successfully. Russian General Vishinsky's hope of landing in planes bearing the red star vanished as the American gliders slid to a halt.

An operation designed in all innocence to simply gather intelligence in the Mihalovich area backfired. The head of the six man OSS unit was headed by a Lt. Colonel. He told Mihalovich his mission was only to collect military intelligence. His presence in no way constituted political support of the Chetniks. In spite of this a Serbo-Croatian paper printed a leaflet stating the visit was intended to show that support.

It had exactly the effect the British had hoped to avoid. Using this as a pretext to cancel all future cooperation with the British and Americans (at the same time Russian troops conveniently arrived), Tito acted. One by one teams with various Partisan units reported they were "tied down" by guides that were always involved elsewhere and could not move out with them.

Various political maneuverings continued. The British and Russians held the upper hand because their missions spoke as official representatives of their governments. OSS operatives did not.

An American team did get into Belgrade while that town was still half held by the Germans, the other half in Russian hands. They managed to gather political and economic intelligence until a State Department representative arrived.

With the final removal of OSS forces from that embattled area it was difficult to properly interpret its overall successes and failures. The fact did remain that over 2,000 airmen were rescued, many thousand guerrillas were supplied and the coordination of aerial bombing with Partisan help did keep the fifteen German divisions tied up in Yugoslavia.

The Fifteenth Air Force planes servicing the Balkans were known as the "Balkan Air Force." It was often confusing to those hearing of this mysterious Air Force for the first time.

The day Eifler arrived was warm. He was sweating as he supervised the unloading of the cargo of weaponry he would soon be demonstrating. A jeep and driver were waiting for him and he was immediately transferred to his temporary quarters. The constant traveling was wearing him down. His head injury left him in constant pain. Though he took his pills faithfully he was finding it more and more difficult to perform his cover story.

He had little chance to refresh himself as the commander of the OSS unit and several junior officers arrived almost at once. They had been looking forward to meeting with the well known colonel who by now had become a legend.

He had dinner with them at which time he was asked his opinion on the first of many problems. An SO-SI agent told him of a problem faced by the Fifteenth Air Force. A river to the north was carrying vast amounts of oil to the Germans. Some 200 barges were being used. The river twisted and turned making it difficult to bomb. The situation called for an unorthodox approach. Eifler had it. To determine the flow of the river was no problem. Bomb the two barges furthest up river so their cargo of oil would be released and flow down the river around the other barges. Then an OSS "City Slicker" bomb could be used to ignite the oil and all of them could be hit at once. Just before he left Eifler followed it up by wiring OSS Washington and asking that fifteen of the special bombs be sent to OSS Headquarters in Bari.

Another example of the OSS character was displayed by Corporal Salvador Fabrega, a paratrooper who had been captured by the Germans. Fabrega was cited for his actions that followed. His citation for the Distinguished Service Cross stated: "T/5g Fabrega was taken to SS headquarters in Belluno for interrogation, but despite ten days of starving, severe beatings and torture by application of electrical charges to his ears, hands and feet, he revealed nothing about the work and location of his unit. On 16 March he was taken by automobile from Belluno to a prison camp in Bolsano for what he was told would be further questioning and torture and probable execution.

As he was being driven to Bolsano his German escort officer stopped at a tavern. Left alone with the Italian driver, a man named Sette, Fabrega was quietly advised it would be wise to escape as he would never leave Belluno alive. Sette said that in addition to driving for the Germans he was also spying for the American mission and had been able to give them some valuable information on various occasions.

Fabrega shook his head and said he could not escape. He realized the importance for the American mission to maintain the services of a spy in the SS command.

His citation concluded: "His unselfish action in refusing to escape when facing further torture and possible death, in order to further the aims of the mission to which he belonged, are in keeping with the highest traditions of the Armed Forces of the United States."

He did survive the war.

Not so fortunate were fifteen Italian-Americans from the 2677 Special Reconnaissance Battalion of OSS. They had volunteered to blow up the main tunnel of the coastal railroad running from Genoa to La Spezia. After their mission they were to be exfiltrated by Navy PT boats who awaited their pre-arranged signal. German E-boats surprised the small PT force, sank one and drove the others off. Other attempts to pick up the men failed. It wasn't until a year later their fate was determined. A search party found their bodies in a slit trench. They had all been shot in the back of the head. One of the party reported they were still in uniform except their combat boots had been removed. The party also reported their wrists were still tied together by rope.

"We untied their wrists before we buried them," was the final statement. (This was the first major execution under Hitler's orders to shoot to kill all Allied commandos and subsequently became the basis of some of the War Crimes Trials. Attorney William Donovan, assisted by Justice Jackson participated in the prosecution.)

Throughout the entire campaign the German SS demonstrated a savagery that always shocked those opposing them. In particular agents working in Italy saw a code of conduct that would have been applauded by Genghis Khan, certainly not a civilized society.

OSS Captain Howard Chappell arrived in the Val Cordovale area in northern Italy on December 26th. He was of Prussian descent and looked the part with his blonde hair and powerful build. He was a former All-State football player and a heavyweight boxing champion at Western Reserve University.

He was to take over a leaderless group that had just seen OSS Captain Roderick Hall captured, tortured and killed even though he had arrived in uniform. Chappell was briefed by Captain Joseph Benucci who had been selected to lead an OSS sabotage operation in northern Italy. It was Mission Aztec.

There were traitors who sold out the OSS men either to gain favor with the Germans or for money. Added to that was the problem of communists who were supposedly fighting the Germans but actually were feathering their own nest and waiting for the war's end when they might assume power.

Chappell was to take command of the Nanette Division which was operating near Bolzano, headquarters of the Nazi SS troops in Italy. A man named Mello was the Nanette Division's local chief. He planned to have Chappell murdered. In addition to that he stole several plane loads of American equipment which was hidden away carefully. When the Germans appeared they did no fighting.

Nearly thirty American pilots were picked up by Chappell's men. They tried to arrive as soon as possible after the pilots had landed in their parachutes. The pilots, when confronted by these men who spoke no English, were apprehensive and often drew their weapons. One pilot reported he saw some characters running towards him and prepared to shoot when one of them screamed the only English he knew, "Jesus-Christ-Lucky-Strike-God-Damn-Chesterfield-Son-of-a-Bitch." Happily he put his gun down.

A series of sabotage and assassinations followed as the loyal partisans and Chappell attacked. The Germans swarmed through the area putting a high reward on his head.

At one point Chappell was captured by a member of a search party. With a gun in his back he was marched toward an SS outpost. As soon as they were alone Chappell disarmed his guard, broke his neck with his bare hands and hid his body. The balance of the search party, knowing he had been captured, would be looking for him. He decided to bluff his way out. Messing up his blonde hair to look even more Germanic he walked toward and then through the other Nazis looking in all directions as if part of the search party. Leaving the area he went to a house where he was hidden.

With the searching going in full force by over 500 Germans Chappell ordered the partisans to break up into small groups and lay low. Benucci reported he was hidden in the belfry of a church in the small town of Mel. Many partisans were captured. Most of them were hung on meathooks until they died.

In San Antonio a youngster who had served Chappell as a guide refused to talk. The Germans took him to the public square, chopped off both hands at the wrists and gouged out his eyes. Then they threw him on the pavement and finally shot him.

As the Germans finally began their retreat from Italy the partisans and local citizens were told by Benucci to dig out every weapon and kill as many as possible. Bridges and ammo dumps were sabotaged and German patrols wiped out. In one action forty SS troops were killed and 90 captured. Among those captured was the sadistic SS Lt. Carl. Later on Benucci was told Carl had been killed trying to escape. "Still later I heard that it had taken him eight hours to die. Knowing how many young boys he had impaled on meat-hooks, what he had done to American flyers, the number of Partisan girls he had sent to SS brothels, I made no further inquiries. It probably would not have done any good if I had. A lot of SS murderers were killed trying to escape," Benucci added.

Benucci, Chappell and other members of their team were decorated personally at war's end by Gen. Donovan.

Eifler slept on the plane, a difficult thing to do with the uncomfortable bucket seats, on his next flight to Cairo, Egypt. He was told that base had been established when it looked like the Germans might succeed in reaching the Suez Canal in 1942 and OSS would need to leave behind small sabotage and intelligence groups. When that threat did not materialize Cairo was ordered to direct SI, counter-intelligence and R&A activities in Syria, Lebanon, Palestine, Transjordan, Iraq, Saudi Arabia, Iran, Afghanistan and Turkey. It was obvious Jews and Arabs would not cooperate in the secret operations missions thus necessitating duplicate staffing in some cases. The Jewish Agency in Palestine offered to transmit, at no charge, reports from its worldwide intelligence network. OSS accepted in early 1944. The Jewish Agency at first suggested placing a representative with OSS–Cairo to handle its material. The Egyptians refused. The results were almost zero and OSS finally canceled the agreement.

At a noon meeting two days after he arrived in Cairo Eifler went through his paces delighting those assembled with gadgets, lectures on new techniques and even threw in a shooting demonstration.

He was allowed to look over the record of the Cairo branch which showed successful operations penetrating most of the countries OSS had on its agenda. Syria and Lebanon were worked with seven SI and three X-2 agents. The French maintained control of these countries and any native agent with secret material in his possession could count on a lot of trouble if not on being shot. As a result, only two OSS teams, comprised of locals, were effective. Their studies of Russian growth in the area as well as the development of the Syrian National Party were important.

In Iraq four SI agents worked together with the British. Reports on the Kurds and strategic terrain analyses were rated as excellent and important. Two agents, "Bunny," and "Buffalo" worked as a team. In April, 1944, a neutral diplomat on his way out of Germany gave "Bunny" a detailed report on the results of the Allied bombings of Berlin. He stated the Berliners had learned to do their day's work between 2 and 5 p.m. when Allied bombers did not come over. Bombing of Berlin between those hours began promptly. The White House and other high authorities gave specific commendations over this vital bit of information which proved agents in place anywhere in the world can come up with valuable information.

Saudi Arabia was handled by two agents but with little success. Communication could be handled only through the U.S. legation at Jiddah, a far distance from the agents.

Eight agents worked within Iran. They were to collect military-geographical information in preparation for a possible German advance through the Caucasus. Their reports were of a more scholarly nature rather than of military value.

Afghanistan was to be handled by two SI agents. But major problems arose. Their lack of training produced nearly worthless reports. Both the American State Department and Minister discouraged and hampered their work. Within a short time they had to be recalled. The poor relations that had developed with the State Department representatives prohibited their useful return.

Twenty nine agents had been put in place in the Middle East by OSS. With the exception of Saudi Arabia and Afghanistan the results were good. The infighting between Jew and Arab, royalist and communist, the French and the British all took its toll on the Americans who wanted only to fight the Nazis and Fascists. They had not received extensive training in psychology and diplomacy from OSS.

Africa lay like a huge empty puzzle. Transportation and problems of communication ruled it out as a likely place for enemy activity, yet an area to keep under surveillance.

The lack of black operatives in OSS made it almost impossible to infiltrate agents under effective cover. The State Department severely hampered the few white agents on the continent and OSS had to be satisfied with a watch and wait mission.

There was an attempt to use people already residing there as agents but it did not work. Most of them were simply unsuited for intelligence work. Many "agents" so selected involved themselves too much in their previous activities. One man was an anthropologist who spent his six month tour of duty acquiring apes and caring for them when they fell ill. In the final run he caught their disease himself.

Only on Africa's northern coast was there activity where the Afrika Corps and British, then the Americans battled. Egypt and the Sudan were covered by the OSS headquarters in Cairo. Agents were put in other areas primarily as observers. Yet they had to be prepared for sabotage should something favorable to the Axis surface.

To cover a continent so vast OSS allocated its men into the following areas:

Tunisia (French)—3 men
Algeria (French)—7 men
Tangier (International)—7 men
Spanish Morocco—1 man
French Morocco—16 men
Canary Islands (Spanish)—1 man
Cape Verde Islands (Portuguese)—2 men
French East Africa—4 men
Portuguese Guinea—1 man
Liberia—7 men
French Equatorial Africa—1 man
British West Africa—18 men

209

Belgian Congo—4 men
Angola (Portuguese)—8 men
The Union of South Africa—5 men
Mozambique (Portuguese)—5 men
Ethiopia—2 men
French Somaliland—1 man

The Catholic church became involved in the situation in Liberia. American troops had arrived in that country to protect it from the Axis. All German nationals had been forced to leave but in the summer of 1942, when the first OSS agents arrived, Axis agents were in place. Early in 1943 a priest was gathering Allied military information and sending it by runner to another priest who was quite active for the Axis in the Tabou area of the Ivory Coast. Colonel Kirchoff and General P. L. Sadler, successive Commanding Officers of the U.S. forces requested extradition of the priest in the Tabou area. Agent "West" following the action was dismayed when the American Legation refused to comply. Instead they asked for more evidence.

The American Legation tipped off the priests that they were suspect causing the priests to set a trap to find out who was on to them. "West" was caught opening a letter and the Charge d'Affaires of the Holy See accused him of opening diplomatic mail. He was obliged to leave Liberia since the American Minister would not come to his defense.

A joint British-American venture became involved in the problem of diamond smuggling from Central Africa. The U.S. Foreign Economic Administration learned Germany had only an eight month supply of industrial diamonds. Since Germany was almost totally dependent on Africa for its diamonds some way had to be found to eliminate smuggling of the stones.

The major source of leakage was the Forminiere mines in the Congo. Investigation revealed diamonds were being smuggled in Red Cross packages. A secondary channel was also discovered in Southern Rhodesia.

Agent "Teton," attempting to obtain more evidence by acting as a buyer, ran into a problem. A pro-Allied Belgian hired by Teton to make a purchase was arrested by the police. A subsequent raid on Teton's house revealed Teton had uncovered a link to the Police Chief in that area. Teton was charged with questionable activities in pursuing illicit diamonds. The case was brought before the Governor General of the Congo. Although the U.S. Consul-General knew of the mission he refused to come to the aid of Teton and the OSS agent was forced to leave.

In the Balkans, the many islands and mountains of Greece presented a special logistics problem in carrying out sabotage against the Germans. Even a greater problem lay in the political infighting. In 1944, the Communists used as a national liberation front the Ethnikon Apeleftherotikon Metopon (EAM). The label was a total misnomer. This was a political movement. The military arm of the EAM was Ethnikos Laikos Apeleftherotikon Staton, (ELAS). They recruited their partisans from the local people. An evaluation of their operations later indicated they spent more time in hiding than fighting the Germans.

Their counterpart was the EDES, the National Republican Greek League, an anti-communist group. The two factions spent time and energies battling each other for control of the countryside.

The country was a British show. Two OSS representatives had arrived in Cairo in April, 1942, to survey possibilities for operations throughout the Mediterranean. In March, 1944 the first SO officers for Greece arrived, followed in May by the first SI officers. The British furnished money (gold), arms and transportation for the SI teams until the time OSS–Cairo was able to handle them themselves. Later OSS afforded help with the clandestine boat service it built up. SI agents penetrated several areas where British coverage was insufficient such as Evros, East Thessaly, Corfu and Euboea.

OSS was also assisted by the Hellenic Information Service (HIS) of the Greek Government-in-Exile. HIS recruited all service personnel for the SI/Greek Desk as well as some agents. In return for this help OSS gave HIS selected intelligence reports on political and economic conditions inside Greece.

One of the first missions of the ELAS people, together with its OSS partners, was to destroy a vital railway bridge which stopped the movement of badly needed chrome from northern Greece to the German war factories.

Though OSS once again found itself on both sides of its warring guerrilla colleagues the divisions in Greece seemed the most serious. The arrival of Americans was timely because both the EAM and EDES had been decimated by fighting between themselves and the Germans. Though the first OSS representatives were nearly all Greek it was decided to use Americans to lead the teams. The reasons were two-fold: American agents would provide less biased intelligence coverage; and native agents would find it more difficult to gain the necessary respect and assistance from guerrilla groups.

EAM had acted with typical Communist ruthlessness. They had called for the people to join under their banner. Because of their callous attitude the people not only feared but loathed them. Those people who refused to join their movement were dubbed traitors and collaborators. Their homes were burned and they were forced to join. Many were murdered.

Amidst these difficult circumstances OSS continued sending its Greek-Americans. Originally twelve parachuted in. Within a few weeks their number was increased to 250. The biggest problem was transportation from Cairo. Air transportation was limited. The answer came in the form of Greek caiques which could transport the agents in about one and half months. The caique was a small fishing and cargo vessel from two to eighty tons. It was manned by crews of from two to six men. At one time as many as thirty six of these boats were operating from Alexandria, the embarkation point from Egypt. Larger caiques sailed to Karavostasi on the northwest coast of Cyprus where OSS hired its crews and stored supplies.

The OSS men blended into the countryside growing beards like the natives. They actively destroyed bridges and railway lines. They were trained in the Second British Commando Group in Palestine and at Oujda, a small town near Oran. Their training included the use of bazookas against locomotives, a tactic which was used with such devastating accuracy that German engineers always slowed down to twelve miles an hour through passes and over bridges that spanned deep gorges.

Some of the Greek-Americans came across relatives they had never seen or known. They also found that the Greek people could match the Bulgarians or Germans in cruelty. They regarded torture as "sport." In some cases the British and Americans shot their prisoners rather than let them fall into the hands of the Greeks who would make death a slow and terrible one.

An example of this was displayed after the capture of some Germans who had just terrorized a village. Nine of the fifteen survived the fight and were marched back to that same village. They appeared terrified when they saw where they were being taken. The reason was evident when the Greeks attacked them as they were led down the dreary dirt street. They spit on the Germans, threw stones and identified them as the ones who had shot up their village. A fifteen year old girl came out to identify three of them as the ones who had raped her, her mother, the cousin and the aunt of one of the OSS members.

The OSS member in charge tried to calm the people pointing out that the Germans were his prisoners. The people were enraged demanding their own brand of justice. Three men were taken out of the small group and marched to a wall. The people demanded the prisoners once more, this time moving in closer with a definite threat in their eyes. Raising his machine gun overhead the OSS man fired a burst to move the people back. With the prisoners now facing him the Greek-American called his cousin and asked if she was sure these were the men. She was. Then his aunt broke through to confirm the fact. Calling on the people to stand behind him he put a fresh clip in his greasegun. Screaming, "You goddamned Nazi bastards," he executed them in three short bursts. Then stepping forward he took his .45 and fired a shot into the faces of each of them leaving them in a pool of blood and torn flesh.

He turned and walked back through the crowd of silent people. They were surprised at the quick justice meted out by the Americans. They were equally disappointed they did not get to torture their captives, then behead them as was their custom.

This incident was never reported nor were other similar ones that occurred in the mountains of Greece. After all. the OSS men who were Greek-American understood their relatives and way of life. And in a way they had even saved enemy soldiers from slow painful deaths.

The Germans made every effort to track down these British and American agents. A patrol of fifteen Germans tracked down an SI agent at Calchi. They took hostages and demanded his surrender. The agent destroyed his codebook and documents, then killed himself.

A special MO team was infiltrated into Volos. They printed a Greek newspaper to boost Greek morale, distributed pamphlets to encourage resistance, sent out poison-pen letters, posted fake military orders and spread rumors.

When a captured German general was killed by Greeks near Sparta the MO reported that the Nazis had killed him while he was trying to escape to a British submarine. He had left a letter saying that Germany had lost the war and that it was criminal to sacrifice further lives. This story was bolstered by rumors, broadcasts, planted letters and newspaper releases.

10

The seemingly never-ending trip next took Eifler back to India. First to New Delhi, then Calcutta where OSS representatives, together with British counterparts, gathered for the Eifler "show." As always those who observed the demonstration all wanted to secure various devices that they found of special interest.

He went back to his original home base, Nazira in Assam where DET 101 was increasing in personnel and activities. Here he was to officially turn DET 101 over to Coughlin and Peers, then proceed on to Simla to give a final show before leaving the Orient.

Prior to this, though, he had one more important stop before pressing on to Algiers. It was to tell Stilwell of his new orders and to offer to take care of one more important piece of unfinished business.

As he was ushered into Stilwell's tent, the General looked up and scowled, "You, Eifler, you of all people—a goddamned brass hat," he said.

Eifler well understood that term and knew Stilwell's dislike for desk officers. The General felt officers belonged at the front in combat, sharing hardships and danger with their men. Eifler did not launch into any lengthy discussions as to what he had been doing. He merely entered into a discussion of some visits in Europe and gave Stilwell a rundown on what he had observed with Allied forces there. It was now May 16, the day the Marauders attacked Myitkyina. An aide came in with a report of the tremendous casualties already inflicted on the Americans. Stilwell knew the losses they had suffered other than in combat. In Eifler's presence he gave what later turned out to be a completely misunderstood order.

"Send every available man into combat." This covered the entire theater.

Knowing he would be leaving the theater, probably for good, Eifler brought up the request he had received to eliminate Chiang Kai-shek. He said he had found the way to do it.

Stilwell shook his head and stated that he had had second thoughts about it and had decided against doing it "at this time."

Eifler noted he did not close the door for reconsidering such action but had definitely ruled it out insofar as he, Eifler, was concerned. If it was to be brought up again Stilwell would have to find someone else. Eifler said nothing further and dismissed the mission from his mind.

Eifler told Stilwell that he was being reassigned but did not give details of his pending mission. The two soldiers said their good-byes, shook hands, and Eifler left for Knothead to spend the night and see General Merrill. The next day both Stilwell and Eifler left in separate planes heading into the battle at Myitkyina.

In leaving Stilwell, Eifler found himself completely in awe that this man was still in command of his wits, let alone a war. While he had said little of the politics surrounding Chiang and his warlords, he had advised Eifler of much that had happened. It was true Stilwell had created many of his problems with his outspoken anger against the Chinese government and Chiang in particular. Even Roosevelt had suggested he stop referring to the generalissimo as "Peanut." In other talks, Stilwell had used such endearing terms as "obstinate ass," "thug," and "liar." A surprising ally turned up in the form of Madame Chiang. "May" craved action on the battlefront. She realized the problems Stilwell was having in getting the Chinese High Command to move. She suggested to Madame K'ung that if she were to move into town, the two women could meet in private with Stilwell to formulate plans.

At this point, Stilwell was reported to be anti-Chinese. The two women knew better. In the privacy of Madam K'ung's home, they signed "an offensive and defensive alliance." Stilwell knew they meant business and took heart that he was to have some friends in high positions. There were more meetings at Madame K'ung's. The two women were everywhere countering the whispering campaign against Stilwell. In his papers Stilwell commented: "May let out that she has a hell of a life with the Peanut; no one else will tell him the truth so she is constantly at him with the disagreeable news. It can't be easy to live with the crabbed little bastard and see everything balled up."

She even resorted to prayer sessions with her husband, but even her faith and feminine wiles were to have no effect in getting him to move his armies against Japan. She told Stilwell she had "done everything but murder him." Eifler shook his head sadly. He could fully sympathize with the problems of a general who wanted only to fight the enemy with every man and weapon at his command.

Stilwell's monumental battles with Chiang Kai-shek were as well known in America as in the CBI theater. While the Chinese leader seemed to lead a charmed life insofar as the White House was concerned there was a special day in Stilwell's life when Roosevelt sent a telegram to Kai-shek. The text is unknown to this day, but it was the most sharply worded American demand for reform and action that the war had evoked.

In a letter to his wife dated Sept. 19, 1943, Stilwell said:

"Mark this day in red on the calendar of life. At long, at very long last, F.D.R. has finally spoken plain words, and plenty of them, with a firecracker in every sentence. 'Get busy or else.' A hot firecracker. I handed this bundle of paprika to the Peanut and then sank back with a sigh. The harpoon hit the little bugger right in the solar plexus, and went right through him. It was a clean hit, but beyond turning green and losing the power of speech, he did not bat an eye. He just said to me, 'I understand,' and sat in silence, jiggling one foot. We are now a long way from the 'tribal chieftain' bawling out. Two long years lost, but at least F.D.R.'s eyes have been opened and he has thrown a good hefty punch."

The following day, feeling even more avenged, Stilwell wrote his wife again including a poem he had been inspired to write:

"I've waited long for vengeance
At last I've had my chance.
I've looked the Peanut in the eye
And kicked him in the pants.

The old harpoon was ready
With aim and timing true,
I sank it to the handle,
And stung him through and through.

The little bastard shivered,
And lost the power of speech,
His face turned green and quivered
As he struggled not to screech.

For all my weary battles,
For all my hour of woe,
At least I've had my innings
And laid the Peanut low.

I know I've still to suffer,
And run a weary race,
But oh! the blessed pleasure!
I've wrecked the Peanut's face."

He concluded by saying, "Rejoice with me and be exceeding glad,

216

for lo! we have prevailed over the Philistine and bowed his head in the dust, and his heart is heavy."

It seemed a hopeless situation. There was nothing anyone could do unless they gave in completely to the corrupt Chungking government.

On May 17, 1944, Eifler's L-1 touched down at Myitkyina where Merrill's Marauders were up against the Japanese Garrison. Eifler had learned much by now about those American soldiers. Originally dubbed Galahad, their name was later changed to Marauders when a correspondent saw them for the first time and said: "Hell, they look more like marauders." Their official name was the 5307th Composite Unit (Provisional). All were "volunteers." Gen. George C. Marshall requested 300 volunteers "of a high state of physical ruggedness and stamina" from the Southwest Pacific and 1,000 each from the Caribbean Defense Command and the army ground forces in the United States. In answer to the request, the South and Southwest Pacific Commands selected 950 men from veterans of Guadalcanal, New Guinea, and other jungle areas. The Caribbean Defense Command secured 950 more troops who had served on Trinidad and Puerto Rico, and a similar number came from highly trained units within the United States. These men constituted two battalions. They assembled in San Francisco. They were to pick up the third battalion on the way to Bombay.

To say they proved to be high spirited would be an understatement. From the very outset, the group raised more combined hell than the army would ever admit. The idea of combining trained jungle fighters with men who had known no combat had its obvious points. What it also included was the indoctrination of the newer troops to the finer points of goldbricking, officer baiting, gambling, and hell-raising. The troopship left San Francisco with 1,950 officers and men. It picked up 650 more in New Caledonia and the balance in Australia.

The Galahad force was to have but one parade in its short existence. At Freemantle, Australia, the men marched from the ship in formation, through the town and back aboard. Without stopping or breaking step, they proved their dexterity by returning roaring drunk. The good people of that town had fallen in beside them with pitchers of cold beer and other spirits. The troops were grateful.

Training grounds were set up at Deogarh, India, in November, 1943. The rugged jungle training spurred the men on to greater things. On Christmas Eve, 1943, the camp remained calm after a routine day of training. A shot rang out from one of the tents. Another gun answered. More guns joined in the shooting, mostly into the tops of each other's tents. Soon automatic weapons joined in. It seemed as if every weapon in the men's hands were now operating at full firing. The skies lit up with tracers from machine guns. Overhead magnesium flares cast brilliant white lights on the wild scene, and colored signal lights added their bit, much like an obscene Christmas tree parody.

Lt. Charlton Ogburn, Jr., summed it up in his story on the group: "Officers sent out by the enraged battalion headquarters to apprehend the miscreants were later found—by officers later sent to find them—dancing about like satyrs, firing their revolvers into the sky. A British major whom we invited to stay over for the night, after apologizing to him that since nothing had been planned it would be a quiet occasion, surveyed the appalling scene with the *sang-froid* of his race.

"'I can't help wondering what it's like hyah,' he observed, 'when you're not having a quiet occasion.'"

The Marauders were blooded at Walawbum. With instructions to cut the road and hold the area the various combat teams, each took up their positions. From tapped Japanese phone lines, American Nisei learned the Japanese were puzzled about the Yankees. They could not figure out what was really going on. The battle across the river took on some comical aspects as well as deadly fighting. Japanese officers were given to shouting battle commands like football quarterbacks. They would announce the time a squad or platoon was to rush the river and at what point. The Nisei of the Marauders would promptly relay this to their officers, who would then move their BARs and other automatic weapons to form a greeting committee. Screaming like banshees, the Japanese would rush across the waist-high river directly into the withering fire. Those that were able to retreat did so leaving bodies floating in the reddening water. Half an hour later the commands would come across the river again. The Nisei would again interpret, and the Marauders switch their firepower to meet the next attack. With a lull in the fighting, the shouting started. No one was quite sure who started it, although the odds would have to be with the Marauders. The jungle was quiet except for the occasional screeching of the monkeys and some confused birds. The sound of voices carried easily across the river with its many bodies. The Japanese "insults" were hardly that.

"To hell with Babe Ruth," one man reported hearing. It was a cry the Japanese had also used at Guadalcanal. Another highly imaginative Japanese was convinced he had the ultimate insult, designed to bring the Americans in a furious, foolhardy attack.

218

"Eleanor Roosevelt eats powdered eggs," he cried.

"Hirohito eats shit," shouted the Marauders.

Several of the Marauders jumped up long enough to extend the traditional American obscene gesture across the water. American insults won the day. With their own Nisei's advice, the Marauders were able to phrase, in Japanese, the most obscene and excruciating vulgarities against the emperor and Tojo. From this came a well-known and oft-told war story of an American soldier on the trail running into a Japanese soldier.

"To hell with Tojo," yelled the American.

"To hell with Roosevelt," retorted the Japanese, according to the story. When asked by his buddies if he shot him, he said: "I couldn't shoot a Republican, so we split a bottle of rice wine."

The battle continued until the Japanese finally broke it off. Walawbum had cost them 400 dead at the river, a total of 800 alto-gether. The Marauders had 8 killed and 37 wounded. At this point 109 were out with various sicknesses, 19 with malaria, 10 with psychoneuroses, 33 with injuries, and 8 with dengue fever. The jungle already was proving the more deadly foe.

Unknown to the Marauders was a diversionary force of Kachins taken in by Lt. Gerry Larsen and Lt. Bill Martin. They had joined the Forward operation under Luce and with their men were disrupting communications and giving the enemy cause to worry about the actual size of the forces in their area.

On March 17, 1944, the Marauders reached NawBum. Curl was advised of the progress of the American troops as they marched and fought their way south into his area. When they finally arrived, he was standing at a bend in the trail. The troops were watching care-fully even though they had been told they were now in friendly territory. They walked up to Curl and studied him carefully. He was obviously white, but was he American or British? His uniform, hair, and beard were completely unorthodox, but so were those of most of the Marauders.

"I'll be damned," one began. "A goddamned white man way down here in Jap territory."

Curl smiled, extended his hand and casually said: "Glad you got here, boys. We've been waiting eighteen months for you to arrive." Now the stories that had been floating up and down the column about American spies and guerrillas in the jungle were borne out. Marauders gladly swapped canned rations for jungle vegetables and chickens and eggs.

They had already been picked up by Kachins who scouted their flanks. They were to know several days free from worry in that portion of the 101-controlled jungle. They refreshed in crystal mountain streams, cleaned their weapons, and awaited further orders. When those orders came, they moved ahead with several hundred Kachins, now known as Myiahprap Hpung (Lightning Force). Pamplin, Curl, Rhea, and Father Stuart moved with them. Father Stuart heard confessions and held special masses for the GIs. He put aside his weapons to don what vestments he still had and gave spiritual comfort to those men who were soon to die. Two soldiers of the 2nd Battalion brought a buddy who wanted to be received into the church. His buddies had instructed him in the necessary doctrine. In midnight service Father Stuart baptized him in the cold waters of the Tanai Hka River, and he was received into the church militant. This stood out as a most meaningful service to the gallant priest, for this 2nd Battalion was soon to be cut off and besieged in a small Kachin village for thirteen days. Nearly all of the men involved in that ceremony fell and were buried there.

One of the war's more ludicrous moments came when the OSS elephants and the Marauder donkeys first saw each other. It was as if both refused to believe any such other animal could exist. They simply refused to acknowledge or look at one another. It was impossible to miss the analogy of the two beasts, both symbols of America's major political parties, going off to war together but still not liking one another. The Marauders, listed as all-volunteers, were not necessarily that. This was loudly made evident one day when a GI tugged at his balky mule who decided he'd had enough of the war and was not going to budge. The GI was heard shouting: "Come on, you son of bitch, you volunteered just like I did."

Tilly was ahead of the Marauders ambushing and harassing the enemy. The guerrilla soldiers were instrumental in the breakthrough and relief of the remains of that 2nd Battalion. Skittles and Hefty also were ambushing relief columns and causing tremendous pandemonium in the Japanese ranks.

Mission followed mission. The Marauder ranks were being rapidly depleted from sheer exhaustion and jungle illnesses. An order came from Stilwell's headquarters: attack and capture Myitkyina. There was a secret trail over the dreaded Kumon mountain range that could give the element of absolute surprise. One Kachin native, Nauiyang Nau, knew it and agreed to lead.

Rising nearly six thousand feet straight up, the mountain proved to be a nightmare. In many spots the trail had disappeared and had to be dug out of the gummy sides. The rains were now falling. Often the men were reduced to crawling on all fours. In a two-mile stretch one Marauder column lost twenty mules that slipped to their death, their terrified whinnies freezing the men until they heard the final crash signifying the end. Badly needed equipment was lost. Malaria and black water fever were also taking their toll as men died and were buried on the mountain.

Blood-sucking flies, leeches, and mosquitoes made life even more miserable. Men with malaria were supported by their buddies. Most men also had amoebic dysentery, further contributing to their weakened condition. Eliminating got to be such a constant chore, they lessened the effort by cutting the entire seat out of their shorts and pants. One GI, observing an entire patrol so attired, commented: "Well, by Gawd, no one can call them half-assed." The American sense of humor still prevailed, but it was hard to believe these exhausted and sick men were actually moving forward to attack and not retreating.

In the weary, plodding column was Lt. Bill Martin of DET 101 with a group of Kachins. The wiry little brown men were equal to the grueling march. They grinned good-naturedly and joked with the Marauders, who taught them many quaint American expressions, then howled with laughter when the Kachins repeated them unexpectedly. As small villages were encountered, the people were not allowed to leave lest some slip away and inadvertently warn the Japanese. Fifteen miles from their objective, in a scene that would be rejected in any movie script, a poisonous snake bit the heel of the Kachin guide. He was too sick to go on. Martin was right behind him and the first to approach him as he suddenly stopped. He called for an interpreter and was horrified to learn what had happened. The Kachins explained their own remedy: dig a hole, put the injured foot in, and cover it with silver rupees and dirt. The American medics disagreed with this treatment and immediately applied a tourniquet. Then the heel was lanced, and two men sucked the poison out. For four precious and agonizing hours the column halted while word spread up and down through the haggard troops. The stricken guide was then put on a horse to continue the march. It was now May 16.

The next day the column halted three miles from the long-sought airstrip. The troops spread out through the tall grass. Excitement returned as they prepared for the surprise attack. At the given signal, the Americans and Kachins sprang forward through the grass, screaming, firing their weapons, and slashing with knives. The attack was a complete surprise. The astounded Japanese fell back into the city. Martin and his Kachins rolled all the way up to the railway station within the city itself. Here they were ordered to break off the engagement and return to the airstrip. The Chinese were to be given the prestige of "capturing" the city.

The Japanese defense was completely disorganized and confused. Columns were attacking from both the south and the west. Both groups now held back as the Chinese were allowed to move down from the north to complete the job. Two battalions from the Chinese 150th Regiment began a pincer movement. In between them were Japanese snipers who began picking them off one by one. The two battalions turned heavy firepower on the Japanese. Quietly the Japanese troops moved out, and the Chinese closed in on each other. The heavy firepower began taking its toll as the Chinese slaughtered each other. Whether they finally realized their great mistake or merely decided to break it off because of their casualties is not clear. In any event, they did both retire from the fight, retreating back to their own lines. As they entered their own perimeter, a reserve Chinese battalion assumed they were Japanese and opened fire on the remnants. When that mistake was realized, the shattered battalions attempted to regroup and return to the battle. It was too late. The Japanese had hurriedly reorganized their lines. With over seven hundred casualties, the 150th Regiment finally had to withdraw.

Unknown to the Allied forces, many Japanese were on the move into the city from outlying areas. Instead of the five hundred troops anticipated there were now some thirty-five hundred. Lt. Gen. Shinichi Tanaka was 18th Division commanding general. Col. Fusayasu Maruyama was commander of the 114th Infantry Regiment and the garrison commander of Myitkyina city until General Mizukami took command of the garrison units, which included the 56th Infantry Brigade. Colonel Maruyama's regiment was reinforced with artillery, engineers, and other units. It was apparent that the Japanese had to throw everything into the battle.

For the first time the 101 guerrillas were standing toe to toe and slugging it out in traditional infantry fashion. The casualty lists were mounting.

The next day Colonel Cochran's glider troops were to come in on the strip. He had been told the strip was mined and to land his gliders crossways. The Japanese had actually staggered columns of fifty-gallon drums along the strip which Martin's men had already cleared. There was no way of stopping the gliders. The first five landed without incident. Following gliders landing ahead of the first units, ran out of room, and crashed into revetments. In some of the planes the heavy equipment, which was behind the troops, crashed forward, crushing them to death. Other glider pilots pulled their craft sharply away from the revetments into the swamps toward Myitkyina. Unfortunately, this was Jap-held territory, and many were shot down as they emerged. Lt. Jackie Coogan's glider came in, spun wildly to avoid the pending crash, and lost a wing. Some Chinese ran out to grab the wings and stop the sliding gliders. The strut from one plane beheaded one of them on the spot. It was at this point the L-1 with Majors and Eifler now appeared over the Myitkyina area.

The scene from the air was impossible to describe. Mortars were bursting around and on the strip. A dozen small battles were in evidence around the perimeter of the beleaguered city. Majors rolled the plane expertly to a stop and pulled it to the side. The two men dashed from the plane for the cover of the surrounding jungle, where excited figures beckoned to them. Eifler learned a plane had landed just ahead of him carrying Gen. Frank Merrill, who had been flown out earlier with a heart attack. He met Lieutenant Martin, who gave him a brief rundown of the situation. The two men walked down the strip, sprinkled here and there with dead Japanese. They came on one dead enemy who had been hit in the stomach with a bazooka. It had caused his eyes to bug out like sausages and had blown off the top of his head, spilling his brains onto the ground. It awakened Eifler to the fact that he was hungry. "Goddamn, Bill, I would sure like some sausages and brains or eggs," he said. "Where is some food around here? I'm hungry." There was no food available, but he did find a can of cheese from a mountain ration and it temporarily killed his hunger pangs.

They tried to flag a ride in a passing jeep, but the driver didn't stop. He moved down the side of the strip and out of sight. Two minutes later the jeep returned with someone else driving. The driver had been shot through the chest and lay in the back. The jeep sped straight to a C-47 being loaded with wounded. Just as the wounded driver was put on the plane, three Zeros attacked the area. Everyone dived for cover. Eifler landed on top of two men. As he lay there listening to the strafing planes churn up the ground around him, he suddenly got angry. "I came here to fight, not hide," he told himself. He jumped up and faced about as the planes began another pass. Armed with only his .45, he stood his ground, trying desperately for a lucky hit. He looked across the strip where a .50-caliber machine gun was firing back at the planes. At that moment the soldier was struck and rolled over, leaving his gun unmanned. Eifler dashed across the strip, oblivious to the fact he was the only moving object visible to the planes. They came after him but, like their brothers at Pearl Harbor, failed to hit him.

Just before he cleared the strip, he looked up to see a bomb lazily dropping toward him. He could see it from the side which told him it would miss him. He knew if you could see only the tip, you were going to "buy it" right then and there. Just before the bomb hit, he hit the dirt. He was about fifteen feet away when it exploded but was safe in the vacuum. When the dust settled he ran once more, clearing the revetment in one quick jump and whirling the machine gun into position. He chuckled as he fired back at the darting, swooping planes. Unfortunately, he did not bring any of them down. The recently wounded jeep driver, now on the plane, was hit once again by the planes. Slowly the C-47 rolled over, and he died with several of those on the ship.

It appeared that the raid was over. On the other side of the strip Martin climbed up the revetment. As he neared the top, he heard the roar again and looked up to see a Zero bearing down on him, guns blazing. The dirt before him was dancing a pattern of death. He had no chance to get out of its path. Behind him a .50 caliber, camouflaged like a tree, opened up dead center on the Zero. Its bullets tore into the cockpit and staggered the light craft, and the blazing guns stopped short of Martin. Slowly the damaged craft rolled out of control past the strip and into the swamps where it crashed in a ball of flame. The other planes flew away—the attack was over. From behind trees and revetments the men now came to see what they could do to help the injured. An American plane had been landing at the time of the attack. It had crashed into another plane on the ground. One man's head was pinned by the tail section. Quickly the injured were carried off the field for emergency treatment. The dead were put aside for burial and last rites. Father Stuart was of help and comfort. This "soldier for Christ" won the undying love and respect of everyone.

The army reported a shortage of 9-mm. ammunition. Could Eifler help? Eifler dug into his memory. He had just come back from six months of lecturing, but he remembered Red Maddox had this kind of ammunition in his camp. He instructed his pilot to fly there and bring it back. Fortunately, the L-1 had escaped damage, and they were able to get the badly needed ammunition.

A terrible toll was being taken of all forces. The Americans were losing seventy-five to a hundred men a day from exhaustion alone. Colonel McGee, commander of the 2nd Battalion, fell asleep three times during actual combat. He was unable to defend himself.

For forty-five days the fierce battle raged. General Stilwell's order to "throw every available man into the fight" was misinterpreted. He meant every man capable of holding a gun and defending himself. It was interpreted that every man who could walk was to return. The hospitals were scoured, and those who could walk, even though wounded and in casts, were loaded onto trucks for the return flight to Myitkyina. In some cases army doctors stood in front of trucks and refused to let their seriously ill and wounded patients be taken back. There was much bitterness mistakenly directed at Stilwell for what seemed a callous order.

Of the 2,750 Marauders who started the original trek, 200 remained. To warrant being evacuated, a man had to sustain a fever of 102 degrees for three consecutive days. The 1,000 men of the 2nd Battalion were now reduced to 12.

To the south the 1,300 Chindits of Morris Force were reduced to 25 men. The Chinese 150th Regiment could muster only 600 men out of 17,000.

Reduction of Allied troops called for immediate reinforcements. Myitkyina had to fall before the monsoons struck in full fury. They were just beginning.

Two battalions of engineers were flown in. Many of them had not held a rifle for two years. Two thousand additional U.S. troops were flown in from Bombay. Many of them were clerical and had just arrived from the United States. Hair-raising tales were told of how many of these men were instructed on the plane how to load and fire their M-1 rifles. They landed under enemy fire and rushed for cover. It was difficult to let them practice with their weapons for fear other troops would think an attack was coming from the rear. An ingenious solution was reached. They were taken to nearby Japanese-held Namkwi. Here they were pitted against the enemy. When the going got rough, they simply were disengaged.

DET 101 men were moved into the battle area. Many were communications men to back up additional OSS units being sent south of the area. Some watched the increasing U.S. cargo planes as they daily poured in supplies and more men. The strip was more secure, but there were still problems and casualties. One C-47, carrying personnel and ammunition, made a routine approach. Suddenly it exploded in a bright burst of flame, throwing cargo and the bodies of the crew and a group of army nurses onto the field. Death was accepted routinely by the men, but the death of these American nurses seemed uncalled for and unreal. It was a sad day for all of them.

As the battle lines moved farther south, Maj. Pete Joost moved his forces around the city of Lashio. One of his battalions particularly raised havoc with the Japanese. So effective were its ambushes that the Japanese turned on it in force. They even used tanks. The battalion commander, Lt. Joe Lazarsky, melted into the jungle, ambushing the enemy at every possible point. Eventually he reached the airstrip where the light planes were flying out wounded.

It was there that a medical-aid man, Sgt. William Brough, a

conscientious objector, was hard at work evacuating the wounded. As a medical aide, he was in as dangerous a spot as he could possibly be but still refused to carry a weapon or take a life.

He ran from the jungle's edge to the landing strip, a wounded guerrilla on his back. A Japanese sniper shot and killed his patient. He returned and picked up another. This one was also shot and killed while on his back. A third time he tried with another wounded man. When this man, too, was shot and killed, he was angry.

"That did it," he yelled over the firing of the weapons. "If that is the way they are going to fight, I am no longer an objector." With that he dropped his armband, picked up the nearest weapon, and joined the fight. He took command of a company. Later on he was commissioned on the field and fought with distinction. He later became an M.D. in England.

One of the DET 101 personnel was airdrop officer Lt. Dennis Cavanaugh. He moved into an abandoned building and established operations in spite of the war. He worked in close cooperation with Lieutenant Colonel Botts of the Tenth Air Force. Because the airdrops were behind the "bomb line" (a designated line beyond which all ground movement was deemed enemy), the pilots of Combat Cargo and Troop Transport Command had to volunteer. There was no shortage of pilots. Many were bored with what they called milk runs and were anxious to get in on the excitement.

By now many of the Kachins were fighting to the south in the flatlands of the Shan states. They were mountain people and could not see fighting in someone else's land. They wanted to return home but carried out their orders. They were nervous about leaving their homes undefended. When they learned the Chinese were moving down, they were greatly upset. They feared and hated the Chinese far more than they did the Japanese. Word reached the Kachins that the Chinese were approaching one of their main cities, Sinbumkaba. They asked to be returned to protect their families. The loss of these brave men would seriously hurt the overall war effort. Something had to be done to show the Americans would keep faith with them.

The threatened village was eight thousand feet high and approachable only by climbing a steep mountain. Cavanaugh and other officers felt it their duty to keep the Chinese from the Kachin town.

At that time 101 was supplying Northern Combat Area Command about 90 percent of their intelligence and designating 65 percent of their aerial targets. Cavanaugh normally supplied this information through normal designated channels. This time, however, it had to be done unobtrusively and without leaving any paper tracks. Cavanaugh, therefore, used the telephone to a Tenth Air Force officer to give the coordinates of the specific mountain now occupied with Chinese troops. The Tenth Air Force gratefully received the intelligence of "Japanese troops" and sent a flight of P-47s loaded with bombs and heavy cannon. They later reported they found the columns of "enemies" right where they were reported and did a beautiful job of blowing them right off the walls. Cavanaugh thanked them for their splendid cooperation, especially in view of the fact they had not had to go through channels, which might have caused them to miss a "golden opportunity." The news was received warmly by the Kachins, who returned to the fight knowing the Americans were solidly behind them. There was no particular problem from this action.

Not so with a similar problem involving Joost's 2nd Battalion to the east. They were near the Chinese border. It was commonplace for the Chinese to cross into Burma and attack and plunder the Kachins. This time they had performed as usual but got more than they bargained for. They had burned nine Kachin villages and retreated over the border when the Kachin Rangers approached. The Kachins, together with their American officers, followed them into China. There, with an eye to being fair, the Kachins burned exactly nine Chinese villages to the ground. This time a cry of outrage came from Chungking. An American colonel and a Chinese colonel were ordered to investigate and report. Their report was correct—both sides were wrong. It did not satisfy Chungking, however. Chiang Kai-shek sent DET 101, and Peers in particular, a bill for $25 million for the damage.

It was a little high for Peers's pay as a lieutenant colonel, and he chose to ignore it. In later years the American press tried to make something out of it but without success. It was dropped.

The monsoons were in full sway now. Conditions were intolerable. The Japanese were slowly being picked off, but resistance was fierce. Nearing the end, the Japanese sought a way to retreat. Their only avenue was the mighty Irawaddy River. During the night they would slip into the river on logs and float under cover of darkness through the troops ringing the city. Troops down the river suddenly realized they had a human shooting gallery. They obtained supplies of beer or native laku and took up positions facing the broad, swift river. When the enemy came into view, they casually laid down their beverages, picked up their rifles, and proceeded to shoot the enemy from the logs. At the beginning they had gone out in boats to try to get prisoners. The Japanese had thrown hand grenades into the boats, so the order went out: "No quarter." Thirty-five miles to the south Martin and former child star Wes Barry set up camp in a two-story home that commanded a sweeping view of the river at a bend. From a teak porch on the second floor they watched for those who had survived the crossfire of the troops to their north. Comfortable in their cane-backed chairs, the men would sweep the water with binoculars till the first enemy troops of the day were spotted. They would then fire with rifles, which alerted the Kachins farther downstream. Here were fifty Bren guns, and they would sweep the river in a hail of bullets. The next step was that of collecting the bodies. This was performed fifty yards farther to the south where dugout canoes put out. The bodies were needed for their uniforms and identification which might furnish information to the Allies. Within a five-week period Martin and Barry had a head count of 556 dead, 29 captured, and 27 Chinese deserters. To prove enemy kills, Martin's men on the trails had been bringing in heads. He discouraged this practice and finally agreed to accept ears, which were not so difficult to carry.

Martin's men had nearly ambushed an "enemy" column, which turned out to be that of DET 101 Lt. Ed Conley. The two compared areas they were to operate from to forestall any possibility of a clash in the dense jungle. Later Conley and Sgt. Art Aubry and their Kachins were surrounded by the Japanese. They were unused to fighting on flat ground and, with all trails blocked, the picture was bleak. One patrol reported finding a narrow opening which they estimated to be ten to twenty yards wide. Was it a trap? wondered Conley and Aubry. They had to chance it. They knew the morning would bring a full-scale infantry attack. Abandoning their elephants, they waited till dusk and moved out one by one. All weapons were at the ready should it be a trap. In single file the men walked, keeping utter silence. The hours passed. Finally they reached uphill terrain, and six hours later the entire group stood on the top of the hill looking down on the area they had formerly occupied. They waited till dawn broke. The early-morning quiet was broken by the flashes and explosions of artillery and mortars. The Japanese attack was sudden and devastating. Round after round poured into the evacuated area. Suddenly the attack stopped, and from the ground below came the yelling of hundreds of voices. It sounded like a football stadium going wild. The Japanese infantry poured into the area in one huge charge. Conley and Aubry would have liked to see their expressions when they reached their objective only to find no one there. The men gratefully turned toward the hills for a return to camp. The Kachins were sure to offer special gifts to the Nats for this one.

A young officer fresh from the States and just assigned to 101 had requested immediate duty at the front. Cavanaugh arranged for him

228

to be flown to one of the primordial strips to the south, and the next day he landed. On his third day in the country he prepared for his first patrol. The Japanese had been scouting the area and lay in ambush as the new lieutenant, accompanied by two other 101 lieutenants, headed for the trail. Unfortunately, they lacked the prescience the Kachins seemed to have. As they reached the trail, the Japanese opened up. One man got away; one was shot in the legs but managed to crawl into the jungle. The other, the newly arrived lieutenant, was killed on the spot. He had left America just six days before.

The Japanese moved into the little village which by now was deserted. The next day a Kachin unit returned with the one lieutenant who had escaped to warn them. The enemy was gone. Evidence of their savagery was apparent, for in the village was a pole with the severed head of the lieutenant impaled. They had cut off his genitals and stuck them in his mouth.

It was small wonder OSS men generally carried sudden-death tablets.

The time was finally at hand. Eifler knew he must depart, turn over command of his beloved DET 101, and return to his new mission. He gave his farewells to those men he could find. Majors warmed up the L-1, and they took off down the battered strip. They both looked down on the pockmarked town and marveled that anyone could still be alive. The enemy was dug in as deep as thirty feet with his guns pointing practically straight up to drop shells on the Allied troops. They headed toward Nazira, where Eifler would land for the last time. On June 9, he officially turned over command to senior officer John Coughlin. OSS in Washington then split the command, putting Coughlin in charge of OSS-CBI and Ray Peers in charge of DET 101.

Eifler and Curl decided to relax and take a flight around the area. Eifler revved up the plane and took off. Unknown to him was the fact the propeller on the plane had been changed since he last flew it. It made a difference. He taxied to the end of the strip, gunned the motor, and headed full throttle down toward the large tree at the end. At the proper point he pulled back on the stick. Nothing happened. He was now committed and would have to either crash on the ground or attempt to pull up. At the end of the strip he finally got the L-1 off the ground. It was all too obvious he was not going to get over the tree. He decided he had only one chance, and that was to go through it. Bracing himself, he pulled the plane directly into the foliage. There was a bump, but the plane continued through, branches dropping into the brush. They had made it. Curl tapped him on the shoulder and pointed to the right wing where a branch was lodged.

"Was that the one you were looking for?" he asked.

The rest of the flight proved no damage had been done to the craft. They landed at Simla, where Eifler was to tell Dorman-Smith he was leaving. In the two years since their paths had first crossed, much had happened. Dorman-Smith saw in Eifler the adventurous man he wanted to be but could not because of age and position. He was glad he had been right in backing the Yankee colonel in the beginning—glad not just to verify his original opinion but also that it was proving to be a most effective method of fighting the Japanese. They spent many hours conversing as Eifler brought him up to date on the various areas he had just visited. Before an assembled group of British troops Eifler went through his demonstration. They were most impressed—both with seeing Eifler personally and with the new weapons. Afterward they met for a final time in Dorman-Smith's office.

"Eifler, I want to personally express my appreciation to you for what you and your chaps have done over here," he began. "I had many doubts when I first heard of you, as you well know."

Eifler did well know and nodded in agreement. He was indebted to the spunky governor for backing him when it could have meant great criticism had Eifler fallen flat on his face. He had proved his spirit with the granting of the Burmese rupees.

"Now you are returning to Europe for God knows what," he went on. "I am sure your duties will take you once more to London. I am making arrangements for you to visit the Right Honourable Winston Churchill to give him an informal report on all activities in Burma."

Eifler was taken aback. A personal visit with the prime minister was something he had never even considered. "I would be honored to do so, Governor," he replied. As he turned to leave, Dorman-Smith had a parting word.

"Oh, one more thing—don't offer to shoot his cigar out of his mouth. I know you can do it, but there are some jumpy aides around him and we need them all."

Eifler promised there would be no such action and left. Now it was back to New Delhi for his final report and flight to Algiers.

On June 12, 1944, Eifler wrote a three page letter detailing his tour to Donovan. It concluded, "I have completely turned over my organization to Colonel Coughlin with the exception of one fund turned over to me by General Stilwell which will be completed within the next few days. I shall then proceed to Algiers according to your instructions. I have not heard anything further on my proposed entry to country X and I have made no further attempts along this line, not knowing what your wishes are at the present time."

He sent on to Donovan a recommendation given to him by Father Stuart at Myitkyina. It concerned CWO Bob Rhea and the work he had done and was still doing in Burma. The letter of commendation, heaping praise on Rhea for the mountains of credit he had brought OSS with his heroic camera work, was duly forwarded. Eifler recommended a letter or wire be sent from Donovan.

Another recommendation was made by Eifler. He suggested a catalog be compiled listing descriptions, pictures, and possible uses of OSS devices. He felt it should be supplied to each theater officer and updated as changes occurred. He knew of opposition to publishing such a catalog but stated, in his opinion, that such opposition could not sustain the harm being done to the men in the field by not having a ready reference of equipment available to them. He pointed out that this, as well as the supply problem, were the main difficulties resulting in delays between the development of an OSS toy and its actual use in combat.

After forwarding this report, Eifler packed his gear to leave the CBI theater and his men once and for all. On June 15, Eifler and Curl left for Algiers, where further instructions would be received.

While many officers had flown the miles Eifler had been logging, it was safe to say probably few had known the accompanying intrigue. The unit of which he had just relinquished command was so much a part of him it was difficult to realize it was really no longer his. From time to time he gazed out the windows at the terrain below thinking of the history that had engulfed the countries. Below were Afghanistan, Iran, Iraq, and finally Algiers, where his plane banked sharply for its landing.

Ahead lay something as challenging and dangerous as anything he had ever known. He did not think in terms of fear. He knew none and was later to remark that he could hardly ever consider himself a hero since he felt heroes were those men who performed above and beyond the call of duty when they were scared to death. In his mind there was no such thing as failure. Everything was possible; he could do it. This philosophy had pushed his men to unbelievable heights and was continuing to do so.

The Allied forces had swarmed ashore in France and were struggling to consolidate their holds on the beaches. The island-hopping MacArthur was moving ahead in the Pacific, and the tide was beginning to turn. How long the Axis could hold out was still conjecture. One thing was certain, and that concerned the Allies' fear of Germany's splitting of the atom. Hitler kept referring to a secret weapon. Obviously, he meant the atom bomb. If the Nazis did get it, England would be out of the war within a few weeks. They would have no choice. That Eifler had been asked to negate this threat stood him in no particular awe. He was simply the instrument to solve this problem. He had no doubt that he would succeed.

He was taken to the Algiers OSS headquarters, where he was to prepare for his next move. His plan was to go first to England to check on some items, then finally head back to his main target, Switzerland. Here he would appear under the cover of studying the customs problems arising out of a neutral country with its warring neighbors. He would then determine the weak link, and at that place he would smuggle in the kidnapped German scientist. He knew his men were continuing their training in America, and when he was ready for them they would be flown over.

His plans were to change quickly. Waiting for him at Algiers were General Donovan and Colonel Goodfellow. From their presence and attitude, Eifler knew something was up. They wandered outside, into the bustling Algiers traffic. There on the sidewalk Donovan put it to him.

"Carl, there's a change in your orders. We have broken the atom secret with our Manhattan Project. We beat the Nazis. Your mission is scrubbed."

Eifler was silent a minute. He had prepared himself mentally for the mission. Inwardly he had already lived part of it. He was not pleased, even though it was a near-suicide mission. "I see, sir," he finally replied.

"Buxton is pleased," went on Donovan. "He said you were too valuable to risk in such a hazardous mission anyway."

"Where do I go from here?" he asked softly.

Donovan paused as if to select his words. It was as if he was forcing himself to say something he didn't particularly like but was duty bound to do so.

"Carl, I've had a request from Gen. Douglas MacArthur for an experienced agent to make contact with the guerrillas on the Philippine Islands. He needs much information and guerrilla action to prepare for his landings. You are obviously that man. When we called off the kidnapping, I gave him your name. You know of the situation between MacArthur and myself. If you go with him I will no longer command you. I will, however, continue supplying you both with equipment and money."

Eifler well knew that there was no love lost between these two men. MacArthur had expressed little appreciation for OSS operatives and indeed had forbidden them in his area of command. Eifler knew Donovan was certainly putting his country's best interests first. Donovan's eyes were now fixed on Eifler, calm but anxious to know Eifler's reaction to this new venture.

Gazing steadily back at him, Eifler spoke slowly: "Sir, for over two years you have been wanting a direct penetration of Japan proper. If you are going to give me a choice between MacArthur or going directly into Japan, I would choose the latter."

In this exchange Donovan had given no order, merely stated some facts. Eifler in turn had simply given a preference. It was obvious both men knew each other very well. Donovan appeared pleased with Eifler's reply. They returned to the hotel. He called in one of his aides.

"Send a wire to Buxton deleting Eifler's name from the MacArthur job. Tell him to send someone else. Eifler will come in on the other project."

In five minutes Eifler had been switched from a direct penetration of Nazi Germany to Japan. The average man would have been reeling at this point. To these men it involved little more than the moving of a pin from one country to another.

Eifler and Goodfellow were to be roommates that night. After the meeting with Donovan, Eifler decided to go in town and see the sights. He invited Goodfellow, who declined, saying he had paperwork to do. Eifler went out, had a few drinks, did some visiting, and returned to the room. By this time Goodfellow had retired and was half-asleep. Eifler entered and snapped on the light. He then began pacing back and forth, his huge hands clasped behind his back, his brow deeply furrowed. He was softly murmuring. Finally Goodfellow was able to distinguish what he was saying.

"I can't get him out of my mind—I can't get him out of my mind," he was saying to himself.

"Who can't you get out of your mind, Carl?" was the puzzled query.

"The last guy I bumped off—I can never get him out of my mind."

Goodfellow thought that one over and finally asked: "Well, what do you do about it?"

"Bump off another one," was the sinister reply.

Goodfellow looked around the room, well aware he was the only other person present. He lay back on his bed and said: "Oh, for heaven's sake, Carl, turn out the light and go to bed."

Goodfellow slept fitfully. Eifler did not. He had problems with the heat. Both men slept on top of the sheets wearing only their shorts. For all the power they possessed between them they looked anything but dangerous.

11

Eifler reflected on his scrubbed German mission with no regrets. He would gladly serve his country where needed for any service in any territory. He felt no special relief at the fact he was almost sent into a sure suicide mission. He never expected to survive the war anyway. Nor did he feel relieved that he had not been forced to assassinate an unarmed scientist. If that man could turn the course of the war in Germany's favor then he had to be destroyed by any means, if that was the only option.

And while Eifler was to have nothing more to do with Germany, it was not so with OSS. In spite of British misgivings and the enormity of the problem of getting agents into Germany itself, they would indeed go. Regardless of the risk, it had to be done. The British actually did not want the fledgling Americans to muddy up the waters in Germany for several reasons. They felt that the Americans worked better as a group, not as lone wolves. After all the Americans had never had the advantage of the English boarding school education where life was a constant battle against authority from age seven on. In addition, the British had compromised the German espionage ring in their country. Not only did they know who they were, they had doubled them causing them to appear active for Germany but actually feeding false information supplied by the British. And the final factor lay in the British knowledge of Germany's ENIGMA which gave them detailed information on Germany's war plans. The Americans, if captured, might give the whole situation away.

OSS, however, was determined.

On September 2, 1944, the first OSS agent, Jupp Kappius, parachuted from a British bomber into Germany. It was scarcely three months since Eifler's kidnapping mission had been called off. Actually planning for the infiltration by Kappius had started years earlier. On December 26, 1941, the black hulled Portuguese liner, Serpa Pinto had arrived in New York Harbor. It brought 178 refugees, mostly Jewish, from central Europe including some German-Jewish nationals. Studying the manifest, made available secretly by the navy, was Naval Lieutenant, Peter Karlow who worked for the Coordinator of Information.

Just out of college, Karlow was multi-lingual and anxious to serve. His COI colleagues were from varied backgrounds. Luck or intuition had caused the COI to study these new arrivals for backgrounds that might be helpful to America in its war effort. Where had they come from? What knowledge had they of personnel, topography or manufacturing that could aid plans to invade Europe? What political knowledge might be exploited should we find it possible to blackmail officials? Which ones might be especially motivated to serve in a most dangerous capacity? In particular, what Germans might be arriving?

Other details were taken into consideration. The types of clothing worn might give an indication of the state of the German economy. The type of steel in a razor could show some change of German industrial processes. The COI wanted everything they could buy—clothing, wallets, shoes, underwear, pens, watches and luggage. If it revealed nothing it could be stockpiled and used for agents operating in German held territory.

Karlow, who wore civilian clothing, put the nervous refugees at ease conversing with them in their native language as he asked about conditions in Wiesbaden or Nuremberg where they had lived. Who had their neighbors been? What landmarks could they remember? What was being manufactured in the area? What was the color of street cars in the town they were supposedly from? Where were the telephone and telegraph offices? As he debriefed them the COI increased its campaign to buy up personal articles from the refugees. A warehouse was soon filled with belts, shaving brushes, dresses, valises, vests, trousers and coats of European origin. From this collection of second hand items Jupp Kappius was outfitted for his mission.

Kappius had been given an assignment before leaving OSS headquarters. It asked a lot: "you will create an underground organization for the purpose of (1) promoting internal resistance to the Nazi regime; (2) committing acts of sabotage against the war effort; (3) encouraging subversion in all its forms...you will cause rumors to be spread according to the following directions: (1) to create dissension between Wehrmacht troops and all political and semi-political formations, e.g., Waffen SS, Gestapo, Hitler Jugend...(2) to create financial panic on the German home front and among troops resulting in a run on the banks...(3) to encourage surrender or desertion..."

Kappius became Wilhelm Leineweber, an architect and section leader in the Todt Organization which performed military construction for the Germans. He was coming from France to find his mother who had been bombed out. Then he was to go to Bochum for reassignment. His identity was "confirmed" with nine forged OSS docu-

236

ments including the customary German ID, food-rationing coupons and blank travel orders to use as needed.

He landed in a tilled field close to some woods where he hid and buried his parachute. Just before midnight that same day he made his way to Burgstrasse 15, a triplex on the outskirts of the town. This safe address was that of a young ISK couple, both of whom had shown their hatred of the Nazis and had been sentenced to hard labor for their outspoken criticism.

Timing was most opportune for Kappius. The German anti-Nazi movement was demoralized after the severe reaction of the Gestapo to the attempt on Hitler's life. Thousands had been arrested, tortured and killed. Allied agents knew all too well the motto of the dreaded SS: "Blest be all that hardens."

For the Germans to know that help was now on the way and that they were not forgotten lifted their spirits in these dark times. As Allied armies approached the anti-Nazis began reforming. Kappius had a close circle of lieutenants that numbered 15. Each had his own subgroup. About 75% of them were factory workers or miners. He dealt with Liberals, Socialists and individual Communists but would not deal with the Communist party.

As this was going on his wife, Anne and another woman, Hilde Meisel completed their training at OSS Camp O outside London. They were escorted to Switzerland by Lt. Anthony Turano. From there they would slip over the border into Germany.

OSS officer Arthur Goldberg had been moved by Meisel and her idealism. He had a foreboding OSS might well be sending her to her death. Her codename was "Crocus."

Anne Kappius traveled to the Ruhr disguised as a Red Cross nurse. She served as a courier to her husband. By not using a radio Kappius cut down the odds of being picked up by directional-finders employed by the Gestapo.

When his wife reached him Kappius had been in Germany only a month but sent back word of resistance cadres spread throughout Bochum, Essen, Witten and other cities in the Ruhr linked to Cologne, Hanover, Breslau, Hamburg, Gottingen, Frankfurt and Berlin. In addition he had a safe address in nearby Dortmund where his London-OSS partner could stay when he arrived.

In addition he had penetrated the security system at the Krupp arms plant and had two hundred fifty rifles available. Also of interest in his reports was the fact the Germans were well clothed and fed. Trains and streetcars ran on time. Utilities were available with no restrictions. Food was rationed but plentiful, even butter.

Allied air power now took over. On November 4, 1944, the city absorbed over 3500 tons of bombs during a 40 minute period. It ended the trains and street cars running on time and nearly destroyed the telephone system. Kappius did report the alarming fact that approximately one third of the 5,000 pound bombs failed to explode.

With a timely tip-off of an impending Gestapo raid Kappius left his first safe house. He never stayed more than a week at any address rotating between five homes in the Ruhr. He was most impressed and appreciative of the OSS briefing including events and life in Bochum and other towns. It enabled him to talk as if he had never left the area.

On two occasions Anne Kappius traveled deep into Germany to return with reports of her husband. Hilda Meisel went to Vienna and established an intelligence chain. As she returned to where the Austrian border crosses into Switzerland she ran into an SS patrol. A sharpshooter brought her down with a shot that shattered both legs. Before they could get to her she bit into her 'L' pill, a cyanide capsule. She died instantly.

Though saddened by the death of this brave lady OSS continued expanding its recruiting of anti-Nazi Germans. Vengeance and hatred were not sufficient. A man intent on revenge might be so emotionally involved he would miss some small sign that could indicate the first opportunity to strike might not always be the best and thus jeopardize his mission and comrades.

Some Germans had been given slight hints, some even promises that working for OSS would gain them a trip to America at war's end. A few OSS recruiters were of the opinion they could even offer U.S. citizenship. When word of this reached Washington these recruiters were told under no circumstances could this be promised as OSS had no such authority. That authority rested with U.S. immigration laws. A final statement, clear but brutal was made: No agent should be recruited without serious thought being given to the means of disposing of him after his usefulness has ended.

Nevertheless, until the war ended both the possibilities of emigration from Germany and U.S. citizenship were dangled before prospective agents.

Many agents were recruited by an OSS team of three men who interviewed newly captured prisoners in preference to those who were already imprisoned. The team had noted the grouping of German prisoners by themselves into small groups—army and Luftwaffe who both avoided the SS. One of the team members, Carl Muecke, entered a POW camp to speak to over 10,000 prisoners through a loudspeaker.

His request was for them to turn in all official papers in their possession such as ration coupons, travel papers and their paybooks. He received the objection of a prisoner who reminded him that under the Geneva Convention they did not have to do this.

Immediately, many other prisoners jumped up to shout, "Be quiet. Can't you see an officer is speaking."

OSS recognized this as the obedience of the Germans. They had a new master now and he was to be obeyed. While they had all sworn an oath to fight to the death of the Fatherland they were told they could still keep that oath by fighting for the survival of their country and save their families from sure death by getting rid of Hitler and his henchmen.

Even at this time Nazi and Wehrmacht officers were dealing with OSS making offers that were certainly worth listening to. One high ranking German officer suggested to OSS that if the Allied forces in the west could be enticed to hold up their advances and withdraw the heavy pressure a deal could be made. The proposal was the Germans would double cross the Japanese and give American forces all intelligence information they possessed on Japan. The Germans could then concentrate their forces relieved from the western front to the east, and defeat Russia which, they said, was to the Allies' interest as well as Germany's.

The Russians, paranoid over the Allies making a deal, voiced strenuous objection to any such meetings with German officials unless the Russians were present.

As the war wound down many German armies preferred to surrender to the Americans and especially to OSS operatives whom they had learned to respect.

Not only were passports, currency, work permits, ration stamps and other official papers counterfeited by OSS but even postage stamps. In 1941 an official German stamp known as the Scott A15 was issued. It was a bright carmine colored, 12 pfennig stamp bearing a profile of Hitler.

As part of OSS operation "Cornflake" Hitler's face on the stamp was carefully redrawn and turned into a Death Mask. The stamp was printed up and sent inside other envelopes for any post office would not have forwarded mail bearing the defamatory stamp on the outside.

Cornflake was a complicated operation devised to bring subversive propaganda into the homes of the Germans through the infiltration of their postal system. The first time it was used, two mailbags containing subversive material were dropped into Hungary.

Then the operation turned directly into Nazi Germany. The plan was to drop mailbags containing the materials alongside shot-up trains. That seemed simple, but it soon brought out the realization that more needed to be known of the German postal system. To obtain this information German POW's with postal service were interviewed hundreds of miles apart in order to cross check their information. The latest German postal regulations were also studied.

The stamps, in 6 and 12 pfennig denominations, were printed in Rome by a firm that had a history of printing stamps for some Latin American nations. Not only were the stamps forged but also mail sacks and sack labels. Armed with the materials and knowledge of the regular postal system, OSS learned that in August, 1944, the Germans had completely reorganized the country dividing it into new postal districts. Old cancelling devices had been changed. Each new district had its own special number. It took weeks of searching in Rome before the post-August, 1944, cancellations could be found.

The OSS propaganda newspaper, *Neue Deutschland*, contained all of the MO propaganda themes. It was to be the principal stuffer within the envelopes. Also included were other leaflets and copies of the Death Mask stamp.

While the operation presented numerous problems, the Air Force freely gave its approval to the mechanics of the plan. A special fighter group of the 15th Air Force had a record of being tops in its low altitude attacks on German rail traffic. They termed themselves the World's Champion Trainbusters. They were selected to augment the operation. The mail they carried had to fit the towns and cities on the rail line of that particular day's train hunt. Postal cancellations were stamped on the envelopes at the airfield prior to each flight. Each mail sack contained 800 letters and contained a small bomb to scatter the envelopes. The bombs were designed to explode fifteen feet over the target to allow the released mail bags to reach their target untorn and undamaged. The technique was to find an enemy train moving north from southern Austria, preferably with a mail car attached. The fighters would then attack the train and destroy several or more cars and demobilize the train. In the confusion the bombs containing the mail sacks would be dropped around the train to be found in the debris.

Back in Rome the research continued. Over two million names and addresses were taken from phone books of Berlin, Dresden, Vienna, Hamburg and Stuttgart. A staff of typists addressed 15,000 envelopes a week. Many were hand addressed to provide a plausible mixture.

Then another hurdle was thrown in their way. The Germans announced henceforth only business and official mail would be permitted through the German postal facilities. The OSS countermeasure was to produce envelopes from German industrial establishments in Berlin, Vienna, Munich, Linz and elsewhere. These envelopes were printed to be in conformance with the revised regulations.

Within a sixty day period in early 1945 over 120 mail sacks had been dropped to targets inside Germany. During ten drops that were later analyzed more than 50,000 pieces of mail containing subversive literature were taken into Germany. Three fourths of that mail either reached the addressees or at least got to German postal officials.

A report on one of the operations said: "No. 7: Target was a fifteen-car train with locomotives and seven or eight passenger cars and seven or eight freight cars on the Vienna line. Strafing took place in the vicinity of Gmund. Front and rear locomotives destroyed and six freight cars damaged. Nine bags dropped on targets."

After the German surrender in Italy an interrogation of German prisoners showed the letters had definitely been received. Some of the letters resulted in German counterintelligence investigating entire units with court-martials following. The German POW's reported seeing the letters as far north as the Baltic ports. It was impossible to accurately assess the confusion and mistrust caused by the Cornflake operation but it was obviously a huge success in weakening the morale and fighting spirit of the enemy.

The pattern of both OSS operations and German reactions, particularly as the tides of war reversed, was repeated in other countries of Europe.

OSS operatives dispatched from London to work in France were recruited in America and England from the ranks of the Army and Navy. They would not need perfect French accents since the men would be mostly working with resistance groups. In addition American officers in uniform would carry more prestige with the Maquis.

During 1943, OSS made an arrangement with SO,E to take American recruits. Many of the Americans had received some training in America but needed additional training before going into France. After completing additional courses the students went to the SO,E Assessment Board. They were given a four day course to test their motivation, intelligence, aptitudes, emotional stability, initiative, discipline, physical coordination and stamina.

Teams of three agents were termed Jedburghs. Of 61 prospective Jedburghs who took the four day course during a given period, only 43 were approved. The rest were transferred to other branches in non-operational duties.

A majority of failures were due to lack of sound motivation which the Board considered the most indispensable qualification of a successful operative. Those who passed went on to parachute school for training. Depending on the weather the course lasted from four to six days. With final tune-up courses they were then readied for their jump into France.

The London offices had their cover stories, false papers, money and clothing from the continent to give them all the cover possible. One agent was arrested by the Germans who did not believe he was a repatriated prisoner from a German concentration camp. So complete had been his training and retention that when questioned by the Gestapo he gave a complete description of the camp where he was supposed to have been as well as the name and description of the camp commander and the doctor. A German soldier who had been a guard at that camp was called in to verify the information. He had to admit every detail was correct. The Gestapo released their prisoner after apologizing for having doubted him.

The thorough training could sometimes backfire as one agent found. He had been picked up for questioning. As he waited his turn he listened in horror as the man before him was telling the same cover story. Improvisation was a real necessity.

In preparation for operation ANVIL, the invasion of France, eighty-five OSS officers and civilians worked to prevent German destruction of factories, bridges and other targets the French would want left intact when the war ended.

OSS and Maquis found many different ways to aid the war effort. When intelligence sources indicated the possibility of new and secret weaponry being manufactured in certain plants, a bombing naturally followed.

After the bombing, the agents, who had become volunteer fire fighters, went into action. Their primary focus, however, was among the debris where they sought any special components that might be of value in the ongoing analysis of the enemy war machine. Even scrap metal might give an indication of the materials being utilized.

Jedburgh agents pretended to be travelling salesmen. With their fake documents that "proved" they were legitimate representatives of existing firms they called on factory managers to request that they be permitted to sabotage certain vital machines. The managers really had no choice, as to say "no" meant that the air force would bomb the plant causing numerous deaths in addition to destruction of the whole facility. This was beneficial to the Allies because it meant that vital parts of certain factories could be disabled with great precision. When the time came for the Germans to withdraw they would hardly bother to blow up a factory that wasn't able to produce anyway. The French *Societe National des Chemins de fer* (national railroad trust), together with the Maquis, cut rail lines, sabotaged turntables, blew up control towers, derailed trains and disabled locomotives. Over 1,000 engines were put out of action. In addition the continuous sabotage by the French underground greatly hampered the Germans.

Between June and September, 1944, 276 Jedburghs were dropped into France, Belgium and Holland. As the French had their own leaders the Jedburghs did not assume command functions but rather helped to plan and took part in sabotage and guerrilla operations. In Brittany the Jedburgh teams armed and organized over 20,000 men.

One Jedburgh team was dropped into Finistere, the westernmost Department of the Brittany peninsula. They knew the Germans had extremely tight control over the area but decided nevertheless to proceed to Brest. Special papers were required for everyone. Curfews were strictly enforced.

Two Frenchmen sent to aid them helped hide them in empty wine barrels. They were driven as part of a truckload of wine for the Germans north of Brest. They arrived two days later at a safe house near Lesneven despite the fact the Germans stopped the driver many times. When a flat tire occurred a German patrol even helped the driver change it.

On August 27, the Maquis prepared an attack on the city of Angouleme. Other forces were brought in from the neighboring Departments of Haute Vienne and Vienne. The preparations called for considerable ingenuity as the Germans numbered 2,500.

Fifty men familiar with the town infiltrated through the sewage system. The parish priest of Torsac provided the means of arming the resistance within the town. Looking solemn and serious he would lead a mournful funeral procession into the Angouleme cemetery where the coffin would be interred with loud weeping and wailing. During the night the coffin would be disinterred and the arms it actually held distributed to the resistance.

One of the teams assigned to operation ANVIL, preparing for the invasion of southern France, was assigned the name "Penny Farthing." After several parachute drops had to be aborted due to enemy action several of the agents finally did make the drop. Radio operator, "Toto," had a wide wartime acquaintance with French Army radiomen and was able to recruit and train operators in clandestine radio procedure. They operated in relief of Toto.

In August, 1944, a severe blow was dealt to Penny Farthing with the arrest of Toto and a colleague in a cafe in Lyon. Someone had betrayed him. During his weeks of interrogation Toto managed to avoid the death penalty that awaited him. The Germans considered him valuable because of his advanced knowledge of radio.

Special interrogators were sent from Berlin to question him. During the many days of questioning Toto not only managed to say nothing of value but at the same time acquired information from the Germans on their directional finders that enabled them to locate enemy transmissions. Toto managed to work a "deal" with one of his captors and was able to delay his execution, day after day, until the invasion of Southern France began.

On August 24, a few hours before he was to be shot, his Gestapo guard and a Nazi colleague grasped him as if taking him to his execution. Once they got in the car they untied him, handed over their guns and declared themselves his prisoner. Toto drove them some 40 kilometers to the Maquis entrenched just outside Lyon. After turning them over to the Maquis he returned to the invading forces and began intelligence missions back through the German lines.

There were other OSS operatives in France who infiltrated from Spain. Ten chains expanded to fifteen chains with some 1,500 agents furnishing more than 50% of all raw strategic intelligence from France. It was some time after these first operations began that SI/France successfully infiltrated its teams from Algiers. One agent landed by PT boat in late 1943. He had been asked to get details on the coastal defenses. As requested by his superiors he dispatched a complete report within a month. It went by pouch through Spain to Algiers. The report consisted of overlays at 1:50,000 from Avignon south to the sea and east to the Italian border.

Another agent gained the confidence of a German officer who commanded nineteen batteries at Port St. Louis. Not only did the German confirm positions and calibers of guns but he gave their range and setting and details on the crews and supply arrangements as well as their command and observation posts. OSS intelligence was so complete that when the air corps requested information on the wall at Frejus, factual data from thirty separate agent reports provided it complete to the sand content of the concrete and the name and address of the Italian engineer who started the wall in 1942.

Not all operations were successful, and agents of the Maquis and OSS could expect no quarter from the Nazis if they were caught. In mid-July near Vassieux the partisans awaited an air drop that came on schedule. As soon as the containers fell to the ground and the partisans ran out to collect them Luftwaffe Me-109 fighters began strafing the area killing and wounding many on the ground. Enemy artillery also zeroed in on the scene and three Wehrmacht divisions which had been moved up slowly began to close in on the redoubt.

In one ambush OSS OG killed more than a hundred of the

244

enemy. Three days later the enemy surprised them by landing a score of Stork gliders with over two hundred SS troops on a plateau in their midst. In a final assault on July 23, the Germans overran the plateau taking no prisoners and burning and torturing. A female assistant of one of the radio operators was caught by the Nazis. So intense was their fear and hatred of the Maquis and OSS that they sliced her belly open and left her to die. The report stated they had "hung her guts around her neck."

In Paris the city eagerly awaited the first Americans. On August 21, the citizens put up barricades around the city. The Nazis countered with tanks sent out to crush them. The Gaullists pleaded for the Allies to move troops in immediately when the German resistance became vicious. General Patton was at Chartres, some 50 miles from Paris. A rumor surfaced that the Americans were actually at Rambouillet, just 30 miles away. The only Americans there were David Bruce and his OSS staff who were traveling ahead of Patton's forces gathering intelligence.

At a local hotel in the village Bruce joined forces with a motley crew of local partisans. With them was their unofficial "Captaine" Ernest Hemingway. The famed author was no stranger to OSS. In London's pubs he had joined Jedburghs in training as they let off steam. Playing the general now, Hemingway gathered local citizens and collected weapons to arm them against the Germans, now only a mile away.

The delay in liberating the city was maddening to many as politics were played out in rear headquarters and Washington. When the day finally came and French Generals Leclerc and de Gaulle received the German surrender, Bruce and Hemingway made their way through the wildly celebrating city to the Ritz Hotel, the finest in Paris. The manager wanted to know if there was anything they might do for the distinguished writer and the OSS Colonel.

"Yes. How about seventy three dry martinis," Hemingway replied.

In many other areas of France OSS agents carried the battle to the Germans in various ways. While their papers could be forged, and used clothing of European manufacture could make them look authentic, one thing that was difficult to alter was the human spirit. Drawn from every branch of the service as well as civilian life the agents of OSS still had their own foibles and beliefs.

One of the Jedburgh's was Marine Major Peter J. Ortiz. His mission was in the Haute Savoie and he was to impress on the

French Maquis that preparing for guerrilla operations to support the invading allied armies was their most important task.

He parachuted into France with British Colonel H.H.A. Thackthwaite, both men in civilian clothing. They had also taken their uniforms as a second thought. That decision nearly caused a catastrophe. The Germans stopped Ortiz on a routine matter. His papers were perfect, not even questioned. But the Germans were interested in his suitcase and demanded he open it. The officer in charge lifted out Ortiz's uniform coat which was folded inside out. He saw only the inner olive drab lining in place of the Marine insignia, campaign ribbons and officers rank pinned to the shoulders. Ortiz slipped his L pill into his mouth as the German also checked out the forest-green trousers, also part of the uniform. Evidently he was looking for weapons for the German then dropped the uniform back in the suitcase and waved him on.

The uniform was to be used in a confrontation in a local bar a short time later. It was evening and Ortiz, acting out his role as a collaborationist, was drinking with German officers. During the course of the drinking the Germans insulted everything that they could think of about the U.S. To Ortiz, however, the Germans finally went too far. They insulted the U.S. Marines.

Excusing himself Ortiz returned to his hideout and donned his uniform covering it with a raincoat. He returned to the bar and ordered another drink. Then turning aside he removed his raincoat taking a revolver out of the pocket. The Germans turned to face a United States Marine officer in full uniform. Calmly Ortiz addressed them.

"We've been drinking toasts to Hitler all night. Now I want to offer a different toast," he proclaimed. He raised his glass in one hand, his gun in the other. With considerable encouragement they all drank a toast to the President of the United States and as an afterthought to the United States Marines.

Satisfied his honor had been restored Ortiz slowly backed out of the bar, his pistol keeping the peace. He returned to his hideout.

It didn't take long for German security forces to determine that one "Jean Pierre" was actually that crazy Marine officer. After he led a Maquis raid that destroyed a troop train and two miles of rail track the price on his head was raised from 150,000 francs to half a million.

To have jeopardized the lives and mission of a unit in the field for a matter or honor would not have won high marks for the officer in OSS records but the Marine Corps had to love it.

In later operations Ortiz and four Marine sergeants were sur-

246

rounded by the Germans in the small village of Citron, south of Lake Geneva. The Germans demanded their surrender or death. Ortiz had to make an agonizing decision. He feared his failure to surrender would result in the slaughter of the local citizens as had been done in Lidice in Czechoslovakia after the assassination of Gauleiter Reinhard Heydrich, the Gestapo overlord. More recently there had been a mass killing of over 700 people of the French village of Oradoursur-Vayres in retaliation for the killing of a German officer.

Rather than shoot his way out, Ortiz surrendered to spare the villagers. Surprisingly the Germans did not execute the OSS men but rather passed them through a series of POW camps. They eventually reached Marlag-Milag Nord, a POW camp near Bremen. All survived the war.

Ortiz received the Navy Cross for his original mission in early 1944, and a Gold Star in lieu of a second Navy Cross. His citation honored him as he "disregarded the possibility of escape and, in an effort to spare villagers severe reprisals by the Gestapo, surrendered to the sadistic Geheime Staats Polizei."

The French bestowed on him la Chevalier of the Legion d'Honneur and awarded him the croix de guerre with palm. He was honored by Great Britain who gave him Officer of the Most Excellent Order of the British Empire.

OSS operatives were needed to gather intelligence on German troop strength in designated areas of Allied landings in Southern France—operation DRAGOON. Jean D'Errecalde, an American of French parentage, parachuted into France in early July, 1944. He was soon arrested by the Gestapo. Fortunately he did not know the date of the landings although it is not known if he broke under torture.

Lt. Geoffrey M. T. Jones was designated to take his place. Jones had lived in the Provence region of France for many years. His home was not far from the place where the Allies were scheduled to land. He spoke French fluently. After his graduation from Princeton he went into the 111th Airborne. Later he learned of the strange OSS and applied for a transfer which was granted. It was a difficult decision to let Jones go into France. He knew too much about the invasion plans and the entire OSS mission at Maison Blanche. Jones pressed for permission to go. There was no doubt he was the best qualified.

Permission was finally granted and he dropped into familiar territory and quickly got together with the Maquis and partisans. He had only a few days to organize his people. He moved to Mont de Malay from where he could view the entire coast north to San Remo in Italy and west as far as Toulon and Marseille.

The local people were fiercely anti-German. There were seven gendarmes in the area. Fortunately the Germans allowed them to move about freely. They became Jones' eyes and ears. Five days before D-day Jones and other agents sent the final Order of Battle telling the Allies what support they could count on from the Maquis, the partisans and OSS. Landing troops had been shown a head and shoulders picture of Jones so they would recognize him as they landed.

On the actual morning a low fog hung over the fields. American paratroopers had already been dropped and were moving cautiously through the area. Jones moved equally cautiously as he knew their fingers were on their triggers and they were jittery. On his first attempt to make contact Jones appeared out of the mist in his pun tans looking suspiciously like a Wehrmacht Afrika Corps officer. The American soldiers were in olive drab uniforms. Finally, arms held high, he surrendered to a suspicious sergeant of the 517th Parachute Infantry Regiment. It was the battalion Jones had originally joined in 1942. After answering numerous questions in headquarters he was accepted for what he was. He offered continued help in coordinating his partisans and Maquis with the Allied troops.

As the battle moved inland Jones flopped in a hayloft and got his first sleep in 90 hours.

There were, as always, plots within plots. Spain was a sterling example. The Allies had to face the possibility that Spain might join the Axis. As a belligerent Spain would certainly close the straits of Gibraltar to Allied vessels. The Western Mediterranean would be an Axis pond. German bombers could fly further west and south to attack allied shipping from Spanish bases. An invasion of southern France would be impossible without heavy loss of Allied personnel.

While the Allied high command prepared its countermoves for such a contingency OSS became more aggressive. Plans to overthrow dictator Franco were considered. A natural thought was to eliminate him and put the blame on the Germans. It was dropped. Locations of huge Spanish arms depots that might require destruction were noted. The possibility of Americans in German uniforms to create something unpleasant and disrupt Fascist harmony was considered, then rejected.

And while the deadly watch and wait game continued, OSS activated operation "Bullfight" in Spain. Its cover was the American Oil Mission under the Standard Oil Corporation.

In April, 1942, the first two SI agents arrived in Lisbon and

Madrid under State Department cover. As oil attachés they were to divide their time between noting the use of fuel supplied to Spain by the Allies, the rest of their time to intelligence. OSS agents had to watch the Germans, the Spanish police and Falange and another source, American Ambassador Hayes. He considered espionage against a "friendly" country to be "un-American." The agent heading over from Washington was advised, that he would probably have more trouble keeping under cover from Americans than from the Gestapo.

Hayes found fuel to further complain of covert operations when two OSS agents were arrested and jailed by the Spanish in mid-1943 for dealing in the black market. They were buying European currency for future OSS operations. Using this as proof that his authority was being undermined he demanded withdrawal of the OSS from the entire Iberian Peninsula. While he was unsuccessful he did gain some concessions. He was granted the right to censor all communications of OSS and authority to approve all agents hired and all contracts and operational plans. But this new authority also worked both ways. Without intending to or even realizing it, Hayes made himself an accomplice of the covert operations.

These restrictions severely hampered SI and MO operations. The agents in place were forced to maintain a low profile.

About the same time OSS agents in Portugal made a major mistake. Not knowing America already had cracked the Japanese code they entered the Japanese embassy and stole a copy of their codebook. Upon discovery of the theft the Japanese immediately changed their ciphers. For too long a period of time America was without knowledge of what the Japanese were doing. The Joint Chiefs of Staff were irate. In this instance the rivalry between various branches of the armed forces was basically to blame. No one had bothered to inform OSS that we were already reading the Japanese code.

A second mistake was made by an OSS agent in Morocco who sent some of his communist agents into Spain without telling the American Embassy in Madrid.

Donovan continued defending his men even in their mistakes. His statement, "I'd rather have a young lieutenant with guts enough to disobey an order than a colonel too regimented to think and act for himself," endeared him to his men but would never find its way into West Point thinking.

By October, 1944, twenty agents had been sent in under private cover. In eight short months agents detailed information of extreme value should military action be necessary against Spain. Updated maps of roads, bridges and airfields, together with photographs, were sent back via the diplomatic pouch. Even samples of sand were sent back from the beaches for possible beach landings. Over 1,000 maps of France and the Iberian Peninsula were made available. They included plans of important cities, aerial photographs, hydrographic maps and some highly secret military fortification plants.

After the North African invasion many Frenchmen found their way into Spain and from there to North Africa to join the Free French in fighting the Germans. OSS in Spain set up a small shipping operation to support their operations in North Africa. They were carrying cargo between Barcelona and Cadiz or Huelva. The ships were rust buckets and had frequent maintenance problems that ruined many schedules. The crews, undoubtedly loyal, had no idea of security. As a result the Spanish police soon learned of this operation and in due time arrested and imprisoned two "directors."

Operation "Aquitaine" was set up in Toulouse. It infiltrated agents over the Pyrenees into Spain. As might be expected the Basques were most cooperative bringing in valuable information on Spanish operations. In one case they advised that the Germans were secreting economic assets in Spain.

In Portugal and Spain tungsten smuggling was uncovered, then stopped. From within Spain came information that enabled a British submarine to sink a German ship loading at a secret port near Bilboa.

X-2 agents arrived in Lisbon in November, 1943. During the negotiations for this, Ambassador Hayes agreed to the establishment of X-2 offices in Spain.

Corruption played its part in the OSS scheme. The Spanish control officer at one of the most important points of entry into Spain from France sold information on important German agents and their missions. His information was excellent as the Germans carried letters of identification which he was required to see. OSS was pleased to add him to their payroll.

Taking a more aggressive position in Morocco, agent Donald Downes went to London to confer with Dr. Juan Negrin who was formerly the President of the Spanish Republic. It was Negrin's opinion that if Franco joined the Axis a strong partisan movement could be launched. The plan was enjoined by Major Arthur Goldberg in Washington. Downes sent an advance team by boat into Malaga in southern Spain. They were to find whatever was left of the Republican underground.

When Downes returned to Morocco information was already coming back from the Malaga team. He then sent a second team of agents to Cadiz and a third team was planned for Cartagena. Malaga asked for some supplies and additional personnel. When these were ready for shipment Downes went to the British to arrange for shipment. The Admiralty in London torpedoed the shipment saying no British ships were to take secret agents into Spain.

Knowing his men in Spain needed the shipment Downes acted in typical OSS fashion and decided to fashion his own "navy." He obtained a fishing vessel, some rowboats and landing craft. His point of debarkation was a small sandy beach on the narrow corridor between Algeria and the Spanish zone. Its garrison consisted of Spanish Republican naval officers and OSS men. But it was too late. The Malaga people waiting on the beach had caught the eye of the pro-German Spanish police. The Spanish had already infiltrated the underground people with whom OSS was dealing. Later Downes' Spaniards met with the Republicans and the police struck. Downes' agents were either killed or captured. The booty recovered by the Spanish included American equipment including plastic explosives, sten guns and other armaments. Under torture the agents named Downes and Arthur Goldberg as the Americans who had recruited them.

As expected the Spanish angrily protested to Ambassador Hayes. The incident became a storm in Washington. Major Goldberg was called into the office of the Secretary of State for an explanation. By agreement with Donovan he denied any knowledge of the actions. It didn't calm the storm.

Finally Donovan said that Downes' actions had been approved in advance by Mark Clark's intelligence division as a security measure. This and sufficient apologies finally put the matter to rest diplomatically. In the prisons of Spain, however, several Spanish Republicans died a slow painful death at the hands of the Spanish Gestapo.

The OSS Barcelona station watched enemy agents closely. They were charged with watching enemy traffic over the Pyrenees and controlling double-agents who worked between Spain and France. Eventually X-2 files listed at least 3,000 enemy agents, 600 suspects and 400 officials of enemy undercover services. Forty five of the latter were under X-2 control. Some highly placed officials of the Spanish Police and of the *Servicio de Information Militar* had been converted to a "more cooperative attitude" by SI.

In addition two invasions of Europe were planned by the Allies. One from the north, the other from the south. OSS-Spain was responsible for the southern attack, termed operation ANVIL. Their objective was to learn if German inquiries indicated a suspicion of the invasion. Also X-2 was to learn all it could of German troop movements into and around the area which would give an indication the enemy had some knowledge of the pending attack.

Of equal importance, BULLFIGHT was charged with discovering Heinrich Himmler's secret agent in Madrid and, if possible, his actual presence should he arrive for consultations. The agents working on the case included a striking young woman. She was 21 year old Aline Griffith from New York who had sought adventure and was taken into OSS. She survived the rugged training schedule and was sent to Madrid via Lisbon. Combining her training, cunning and beauty she worked her way into Madrid society and was invited to the gala parties at some of the villas on the outskirts. She hobnobbed with the enemy all the while posing as an employee of the American Oil Company. She was courted by one of the top bullfighters in Madrid which immediately gained her notoriety and soon she was in competition with some of the beautiful German women serving the German interests. She survived several attempts on her life.

Though operating under the restrictions of Ambassador Hayes, OSS was able to carry out its missions. Operation ANVIL was a complete secret until the minute Allied troops hit the southern beaches.

Communication from the agent in the field was a problem in many ways. One was the frequency of damaged transmitters in the initial drop. One SI desk attempting to put sets into Germany had seven out of twenty-two sets smashed. When this happened the entire mission was worthless since the agents could not send whatever intelligence they had been able to gather.

In the occupied countries it was not too big a problem to drop parts or spare sets. In France the agent transmitted from safe houses and moved his base frequently.

In Germany, however, it was different and presented a major problem. With a hostile population and tight controls it was all but impossible to move the transmission equipment, its necessary code books, aerials and power supply. Wireless transmission signals were easily picked up and the German directional finders were greatly feared.

In the fall of 1944 the solution was found with the invention of the Joan-Eleanor (J-E). This enabled the agent on the ground to talk directly with a plane flying overhead even at an altitude of 30,000 feet. J-E's four pounds and compact size made it ideal for transmission. It used small powerful batteries that eliminated the need for an outside power supply. The high frequency and vertical cone-shaped directivity virtually nullified the advantage of the enemy's directional finders.

To utilize the J-E missions, three British "Mosquitoes" were

252

secured during the Autumn of 1944. The tail sections were remodeled to include oxygen systems, secondary inter-communication, direction indicators and emergency lights. Also provided was space for the J-E operator and his equipment.

The first time the new J-E system was used was in November, 1944 in Ulrum, Holland. From then until VE Day, a total of fourteen J-E teams were sent to Stuttgart, Berlin, Munster, Regensburg, Munich, Landshut, Leipzig, Plauen, Straubing and Bregenz. The majority of these teams were not heard from either because their equipment was smashed in the initial drop or they were captured.

Agent "Bobby" was the first one to parachute into Ulrum. His job was to lay the foundations for an underground railroad which would infiltrate OSS agents from Holland into Germany. Bobby was also supposed to report any intelligence he might incidentally gather. His early contacts were good, revealing German intentions to flood the Polder river, enemy troop movements at Arnhem, direction of water barriers between Ens and Winschoter Diep and the results of Allied air raids on the Gaarkeuken docks.

Early in February the Gestapo picked him up. His subsequent broadcasts were controlled by the enemy. Curiously his capture was not due to a security breakdown or even the German's directional finding equipment. It was due to a mistake in identity and no doubt saved his life.

Convinced Bobby was a traitor a group of Dutch underground workers were on the way to kill him when the Gestapo picked them up. The Dutch had confused him with another Allied agent, also called "Bobby," who was a traitor. When the Germans told Bobby that the Dutch underground was going to kill him he recognized the problem and feigned indignity at such "treachery" and agreed to "help" the Germans.

On February 10, 1945, the Germans began using Bobby under their control. He immediately flashed his prearranged control signal, the frequent use of profanity. He said he did not want any additional assistants and pointed out that the enemy had one of the "other" J-E sets being used by his men. There were no such other sets.

The Germans believed him when he said the Americans would be less likely to believe he was under German control if he broadcast with cautions.

Knowing their agent was in enemy hands the OSS began the standard operation of keeping an agent alive by sending false information with just a touch of truth in it.

In April, the Germans, seeing the handwriting on the wall, sent Bobby back to his lines to open negotiations with OSS for a joint

OSS-Gestapo operation to be directed at penetrating Russia and Japan. Bobby was able to maintain his spirit of cooperation all the while not revealing anything to the Germans they did not already know.

Only four OSS agents were able to report on a regular basis from Germany. They all used the J-E system.

Neutral Sweden and occupied Finland and Norway presented special problems. It was obvious that Sweden needed to be used for gathering information on Germany which depended on her for needed supplies, and also as a base to send agents into Norway and Denmark.

The Finns were an enigma. They considered themselves at war with Russia which had invaded them in November, 1939. In their fight with Russia they considered themselves a co-belligerent with the Germans. In early 1942, the Germans used Finnish territory as a base for operations against Russia. Finland became dependent on German supplies.

Russia put pressure on England and in December, 1941, a reluctant Churchill declared war on Finland. America did not and in fact maintained a legation in Helsinki. It had little effect as Finnish strongman, Marshal Karl Mannerheim and his officials were under strict Gestapo surveillance.

To counteract this, OSS obtained the services of Therese Bonney, a most attractive and energetic American of high social status—particularly in Paris. She was a free lance war correspondent and established a close rapport with Mannerheim when she covered his country's war with Russia.

In June, 1942, she agreed to return to Finland to see her friend, Mannerheim, and see if she could get him to persuade his countrymen to drop ties with Germany. Her cover was that of a correspondent for *Colliers* magazine. While the British did all in their power to delay her trip it was accomplished but only after the British Ambassador in Washington had been called in for a dressing down.

When she arrived in Stockholm she found another enemy—the Gestapo. They had arrested her in occupied France earlier and were not about to let her have free reign in Finland.

Finnish army officers helped her sneak into Helsinki for an appointment with Mannerheim. She was unable to make her point but she did return to Washington with information on the Finnish military posture and German influence within that country.

Before returning to Washington she returned to Stockholm and dropped in on a Foreign Service Officer she had known for years.

254

Without revealing her OSS affiliation she asked his opinion of the OSS organization and its people. The State Department official said, "I can always smell an OSS officer. We never give them any help."

OSS found itself battling the State Department once more. American Ambassador Herschel Johnson regarded the OSS as almost satanic. The SKF Company in Sweden was secretly transporting ball bearings to Germany. When OSS persuaded their employees to launch a strike Johnson threatened to have all OSS personnel declared persona non grata unless the strike was called off. It was.

OSS did continue its operations in Sweden, although judiciously. The OSS man in Stockholm was Calvin Hoover, former economist from Duke University. He had spent several years in Russia earlier and had come away with a strong dislike of the Soviet political system. Seeing the chance to get back at them he began probing into their activities. The Russians had refused to divulge any information about their military forces or capabilities to America or Britain. Hoover was delighted to meet with Finnish military men in Stockholm and purchase the Russian Army's Order of the Battle and the register of the entire Soviet Navy.

Recognizing the delicacy of covert operations against the neutral and friendly Swedish government, Hoover trod lightly. The principal goal of Swedish operations was operating from there into Norway.

There was opposition from the British whose SO,E had been active with the MILORG since the initial German invasion in 1940. But a rift developed between the two groups over possible political ambitions of some resistance leaders. A reconciliation was in the mill when the first OSS operatives appeared. The British considered the timing inopportune and did all they could to keep them out. In late 1943, a pact was reached with the British that allowed an OSS mission, "Westfield," into northern Norway. The British felt this would not interfere with their operations.

Even with this new pact the British continued their obstructionist tactics. The Americans were denied permission to fly their unmarked aircraft off of British fields into the Norway area of operations. Negotiations were stalled until it went to Churchill personally for his permission. In June, 1944, the drop of hundreds of tons of supplies and weapons into Norway began.

Towards the end of 1944, OSS decided to send an operational group into Norway to disrupt German railway shipments and troop movements. Again there was a problem with the British. The mission was held up for "political considerations." Then the British refused to let RAF planes flown by Norwegian pilots drop the agents.

Out of necessity the drop was finally made by American flight crews who had no experience in such operations. Two of the planes crashed killing ten OSS men. An oversight by SFHQ Air Operations was the problem. Many of the special crews that had flown these unique operations had reached their fifty mission status and been rotated back to America. The replacements were completely untrained for such a mission and SFHQ had not seen to a special training program. On top of that the weather conditions close to the Arctic Circle were at their worst at that time of the year.

The group commander, William Colby, and nineteen of his men including Lieutenants Farnsworth and Strather were forced to operate with meager supplies. Some of their badly needed containers had not been hooked properly to their chutes and free dropped to their destruction. Others were dropped off course—in neighboring Sweden.

After the Americans had blown their first bridge and some of the track the Germans began a vigorous pursuit. It was late April when the Germans were trying to organize their withdrawal from Norway. Their 400,000 troops could prolong the war on the continent and Colby was determined to keep them in Norway.

Colby advised he was going to dig in at a small village and hold it. SFHQ was brief and adamant in its reply. "No."

Colby was equally adamant. He knew he was on the firing line, not the SFHQ man secure in his headquarters. "I am here, I know what I am doing. I know I can do it, the resistance wants me to do it, and I intend to do it," he sent defiantly.

London replied simply that Colby had his orders and was expected to obey or face disciplinary action upon his return. It was resolved—several days later—when the Germans surrendered *en masse* and the agents had the honor of accepting the surrender of hundreds of thousands of German troops. Colby received the Silver Star for "gallantry in action." His disobedience of orders that would have brought a court martial in the regular army was overlooked by OSS.

The resistance in Denmark remained under British control which had been established prior to the arrival of OSS. The Westfield mission carried out sabotage and espionage and maintained the only clandestine boat service bringing in agents, supplies and messages. Attacks on the railroads were especially effective in January and February, 1944. Eight saboteurs attacked the Charlottenlund factory making V-2 radio parts. They damaged it so severely it was abandoned.

In October air assistance was needed for a serious problem. The Gestapo had been taking a heavy and deadly toll of agents, especially in the Jutland area. Their counter-intelligence was excellent. At the request of agents in the field 26 Mosquito bombers roared in just above the tree tops and attacked the Gestapo and Sicherheitsdienst headquarters in Aarhus to destroy the files on resistance activities. The headquarters were demolished and 150 German Gestapo and counter-espionage officers were killed. Similar operations were repeated at Copenhagen in March and at Odense in April. As was the case in DET 101's deadly fight against the Japanese in Burma, this use of closely coordinated air power was of critical importance for the OSS in the Danish operations.

12

On June 27, Eifler's 38th birthday, he left for Washington and his new assignment. He learned his father-in-law, CPO Millard Kern, was in New York and headed for overseas duty. He requested that Kern's C.O. give him a three-day pass that they might spend some time together. It was granted. On the day the two got together Eifler was in New York addressing a group of three hundred from the CAP. Kern entered the room during his address. Eifler excused himself, walked to the back of the room, and brought Kern forward to be introduced. He tried to introduce Kern as his father-in-law, but the sight of a full colonel with his arm around a CPO brought gales of laughter, and he got no further then the word "father." After the talk they began a train trip to Washington, D.C. As "junior member" of the group, Kern was told he had to be responsible for all luggage and the briefcase. He departed in one cab with his luggage, and Eifler followed with Curl and Richmond in another cab. Kern made the train, but the other men did not see him and thought he missed it. Eifler called ahead to Frazee to meet the train just in case they had missed him. He did meet Kern and took him to the preselected hotel. Kern was jubilant. He chided Eifler for not being able to handle himself and getting the details all fouled up. Eifler said little.

Kern had been former heavyweight champ of the Pacific Fleet. When Eifler had married his daughter, he had made it clear that the first time they met Eifler would get a few lumps. Within twenty-four hours of that first meeting they did indeed each exchange lumps, although it was not done in anger or hatred. Each of them simply had to test the other. Now the scene was years later. They each had several drinks. Without a word being spoken they drifted to the center of the hotel room, removed rings, watches, and ties, and began once more slugging it out. It was already agreed they would stop when first blood was drawn. Kern was in his early fifties, Eifler about fifteen years his junior. In addition, Eifler had just come from years of strenuous physical training and activity. It didn't take long for Eifler to knock him down. Kern bounded up, threw a few more punches, and soon was knocked down again. Four times Eifler knocked him down before Kern finally gave up. They laughed, threw their arms around one another, and had a few more drinks.

Two days later Kern had to return to his ship, and the men exchanged handshakes. Kern left for his overseas assignment. Eifler went back to his new mission.

It was to be known as "Napko." The OSS men who had been recruited and trained for the kidnapping plot would constitute the nucleus of the Napko project. In addition, Korean natives were needed to implement the plan. The penetration would come from Korea. Eifler knew the majority of Koreans hated the Japanese and would be only too glad to help in any way possible. He also knew there were some traitors in that occupied territory as in all other enemy-occupied countries.

Actually it was almost as if Eifler's original plan had been given back to him. In the beginning he had anticipated entering China and from there penetrating Japan. Now it was to be from Korea.

He brought back agent Alex from the Orient and put him in Camp McCoy, a POW camp for Koreans. Eifler had okayed his plan of bringing the "escapees" from that compound into OSS. The adjutant general and the camp commander were to be the only two who knew Alex's true identity. The escapees had to be officially reported to the Swiss Red Cross in accordance with international law.

When Alex reported suitable candidates to the commander, they were removed to the hospital for some health problem. From the hospital they were transferred to the Sherman Hotel in Chicago. They remained there for several days while their passports were being prepared. What they did not know was that they were also undergo- ing further scrutiny. Their rooms were bugged. After their short stay, and approval, they were flown to Los Angeles, put into the Biltmore Hotel, also bugged, and transferred to Catalina Island, where their training was to begin in earnest.

The recording equipment was giving Eifler problems. It was designed to begin recording when someone talked and stop when the voices did. It was not doing its job. A specialist in the East was sent for. He was overheard telling someone of his ordeal. "I never saw anything like it. I'm flown into Los Angeles where a car whisks me to Newport Beach. Then a boat takes me to Catalina Island where a jeep picks me up and takes me to a large building. A full colonel is cooking, a major is washing dishes, and a bunch of lieutenants are sitting around asking when the coffee will be ready."

The specialist was immediately returned to the East when he could not solve the problem. Eifler had a long-time friend, Margaret Turner, whose brother-in-law was interested in recording equipment. He decided to put the problem to him. He was P.O. 2/C Dave Bronson of the Coast Guard. To each problem presented he had the irritating habit of replying: "Elementary."

"Okay, if it's so goddamned elementary, let's go solve it," Eifler told him.

True to his word, he solved the problem at once. Eifler then wanted him flown to Washington, D.C., to work with Major Huston, now back from Burma. The coast guard said no. Only officers flew. Eifler unraveled that problem in a hurry. He instructed Frazee in Washington to transfer him from the coast guard into the army at the same rank. The problem was a bit complex, and they had to go through both the secretaries of the navy and the army to get it accomplished, but in short time he was in the army. How he explained the switch in services to his wife without telling her what was going on must have been one of the war's more interesting stories.

Another hotel was utilized for the transfer of the Koreans. It was the Palace Hotel in San Francisco. An office was also set up in Los Angeles with Aitken in charge. The only other office was one in Washington, D.C., which Frazee commanded. Eifler worked between the two and the training camps on Catalina where Curl was stationed. The head of security at the Biltmore was a former Los Angeles police captain whom Eifler knew from earlier days. He also had run into a man he had known in Hawaii, Coast Guard Admiral Towl. To the chief of police in Los Angeles he confided his plans of having his Korean agents penetrate the Los Angeles harbor with a two-man submarine.

"What about the FBI?" was his astounded inquiry.

"I'll just take my chances with them," he replied. "If either of you hear of my men being captured, please let me know.'

Admiral Towl shook his head slowly. "Only you, Eifler, would dream of such a stunt."

While none of the men were captured entering the harbor, some were discovered.

One unit set up its transmitting equipment on the roof of the Los Angeles Biltmore. They would beam their message to an overhead airplane or to their special radio station in the state of Washington, just south of the Canadian border. Their messages would then be relayed to other units in the southern California area. This was to familiarize them with sending and receiving to and from stations fifteen hundred miles distant. The security officer at the Biltmore discovered them one day and made his report to Eifler. For all intents and purposes, this unit had been discovered and would have been dead—had it been in enemy territory.

Another unit with three Koreans was sent into the San Diego area. They checked into a hotel and proceeded on their mission to set

260

up a radio site near Balboa Park. They rode the streetcar to the park and walked through it into the most heavily wooded section. Here they set up their small site. Their equipment included the telegraphic key and a hand generator. They did not check the area carefully, unfortunately, for their little station was set up just two hundred yards from a U.S. Army communications center. It was time to make radio contact, and they proceeded. One agent worked the key, while another straddled the little stool-like bench and worked the hand generator at a steady pace. The third agent stood apart, watching for intruders.

From behind all three men stepped an army captain from the communications center. He viewed the scene with amazement. Their transmission had been picked up immediately. He walked over to the one Korean and said: "What's going on here?"

The man sending did not break rhythm, nor did he turn around. He waved his hand behind him as if to shoo off the intruder. The captain then walked over to the third Korean, who had turned around to see what was going on. "What are you doing here?" he repeated.

"I watch," was the simple reply.

"Get the hell out of here," the captain said. He then turned back to the other two men, taking out his .45 automatic. The third man wisely disappeared into the bush as his two comrades were put under arrest.

As soon as he could, the Korean called the one phone number he had been given. It connected him with one of the OSS officers. He told what had happened.

"What are your next instructions now?" he was asked.

"Clear out room and move," was the unhesitating reply.

"Then do so and go to your next contact point."

He immediately complied and moved to an area in north San Diego where he was picked up.

By now the FBI had the two Koreans and could get nothing out of them except a phone number. It was the OSS lieutenant again. Yes, he knew the two men. They were employees of the U.S. government. He would give only that information plus his name, rank, and serial number.

"Lieutenant, who is your superior officer?" they asked.

They were referred to Major Bob Aitken. Aitken gave them his name, rank, and serial number and confirmed the Koreans were employees of the U.S. government.

"Major Aitken, who is your commanding officer?"

"He is Colonel Carl Eifler," Aitken replied.

"Where can I get in touch with him?"

"Somewhere in the Washington, D.C. area."

At the time Eifler was sitting beside Aitken in the Los Angeles office but saw no reason to get involved. So far as Eifler knew, the FBI never pursued the matter. No doubt they did check with Washington and found out Eifler was OSS and decided that explained the whole thing.

Special equipment was being investigated by Eifler. One involved getting the men ashore. There was a nylon inflatable boat that was to be attached to the agent's back. The agents would be released from a submerged submarine, float to the surface, and inflate their boat. Another special boat was designed with an extremely low profile to avoid radar detection. It had a hundred-mile radius and could be released by a sub fifty miles at sea. The boat would then take its load in, and one man would return in it to the sub, which would resurface at a given time. The students had to have Japanese glasses and clothing of Korean or Japanese manufacture. Once ashore, they would have to bury their radio sets and other identifying equipment until they had established safe bases.

Two listening posts were to be established, one in North China and the other in the Philippine Islands. The possibility of failure of the listening posts' equipment had to be taken into consideration, and it was felt that two, in opposite directions, would take care of such an eventuality. It would also take care of atmospheric conditions that might prevent transmission.

The Napko plan called for ten groups to go into Korea. They would differ as to specific goals. Of the ten groups, it was estimated seven would make it, the other three be caught. Of the seven that got into operation, one would soon prove to be the most successful. That would be the one into which OSS would immediately pour all its effort and support.

July was now past, and the heat of August made itself felt in Southern California. Eifler was going over plans and reviewing the personnel who had completed their training. Napko, he had decided, must first begin its espionage and establish its rhythm of violence against Japan. Then the final phase would come—the fomentation of a revolution to tie up Japanese troops, disrupt their communications, and prevent troops from leaving Manchuria to return to Japan. Intelligence reports from Korea were exiguous. Much of the information on hand was that which Eifler himself had relayed through the confessional booth of Chungking. There was a leading businessman with a string of pharmacies throughout the country who had made known his willingness to serve. He would be invaluable since his stores would give him reason to travel.

Eifler did not want to get tied down to Korea in a series of guerrilla and intelligence operations such as his DET 101 had done. He was anxious to get into Japan as soon as possible. A strong organization first had to be established on the Korean peninsula, he realized. The more problems the Japanese could suffer there, the better his chances in Japan. He had decided on personally going ashore from the two-man submarine, to be launched from its mother ship. Already the plan had gone from OSS Washington to the U.S. Navy for their opinion and approval. America had no such craft. It was necessary to build one, and work was already under way. The cost was $20,000.

From continual research, investigation, and analysis, Eifler was preparing a manual for Napko. It contained charts of the coastlines, photographs, natural obstacles, tides, topography, average temperatures, and a host of other information. Through August, September, and October he assembled a plan that was to be nearly three inches thick. It included costs down to the last spoon. It was presented in Washington to the Planning Commission. The commission included a general officer of the chief of staff, an admiral, another army general, and an OSS representative. After the presentation, the admiral sat back and said: "Colonel, this plan you have just presented makes every other plan we have seen just a scheme." It was fully accepted.

It was at this time that the news officially broke that General Stilwell was being recalled from China. He was to be replaced by General Wedermeyer. Chiang Kai-shek had finally won out over Stilwell and General Marshall. Visits to China had been made by former presidential candidate Wendell Wilkie and Ambassador Patrick Hurley. Many Americans winced when Hurley arrived. He enjoyed giving out with Texas war whoops and referred to Mao Tse-tung as "old moose dung." The war was something Stilwell was capable of fighting. Intrigue and double-dealing were beyond him because he did not care to stoop to them. He stated exactly what his thoughts were, but this was not the way of the Orient.

Eifler felt deep sorrow for his friend. He knew what it must have done to this man who tried so hard to do what was best for his country and, of course, for China. He knew Stilwell would first come to Washington, D.C., and from there it was anyone's guess where he would be headed. Eifler would not be able to see him in Washington, as he had to return to the West Coast. He looked forward to sitting down with him once more to discuss not only the problems of the CBI theater but getting his advice on Eifler's new mission. Eifler still considered him a military genius, indeed he felt his ability to keep

China afloat was proof of that. After all, he had his biggest problems with the Chinese government and many Americans. The Japanese at times were almost welcome adversaries. At least they were supposed to be his enemies.

Eifler flew to San Francisco to visit with a man he had worked with in earlier years. While there, he ran into Leo Stanley, who was now a commander in the U.S. Navy. Many years had passed, and much had happened since they had parted. They met in Eifler's hotel room. Stanley had been hospitalized for a fungus of the lungs he had picked up while stationed on Guam.

Eifler told him as much as he felt he should about his work. Then he posed one of his point-blank questions.

"Leo, I am working on a unit now that is going to penetrate Japan directly. I have several other men with me that I worked with before the war. I selected them because they have the talents I need. So do you. Would you like to join my unit?"

Stanley said nothing. He picked up a drink, turned, and walked over to the window. For a long time he stared thoughtfully into the San Francisco night. Eifler said nothing to interrupt his thoughts. Finally he turned and walked back to his chair. "Carl, I've made it a point to never work for a man who once worked for me—but in your case I'm going to break it. Yes, I'll be glad to join you."

They shook hands, smiling. Eifler was pleased with this new addition to Napko.

In short order Stanley was appointed as head of intelligence for the unit and filled in on the project to date.

There was a silence from Stilwell that disturbed Eifler. He had tried to communicate with the General but without success. It was reported that he was returned to Washington, D.C., practically under guard. He was not allowed to talk to the press. Ranking American generals failed to meet him, and he had been hustled to officers' quarters at a remote base. His trip to Washington and thence to his Carmel home was made with accompanying MPs and instructions not to talk.

In late November, Eifler secured an appointment with him in his Carmel home. The day was overcast, and a fog appeared waiting only a few more hours before descending into the little valley. The two men happily greeted each other at the front door and went inside. A fire crackled in the living room, and they sat down to catch up on much that happened since they last had met some five months ago.

Stilwell felt betrayed by President Roosevelt. To him, there was no doubt Chiang had pulled the rug out from under him. General Marshall had continued his best efforts to back Stilwell, but it was too late. The election, now concluded, could have been influenced strongly had Stilwell returned to speak as bluntly as he was known to. Stilwell's return had been arranged for the day after the election. All that he had worked for and hoped for was past. Now he sought a division he could lead in combat in Europe—anywhere. General Boatner had been told by Roosevelt that the White House informed Chiang he should take over all of Indochina right after the war. The reason he gave was simple: he, Roosevelt, said the French had forfeited their right to rule by neglect. Knowing Chiang could not rule his own nation, Stilwell shook his head sadly.

There were stories that brightened the day, also. They both roared with laughter as Eifler recounted two more stories he had heard of his fighting priest, Father Stuart. The good Father was visiting an American army hospital. He was in a plain khaki uniform with nothing to designate what he was. All present, however, well knew who and what he was. The American nurses decided to have some fun with him. He was sitting on an army cot when one of the nurses walked in, and sat down as close to him as she could get. He looked a little bewildered and continued talking, but moved slightly away. She promptly moved with him. He continued edging sideways, always accompanied by the nurse. Finally he was at the edge and could go no farther. He couldn't figure it out. She leaned over and kissed him soundly. He continued with his discussion, and finally time came to leave. He stood and headed toward the door, then stopped and turned around to speak.

"As all of you know, I am a priest. We are under oath of poverty and not supposed to accept anything. This young lady has given me a kiss. I must return it."

He walked over, planted a Hollywood kiss on the nurse, and walked out.

Later on, after part of north Burma had been cleared of the Japanese, Father Stuart and Father MacAlindon were in a jeep just above Sumprabum. The two had been conducting business with the natives of that area and also partying a bit—both with the natives and with some American personnel. A bit of native wine had been consumed, plus some American bottled spirits. Father Stuart had told the story himself.

"As we were driving up the narrow dirt road, I noticed we seemed to be weaving back and forth quite a bit. I calmly remarked to Father MacAlindon that his driving seemed a bit erratic. The good Father said: 'But Father Stuart, you are driving.' So I looked down and, sure enough, I was."

Of far more importance to the two officers was the war and their new roles. Stilwell had been told he was to be given command of the armies invading Japan. With Eifler's mission to penetrate Japan, it appeared the two would be working together once more. Neither spoke of the danger involved in Eifler actually landing in Japan. Stilwell walked over to a long oak table and picked up a rolled map. He walked to the middle of the living room, knelt down, and spread the map out. It was a military map of Japan and surrounding areas, including Korea, Manchuria, and Russia. Eifler dropped down beside him, and soon both were lying flat on their stomachs examining the enemy islands. With pencils they probed harbors and shorelines. Stilwell spoke first concerning Eifler's actual mission.

"What are your immediate plans, Eifler?"

Eifler pointed at Korea. "To land in Korea and from there penetrate Japan proper."

Stilwell, the supreme strategist, looked at Eifler and said, "take this into consideration...the Russians will be coming in. When they do the Japs will move north from Manchuria to cut the rail lines to Vladivostok and then take that city as it is the geographical center of the sphere of influence of Japan. When they take Vladivostok they will be free to move their troops to Japan for defense of their homeland. At this time a revolution in Korea would not only prevent free movement of troops back to Japan but tie up troops to control the revolution. Take this into consideration in your plans."

Eifler quickly digested this and knew it would somewhat alter his plans and timetable.

"How far are you with your plan, Carl?" asked Stilwell.

"We are well into the training on Catalina. My officers are all selected, and the unit is complete insofar as the T/O is concerned. General Donovan has taken the plan to Admiral Nimitz for the use of a submarine to put me in Korea."

"How soon do you plan on this?"

"I would estimate a good six months more."

They stood up. Stilwell put his hand on Eifler's shoulder. "I wish my plans were more definite, Carl. I don't know from one day to the next just where in hell I'm to be. I envy you."

They walked to the door and together looked at the rapidly lowering fog. They shook hands again, and Eifler left to reconsider his plans with these new thoughts from his friend.

In December another OSS group was also put on Catalina. Its mission, while dealing with the Far East, had nothing to do with Eifler's mission.

Training schedules were set to prevent the two groups from colliding with each other on training missions. One of the members of the new group was Captain Clair Weeks who knew Catalina well. Before the war he cruised the island regularly on his 36 foot sailing cutter. He knew the coves and bays but was unfamiliar with the rugged interior. He was to learn that part very well.

Weeks had taken his training at Area F, then traveled by rail to Los Angeles for his new assignment at the "secret west coast training center." He went to the San Juan Capistrano Beach Club in Orange County which processed OSS personnel. His next stop was Toyon Bay in Catalina.

His group of 35-40 men came from various military branches but also included some civilians, and a few foreigners.

The training focused on potential assignments to S.E. Asia, Burma, China, Thailand, Malaya and Indochina. As an MO officer, Weeks received special training in psychological warfare, propaganda (both black and white), radio programming and broadcasting, script writing, preparation of posters and leaflets and other kinds of disinformation.

The main training program concentrated on Secret Intelligence (SI) and Operational Groups (OG) with the later addition of the Maritime Unit (MU) operations.

The training calendar included weapons training, demolitions with plastic explosives, prima-cord and time delayed detonators. There was close combat with knife fighting, the art of stealthy approach for killing with a knife or by snapping a victim's neck with bare hands or special blackjacks.

The course ended with a three day survival skills exercise. The trainees were to live off the land with only a knife and fishing line. At least one of the trainees was rumored to have infiltrated into Avalon in search of food. When their training was completed, the group left Toyon Bay shortly after Christmas that year.

Napko continued training its Koreans.

The new year arrived and with it a growing string of victories and advances for the Allied armies. MacArthur's island-hopping in the Pacific was leaving hundreds of thousands of Japanese troops cut off and with limited supplies. Eifler carefully followed all news he could get on his former command, DET 101. The newspapers gave little information, but Eifler was able to glean many facts from returning 101 personnel. The guerrillas were now into the southern Shan and Karen states in units of one hundred to three hundred men each. Commanding them were Lieutenants Powers, Coussoule, Conley, Martin, West, Hansen, Larum, Truex, Meade, Pangborn, Poole, Romanski, Stein, Wright, Brophy, Milton, both Pamplin brothers,

Burma Sam (Maj. Saw Dhee Htu), and Lieutenants Scott and Weld, who had transferred over from the Marauders along with Captain Brunstad. Also included in the striking forces were thirty-five enlisted men. A great many of the men were unknown to Eifler, having come in after he had left for his new missions.

The two-man submarine was completed, and, true to his word, Eifler began penetrating the Los Angeles harbor. Not only did the strange craft penetrate the Los Angeles and San Pedro areas, it was also active off the coast of Orange County. In some instances it would land agents on Newport Beach or San Clemente. They would then proceed to the coast highway where they would be picked up or hitch a ride to their destination. In other training missions they penetrated as far as Santa Ana and Anaheim before being picked up. The good people of sleepy Orange County were no more aware of their invasion by "OSS spies" than were the citizens of Los Angeles cognizant of the fact their Biltmore Hotel was bugged, playing host to spies, and harboring illegal transmitting equipment on its roof.

In the many missions of the two-man sub against California, there were no problems and no Korean was ever captured or questioned. Clearly, the Koreans were ready to land in their own country now.

One unit was named "Einec." This unit was to penetrate the Korean west coast, about twenty miles from Seoul. It would primarily report on economic conditions and the Japanese units that were there. Five agents—A, B, C, D, and E—would compose the group. A was the pharmacist with his stores throughout the city. B, C, and D had a good background in farming, and this would be an excellent cover for them. While the Japanese had an extensive identification system on farm workers, the unit's designated area was heavily agricultural, and they felt it would be easier to mix in that way. It was also known the Japanese did not have dossiers on B, C, and D, which would be important if they were interrogated. For substitute covers they adopted occupations of woodcutters and fishermen. E also was from the Seoul area and had friends there. The plan had photographs of the Korean littoral where the men would land.

"Charo" plan involved agents A, B, and C. This group needed physical alterations such as glasses, dental work, moles removed, and even minor surgery to correct nervous blinks and concave noses. This group would enter yet another area, as would eight other units. All faced similar problems.

The next big step was introduction of Korean agents into Japan proper. There were over 2 million Koreans impressed into labor forces in the Yokahama-Kobe-Yasaka manufacturing districts. In addition, a large number of Koreans had been assigned to farms as laborers to replace Japanese men in the service. The opportunity to penetrate lay with these large numbers of Koreans who would have even more reason to hate their Japanese masters.

Whichever way the men were eventually introduced into Korea and Japan could serve as a reverse corridor for bringing out scientists, politicians, and military leaders of value to the Allied cause. As in Burma, it was also assumed a great number of downed Allied pilots would be rescued and returned to safety. The lessons learned in Burma and China would be of great help.

The voluminous report on Korea was constantly updated with fresh information. Planes flying on bombing raids from China to Japan were making aerial photos of coastal approaches that could be utilized both in Japan and in Korea. The U.S. Navy was making daring approaches via submarine and contributing information. The administration and training were part of the overall job, but Eifler was a man of action and longed to get back into the thick of it. Through March and April a plan was considered involving a small group nearly ready to penetrate Korea. This was dubbed the "Mooro" plan. To report how strongly he felt about this group and its readiness, Eifler sent a secret order on May 1, 1945, to General Donovan. Its points were:

1. Enclosed is a copy of the preliminary report of Mooro plan. The original of this plan has been sent forward to Washington office and will reach you through official channels.

2. I consider this plan so important that I wanted to acquaint you with the general outline immediately. This group was originally contacted with the idea in mind of having them take over an island off the coast of Korea. This island has been decided upon. It is inhabited by about 18 people, whom we believe can be converted to our ideas. If they cannot they will be eliminated and the island will become one of our first bases in our chain of smuggling.

3. While working on this plan it was determined that one of the members knew of a possible landing site in North Korea. After the possibilities of this landing site were investigated it looked so good that about six of the American officers of this unit have requested permission to accompany the agent when he is dropped in. I believe that it is so near what we have been looking for that I should not hesitate at all in accompanying this agent.

4. Present plans indicate that I shall need two more schools, making a total of five schools, with necessary per-

sonnel. The fourth should be ready by June 15 and the fifth not later than July 1.

5. It is requested that your permission be given for these schools and that orders be issued authorizing the necessary personnel as camp complement and instructors.
/s/ Carl F. Eifler
Colonel, Infantry

Meanwhile, in Europe OSS activities increased. Far from the destruction and confusion of bombing, the delightful town of Innsbruck, Austria was nestled high in the Alps. It was a place of rest and recreation for German troops. Its Offizierkasino was used by members of the 106th High Alpine Troops.

On the night of April 3, 1945, a small group listened in total boredom to an army engineer, in his cups, talk of his recent service in Berlin. Among them was First Lieutenant Frederick Mayer. At first glance Mayer was all he seemed to be in his grey German uniform. Actually he was considerably more. He was an American, he was Jewish and he was an OSS agent.

The evening ended and Mayer retired to his room where he wrote out a message for military intelligence. It was picked up by a courier and taken to the OSS radio operator in a small village called Oberperfuss nearby. Mayer was a German national who had fled with his parents from Freiburg, Germany in 1938. His father was deeply troubled, having served honorably in the German Army in the first World War, but unwilling to face the persecution the Jews were subjected to.

Arriving in America, Fred Mayer had gone to work in a Ford plant. After Pearl Harbor he enlisted and was with the Rangers when OSS tapped him because of his background. While a friend described him as a man whose "fear nerve is dead," Mayer felt no deep hatred for the Nazis. In particular his analysis indicated he was cunning and possessed of a high spirit. Taken to Bari, Italy, the jumping off point for covert missions, he was teamed with a Dutch Jew, Hans Wynberg and a third man, Franz Weber. They comprised the GREENUP team.

Their area was to be Innsbruck but the problem of finding a suitable drop location was considerable. All of the flat areas were occupied. Finally Mayer recalled a small lake between two mountain peaks that would be frozen over at that time. The air force was disturbed at the hazards dropping between those peaks in winter would entail. Finally one pilot agreed that if these men were crazy enough to jump in that area he would be crazy enough to take them.

Dropping down through a cloud cover the pilot dropped the men at a spot he thought was over the frozen lake. He barely cleared the mountain peaks after the drop. The men were not dropped where intended but rather on a glacial ridge, the Sulztaler Ferner, at a little over 10,000 feet. On the mountain the men searched for the containers dropped with them. They found all but one. The missing one contained their skis. They were forced to plod along in snow sometimes over their waists. Some hours later, totally exhausted, they came upon a lodge that had been established for skiers. It was so far up no one came to it at this time of the year. The men broke in and rested for two days, then moved on.

Their next stop was in the village of Greis. Weber wore the uniform of a German officer, the other two were nondescript uniforms. Could they find transportation to the bottom of the mountain, they asked. They posed as men separated from their units.

The Burgermeister could offer only a sled. Thinking it better than nothing they accepted and began a harrowing three and a half hour trip down the mountain at speeds of up to 60 miles per hour. At the bottom they made their way to Oberperfuss.

Mayer was anxious to get into Innsbruck and start operations. Weber had three sisters there who would help. One of the sisters, Aloisia, produced papers from her hospital job saying Weber was on convalescent leave. He traveled within Innsbruck, his face in bandages so local residents who knew him before would not recognize and compromise him. Webers other two sisters were helpful in leading the GREENUP team to anti-Nazis who were already doing their own subversive work.

Aloisia produced a uniform for Mayer from her hospital. It was the uniform of a lieutenant in the 106th High Alpine Troops. Lacking documents, he simply said the Italian partisans had robbed him of his money, papers and paybook.

The intelligence he secured was good and flowed freely.

During this time another OSS team, POEN, became active. It was comprised of two men, Fritz Molden and Ernst Lemberger, an Austrian Socialist. Molden was young, articulate and brash. Molden had worked with OSS but always wanted his own terms. He wished to be accepted as an Austrian working with Allied authorities, not just an OSS agent. His intent was to have Austria recognized as a subjugated nation and therefore not to be occupied after the war.

On one occasion OSS had asked him to take a female agent into Italy through his underground. Molden was upset that she spoke no Italian and had only one leg. He carried out the request but afterwards complained that on any such other mission the agent must speak the local language and have two legs.

The two men were entirely dissimilar not only in their 18 year age span but also in temperament. On February 16, 1945, they left Switzerland for Milan where they received their new identities, uniforms and papers. Their story was that they were on a secret mission for the Abwehr. On February 25, they arrived in Vienna and began making their contacts and obtaining intelligence. Things went smoothly until a mass meeting in Grinzing, just outside Vienna. The Nazis, alerted to something unusual, moved in. There was a fight with the underground and an SS man was killed. Molden and Lemberger had to flee at once.

On the train a military policeman moved down the aisle checking papers. He examined those of Molden and Lemberger, made a few notes and disappeared. Molden, sensing a problem, said to Lemberger, "we'd better get off at the next station."

Before they reached it, the military policeman approached them and said they were to report to the train commander. Molden was sure the shootout they had just left had compromised them. He advised Lemberger they would have to jump. Before they could do so, the train entered the Vienna Woods. In the dark Molden unsnapped his pistol holster and whispered to Lemberger to do the same. They would at least take some Germans with them.

They were taken through several more cars until they reached the last one. Here, the Captain said he was sorry to inconvenience them but he was understaffed and noticed they were Abwehr. They would have to help check papers of the troops on the first half of the train.

To the highly sensitive and trained men it was an intelligence bonanza. They checked the travel orders and made mental notes of various armored, infantry and artillery units moving from one area to another.

On March 4, 1944, the two men were back in Switzerland. They made their report to Allen Dulles. Included with other details was the fact that many of the conscripted laborers in German industry were not conscripts at all but actually workers who had gone voluntarily to seek employment, including many French. Also the Germans were not nearly as bad off as the Allies thought insofar as food and services went.

Other agents recruited, by OSS fit into various categories, not all good. Two who had been interviewed, then given training, turned out to be possible security risks. They had been taken from a group of Dutch recruits. As part of their training they had been inside the highly secret OSS Grosvenor offices. But the haunting question remained as to their loyalty. Could they be doubles sent in by the Nazis?

So strong was the feeling that they could not be trusted that OSS agreed to dismiss them. But there was the problem as to what could be done with them. The Dutch refused to take them back. The British did not want them. In fact they felt they should be entirely removed from Europe. The solution was typically unique. OSS put the two men on Catalina Island. To further soften their war experiences they were each paid $500.

In Innsbruck Mayer felt his role as a German officer might be wearing out. He decided to join the foreign workers fleeing from the Russian advance. He would be an electrician. With newly forged papers and clothing supplied by one of Weber's sisters he found a job with an anti-Nazi who operated a radio shop and worked for the Germans.

Fate changed the script with the arrest by the Nazis of a small time black market racketeer. He broke down almost with the first slap and said he knew of a high ranking American agent in the area. Within minutes Mayer was arrested and taken to Gestapo headquarters.

At first the questioning was polite. Mayer stuck to his cover story. Slaps were followed by severe beatings till his face became a swollen mass. Sticking to his story of being a French laborer Mayer spoke in French which had to be interpreted for the Germans. It gained valuable time.

The man who had betrayed him was brought in and told Mayer that he had told them everything, it was all over. Mayer knew, however, that that man knew only a small part of the story. Now he switched to German and finally admitted he was an American agent but that he was working alone and had no radio operator. More beatings followed, but he stuck to the story.

Agents had been told to try to hold out for 48 hours if caught. By then their compatriots should have word of the arrest and have cleared out. The 48 hours came and went, but still he did not break his story.

Mayer was stripped and forced to sit on the floor, his knees bent. His handcuffed arms were looped over his knees. Placing a rifle through the triangle formed by his arms and legs he was then turned upside down. He was then bullwhipped. Water was poured into his nose and ears, one of which was ultimately punctured.

After six hours they gave up and dumped him on a bed of straw crawling with vermin. He lay there for twenty four hours, his hands tied behind his back.

Another agent was tortured in a nearby cell. Mayer heard his screams throughout the night. Finally they stopped. He had been tortured to death.

As Mayer took a breather from his brutal captors other forces were at work. One of them involved the Kreisleiter of Innsbruck, leader of the Nazi party, Dr. Max Primbs. For a Nazi he was decent, intelligent and not without compassion. He did, however, accept Hitler as almost God and believed fervently in his leadership. He had practiced medicine earlier.

Primbs had seen the original beatings of Mayer and had asked his captors to go easy on him. It had little effect on Mayer's interrogators.

A strange twist of fortune, caused by the propaganda efforts of both sides, however, did influence Mayer's captors and led to one of the most unusual events of the war.

The game of disinformation along with black propaganda played a major role in the intelligence operations of both the Allies and the Axis. Rumors are always rampant in war time. A piece of disinformation put out by one of the Allies might later be picked up as possible truth by another. Even within a country's own ranks a rumor started by an intelligence organization might well surface in another branch of that same country.

Unwittingly it was an OSS report that created a situation that the Germans were quick to take advantage of.

In September, 1944, the front office of OSS received a report from R & A posing the possibility of the Germans fortifying their Alpine areas for a last ditch stand. Included in that report were intelligence observations that there was military activity underway in some of the more remote mountain areas. Tunnels were being blasted through the mountains. Heavy construction machinery was heard in the area. The blasting could be heard almost all the way into Switzerland.

Within Dulles's headquarters his officers had seen the fortified mountains maintained by the Swiss. Their system of fortresses was most efficient. It didn't need to be pointed out that if the Swiss could do it so could the Germans.

The R & A report added that while the European war would probably end in the middle of 1945 the Germans could hold out in a mountain redoubt and make victory very costly. And it could prolong the war by six months.

The report was actually along the same lines as German thinking. They had considered using the mountains as the place for their last stand—but with only a few troops. The Nazi leaders had proposed to Hitler that they place their troops and seat of government in the alpine area. Here, they felt, they could hold out for a long time. At least sufficiently long to bargain for better armistice terms with the Allies. The R&A report was picked up by the western press who told

274

stories of Hitler's "redoubt" and plans to dig in and prolong the war.

The Germans were doing their usually efficient research and came up with the story out of the western press and made use of the fears of the Allies. They decided the idea of a final redoubt made good sense.

Master propagandist Joseph Goebbels cranked up his machine and leaked several stories about all the construction going on. Top Nazi military leaders, who should have known better, began believing the Goebbels' stories.

The Allies began trying to pinpoint the sources of their intelligence and find the precise area of construction.

In the midst of all the "leaks" from Germany and intense digging by Allied intelligence, the Abwehr "leaked" phony plans and "facts" about the redoubt.

In January, 1945, *Collier's* magazine gave a detailed report on immense caverns, tunnels, special roads and the fact the best of the Hitler youth was being trained for guerrilla work. They were to be termed, "Werewolves."

The usually cautious *New York Times* printed a story by their reporter, Hanson Baldwin, that after the fall of Berlin the Wehrmacht would move its forces south to the *Alpenfestung* or mountain fortress.

There was a division of thinking among OSS ranks. Those agents in Europe began seriously doubting the whole story. But OSS Washington, along with American military leaders, did not.

Differing press reports brought about a report from the Seventh Army's G-2:

> "Himmler had ordered provisions for 100,000 men and the area was to be defended by eighty crack units of from 1,000 to 4,000 men each. Himmler was seeing to it that the best arms Germany could produce were earmarked for the Redoubt and sealed trains bearing armaments were arriving from the Skoda works. Many of these trains were seen to be carrying a new type of gun. Elaborate underground ordnance shops run by hydroelectric power were being built and a report alleged that an aircraft factory capable of producing a 'complete Messerschmitt' was in operation. The terrain would aid the defense and the Nazis could draw upon the Po and Danube valleys, western Czechoslovakia, and the upper Balkans. The Redoubt Center's combat personnel would number between 200,000 and 300,000 veterans of the SS and special mountain troops 'thoroughly imbued with the Nazi spirit' who could expect to fight fanatically to the last man."

In April, 1945, the *Times* once more reported on the *Alpenfestung*. Supposedly it was more heavily fortified than the Monte Cassino where American forces had fought one of the fiercest and costliest battles in Italy. Arguments raged regarding the truth of these reports.

Finally in mid April the American military began siding with OSS Europe in the belief there was no substance to the story. Their thinking was enhanced after surrender discussions with German General Wolf.

Mayer's captors were unwittingly duped by their own Nazi propaganda. A message from OSS Berne had been sent to Washington concerning the construction of the supposed fortifications in the Alps where top Panzer and SS divisions would hold out after Germany's armies were defeated.

The message was intercepted by the Germans and brought to Primbs' superiors who would be interested as Innsbruck sat in the center of this alleged Redoubt. The Germans knew nothing about it.

Primbs and his superior, Gauleiter Hofer summoned Mayer for a discussion. Although they still believed in Hitler they were not stupid men. With the advancing Allied forces in Italy and on German soil they saw the handwriting on the wall. American troops were not far from Innsbruck.

Mayer's painfully swollen face was ignored as they talked. Hofer wanted to discuss the possibility of negotiating for the surrender of his province. Mayer relayed the request to his OSS headquarters.

Following this Mayer was taken back to Reichenau prison. Finding his cell door unlocked he slipped out and found two of his underground contacts waiting for him. It was assumed Primbs had arranged the escape.

And then the startling news reached Mayer that Hofer had decided to heed the request given by Grand Admiral Karl Donitz the day after Hitler's death. He was going to broadcast that Hitler had fallen to save the nations from Bolshevism and Germany would surrender to America and England but never to Russia. The Germans were to fight on.

Mayer went back to see Hofer and argued that further resistance was futile and would only result in many more deaths on both sides.

Hofer agreed to soften his approach with one proviso—that Mayer place him under house arrest until the Americans arrived. This would protect him from the Austrian anti-Nazis. Mayer agreed.

Hofer made his broadcast. There was to be no further resistance. Innsbruck was to be turned over to the Americans.

276

Innsbruck was in an uproar. Mayer went to Oberperfuss to pick up his radioman, Hans Wynberg. They sought out what American uniforms they could find. They roamed the streets of Innsbruck with Austrian patriots and unnerved SS men.

That night, Mayer, Wynberg and Primbs went to Hofer's home to make sure he had not changed his mind on the surrender. They found he had retired for the night. His personal guards, however, wanted to talk. They could not understand the harsh reality of what had happened to them. They were really the victims, not the brutes they appeared. The Poles had started it by killing large numbers of Germans. Hitler's fight was America's fight, and, with his death, war with Russia was inevitable for the Allies. Happily the Germans said they would fight alongside the Americans when that time came.

Mayer and Wynberg, the two American Jews listened in amazement as the Nazis poured forth their troubles and problems, totally insensitive to the horror they had caused. It was a satisfying end to their mission.

The next morning, May 3rd, the American 103rd Infantry Division of the Seventh Army moved towards Innsbruck with orders to take the town.

On the western side of the city the Germans had turned their heavy guns to face the enemy. Both sides were heavily armed and well trained. It promised to be a bloodbath.

Just before five o'clock that afternoon the American troops summoned their intelligence officer Major Bland West to the head of their column. They pointed out a car bearing down on them with two German soldiers standing in it and waving a huge white banner. It approached them.

Major West returned the salute of the driver who now jumped joyfully from the car. He introduced himself as Lt. Fred Mayer of OSS and he had personally come to take the Major back to arrange for the surrender of Innsbruck and the province. Looking at the battered face of Mayer and the flag of truce, actually a bed sheet, White could only shake his head and wonder about the vagaries of war. He was later to be more shocked to find out Lt. Fred Mayer was actually Sgt. Fred Mayer. The German Army in that area had in effect surrendered to an OSS Jewish Sergeant.

Czechoslovakia was an area not penetrated by any Allied intelligence service. Both the British and Americans were greatly hampered by lack of intelligence and ability to use covert methods and sabotage the German war machine. The Russians, the State Department learned, had staked out Eastern Europe and the Balkans as their postwar areas of influence and would not look kindly on any British or American intrusion into those areas.

In 1944, America formally asked Russian permission to deploy "military missions" into Czechoslovakia, Rumania and Hungary. The reason for this mission was to locate and exfiltrate American pilots. Finally in late July, 1944, the Russians agreed. It was all OSS had been seeking.

Under the cover of the "military mission" two OSS teams had been organized, briefed and otherwise prepared. In mid-September the DAWES mission, headed by U.S. Navy Lieutenant Holt Green with Sgt. Joseph Horvath, Slovak interpreter and Pfc Robert Brown, radio operator, proceeded into the eastern part of the country to aid resistance and gather military information.

The western part of Czechoslovakia was assigned to operation HOUSEBOAT commanded by SI Lieutenant John Krizan, the nom de guerre for Czech-born U.S. Army Private John Schwartz, Lt. Jerry Mican as a second SI agent and Navy radioman Sp(X)2/c Charles Heller. They were instructed to go as far into Bohemia as possible to collect intelligence.

On September 17, 1944, the six OSS agents, dressed in military uniforms, boarded three B-17s of the Fifteenth Air Force Special Group at Brindisi. The planes were loaded with arms, ammunition, and medical and food supplies for the partisans. At 0600 the planes took off and slipped into a formation of other American planes headed for a bombing mission elsewhere. Six hours into the flight the three B-17's peeled off from the formation and landed one by one at the abandoned Tri Duby air field. It was six miles from a Luftwaffe base. They were cheerfully greeted by the partisans and a group of fifteen American pilots. The pilots flew out with the returning planes.

In late 1944, a Slovak resistance movement erupted. They had been watching the Russian advance and felt the time right. Two divisions of the Slovak Independent Army slipped their chains and turned their weapons on their German conquerors. Aided by partisans they seized Banska Bystrica and established their own headquarters. Utilizing the local radio station they sent out word the resistance had been stepped up.

Twenty days later six B-17's arrived bringing sixteen more OSS personnel and twenty tons of weapons. This time 28 Allied pilots were evacuated.

The OSS DAWES mission was multi-purpose. The collection of military information was obvious. There was the training of the partisans and to arrange for their needed supplies. There was the

278

need to set up an evacuation unit for Allied pilots and to commence sabotage and covert operations.

Between October 13 and October 20 over 1,000 words per day on German troop disposition and positions were radioed out along with targets for bombing missions.

The Germans were not ignorant of what was going on in the area just south of them. Their commander felt it was time to wipe out all resistance and in the late fall prepared to move against the agents.

Playing the game of chess for real stakes the commander of the first six OSS men radioed for help. Five additional teams had already been trained and were ready. They were sent in with orders to fan out and work with other guerrillas.

Lt. Krizan of HOUSEBOAT was all too aware of how the Communists were tightening their control over the resistance movement. Through promises of supplies and Red Army troops, neither of which ever materialized, they made their presence felt.

Two other agents expressed their concern when they attempted to teach the partisans how to handle the bazooka.

"They're afraid of these weapons," SO Captain McGregor reported. "We showed them how to use these tank busters and the next day we found them strewn about the area."

Krizan learned Soviet agents and their fellow travelers who controlled these partisans had told them they were not to accept American weapons and throw them away which they did.

This was occurring even as the German units moved into the partisan territory. The resistance fell apart. On the 26th of October the Slovaks abandoned the Banska Bystrica area. By now the Americans numbered 37 and consisted of both OSS men and pilots. They agreed to divide into four units to move out with the partisans in hopes they would not suffer major casualties.

Of the five last OSS teams to arrive only one was to survive—the Hungarians.

The partisans panicked. Throwing away their weapons they seized the American supplies and retreated through the snow covered mountains toward the Russian lines. But there disaster awaited them in the form of the freezing weather. On one day 83 of the Slovaks froze to death waiting for the return of one of their patrols.

The remaining OSS men reunited and continued trudging through the mountains. Each day they lost another of their numbers. Five aviators and one OSS agent were captured by the Germans while on patrol. One by one the other OSS agents and pilots were captured.

Krizan outwitted his captors claiming to have been merely a pilot. When the Germans asked about a code he had in his pocket he told them it had been given to him by a British Major for delivery to someone on another mountain. Luck was with him as the Germans knew they had killed a British Major and there had been some partisans on the other mountain who were also killed. They had no way to check up on him.

The Germans took the other OSS men and pilots to the Mauthausen Concentration camp near Linz, Austria, where they were tortured for whatever information they might divulge. On January 24, 1945, they were all executed.

Mauthausen was a camp from which no prisoners were intended to ever leave. It contained a building named by its inmates "Death House." Each day at 9:00 a.m. and 5:00 p.m. prisoners were ushered into the facility—120 at a time. SS men battled one another for a view through the small window to watch the death agonies as the cyclone cyanide was released. One time a total of 220 prisoners were gassed.

In addition to the gassing, prisoners also were shot or hung. Another favored method of execution was taking the prisoners into a room supposedly to be photographed. An SS man stood behind a camera mounted on a tripod. While the prisoner faced the camera SS officer Franz Zieris, standing behind them, shot them in the back of the head with a carbine. Zieris enjoyed this activity and boasted he had executed at least 400 men by this method. The OSS men of DAWES and HOUSEBOAT were executed in this manner.

Three months after their deaths OSS agent Jack Taylor was thrust into Block 13 at Mauthausen. He was the agent the DAWES and HOUSEBOAT teams had desperately tried to contact prior to their capture.

The inmates believed Taylor to be the one American who might survive and some day be able to tell the story of the SS inhumanity. They felt any story they might tell would be dismissed as propaganda while an American would be more inclined to be believed.

One by one they told him of men being torn to pieces by trained dogs as the SS watched and cheered. They related how men were tossed into concrete mixers, or injected with magnesium chlorate in the heart or given steaming hot showers, then put outside in sub-zero temperature while hoses were turned on them.

Taylor committed the stories to memory after insisting on at least two eyewitnesses to each account. He did not need witnesses other than himself the day 367 Czech Jews arrived after a long march into the camp. They were immediately stripped and put into the gas chamber, then into the new crematorium.

As a grisly note Taylor reported the old emaciated prisoners gave off a pale, yellow smoke. The younger healthier victims produced black, oily fumes. The smoke stacks cast these tragic evidences of Nazi inhumanity indiscriminately into the grey skies.

Krizan, still in his cell, convinced the Germans he might save their lives as the Russian forces drew near. He said in exchange for his freedom he would give them a letter stating as an American officer he had been treated with kindness. It worked. He was freed and he and two American pilots hid out with the partisans until Vienna had been liberated.

An analysis of the Czechoslovakia debacle indicated a lack of planning by both the Allies and the insurgents. A swift advance had been promised by the Russians. The end result was a two month campaign to reach the partisans through the Dukla Pass whereas only two weeks had been allotted. The Russians did make a valiant attempt, however. In that attempt they suffered 120,000 casualties.

The British made no attempt to help. They did not want American successes which could lead to American influence in central Europe. OSS did fly emergency supplies from Cairo to Bari but bad weather prevented them from getting them to the men on the ground in time.

It was in mid-May that Germany, divided by the Allied and Russian armies, finally surrendered. The war in Europe was over after nearly six bitter, devastating years. The streets of the Free World were alive with shouting, cheering people. For a few glorious moments the war with Japan was all but forgotten—save for those troops in the Orient still facing this deadly enemy. The logistics of transferring the great war machine to the East loomed ahead now for the armed forces. The rebuilding of badly decimated units and air units would have to be started.

OSS found itself in a similar but smaller situation. With the German surrender the OSS agents in Europe took on new assignments. While many went on to China to work against the Japanese, others remained in Germany to spearhead the search for missing art treasures purloined by the Nazis. OSS Captain Baron Rudolf von Ripper of SI was assigned to track down those Nazis who had escaped. As an aerial gunner he had fought against Franco during the Spanish Civil War. He accepted his new assignment with understood enthusiasm.

What agents from the European theater could be utilized against Japan? Since MacArthur refused to use them and they were not welcome in China, it appeared only DET 101 in Burma and its new sister units DET 202 in Calcutta, DET 303 in Kunming, and DET 404 in Ceylon plus Eifler's Korean plan could utilize them.

There was no reason to alter Napko. Eifler proceeded on course. He began looking daily for the entry of Russia into the war now that its western borders were secured.

13

While Donovan's agents dealt with the infighting between communists and royalists in Europe there was even more of a problem in China. It was first evidenced in mid-1942 when Eifler reported to Stilwell only to find the OSS men could not operate within that vast country. The problem then, as always, was Kai-shek and his chief of Secret Police, Tai Li.

Tai Li offered to use his 400 agents within China to provide intelligence but OSS was to pay for it. The British had found such an agreement absolutely worthless insofar as the value of the "intelligence" Tai Li delivered while continuing to demand more money. Admiral Milton Miles of the U.S. Navy was in Chungking with Navy personnel monitoring the movement of Japanese ships off the coast as well as of troops on land. In an attempt to cooperate with Kai-shek and Tai Li, Miles worked with them as closely as possible. While OSS regarded Tai Li as every bit as crooked as Kai-shek, Miles felt he had some merit and could be handled.

The situation got to the point where the Navy gave so generously of its supplies to the Chinese they could or would not even supply OSS. Miles had been assured of 150 tons of supplies a month and was to control their distribution to OSS, Chinese elements and the Navy. One month the total received was 130 tons. OSS got nothing.

While OSS was kept from operating its intelligence groups, Tai Li provided such information from his own men to the Navy. The Navy personnel spent considerable time examining and processing the reports before sending them on to Washington. Miles held the information until he was sure it had been cabled to the Navy Department in Washington before releasing it to OSS. OSS asked for copies of the reports that were forwarded to the Navy group. Tai Li's reply was to the effect that it was impossible because the Chinese did not use carbon paper and lacked office supplies. It was increasingly evident the Navy sided with Tai Li in trying to keep OSS from functioning and supported all of his obstructionist tactics.

In order to reduce friction the Sino-American Cooperative Organization (SACO) was formed. It combined the activities of OSS, the U.S. Navy group, China and the Chinese intelligence service. It was directed by Tai Li and based on the resources of his agency.

OSS had two problems with SACO: to induce Tai Li to use his men against the enemy and to train his people to operate efficiently. The first was only partially achieved and then by use of threats and bribes.

If Tai Li did OSS's bidding he would continue receiving supplies. If he didn't then OSS would withdraw from SACO, start its own separate organization and cause Tai Li to lose considerable face.

Recognizing that OSS had the complete backing of Stilwell and was indeed capable of operating without his help, Tai Li finally did a turnabout.

In order to penetrate Manchuria, Korea and finally Japan it was necessary to enter operational bases in Communist-held areas. Operation DIXIE, formed in July, 1944, was the OSS vehicle to accomplish this objective. Its goal was to estimate the potentialities of the Communist Chinese to aid American plans, to be involved in possible military action, and as an intelligence gathering resource.

As expected Tai Li did everything in his power to keep the liaison from developing. But, by now, OSS was flying under its own power and beginning operations together with the communists.

During the first eight months the OSS men attached to DIXIE produced eighty per cent of the mission's intelligence data. For the first time details were available on Japanese order of battle information, train counts on the strategic North China rail lines and Japanese intelligence and counter-intelligence units in China.

While the information was gratefully received by OSS, Tai Li and Chiang Kai-shek looked at it quite differently. Their only concern was how deep was the cooperation between Mao Tse-tung and OSS. Donovan tried to improve the deteriorating OSS position by an amendment to the Joint Chiefs which would allow the OSS more freedom under Stilwell. There was no formal amendment but rather an "understanding" which was reached on December 9, 1943, in Chungking. Personnel from OSS, the U.S. Navy and China came to an agreement regarding specific areas of activity. After this agreement was reached, Donovan took a more definitive stance. On December 17th he ordered activation of OSS DET 202 in Hsian, China, staffing it with several men from OSS DET 101. By April 9, OSS had divided China into three large zones: Zone 1, Hsian Unit Field Command, north of the Yangtze River with base headquarters at Hsian; Zone 2, Chihkiang Unit Field Command, south of the Yangtze River with base headquarters at Chihkiang; Zone 3, Szemao Unit Field Command, comprising Indochina south to the 16 north latitude with base headquarters at Szemao.

The Commanding Officer of Zone 1 was Lt. Col. Gustav Krause.

With this masterstroke, OSS now became virtually autonomous under SACO. Basic control by SACO, still in Tai Li's hands, continued to be an obstacle. When OSS set up its training schools the Chinese sent recruits who were of deliberately inferior calibre, sometimes completely illiterate.

Starting with a handful of men DET 202 grew into a unit of 200 Americans and over 3,000 Chinese guerrillas. Though hampered continually by Tai Li, when DET 202 reached its full complement of men it began producing dramatic results. Teamed with the 14th Air Force under Chennault it rescued downed pilots on his behalf and began making its guerrilla operations felt by the Japanese.

As was often the case with OSS operations, Krause had entered the organization for an entirely different purpose than that in which he now found himself. He had been recruited because of his knowledge of the German language. He was to join other German speaking OSS men for an operation against the Spanish government. With the eventual scrubbing of that plot he was sent to China.

His knowledge of German was not lost as many of the Chinese officers, trained by the Germans, also spoke German giving them a common language in which to communicate.

Through OSS personnel moving back and forth Eifler kept as up to date on his DET 101 men as possible. Regardless of the current mission he might be involved in, his heart remained with this first group of Americans, trained in all manner of un-American policies and fighting for their lives against a ruthless enemy.

He fully sympathized with General Stilwell and well knew of the corrupt Chiang Kai-shek government. He was not prepared, however, to realize the depth of betrayal Kai-shek would stoop to for personal gain.

The story began with the 3rd Battalion of American Kachin Scouts, OSS DET 101, under the command of Lt. Tom Chamales, author of *Never So Few*.

Numbering eight hundred guerrillas they were high in the hills of Sinlumkaba, No. Burma. They were to head south for the fighting near Lashio. To the south was the 2nd Battalion of Kachin Rangers with whom the Chamales force was to rendezvous. On January 6th a Kachin scout reported Chinese bandits near Lewje, China. It was further reported these Chinese were dealing with the Japanese.

Chamales reported to the 2nd Battalion what had been discovered and that it was his intention to attack and disperse those bandits. Major Pete Joost, commander of that group, agreed.

Chamales set up his headquarters in an abandoned Buddhist

temple. Around ten o'clock that evening a group of Kachin civilians came in to report those Chinese, supposedly our allies, had crossed the border, raided their villages and carried off their women. The Kachin guerrillas hearing this wanted to attack at once. It was denied. The plan to attack at dawn was to be adhered to. They would move out at 2:30 a.m. the next morning.

Other reports indicated there were at least a thousand guerrillas dispersed throughout four camps. The city of Lewje was deserted. The people had fled to the hills to escape beatings and, quite possibly, death. Chamales ordered the full strength of four companies was to be used. He would take command of the 1st Company; 2nd Company to be headed by Al Freudenberg; 3rd Company by Japanese interpreter, Kenneth Shigeto Mazawa, a Nisei from Chicago, and 4th Company by Donald Niven.

Promptly at 2:30 a.m. the Kachins moved out sneaking through the tall grass to their target. At 4:45 a.m. the first firing was heard. By 5:00 a.m. all companies were engaged. Fires began rising from the tall grass and huts where the guerrillas were bivouacked. From 4th Company Niven radioed in, "We're slaughtering them. It's slaughter."

Chamales wanted prisoners for questioning but it appeared none were being taken. Finally about 2:00 o'clock that afternoon six Chinese prisoners were brought in. Their heads were shaven. Two had pigtails. They were dressed in black coolie pants with padded black jackets and black coolie hats. None seemed to be over 20.

An hour later 2nd, 3rd and 4th companies returned, their Kachins grinning and loaded down with booty they had taken. There was a total of 26 prisoners. The total Chinese killed were close to 300.

Freudenberg was inside a church where the prisoners had been taken. He came out with one of the captured documents.

"Do you know what this is?" he asked. Chamales said he did not.

"It's a warrant from the Chungking government—from Chiang Kai-shek himself. It gives these guerrillas the right, actually the license, to raid, loot and pillage anything, including American convoys. The loot is to be split fifty-fifty with Kai-shek."

Freudenberg had one of those stupefied looks on his face. He couldn't grasp the evil a human could stoop to. Chamales likewise found it hard to grasp. Nautaung, a 22 year old Kachin came forward and took the document. He examined it a minute, then said it was a bona fide document, he had seen others. Many warlords carried them.

Freudenberg said many of the prisoners inside the church had American equipment including personal effects such as wallets,

286

letters and bracelets. One of the prisoners said they had raided and looted American convoys supplying the Chinese Nationalist Troops. They then burned the convoys along with some of the GI's while they held others for ransom. The GI's they had burned had been bound hand and foot.

Rage swept over the Americans. Sheer hatred and rage with a natural desire to kill all the prisoners immediately. For several hours Chamales fought with himself. About eleven o'clock a Subadar Major came in and asked for the prisoners. Chamales knew why he wanted them but needed to keep some for interrogation. He did release ten to him, however.

The Americans had lost considerable face by not killing the Chinese immediately. The Kachins could not understand it. A short time later there was some shouting, then screaming, then firing of weapons. The Subadar explained they had all tried a mass escape and of course had to be killed.

The next morning a message came in. Chamales was ordered to release all prisoners at once, destroy all captured documents and prepare to receive a Major Dong, a personal representative of Chiang Kai-shek himself. It was also stated Chamales had jeopardized his position as an officer and if he did not placate the Chinese there might be personal repercussions against him.

Angered at first at Col. Peers, commander of DET 101, Chamales then realized it was not a message Peers would send and that the matter was out of his hands. The Subadar Major returned now to ask for the balance of the prisoners. Chamales agreed saying he was to take them to the edge of the town and release them. The Subadar Major grinned, saluted and left with them. Later the same report came back—a mass escape had been attempted and all the prisoners had been killed.

They waited all the next day for Major Dong to arrive. He had to be flown to a nearby airstrip and arrived the following morning. He was in a Chinese Nationalist uniform but his equipment was all American. He offered his hand. Chamales refused to take it.

Dong said the OSS men had committed grave and atrocious acts against the good people of China and wanted an explanation. He added he knew Chamales had been told to cooperate with him fully and he wanted Chamales report along with an apology in writing. Chamales told him to go to hell. Dong said Chamales could not tell him that, it would cost him face. Chamales told him that was tough.

The meeting broke up but was started later at the request of Dong. Again he demanded a written apology and this time added the Chinese government was demanding triple indemnity for the damages inflicted by the attack. Chamales brought up the question of warrants issued to the warlords. It was ignored. Dong said the Chinese were endorsed by Chungking and Chiang Kai-shek and had rendered a great service to China.

Chamales asked if the raiding and looting of American convoys and skilled American soldiers was rendering a truly great service to the Nationalist cause. Also, was it the policy of the Nationalist Government that those licensed guerrillas be allowed to sack and pillage the peaceful villages of China? Dong said no such thing had ever occurred. There was an impasse until the next day when Chamales received another message from the OSS base. It said the American High Command and the Chinese High Command felt maybe he had been in combat too long. Chamales knew Peers was caught in the same web he now found himself.

At a meeting later, Dong said maybe if Chamales would just sign a statement to the effect he had not been feeling well it might save sufficient face for the Chinese. He then amplified it with the reminder of the tremendous influence Kai-shek had with Washington and if he could get Stilwell removed then certainly Chamales would be no problem.

Chamales showed him the warrant, that he had proof of the Chungking duplicity. Dong angrily said he had been ordered to destroy all documents. Chamales had never wanted to kill anyone as badly as Dong. His hand twitched several times as he patted his .38 but he restrained himself.

Early the next morning Dong requested another meeting. A Chinese agent, a lesser representative of Kai-shek had been captured but kept out of sight. He was also known to be a supplier of goods for the Japanese army and confessed it. He was with two other Chinese. Chamales agreed to the meeting if Dong would permit a photograph of the Chinese and Americans. Dong agreed. After the picture was taken the Chinese traitor and his two colleagues were told to move out of the group. They were immediately blown apart by the Kachins. It was the final answer to Dong.

Chamales knew the warrant was his bargaining chip. He sent it on a mule with a special guard to make sure it did not get stolen or just disappear. He had a concern that he just might be court-martialed but it never happened. Such a happening would cause the material in the warrant to be made public. It was embarrassing to the American High Command who could not now give the Chinese the apology they felt so essential. Peers was severely criticized for the men under his command. The Americans in Burma and China, both OSS and regular forces, could never understand the American

288

government tolerating the robbery and murder of American forces and the power the Chinese lobby held over Washington. Eifler, enraged by the story of betrayal, tried to turn his mind to positive things. There was nothing he could do.

OSS working in China, the largest nation shared the same interests and determination to succeed as agents working in the smallest nations. Romania, though tiny, provided a treasure of intelligence information as the Germans left. The small nation of Romania had considerable interest to the Allies for two reasons. First was the large number of U.S. and British airmen imprisoned there. Second was the intelligence gathered by Romanian intelligence on the Germans. In addition the Allies were anxious to determine the damage done to the Ploesti oilfields in the massive bombing attacks against it.

On August 23, 1944, there was a coup against the Germans. With the flexibility OSS had been allowed they were able to fly 21 agents into the Popesti airport on August 29th, just six days later. The Russians arrived a few days after them. The British already had an SO,E agent who had jumped into the country in 1943.

OSS knew over 1,000 airmen were located near the Popesti airport. Trucks were brought in from Bucharest by the Romanians and the prisoners brought to the airfield. On August 31 over 1,100 men were flown out on B-17's of the Fifteenth Air Force.

Fighting was still going on in the outskirts of Bucharest. Even with that going on OSS men, together with the now arrived Russians, combed the hospitals for other airmen. Within the next few weeks the number of rescued airmen was 1,350.

Following this a team of experts began examination of the oil fields on September 3rd. The official German oil mission in Bucharest was Ruminoel. From its records it was determined that shipments of processed products to Germany declined by sixty-two percent during the time the oil fields were under attack. Of unexpected help was the destination of some shipments to German forces which gave the Eighth and Fifteenth Air Forces some new targets.

Rummaging through the material and records discarded by the retreating Germans the agents found manuals and equipment. From records in the Schenker and Co., the center of German espionage in Romania, they gleaned valuable information. OSS was able to provide the air force in Italy with ninety percent of its information on Romania.

Sifting through information the agents found and catalogued 10,000 dossiers from the Nazi Party in Romania. They were combed for evidence to be used in the coming war crimes trials. Also found were the Gestapo files which proved a true bonanza.

Sixty former Axis agents, some of them doubles, were identified along with 4,000 Axis intelligence agents and officials. More than one hundred subversive organizations and 200 commercial firms used for espionage were identified.

Supply depots, tactical targets, airfields and communication centers were pinpointed and turned over to the air force for action.

After an examination of the damage to the oil fields the air force was notified that in future oil field attacks their bombs should be fused no longer than 1/100th of a second.

Valuable information was also picked up about the Romanian fleet in the Black Sea and the coastal defenses in place.

One of the first Americans to enter Romania was Beverly Bowie, an assistant editor of the *National Geographic*. His colleagues were surprised to find out he had immediately become a regular at Romanian Cabinet meetings. As many OSS agents were the first and only contacts in occupied countries they were looked on as official representatives of the United States whose advice was officially that of their government.

"Before they vote on anything they ask me what I think," Bowie said with a grin. "I go into a trance and try to figure out what Franklin Roosevelt would do, then I give 'em an answer. They pass all my laws unanimously. I never thought running a country was so easy."

The OSS mission had entered under false colors. It was termed an Air Crew Rescue Unit when it first went in. On November 9th the U.S. division of the Allied Control Commission arrived. Up until this time OSS had been the only official U.S. representative. Lacking official approval to continue the OSS unit was closed in September. In thirteen months it had done a remarkable job in culling through the mass of paperwork left behind and making sense of it.

On May 18, 1945, Eifler received a copy of a recommendation to the office of the adjutant general, War Department, Washington, D.C. It recommended him for the Distinguished Service Medal:

SUBJECT: Recommendation for Award of the Distinguished Service Medal to Colonel Carl F. Eifler

TO: The Adjutant General War Department Washington 25, D.C.

1. It is recommended that the Distinguished Service

Medal be awarded to Colonel Carl F. Eifler for exceptionally meritorious service to the Government in a duty of great responsibility while serving as Major and subsequently higher grades in the CBI theater.

2. The service of Colonel Eifler has been of such distinction that it has been broadly acclaimed throughout the limited channels which rigid security regulations require.

3. It should be emphasized that in the planning, development and operation of the program for which Colonel Eifler was responsible, his own imagination, ingenuity, determination and brilliant ability and adaptability were sources of inspiration to his associates and were directly responsible for the amazing success of his operations.

4. Following is a specific, though condensed resume of the services of Colonel Eifler upon which this recommendation is based:

On 20 March 1942, Colonel Carl F. Eifler, then a Captain, reported to the office of the Coordinator of Information, and was given the task of organizing a small group of officers and men for the purpose of espionage and sabotage activities behind enemy lines in the Far East.

A group of twenty-one officers and enlisted men were personally selected by Colonel Eifler in the United States, and were trained in British and American schools on secret operations. On 28 May 1942, this group left the United States for the Far East. The unit was known as Detachment 101, or Task Force 5405-A.

On 12 June 1942, Major Eifler reported to General Stilwell's headquarters in the CBI theater. In September 1942, General Stilwell directed that operations begin in Burma by establishing radio bases in enemy occupied territory. It was the General's desire to make friends with the natives, prepare to sabotage the railway in northern Burma, and establish an intelligence unit which was to operate in support of his command. Headquarters were established in Northern Assam in October, 1942, and a training program was immediately put into operation. Twenty-six separate schools were established for the purpose of teaching espionage and sabotage, and agents were recruited from among natives of the areas occupied by the Japanese.

Agents were taught modern radio communications, demolition, use of small arms, and to maintain communication with Allied headquarters, sending and receiving mes-

291

sages in English without being able to read English, despite
the fact that they coded and decoded all messages. Natives
were also taught to jump by parachute into areas occupied by
the Japanese.

On 26 December 1942, Major Eifler led the original
operational group to return to Burma, consisting of two
American officers, seven British officers, and five native
agents, to establish a radio station in northern Burma. This
base station was established 10 January 1943, to handle all
radio communications from sub-stations in the field.

7 February 1943 the initial agent radio station was established in Japanese occupied territory. This original station
was approximately 250 miles south of the foremost Japanese
outpost. Agents mined the railway in northern Burma, and in
the first weeks of February, cut this railway line in twenty-
one places .

Four air strips for light planes were completed while the
Japs controlled the territory where they were located. These
airports were camouflaged, and were not discovered by
Japanese troops. All of these strips were later used by military forces during the battle of northern Burma; some for
evacuating wounded by light plane, and some as headquarters for advancing troops. The use of these permitted the
generals commanding the troops to have easy access between
their troops and the commanding general's headquarters.

On 1 October 1943, the first plane controlled by 101, with
Colonel Eifler as a passenger, landed in Japanese occupied
territory. Colonel Eifler was able to make contact with the
agents in a matter of hours, which previously had taken about
six weeks.

In November 1943, the second field was completed
approximately twenty odd miles from the Japanese headquarters in northern Burma. This field was afterwards used by
General Merrill as his headquarters, and allowed him to
communicate with General Stilwell's headquarters in a
matter of minutes.

Also, in November the third field was completed, thirty
miles north of Myitkyina. This field was later used to evacu-
ate wounded to base hospitals.

The first Japanese Pilot officer to be captured in this
theater, was kidnapped in November 1943, in occupied
territory, and was flown from Burma to India by Colonel
Eifler in a small single-seater civilian plane. The Japanese

officer had landed two miles from the Japanese strong point of Nsopzup believing he was landing in his own or friendly territory. The natives who had been organized into an agent chain under Colonel Eifler's direction led him instead to the spot where Colonel Eifler took him into custody. This whole remarkable episode was made possible only by the superior planning and execution of Colonel Eifler's program for that area. Further, as a result of the capture of the officer, information was obtained definitely locating the position of Japanese air fields from which the enemy operated in their molestations of Allied cargo and passenger planes flying over routes, commonly known as the Hump between China and India. This, of course, afforded the Allied Air Forces an opportunity to attack the areas of the fields thereby greatly diminishing the effectiveness of enemy air opposition.

Towards the latter part of 1943, 101 had grown to where 84,086 lbs of equipment, food, ammunition, radio supplies, etc., were introduced into enemy occupied territory in a period of thirty days. This was doubled in the early months of 1944. Also during this period of thirty days, a total of thirty-five agents, officers, and enlisted men assigned to 101, were introduced into Japanese territory. A total of twenty-six air-corps men who had been shot down by Japanese aircraft, were rescued or assisted by agents of 101 during this thirty day period.

In addition to its normal duties of securing and passing information during the month of May 1944, members of 101 led the Galahad Forces under General Merrill via unknown paths to Myitkyina.

By May 1944, hundreds of agents were operating under the direction of Detachment 101, in addition to a native population of approximately 15,000 directly influenced by this organization.

5. Colonel Eifler's personal indomitable courage, fortitude and bravery along with his amazing stamina further enhanced and inspired the agents who assisted him in operations he introduced and directed.

6. This recommendation is based on my personal knowledge, the records of this office and the records of the CBI theater.

7. Colonel Eifler's service subsequent to the time of distinction has been honorable.

M. PRESTON GOODFELLOW
Colonel, GSC
Deputy Director, OSS

CERTIFIED A TRUE COPY

/s/ Graham G. Campbell GRAHAM G. CAMPBELL Major, Inf.

WAR DEPARTMENT
The Adjutant General's Office
Washington 25, D.C .

In reply refer to
AGPD-B 201 Eifler, Carl F.
(18 Apr 46) 0 288 691

20 May 1946 subject: Legion of Merit (Oak Leaf Cluster)

TO: Director, Strategic Services Unit 25th and E Streets, Northwest War Department Washington 25, D.C.

1. Reference is made to your recommendation of 26 September 1945 that the Distinguished Service Medal be awarded to Colonel Carl F. Eifler, 0 288 691, Infantry, for services from March 1942 to May 1944.

2. The recommendation has received careful consideration in the War Department and the Legion of Merit (Oak Leaf Cluster) was deemed the appropriate award.

3. By direction of the President, in addition to the Legion of Merit awarded to Colonel Eifler, as published in General Orders No. 6, China-Burma-India Theater, 31 March 1944, a bronze Oak Leaf Cluster was awarded to him by the War Department .

4. The Commanding General, Philadelphia Quartermaster Depot, has been directed to forward to you, complete in container, a Legion of Merit (Oak Leaf Cluster) for presentation to Colonel Eifler. The official citation pertaining to this award is enclosed for presentation with the decoration.

BY ORDER OF THE SECRETARY OF WAR:

A. J. VALENTE Adjutant General.

1 Incl.
Citation

A TRUE COPY:

WM. L. BESWICK

Lt. Colonel, M.A.C.
Adjutant

June and July saw no letup in the mission. In early August, Eifler stated the Koreans were ready and requested a submarine be assigned to his unit. He was to fly to Honolulu to meet with Donovan, who had flown ahead to get approval from Admiral Nimitz. The Koreans on Catalina were put on alert. There were no leaves. All mail was to be even more tightly censored. It was now August 19, 1945. After Eifler's departure from San Francisco in a few days, the Napko unit was to follow immediately and be introduced into Korea.

The news the next day was stunning. At 0915 that morning Japanese time, an American superfortress dropped history's first atomic bomb. It fell on the bustling city of Hiroshima. Sixty percent of the city's built-up area, 4.1 square miles, simply disappeared. The final death toll was 71,000, with 68,000 injured. It was simply incredible, reported the crew of the *Enola Gay*. The world was stunned.

Three days later another superfortress, *Great Artiste,* was sent on a similar mission. Its primary target, Kokura, was socked in. Its secondary target was Nagasaki. An even more powerful atom bomb was dropped, which destroyed only one square mile of the seaport but was said to have been more devastating than the first. It killed 35,000 people and injured 60,000. What would Japan now do? It was clear she could not take many more of these incredible raids. With no word of negotiation or surrender, the United States could only continue to press the war. Napko was to go in as planned. Three days later Eifler had his orders and time of departure confirmed. At 2200 on August 26, he was to depart from the United States. The next day he would arrive at his base, be prepared to immediately board the waiting submarine and head for his rendezvous just off Japan where he and another agent would board the two-man sub and land on the coast. He felt the Japanese war spirit would only be more adamant and more unified in the face of the terrible bombings.

That afternoon came another startling pronouncement—Japan was surrendering. The war was over.

Eifler stood at the window of his room in the Palace Hotel in San Francisco. Words were beyond him—tears streamed down his cheeks. The tremendous relief was not because he had been spared a near-suicidal mission but that the killing would now stop. The invasion that was estimated to cause over 2 million casualties now need never happen.

The tremendous problem America faced in diverting her energies to peace was monumental. Twelve million men and women were in uniform. Psychologically, Eifler faced the same problem in gearing himself back to peacetime activities. He had used every ounce of energy and will in training himself to be a superb fighting machine. The fighting units he had commanded had turned in outstanding jobs: "K" Co., 35th Inf., the 811th Military Police, and DET 101 in Burma. His Korean units were ready to prove themselves. He would still go to Honolulu to meet General Donovan, but it would be for a much different purpose this time.

Wartime Honolulu was still leaving its nighttime lights out. Though beaten, some Japanese commanders well might try to make one last retribution attack somewhere. Upon his arrival, Eifler found Donovan had already returned to the States. He had much to do now with winding down his secret organization. The future of OSS, if there was to be one, was dim. Of prime importance was the return of its talented and highly trained men to peacetime pursuits.

Eifler returned to Washington, D.C., to wind up his own affairs with OSS. He would then have to be turned back to the army for discharge and his return to civilian life.

One problem awaited him—the "missing" Korean agents. Not knowing what course of action to take, he went to the provost marshal to ask his advice. He stated his problem and asked the provost marshal just what he should do with these men.

"What men?" was the reply.

"The Koreans you and I discussed eighteen months ago—the ones that we took from Camp McCoy," pursued Eifler.

"Colonel, I don't know anything about it," was the final statement.

Eifler knew he well knew all about it. The two had gone into great detail discussing the plan at its inception. The war was over, and it was a problem, so the general simply feigned ignorance and

296

dumped it back into Eifler's lap. There was nothing to do, so Eifler left to solve it himself. He also faced the problem of explaining the situation to the Swiss Red Cross, who had dutifully recorded the reports of the many "escapees."

It would be impossible to tell the true story to all the involved agencies. In addition, Eifler knew the State Department would soon enter the picture with questions about illegal passports gained from false information. Having tried to do what he considered the proper thing in reporting the incident to the right authorities, Eifler now took other steps. He instructed Aitken to smuggle them in with the returning POWs as they were shipped home from America. A combination of OSS and customs talents eventually did the trick. Neither the Red Cross nor the State Department were ever the wiser on this batch of men.

In September, 1945, over the protests of many high government officials, the OSS was abolished. It was felt it had done its job well but would not be needed in postwar years.

Eifler continued filling out the numerous forms required. News reached him of a final ceremony for the Kachins. They were to be honored, given decorations and presents for the tremendous help they had given to DET 101 and to the Allied war effort in general. One award had its genesis in an amusing and peculiar fashion. It actually began in early 1943 when Eifler had been visiting Wilkinson's camp. Eifler had been definite in instructing all OSS men to never promise the natives anything they could not deliver. The natives, much like children, could never be allowed to lose respect for the Americans.

Wilkinson had promised the natives weapons, medals, and supplies. These would be given them at war's end in appreciation of their help. In transmission of messages, the comma is shown as CMA, so that portion of his message came through reading WEAPONS CMA MEDALS AND SUPPLIES. Someone unfamiliar with transmission procedures at New Delhi came up with the idea there was a CMA medal and sent it on through. Word at once came back there was no such medal in America's awards. When Eifler found out about it, he was preparing for one of his trips back to the States. Realizing the natives would expect a CMA medal, he petitioned Washington for one to be created. Washington refused even though he appeared before the men who design and approve of the medals and awards for America's fighting forces. When he returned to India, Eifler continued pursuit of the elusive medal. If Wilkinson had promised it and the natives expected, then, damn it—there would be one. Finally his desire for the medal was satisfied with approval of General Stilwell.

New Delhi was instructed to design a medal befitting the occasion. A silver emblem with the peacocks of Burma across it was struck. It also bore the initials *CMA*, which were to stand for Citation for Military Assistance. One more problem arose. There was nowhere to pin the medal since most of the Kachins wore nothing above the waist. The large ribbon like the one used on the Congressional Medal of Honor was decided on, since it could be slipped around the neck. A bright green ribbon beautifully offset the silver medal with its peacocks.

The ceremony was impressive as Kachin leaders and chiefs stood proudly at attention. The medals were put about their necks, and they were given other gifts—gifts that nearly created an international incident. One of the most valuable possessions a Kachin could claim was a good rifle or shotgun. There was a surplus of weapons and, wanting to aid the brave Kachins, 101 made gifts of rifles and shotguns to many of these men. The Kachins needed them for hunting but also for protection against sporadic raids by the Chinese as well as occasional forays by other tribes and the Burmese themselves. The British were disturbed and expressed their concern. Also, the Burmese government made unhappy sounds to the American officials.

Eifler was pleased that at least this much had been done to help the Kachins. He was unhappy, however, because he had promised the Kachins much more, and now his promises were not be carried out. He buttonholed and cajoled everyone he could reach but to no avail. The American government was not anxious to offend its British allies or the Burmese, and Eifler's promises were not to be kept. Eifler debated whether or not he might on some pretext get back there and carry out his promises personally. It proved to be impossible, and he watched in frustration and anger as the Kachins were not given what he had promised in the name of his country.

At war's end realizing the Communists were destined to take over the corrupt and deteriorating Nationalist government, OSS instructed Krause and some of his men to stay behind and set up teams of Chinese for listening posts in northern China. It was more hazardous duty than anything they had ever done against the Japanese.

The 22 men who remained with Krause found themselves in a precarious situation. In violation of the Potsdam agreement the Russians had sent two Divisions into China just north of Peking. The Russians had brought stencils and seized every piece of American equipment relabelling it, "Made in the Soviet Union."

In addition they took watches and money from the DET 202 men at gun-point and slashed the tires of OSS jeeps and trucks.

Fearing for their lives the Americans appealed to President Truman to send the First Marines encamped in Tientsin, some 60 miles away.

Truman's reply was not to worry, good old Uncle Joe's boys are just letting off steam. No Marines would be sent.

In order to protect themselves DET 202 found it necessary to re-arm the Japanese and some of the Germans they had held and set them out as their perimeter. And so the OSS-China mission ended, its former enemies now its protectors against its questionable allies.

Observation stations, however, were established in Peking, Nanking, Hong Kong, Canton, Mukden, Tientsin, Hankow and Tsingtao.

For some time prior to the end of the war, the North China OSS base at Sian had been watching a notorious Japanese POW camp housing allied prisoners. It was too heavily defended for an attack. Even had they been able to free the prisoners, the problem would have been how to get them back to Allied lines. They would have required more provisions than the base had and would be in need of immediate medical treatment. Nor did they have the transportation they would need to move the prisoners out before the Japanese attack that would surely follow.

All they could do was monitor the situation closely and wait for the right time to make their move.

The Feng Tai Camp in Hopeh Province, North China, housed roughly three hundred fifty assorted prisoners of war. The Japanese captors carried out their customary ruthless treatment of the prima-rily American and Australian prisoners.

Thirty seven huge warehouses with corrugated roofs, known as go-downs, held ammunition for the Japanese Imperial Army. Go-down 37 was filled with prisoners held as human shields. On the 15th of August 1945 the prisoners listened intently to the sound of gunfire as it drew nearer. Their hopes were for Chiang Kai-shek's troops to overrun their camp. The truth was, however, it was the probing thrusts of the Communist 8th Route army moving south from their northern hideouts.

The Japanese commanders made the prisoners line up and count off. Two trucks stood nearby and soon left taking troops into Peking for a days leave. "Goofy," so named by the prisoners, was a less than normal farmboy attached to the Japanese forces. Considered too stupid or too insignificant to fight he was merely tolerated.

He managed to scramble aboard the trucks as they pulled out. Actually the Americans had been grooming Goofy. He was told when the war ended America would make many films about the fighting and would need Japanese. In short order they convinced him they were the key to his becoming a film actor and in turn got him to do things for him he ought not to have done.

The trucks sped by the electrified fence and past the field where Colonel Odera, the camp commander, was giving bayonet instructions to two hundred Japanese girls being trained to kill Americans on the beaches of Japan. It was Japan's hope that they could make the invasion so costly that Washington would agree to a negotiated peace.

Fourteen hours later the trucks returned. Goofy instantly sought out his American friend, an ex-marine named Hanvey. He was one of two Americans grooming Goofy.

"Everything fine. Japan America friends now," Goofy exclaimed.

"Go to hell," Hanvey retorted.

"No, I hear Emperor on radio," Goofy insisted.

Hanvey did remember seeing some officers come out of the Colonel's quarters and bow towards Tokyo. It might be true. Two days later an air raid alarm sounded. The prisoners were all herded into go-down 37 as Japanese gunners manned their weapons. Through cracks in the wall the prisoners looked out. A cry went up as the first plane approached and huge canisters and then men parachuted down. It was an OSS team of Operation Magpie sent from the Sian command by Colonel Peers. It was commanded by Major Ray Nichols of Mississippi, and Captain Carpenter of Delaware. They were to investigate the condition of the prisoners and see if the Japanese were going to observe the cease-fire order from Tokyo.

The Nichols-Carpenter team, carrying only side arms, were dropped into the midst of a swaggering army that had never been defeated and was quite capable of murdering all the foreigners in China and taking to the hills to carry on the war. For half an hour the Americans were pinned down by machine gun fire while radio transmitters sputtered between the command in Sian and the Japanese headquarters in North China. Suddenly the firing stopped. Major Nichols had won the first round.

A few hours later, scattered Japanese officers began bringing in living skeletons, dumping them onto Colonel Odera before Major Nichols and his men could get wind of them.

One of them was Commander Winfield Scott Cunningham, the naval governor of Wake Island. After a torture period in Nanking he was shipped north to a cell where he could hear four dying Doolittle pilots scream. "One of them quit moaning three days ago and we are going to have to do something if we want to save the others,"

300

Cunningham explained.

Two days later Odera packed his starving charges on trucks and moved them into Peking before Major Nichols and his medical officers could see them.

A passing Italian Priest was given a note to be sent to the Sian command telling them of the plight of the Doolittle survivors. He got through and the Japanese were forced to comply.

Major Nichols and Captain Carpenter and the young officers around them looked like gods to the prisoners who watched spell-bound through the open door that Monday as the two OSS leaders slowly backed Col. Odera and officers of the Peking command into a corner and forced them to hand over the four Doolittle survivors.

For a short time, peace hung in the balance. Major Nichols, never raising his voice, pretended not to notice when Colonel Odera, still standing, removed his sword, then sat down on the sofa. Odera began to perspire and took off his coat as the major continued, asking questions about the prisoners who had died when Odera was moving them north. The Colonel mopped his brow and Nichols leaned over to offer him his fan. For two seconds all breathing stopped. Odera took it and the roomful of Japanese officers and the prisoners in the hallway knew that the handsome major from Mississippi and the young captain whose father was on the board of directors of Dupont de Nemours in Delaware had won.

Major Honda moved to sit down also. For the first time Major Nichols' voice changed. "You stay where you are. You have been posing as an officer of the Japanese army. You are really a legal officer of the gendarmerie." The gendarmerie were the Kampetai who handled torture and executions. Honda's hands began to tremble.

It was from the OSS men the prisoners learned of the A-bombs that had ended the terrible war.

The prisoners now realized why the Japanese had carried gaso-line cans out to the air-raid trenches a few days earlier. News of the A-bomb had reached the guards. Orders had been assigned to kill all prisoners at a later date in order to release troops for the defense of the home islands. They wanted to burn their captives and get it over with. Odera, however, had convinced his superiors that the game was up and that they would be held responsible.

Unfortunately, the Japanese Commander in the Philippines had carried out the horrible task of dousing American POW's with gaso-line and setting them on fire. Many of the dying Americans pleaded with the Japanese to shoot them and end their suffering.

It was several days later when the Imperial Chief of Staff, General Seizo Arisue turned command of the Atsugi Air Base over to Colonel

Charles Tench. Arisue had to think ruefully of the day he took physicist Dr. Yoshio Nishina to Admiral Tojo and begged for funds to make an atomic bomb. Nishina, who had worked in Copenhagen under Niels Bohr, said he had solved the technical problems and was ready to start assembling an atomic bomb that would make Japan the "arbiter and winner of all wars." All he needed was a hundred million yen, approximately $50 million at the time.

Tojo fidgeted, then said the cost was prohibitive and that alone failed to give Japan the bomb for which self righteous Westerners have heaped guilt on America ever since.

The wife of General Dan Pao-tchao blessed the Americans for their A-bombs and the rations she had received from OSS officers. She had been born Princess Shou Shjan, the sister of Princess Der Ling and taken to the court of the old Empress as a little girl to be brought up as a lady-in-waiting. It was a period full of hope. Peking was basking in the setting sun of an era no one thought would end. Prince Teh, of the Mongols, the descendant of Genghis Khan, with his squadrons of horsemen following the nine-yak-tail banner, was in a spacious house in a narrow hutung, negotiating treaties with emissaries from tribes in the northwest as though nothing had changed in his world. Dignitaries of the hui-hui, China's Moslems (the name means return-return) came from the old mosque on the Street of the Cow and the mosque on Morrison Road to pay courtesy calls on the young OSS officers.

Several days later in the Grand Hotel des Wagon Lits, another OSS officer entered the door, his face white as he clenched a report. It explained one of his finest officers, a young man named John Birch, had been killed along the railroad track to Hsuchow. Sian Command knew where the murderers were and was about to send a detachment after them when orders came from Area Command to halt everything. From the hills the 8th Route Army sent student cadres into Peking to plaster walls with crude posters calling on the people to kick out Chiang and his American imperialist allies.

14

The dismantling of the espionage machinery finally made apparent the great contribution of women. As would be assumed, they had served well in a variety of clerical and analytical positions. Not as well known was the fact many had served courageously and brilliantly along with their OSS brothers.

While many scoffed at the idea of women as agents those same women were proving their mettle in action.

Richard Scorge, the Soviet master spy in Japan before World War II said,

> "Women are absolutely unfit for espionage work. They have little understanding of high politics or military affairs. Even if you use them to spy on their husbands, they do not really understand what their husbands are talking about. They are too emotional, sentimental and unreliable."

Women of OSS and other nations were to prove him wrong.

The Japanese soldier was indoctrinated to fight until his death. Surrender was dishonorable, for his soul could never return to the national shrine of Yasukuni.

A careful monitoring of Japanese internal affairs showed there had just been a change of top level government leaders in Japan. It was a perfect time to work some psychological mayhem.

A document was cyclostyled by Marjorie Severyns (Ravenholt), a Japanese prisoner of war and a Japanese scholar. It was designed to encourage the surrender of Japanese soldiers. Its message was that it was not dishonorable to surrender if overpowered by the enemy or if the soldier was isolated or wounded. Then the question of how to implement it arose. It called for the services of a native in the form of a Burma scout who was working for OSS. He killed a Japanese courier on a jungle trail and planted the document on his body. Then he went to the nearby Japanese headquarters to report finding the body and agreed to lead them there.

Upon arriving they discovered the document in the courier's pouch. It was logical that with the new leaders there could well be a change in policy. It seemed that there was a direct effect on the

Japanese soldiers from that day on.

The village of Bhamo fell without a fight. During this time many unusual incidents were reported of Japanese feigning unconsciousness. The prisoner of war stockades, normally empty, now were crowded with Japanese who voluntarily surrendered when "surrounded by superior forces."

Reports of fanatical last ditch fighting and crazed banzai charges were almost unheard of as the Burma campaign ended.

Another counter espionage mission ended both in success and tragedy. Three people were assigned to search within the Nationalist Chinese Embassy in New Delhi to see if Japanese agents were operating. They were Major Oliver Galdwell, Miss Rosamond Frame and Miss Joy Romer. They were all longtime residents of China. In addition they were bilingual in English and Mandarin.

A thorough and brilliant investigation turned up two Chinese employees in that Embassy who were sending classified information to the Japanese in Shanghai. A few days later after the guilty were revealed Miss Romer was brutally attacked while walking down the street. The thugs who severely beat her obviously intended to kill her. She lingered for nearly a year before succumbing.

As there was no robbery some OSS sources (not all, however) could only assume it was at the direction of Gen. Tai Li who resented American intervention in a Chinese internal matter.

A similar operation was conducted in Italy against the Germans. Barbara Lauwers (Lee Podoski) was a WAAC assigned to OSS in Rome. The allied armies were moving north towards the heavily industrialized Po valley.

Included in the German forces were thousands of unwilling Czechs. Seeing the chink in the German armor Lauwers went to work.

She created five "speeches" from "fellow Czechs" who supposedly had defected. They had "joined" the Czech Army of National Liberation which was fighting alongside the allies.

BBC broadcast these "speeches" to the Czech garrisons in northern Italy. In a two pronged movement German prisoners of war, now working for OSS, infiltrated their own lines to pass out surrender passes. Six hundred Czechs defected and joined the Liberation Army of their compatriots. Lauwers was awarded the Bronze Star for her part in the plot.

Hollywood was turning out war films to bolster American morale. Full length features extolled the valor of our armed forces. Special features and documentaries showed actual combat footage and sold war bonds. Even cartoons ridiculed Hitler and the Japanese, all too often invoking severe racism.

OSS was looking for ways to tap America's talent for its own black propaganda purposes. Playwright Robert Sherwood was put to work writing special material. But the idea of music, used clumsily by the Germans, was given special consideration. Music had a special way of getting to the emotions and thoughts of fighting men of western cultures.

"Musical warfare" was a special innovation. First it was necessary to violate America's copyright laws and use the music of American composers. Their songs were translated into German without the composers' knowledge. They were then played over clandestine radio broadcasts from England into Germany where they boosted the American way of life and undermined the Germans.

The lyrics were rewritten to send the message OSS wished to convey. The next step was to find the artists to sing these tainted words. European-born opera singers and Hollywood stars of German ancestry were used without being told what they were doing. Most notable of the singers were Lotte Lenya and Marlene Dietrich.

To find the person most capable of reaching the German personality composer/arranger Kurt Weill was used. He was the husband of Lenya and composer of several Broadway musicals.

The New York advertising agency of J. Walter Thompson was employed to recruit back up singers for the clandestine operations. This was done without the knowledge of the American Federation of Musicians. During the summer of 1944 the OSS made as many as eight recordings a week of complete Broadway shows and the hit songs of the day.

Among those songs were some still popular today such as "I Told Every Little Star," "I'll Get By," "My Heart Stood Still," and "Is You Is or Is You Ain't?"

Documents released forty years after the war indicated the OSS concern over violation of U.S. copyright laws in not asking for the consent of the song-writers to use their work. One special memo from an OSS official in Washington, D.C. said outright that only Marlene Dietrich was to be trusted enough to be told the entire story. It added she must be most discreet in connection with the copyrights.

OSS used a man known only as "Metzyl" to rewrite most of the songs into German. In August of 1944 he approached burnout as he was doing eight new lyrics a week. The search went out to find someone to help him.

There was little doubt OSS loved Dietrich the most of all the artists used. An August 24, 1944, memo from OSS officer Edward Cushing in Washington, D.C. to OSS officer David Williamson in New York said, "Dietrich is the only one of our artists who, so far as I know, has been told for whom she is working but even she has not been told the nature of the operations in which she is engaged. I urge you to bear it in mind."

Without doubt one of the most sensational OSS women was Virginia Hall. She was the only American woman to receive the Distinguished Service Cross for heroism. In addition she was also awarded the British MBE. She had a mind of her own and found she did not fit into the restrictive academic life at Radcliff and Barnard. She talked her family into letting her study in Europe where she attended schools in Vienna and Paris. She returned home to do graduate work at George Washington University in Washington.

It was her great desire to work in the foreign service. While she did well in her exams she could not secure an appointment in the nearly totally male diplomatic corps. Not accepting it as final she took a job as a clerk in Warsaw, in the American Embassy. In later years she worked in Estonia, Italy and Turkey.

A hunting accident outside Izmir, Turkey cost her the loss of one leg below the knee. Unfazed she simply learned to walk with an artificial limb and a slight limp.

When the war began she became an ambulance driver in Paris. With the evacuation of British forces as France fell she went to London where SO,E correctly evaluated her courage and ingenuity and sent her back as an agent. Her cover story was that of a foreign correspondent for the New York Post in Vichy. While she did that she set up an espionage network and aided downed pilots.

With the German declaration of war on America she fled on foot through the Pyrenees to Spain. SO,E reassigned her to Madrid but she craved action and returned to London to request transfer into OSS. It was granted.

A few weeks later she returned to France in a motor torpedo boat with her own radio which she had learned to operate. Her code name was Diane.

Someone had reported her to the Gestapo but even so she was able to elude them working the rural areas of Chev, Nievre and Preuse in Central France. She had to pose as a milkmaid, taking cows to pasture, doing laundry in rocky streams and cooking meals for her farmer hosts. She continued sending radio messages and organizing parachute drops of weapons and supplies. Next she was assigned to the Haute Loire in the Massif Central, an extremely rugged terrain. She had never had training in sabotage but prior to the Allied advance for six months her teams blew four bridges, destroyed a key rail line and cut telephone wires and derailed freight trains.

With the arrival of allied armies she was reassigned to Austria. While in Italy, however, her mission was scrubbed.

She was so modest that after the hostilities she did not want to accept her medal but finally did in the privacy of the OSS office.

Julia McWilliams Child, as a civilian, served as head of the Registry of the Secretariat, OSS, in China. Her duties included registering, cataloguing and channeling vast volumes of documents, all highly sensitive. She was noted for her accuracy and, especially, for her cheerfulness. She raised the morale of her unit considerably and brought out the utmost efficiency of all her coworkers. For her outstanding work she was awarded the Emblem of Meritorious Civilian Service.

Another OSS woman who contributed in a different manner was the late Rosamond Frame (Mrs. Thibault de St. Phalle). Though living in France she had been born and raised in China. Because of this she spoke fluent Chinese. She became part of the Research and Analysis group in Chungking, China. In fact she became the first OSS agent to fly the "Hump" across the Himalayas into China. She was able to bridge the cultural gap between the Oriental and Occidental women at the elegant parties thrown in that city. And while it sounded terribly social she was looking far deeper than the social talk, keeping a sensitive finger on the pulse of intrigue and interpreting what she heard to her superiors.

The British sent a total of 53 women agents into France. Twelve were executed by the Nazis after extensive torture. Twenty nine were arrested and many died in captivity.

One of these women who survived was Christine Granville, the Countess Krystyn Cizycka Skarbek who worked in Poland until its fall. From there she went to France and finally to Africa. She was the first woman to parachute into a Middle East theatre. She was arrested twice but obtained her freedom each time. One time she skied away from her captors in a hail of machine gun fire. Another time she bit her tongue until it bled profusely. Pleading that she was tubercular she was taken to a hospital and later released. She next went back to

France. She pulled off an amazing coup in freeing two SO,E agents. As a "new courier" she persuaded the captors that the arrival of American troops was imminent. By guts, gall and cunning she secured their release three hours before they were scheduled to be shot.

Ensign Nancy Wake, won the U.S. Silver Star for gallantry in action. In one specific incident, cited in her award, it was noted that "Ensign Wake herself led a section of ten men after their leader had lost his head, resulting in the death of four of them. She led the section to within the face of the enemy, ordered their fire, and withdrew them in good order, showing coolness and courage in the face of enemy fire. She also saved the lives of two American officers in this engagement."

The WAAF, Women's Auxiliary Air Force, had officer Constance Babington-Smith as one of its officers at the secret KIF headquarters in Hedmenham. She was in charge of aircraft and airfields. Her job was to examine reconnaissance photos taken over Germany. This branch of intelligence was important in the selection of new targets as well as following enemy movements. In May 1944 she spotted something most unusual in photos just taken over Peenemunde, a German island in the Baltic. Employing a stereoscope and magnifier she mapped out the oddly shaped shadows which she correctly figured were launching pads with unusual tiny airplanes bunched about them. Her detailed work in searching through thousands of photos resulted in her locating the site where Hitler's deadly V-1 and V-2 bombs were being developed. The RAF bombed them heavily causing at least a six month delay in the buzz bomb attacks on London.

Maria Gulevics was a 23 year old Czech woman of fantastic courage, insight and bravery. She was fluent in Czech, Russian, German, and Hungarian. She joined the OSS men and partisan group that consisted of Jewish refugees from Hungary, women and children. She was assigned to the group as an interpreter. Atop a 6,000 foot high mountain they were joined by other partisans, French and Russian, who were collecting weaponry to attack German forces.

As the group moved through heavy snow, sleet and freezing temperatures many cases of frostbite and pneumonia developed. Moving through waist deep snow the group was severely hampered by the women and children as well as those severely ill.

Maria moved constantly using her linguistic skills to seek out safe houses, find food and even medical aid. As the numbers of the partisans thinned out through capture and death at the hands of the pursuing Germans she remained steadfast, running through chilled streams, helping treat the ill and wounded.

She held up with the strongest of the men During the five months of hit and run action she never wavered.

A tribute was given to her by the men with whom she served who said "her daring adventures into and through German infested areas in our behalf was something that would have been impossible for us. She is undoubtedly most responsible for our being alive today."

In France, the notorious Ravensbruck prison was used for female prisoners. Here the Germans carried out abominable tortures against their female captives, then took them outside and shot them. In this prison it was reported upward of 100,000 women perished. The Germans saved their worst treatment for female agents, most of whom endured severe and excruciating torture before being executed.

15

One day Eifler received the phone call from the State Department he had been expecting. Could he come over and help them solve a problem?

Agent Alex had gone to the State Department to get a passport. He had filed his papers for an American passport in place of his alien one. All aliens who had fought with the American forces were given automatic citizenship. The information he had filed was correct but did not agree with that in the State Department files. He had been asked the reason. He was enough of an agent to tell them nothing. He simply said they would have to ask Colonel Eifler to explain the reason. And now Eifler sat at the official's desk. This man was surrounded by books and codes of his department. From his manner, Eifler felt he could quote entire sections without looking them up. He obviously did not appreciate intrigue and was disturbed that he was having to take the additional time to straighten out the problem. He told Eifler of the problem and then lay down the two differing passports.

"Colonel, do you know anything about these?"

Eifler said he knew all about them. He paused to let that sink in and noticed the irritation across the desk.

"During the war I needed passports to take many agents out of the country. They were both alien and naturalized men. I didn't have time to get all of the background information, so I put in the information I knew would satisfy the State Department." He sat back and said nothing further.

The official was aghast. Finally he pulled himself together. "You know that this is a violation of the law, Colonel?"

Eifler allowed that he did.

"And yet you went ahead and deliberately violated the law?" he pursued in rising tones.

Eifler leaned forward, his huge hands folded on the desk. "Let's put it this way. I didn't expect any of us would get out of this project alive. I figured we would all be killed. I really wasn't concerned about whether or not I was violating any law. But I didn't get killed, nor did these men. Now I am here...what are you going to do about it?" He finished with his famed walnut-cracking smile.

310

The man gulped several times and looked at his numerous books as if to seek help. He had never been confronted with such an individual or situation. Finally he gathered sufficient strength to reply.

"Are there any more like this one, Colonel?"

"Yes, there are," replied Eifler.

"Aliens?"

"Yes, all aliens."

The official was incredulous. No ratiocination was possible here.

"For God's sake, will you give us the right information so we can correct our records?"

"I'll be glad to," Eifler concluded.

Considerable paperwork was required to settle the affairs of many of these aliens, but eventually the records were straightened out to everyone's satisfaction.

He returned to his paperwork. One form before him required an accounting of all government property that was under his command. He had dispensed millions of dollars in cash, innumerable stacks of weapons and munitions, as well as all kinds of electronic gear and other supplies. The report was lengthy and time-consuming. When it was completed, it was submitted and subsequently audited. The government decided, with a straight face, that he was short one Parker fountain pen: "$12.50 please, Colonel." With that he was released from OSS and instructed to report back to the army. Allowed sufficient time for a return trip, he bought a 1939 LaSalle and proceeded to drive cross-country. He found the change in pace exhilarating. For so long he had lived a life of violence now he could observe the small peaceful towns in America and be thankful they were spared the carnage he had witnessed.

He spent Christmas with his wife and his parents in Los Angeles. It was good to be alive.

The passport problem Eifler had resolved with the State Department was but the tip of the iceberg as America began trying to tie up all loose ends, not only of the shooting war, but the political wars OSS agents had been thrust into.

The situation in Vietnam was one of the thorniest problems to face and for which there was no answer. The seeds for future conflict were sewn well before America was even drawn into World War II.

In May, 1941, a group of Vietnamese revolutionaries met in south China to organize into one political group. They called themselves the Viet Minh. Their leader was a man named Nguyen Ai Quoc. Three months later Tai Li's police, aware of Quoc's background in Communism, arrested him. Even more important, however, was the fact the Chinese themselves had territorial ambitions for Vietnam.

After his arrest his compatriots continued strengthening their Viet Minh group. In September, 1943, after a year in jail, Quoc secured his release agreeing to work for one Chinese war lord. Quoc then cloaked his identity with a new name—Ho Chi Minh.

Taking the Chinese funding of one hundred thousand Chinese dollars a month for espionage operations, Ho put most of it into his Viet Minh. It was transformed into a small guerrilla army by Vo Nguyen Giap, a former school teacher. His wife had died at the hands of the French police.

As the Viet Minh solidified they broke off with their Chinese paymasters. In 1944 they sought Allied sponsorship at the Kunming headquarters of OSS. By this time the Americans were tired of the French politics and bickering between their various services. They agreed to see if this new approach just might be the answer to fighting the Japanese.

While various French factions scurried to make sure they maintained their "colony," Ho Chi Minh and Vo Nguyen Giap had solidified their Viet Minh and now moved it to Tonkin. They supplied intelligence and helped rescue downed pilots from Chennault's Fourteenth Air Force. The French, however, refused to have anything to do with the Viet Minh.

OSS Colonel Paul Helliwell in Chungking was contacted several times by the Viet Minh. He denied giving them aid other than a few weapons and ammunition. He refused to give other help unless the Viet Minh would agree not to use them against the French. Such an agreement was not forthcoming.

The Japanese watched the growing Viet Minh organization but even more so the French under their control who were showing more and more support for the resistance. Finally they could take no more.

Calling in French Admiral Decoux on March 9, 1945, they gave him an ultimatum. All French forces, military and police, were to be placed under Japanese command. He was given two hours to reply. When he asked for more time to study the command the Japanese responded by arresting him and all French forces. Only one major resistance force now remained—the Viet Minh.

While the Japanese had indeed arrested most of the French officers and their men, Generals Allesandri and Sabattier were able to escape from Hanoi. Taking their units with them they went north to the Dien Bien Phu airport and from there contacted the American forces in China asking for help.

Help was withheld by Wedemeyer's headquarters who stated no arms or supplies would be given under any circumstances. The political jousting was increasing. OSS Lieutenant Robert Ettinger, a Frenchman of Jewish descent, flew into the airfield and prepared to march out to China with the troops. They were to face hunger, disease, Japanese troops and hostile Vietnamese who were anxious to get rid of their French masters. Many died on the way before they reached their destination, Chungking.

In Chungking many OSS officers of French descent championed their cause. In addition other OSS men who had fought alongside the Maquis in France were sympathetic and began talking of launching attacks against Tonkin from the Chinese coast. They were dissuaded by the French.

Col. Helliwell said, "The French were infinitely more concerned with keeping the Americans out of Indo-China than they were in defeating the Japanese or in doing anything to bring the war to a successful conclusion in that area."

In a sad verification of that statement the French gave faulty information to the first OSS sabotage team to infiltrate Tonkin. It was ambushed by the Japanese.

Giap's forces remained untouched by all this activity. By June six Tonkinese provinces were under his control. The Allies had to accept the fact the Viet Minh was a military reality.

OSS dropped one of its men into Ho Chi Minh's headquarters in May. He spent several months with the leader and was surprised that Ho showed a great interest in the American Declaration of Independence. "He kept asking me if I could remember the language of our Declaration. I was a normal American. I couldn't. The more we discussed it the more he seemed to know more about it than I did. He was an awfully sweet guy. If I had to pick one quality about that little old man sitting on his hill in the jungle, it was his gentleness." Ho was sincere in wanting to cooperate with both France and America.

While the friendship of OSS and Ho Chi Minh grew the French became increasingly angry. They wanted nothing to interfere with their "territory" and held to the belief the Vietnamese would welcome them back with open arms once the Japanese were gone.

In the summer, OSS China sent an officer with a radio operator-interpreter as liaison to Ho. At the insistence of the French one of their officers also joined them. Knowing of the hostility of the Vietnamese towards the French the Frenchman posed as an American officer.

Arriving in Hanoi they were taken to Ho's camp where they found the leader near death. Emaciated, he was shaking and running a dangerously high fever. The OSS men did what they could to keep him alive while they radioed China for a medic.

Two weeks later the medic, Paul Hoagland, arrived with three other agents. He took a look at the ailing Ho.

"This man doesn't have long for this world," he proclaimed. Ho was suffering from malaria, dysentery and various tropical diseases. By use of sulfa and quinine the leader was soon back on his feet and walking about. His life had been saved—a fact he often acknowledged in later years.

At the first formal meeting with the OSS team following his recovery Ho surprised them. Pointing to the French officer he proclaimed, "This man is not an American." The OSS officer and his men denied the accusation.

"Look, who are you trying to kid," Ho persisted. "This man is not part of the deal."

Following that he identified the man as Lt. Montfort of the French army. Amazed at the depth of Ho's intelligence the Americans now feared for Montfort's life. To their surprise Ho sent him to the Chinese border under guard.

"It will be interesting for the French reaction. Perhaps now they won't think of me as a murderous bandit," was Ho's final remark.

Happily the incident did not harm OSS-Viet Minh relations. Ho offered pretty young Vietnamese girls from Hanoi and jungle aphrodisiacs to the Americans. According to military custom they sadly declined.

Donning guerrilla garb the Americans helped the Viet Minh with arms and military training. Giap complained of the poor weapons his men were using. The OSS team obtained rifles, machine guns, mortars, grenades and bazookas. In addition they held training sessions for 200 troops, the elite of Giap's guerrilla force.

During bull sessions Ho spoke of his days in America. During the 1920's he had worked as a waiter in Boston and New York. He was well versed in American history and ideals. He felt America would be on his side in throwing out the French and getting their independence.

"I have always been impressed with your country's treatment of the Philippines. You kicked the Spanish out and let the Filipinos develop their own country. You were not looking for real estate, and I admire you for that," he said to Rene Defourneaux, a French-American from New York.

As the war ended Ho sent a message to the U.S. authorities asking they inform the United Nations, "We were fighting the Japs on the side of the United Nations. Now Japs surrendered. We beg United Nations to realize their solemn promise that all nationalities will be given democracy and independence. If United Nations forget their

314

solemn promise and don't grant Indochina full independence, we will keep fighting until we get it."

While the Viet Minh was more secure in the north there were other Vietnamese factions to the south wanting their piece of the action. In particular the Trotskyites were calling for violent revolution. Causing a riot in Saigon as Allied representatives were about to arrive they brought about the death of both French and Vietnamese citizens. This was followed by a riot where French homes were looted and pillaged.

With rumors the British intended interfering to back up a return of French colonial rule the situation became more and more volatile. The French imposed censorship and martial law and banned all demonstrations and public meetings.

OSS, geared for a shooting war, now found itself involved in trying to maintain what they had fought for in the political arena. In July, 1945, OSS Colonel Peter Dewey had been chosen to head a team of 50 OSS officers to enter Saigon after the Japanese surrender. British General Douglas Gracey, seeking to bar all OSS involvement, objected. An OSS appeal to Mountbatten was successful and in September, one month after the atomic bombs ended the war, the OSS team entered Saigon.

Twelve days later Indian Gurkha troops of the British Army arrived and joined forces with the French paratroopers who had also just arrived from Calcutta.

The Vietnamese Committee of the South, feeling they were in control, welcomed General Gracey. The General was not at all favorable to nationalism and promptly "kicked them out."

Gracey's orders were specific—to disarm the Japanese. But he took it upon himself to "restore order" in much the same way OSS had taken it upon themselves to help the nationalists.

Gracey was no friend of the French. In meetings with the French he involved OSS Captain Joseph Coolidge not only as a representative of the United States but also a buffer.

The situation deteriorated and a general boycott was called by the Vietnamese. Gracey released over 1,000 interned French soldiers, armed them and turned them loose. They began a program of brutality against the Vietnamese people, raping and looting. The Vietnamese reacted with violence against the French.

Knowing of OSS meetings with the Viet Minh, newly arrived French General Leclerc decided it was time for them to go and ordered them out of the country.

Before they could go Dewey was shot and killed by a native who evidently thought him to be French.

The day after Dewey's death General Gracey arrested the Japanese commander in Saigon. He was told his troops would be expected to join the British and French in "pacifying" the Vietnamese or he would be tried as a war criminal. With an offer that he could hardly refuse the Japanese officer added his units and the campaign to return colonialism began. It was the beginning of the Indochina war.

The U.S. State Department announced it was selling $160 million in weaponry for the French to use against the Viet Minh. OSS officer George Sheldon was embittered at this declaration. Upon returning from Saigon he said, "For one who has been there the conclusion is inevitable that the French have learned almost everything under Hitler except compassion."

To the north the situation was almost reversed. With no French to harass the nationals Hanoi was the capital of the Democratic Republic of Vietnam and the French there walked lightly.

The French in China requested an OSS plane to take them to Hanoi to establish their presence. Delay after delay was encountered but finally a party of five French and seven American officers flew from Kunming to Tonkin. Sullen Japanese troops, heavily armed, greeted them. The Japanese were told the Allies were there to make arrangements for the Allied Surrender Commission. The French were astounded by the display of red flags and soon realized the Vietnamese were solidly in control of the area.

The Allied entourage was taken to the Metropole Hotel. A short time later a Japanese officer arrived to advise a very hostile crowd had gathered in front of the hotel and his small forces were holding them off at gunpoint. The object of their wrath was, of course, the French. Subsequently the French were taken to the palace of the Governor-General from where the French had long ruled. In essence they were being held under armed guard for their own protection.

With the OSS and French officers ensconced in their quarters a new page in history was being written. Ho Chi Minh had begun his victory march into Hanoi. With him was the OSS group of Major Thomas. The "sensitivity" of Ho that OSS had commented on had to be examined again, however. On the march the OSS men came across many villages where chiefs had been slaughtered, buildings destroyed. Viet Minh troops moving ahead of Ho had been "securing" the area. There were definitely two sides to the new leader.

Arriving in Hanoi a crowd of several hundred thousand heard Ho declare his Declaration of Independence. Echoing America's own words Ho began, "All men are created equal," then went on to add his further interpretation.

Later that afternoon Giap stood beside OSS officer Archimedes

Patti in reviewing Viet Minh troops. The band struck up "The Star Spangled Banner." Patti saluted, Giap raised his clenched fist in the communist salute.

Understandably the French were angry saying the Americans had been duped by the clever Vietnamese. Other factions of OSS were displeased at the strong nationalistic stand taken by other OSS officers. The French, however, did realize the OSS presence in Hanoi had prevented their massacre at the hands of the Viet Minh.

Some of the more pro-Viet Minh officers were replaced by OSS who realized the international problems they posed with their close Viet Minh identification. While those officers leaving had expressed they felt Ho Chi Minh was more nationalist than communist the new officers were not buying it. OSS Major Frank White who had been part of the Dewey team met with Ho and heard his complaints about the French.

Upon returning to Hotel Metropole White found an invitation to a reception given by Ho at the government palace that same evening. High ranking members of Ho's Cabinet were already there when White arrived. Also in attendance came the French with three army generals. Then two Chinese generals and Colonel Trevor Wilson who was chief of British intelligence in Hanoi. White was frankly out-ranked by everyone.

He waited until the last minute to go in and looked for an empty seat. He saw none and was prepared to just fade out. But then some-one pointed to an empty chair...right beside Ho. He sat down gin-gerly.

He reported the dinner was a "horror." The French talked only among themselves and the Chinese became drunk immediately. Sensing the tension in the room White told Ho he felt there was some resentment over the seating arrangements, that he did not belong next to Ho.

"Yes, I can see that, but who else could I talk to," was the leaders reply.

The subsequent horror of war and slaughter of French, Vietnam-ese and American forces and civilians calls for deeper analysis of the final days of European colonialism.

While Eifler was hanging up his cloak and sheathing his dagger so were the balance of OSS agents throughout the world. The fears voiced about many concerning Communists in the spy organization began materializing. While most of them had courageously fought the Axis forces their energies now turned to consolidating their present positions. In putting down the cloak and dagger of OSS they now reached for their red cloak complete with hammer and sickle.

With the knowledge of many patriotic people who had fought along side them against the Nazis and Fascists they could evaluate those who had leadership abilities but would not go along with any communist leanings. It did not speak well for the security of those who chose not to join forces with the "new order."

The death of OSS agent John Birch in China signalled a new change in the American media. In a sudden turn the UP ran an April 2, 1946 story headed "No Glory In Birch's Death." In Billings, Montana a small time broadcaster who had been in OSS rushed to smear both Birch and the Chinese Nationalist with the statement Birch "did not have a high regard for the Chinese," and that his "brash manners" had brought on his death. On April 3 AP issued its syndicated story with the same slant. William P. Weiss and Col. Gustav Krause of OSS were quoted as saying Birch was responsible for his death. *Time* magazine joined the fray on April 14 after which UPI commissioned George A. Does, Jr. to do a story picturing Birch as a trouble-maker in his youth. The *Dallas Morning News* of April 23rd reported that he had "fought faculty" and was a "Center of Storm as Student."

General Wedemeyer was quoted as saying the Chinese reds had acted in anger over Birch's arrogance. It was an unusual statement. Those who lived in China long enough to learn the language knew that in times of peril you either bowed low or stood high. If the latter course, which Birch had employed, did not work then it was because the time had come to test America—or to kill Americans. And with this event a full drive against anti-communism began.

The most highly praised OSS officers in books written today are those who in that period advanced communism in China and Indo-China and worked to destroy a liberal king in Yugoslavia.

In a clever ploy that OSS operatives could appreciate, the leftists brought Brian Crozier, founder of the London "Institute for the Study of Conflict" to America to lecture. His mission was to appear dedicated to the West without bringing leftist fire down on his head. He was the "enemy of extremism, both left and right." It was safe to report on Russia's growing might but never on the parallel internal communist threat. The self-proclaimed non-communist must be presented as the only valid anti-communist. By denouncing real anti-communists as extremists and threats to peace, communists and their allies maintain a monopoly on the anti-communist fight and can direct it as they will. This became the doctrine of the anti-anti-communists and was cleverly used to protect the true conspiracy.

OSS agents who attempted to build the "peace movement" in Germany to create dissension with little success could only watch in

318

dismay as they saw the same tactics successfully used against America aided by leftists, radical students and well meaning citizens.

J. Edgar Hoover saw the chance to get rid of his nemesis and put pressure on the new President, Harry Truman, to dismantle OSS. Anxious to reduce the federal budget by eliminating wartime agencies Truman issued an executive order disbanding OSS on Sept. 20, 1945 declaring America had no need of a "Gestapo."

The various branches of OSS were assigned to other departments who were delighted to receive them. Covert and espionage units went to the War Department as a "Strategic Services Unit." Actually it was merely a caretaker body to preside over the liquidation of the OSS espionage net. The Research and Analysis Branch of OSS went to State. Congressional and presidential budget cutting quickly decimated it.

Truman, however, soon realized he was wrong. There was really a need for such an organization as OSS. America had the advance information of the Pearl Harbor attack but did not get the information to the proper parties. Army and Navy intelligence seemed to be at war with each other. And so four months later, in January of 1946, Truman established the Central Intelligence Group. Its ranks were filled with former OSS people. The base was flawed, however. The CIG's budget and personnel were drawn from War, Navy and State. In this manner the old departments kept control over CIG.

While CIG was to provide guidance to the President they found the obstacles insurmountable. The armed forces not only refused to provide information on overseas events, they would not even tell CIG what American capabilities and intentions were. State Department likewise refused to cooperate.

Obviously a change was necessary. In July, 1947, it came with the passage of the National Security Act. Among its provisions was a name change for CIG which became the Central Intelligence Agency. Of greater importance was the fact it was to be an independent department, responsible to the President and not the Secretary of Defense.

Severe criticism was leveled against the U.S. intelligence community for its work with former Nazis, even Wehrmacht officers.

One of their top men was General Reinhard Gehlen, Chief of Military Intelligence on the eastern front. His attention to detail was so precise he was able to predict the battle of Stalingrad as early as the summer of 1942. Angered at his defeatist attitude, Hitler dismissed him.

Foreseeing the defeat of Germany and with a deep hatred of

319

Communism, Gehlen began preparing for the sure arrival of the Allies. His in-depth files on Russia's weaknesses, strengths and political ambitions were carefully packed into fifty steel cases. They were taken into the Bavarian Alps and secretly buried for an eventual bargaining chip with the Allies.

After his capture he met with Brigadier General Edwin L. Sibert, Senior Intelligence officer in the U.S. zone of occupied Germany and told him what he, Gehlen, could offer.

The Eastern division at the Pentagon was alarmed over Russia. While America had demobilized its forces from 12 million men to 1.4 million the Russians had failed to diminish their numbers. Their 6 million men, 50,000 tanks and 20,000 aircraft posed a dangerous threat. But America had no window into that country

Gehlen's knowledge and professionalism delivered to the Allies their sole source of the Soviet's political and military aims. Without him and his files America would have been even more unaware of the new adversary they faced as the war ended.

At the request of the War Department Gehlen was sent to Washington in August, 1945. He was allowed to take five of his men with him. Arriving in Washington in September they found a rapt audience in the American military. Truman had just disbanded the OSS and America needed that window in Russia. In short order the U.S. generals granted Gehlen almost everything he proposed.

The outcome was for the U.S. to give him $7,000,000 and turn him loose against the Soviets once more. For several years he was America's main source of information on Russia.

His system for debriefing German POW's from Russia was a masterpiece. He had the ability to drain them dry of every bit of information they might have observed or participated in as they served in factories, cities and airdromes. His analysis of the millions of bits of information enabled him to detail the planning goals for the new East German army in 1949.

He stated there would be twenty four infantry regiments, two engineer regiments and three signal regiments. Each units strength would be 1,250 men—a grand total of 48,750 bodies. Pentagon records showed his figures were exactly 103 short of the eventual total strength of the "Barrack police."

As brilliant as he was, he was not a likeable man. He was the stereotypical Prussian officer. He sought after power and gained it. Then he used that power to build a secret government surrounding himself with former SS officers and men as well as former Nazis who really belonged in prison.

America's continued use of Gehlen was questioned by many,

320

damned by most outside the intelligence community. Pragmatism outweighed revulsion in matters of national interest.

When President Truman was heckled about use of Gehlen by a leftist Congressman, he replied, "Well, we've also worked with another Hitler collaborator, a man you admire." "Who?" demanded the Congressman.

"Joe Stalin," replied the testy President. "Remember he signed on with Hitler in 1939. This Gehlen fellow, I don't care if he fucks goats. If he helps us, we'll use him." A similar point had been made in a less earthy manner by Sir Francis Walsingham who centuries earlier had served the first Queen Elizabeth. When she complained of the high cost of spying he replied, "Knowledge is never too dear."

What happened to these men and women who had tasted of the OSS wine? Those who had power of life and death, who had practically unlimited funds? Whose training reversed all morals and ethics that were the foundation of Western society?

Were they able to hang up their wartime cloaks and reenter the main stream of society? Did they find their views or philosophies warped or twisted?

While the black arts including assassination, forgery, counterfeiting, arson, blackmail, intimidation, lock picking and safe cracking were easy to put off, what of the more subliminal philosophy that guided them during the war—the end justifies the means? It was made quite clear that the only rule agents must observe was to win. A large number of the newly formed CIA personnel came from OSS ranks. A large percentage of them went on to become congressmen, judges, authors, inventors and sports figures.

There are no known cases of OSS operatives turning their wartime talents into illegal activities. Psychologically there were no unusual problems as the reversal process back to civilized mores began.

America's unique wartime experience exhibited America's strength through the diversity and ingenuity of its people. The freedom of expression and thought Americans enjoyed enabled them to start late in the espionage game and compete with the top organizations of England, Germany. France, Japan and Russia.

So secret had been OSS operations and records of those operations no one really knew how many men and women had served within its ranks—nor the amount of those killed or wounded. Various sources estimated its numbers at 13,000–22,000 and at most 30,000. The Special Operations Division which sent agents behind enemy lines could tell it had 1,600 in action but no one could then say how many teams of fifteen to twenty OG personnel operated behind the lines or even those agents who assumed special identities for operating in German and Japanese occupied territory.

The British SO,E sent over 500 liaison officers into northern Italy. The "useful life" of these agents, before "expenditure," was estimated at six months.

OSS decorated at least 831 men and women for bravery. Several received the nation's second highest decoration for battlefield heroism, the Distinguished Service Cross. None received the nations highest award, the Congressional Medal of Honor although several who deliberately allowed themselves to be captured to spare the lives of civilian hostages certainly ranked with those who did receive it.

Three weeks after the war ended the R&A division of OSS was reduced to a few people and empty desks and chairs. In a later review of the situation McGeorge Bundy stated that, to a large degree, "the area study programs developed in American universities in the years after the war were manned, directed or stimulated by graduates of the OSS—a remarkable institution, half cops-and-robbers and half faculty meeting."

R&A was the core of OSS and had a great impact on Government policy-making. It proved that scholarly research and analysis could produce information unavailable by espionage.

One thing all OSS personnel did take with them was memories. They had been privileged to participate in a unique American experience that had never happened before nor would again.

They had been allowed to play the game of chess for the greatest of all stakes—their own lives and those of their colleagues.

The news of the disbanding of OSS brought sadness to the men who had breathed life into its pirate sails. As might be expected they foresaw the continuing need to maintain a vigilant America. In particular they recognized the menace of communism and the belligerence of Joseph Stalin.

Donovan lobbied long in the backrooms to reverse the order that called for the demise of his organization but Truman was adamant.

It was then that the first rumors of a private OSS surfaced. A private organization, funded by wealthy individuals and corporations with overseas interests. Certainly the personnel were available and many were willing to continue. Even accepting the fact that they would continue being at odds with the FBI as before, except this time they would have no legal backing, the interest did not waiver.

The secret organization, headed by Donovan, was purportedly to continue its intelligence gathering activities and where necessary for the best interests of America, conduct covert operations in which it was all too well versed.

With the resurrection of an intelligence service under the new banner of the CIA the possibility of a shadowy OSS group not only was not negated but increased. It was felt the constraints and oversight of CIA operations would greatly hobble America's ability to take those actions necessary for security. What better way to handle them than by an organization responsible to no one and requiring no funds overseen by Congress?

Few people ever knew how far such a secret organization ever got or, indeed, if it ever got started at all. It was a logical assumption for those men who recognized the continuing threat to America's security while most Americans were anxious only to return to peace time pursuits and forget the devastating war just fought.

The term "cowboy" was hung on OSS operatives by some in the CIA who had never carried out wartime activities. Generally it inferred the OSS philosophy of the ends justifying the means. It was applied to Bill Casey who went from his OSS service into the CIA and later became its chief. Many in felt he continued in the wartime venue.

Many agents said their experiences gave them the only total freedom they had ever known or would know. The instructions they received, to carry the war to the enemy, freed them of any previous restraints they had known from ethics, morals or even decency. To their credit they eagerly abandoned that barbaric code to reenter a civilized society.

As with their brothers who fought in the regular branches of the armed forces the OSS people proved their willingness to fight and die for the principles of democracy.

It was the worst of times—for a few it was the best of times.

Appendix A

Eifler's DET 101 was unique in its size and varied operations. It was likewise different in that it was the only OSS unit to receive a Presidential Citation.

Though the specific time period mentioned occurred after Eifler had departed it still was a tribute to the spirit and courage he brought to his men through his own actions and bravery.

* * *

The citation issued in the name of the President of the United States reads as follows:

"*Service Unit Detachment No. 101, Office of Strategic Services* is cited for outstanding performance of duty from 8 May to 15 June 1945 in capturing the strategic enemy strong points of Lawksawk, Pangtara, and Loilem in the Central Shan States, Burma. This unit, composed of approximately 300 American officers and men, volunteered to clear the enemy from an area of 10,000 square miles. Its subsequent activities deprived the Japanese 15th Army of the only East escape route and secured the Stilwell Road against enemy counterattack. Although Detachment No. 101 had been engaged primarily in intelligence and guerrilla activities, it set about the infantry mission of ousting a determined enemy from a sector long fortified and strategically prepared. These American officers and men recruited, organized, and trained 3,200 Burmese natives entirely within enemy territory. They then undertook and concluded successfully a coordinated 4-battalion offensive against important strategic objectives through an area containing approximately 10,000 battle-seasoned Japanese troops. Locally known as the "Kachin Rangers," Detachment No. 101 and its Kachin troops became a ruthless striking force, continually on the offensive against the veterans of the Japanese 18th and 56th Divisions. Throughout the campaign, the Kachin Rangers were equipped with nothing heavier than mortars and had to rely entirely upon air-dropped supplies. Besides a numerical superiority of three to one, the enemy had the advantage of adequate supplies, artillery tankettes, carefully prepared positions, and motor transportation. Alternating frontal attacks with guerrilla tactics, the Kachin Rangers remained in constant contact with the enemy during the entire period and persistently cut him down and demoralized him. During the vicious struggle for Lawksawk, 400 Rangers met 700 Japanese veterans supported by artillery and, in a 12-hour battle, killed 281 of the enemy while suffering only 7 casualties. They took Loilem, central junction of vital roads, despite its protecting system of bunkers and pillboxes after 10 days of unremitting assaults. Under the most hazardous jungle conditions, Americans of Detachment No. 101 displayed extraordinary heroism in leading their coordinated battalions of 3,200 natives to complete victory against an overwhelmingly superior force. They met and routed 10,000 Japanese throughout an area of 10,000 square miles, killed 1,247 while sustaining losses of 37, demolished or captured 4 large dumps, destroyed the enemy motor transport, and inflicted extensive damage on communications and installations. The courage and fighting spirit displayed by the officers and men of Service Unit Detachment No. 101, Office of Strategic Services, in this successful offensive action against overwhelming enemy strength, reflect the highest traditions of the armed forces of the United States."

Dwight D. Eisenhower,
Chief of Staff

Bibliography

Alsop, Stewart and Thomas Braden, SUB ROSA, New York, 1946.
Baldwin, Hanson, THE CRUCIAL YEARS, New York,1976.
Barrett, David, THE UNITED STATES ARMY OBSERVER GROUP IN
    YENAN, Berkeley, 1970.
Becker, Henry, THE NATURE AND CONSEQUENCES OF BLACK
    PROPAGANDA, *American Sociological Review*, April, 1949.
Becket, Henry S.A., THE DICTIONARY OF ESPIONAGE, New York,
    1986
Bergamini, David, JAPAN'S IMPERIAL CONSPIRACY. New York,
    1971
Bidwell, Shelford, THE CHINDIT WAR, New York, 1979.
Casey, Bill, THE SECRET WAR AGAINST GERMANY, Washington,
    D.C., 1978.
Chamales, Tom, NEVER SO FEW, New York, 1957,
Corson, Wm. R., THE ARMIES OF IGNORANCE, New York, 1977.
Craig, William, THE FALL OF JAPAN, New York, 1967.
de Gramont, Sanche, THE SECRET WAR, New York, 1962.
Dulles, Allen W., THE CRAFT OF INTELLIGENCE, New York, 1963.
Dunlop, Richard, BEHIND JAPANESE LINES, New York, 1979.
Eldridge, Fred, WRATH IN BURMA, New York, 1946.
Fellowes-Gordon, Ian, THE MAGIC WAR, New York, 1971.
Ford, Corey, DONOVAN OF OSS, Boston, 1970.
Goodfellow, Millard Preston, *Papers and Correspondence from the
Hoover Institute*, Stanford University.
Hart, G., H. Lidell, HISTORY OF THE SECOND WORLD WAR, New
    York, 1974.
Haswell, Jock, SPIES AND SPYMASTERS, London, 1977.
Hohne, Heinz and Hermann Zolling, THE GENERAL WAS A SPY,
    New York.
Hunter, Charles, GALAHAD, San Antonio, 1963.
Hyde, Montgomery H., SECRET INTELLIGENCE AGENT, New York,
    1983.
Hymoff, Edward, THE OSS IN WORLD WAR II, New York, 1986.
Icardo, Also, AMERICAN MASTER SPY, New York, 1956.
Japan Defense Agency, War History Office, *Battle of Irawaddi*, 1955.
Joost, Pete, THE BURMA MISSION, *Bluebook Magazine*. June, 1947.

326

Kirkpatrick, Lyman, THE REAL CIA, New York 1968.

Kobler, John, HE RUNS A PRIVATE OSS, *Saturday Evening Post*, May 21, 1955.

Leckie, Robert, THE WARS OF AMERICA, New York, 1968.

Lovell, Stanley P., OF SPIES AND STRATAGEMS, New Jersey, 1963.

MacDonald, Elizabeth, UNDERCOVER GIRL, New York, 1947.

McIntosh, Elizabeth P., THE ROLE OF WOMEN IN INTELLIGENCE, Monographs from the Association of Former Intelligence Officers, Virginia,1989.

Mao, Tse-tung, ON GUERRILLA WARFARE, New York, 1961.

Miles, Milton, A DIFFERENT KIND OF WAR, New York, 1967.

Miller, Nathan, SPYING FOR AMERICA, New York, 1989.

Moon, Tom and Eifler, Carl THE DEADLIEST COLONEL, New York, 1975.

Morgan, Dr. William, THE OSS AND I, New York, 1957.

Mosley, Leonard, HIROHITO EMPEROR OF JAPAN, New Jersey, 1966.

Nicolson, Harold, THE WAR YEARS, New York, 1967.

Ogburn, Charlton, THE MARAUDERS, New York,1956.

Palmer, Raymond, THE ENCYCLOPEDIA OF ESPIONAGE, London, 1977.

Pash, Boris, THE ALSOS MISSION, New York, 1969.

Peers, Wm. R. and Dean Brelis, BEHIND THE BURMA ROAD, Boston, 1963.

Persico, Joseph E., PIERCING THE REICH, New York, 1979.

Rooney, D.D., STILWELL, New York, 1971.

Roosevelt, Kermit, WAR REPORT OF THE OSS, VOL 1 & 2, New York, 1975.

Salisbury, Harrison T., WAR BETWEEN RUSSIA AND CHINA, New York, 1964.

Schultz, Duane, THE MAVERICK WAR, New York, 1987.

Seagrave, Gordon S., BURMA SURGEON RETURNS, New York, 1946.

Smith, R. Harris, OSS, Berkeley, 1972.

Smith, Nicol and Blake Clark, INTO SIAM, New York, 1945.

Stevenson, William, A MAN CALLED INTREPID, New York, 1976.

Stilwell, Gen. Joseph W., THE STILWELL PAPERS, New York, 1948.

Stratton, Roy, THE ARMY-NAVY GAME, Massachusetts, 1977.

Swinson, Arthur, MOUNTBATTEN, New York, 1971.

Terraine, John, THE LIFE AND TIMES OF LORD MOUNTBATTEN, New York, 1980.

Thayer, George, THE WAR BUSINESS, New York, 1969.

Time-Life Books, THE RISING SUN New York, 1977.

Time-Life Books, PRELUDE TO WAR, New York, 1977.
Time-Life Books, CHINA - BURMA - INDIA, New York, 1978.
Time-Life Books, THE SECRET WAR, New York, 1980.
Toland, John, THE RISING SUN, Vols. 1 & 2, New York, 1970.
Tuchman, Barbara STILWELL AND THE AMERICAN EXPERIENCE
    IN CHINA, New York, 1970.
Tully, Andrew, CIA THE INSIDE STORY, New York, 1962.
THE SUPER SPIES, New York, 1969.
Sun Tzu, THE ART OF WAR, New York, 1963.

Added sources consulted:

Aubry, Arthur S.
Cavanaugh, Dennis
Corvin, Mel
Coughlin, John
Dorman-Smith, The Right Honorable Reginald
Eifler, Carl F.
Flaherty, Robert
Ford, John
Goodfellow, Preston
Haimson, Fima
Hengshoon, Harry
Ikeda, Setsuo (Japanese 18th Division)
Larsen, Jerry
Luce, James C.
Martin, Bill
Martin, Harry R.
Ong, Jo
Pamplin, Jack
Rhea, Bob
Richmond, Walter
Richter, Allen
Scharf, Ed
Schreiner, Sam
Shaheen, John
Stilwell, Mrs. Joseph W.
Tanaka, Shinichi (Lt. Gen. Japanese 18th Division)
Tilly, Jim
Walden, Jim
Wolbarst, Roger K.

Index

K

L

M

Peers, Captain Ray   45, 47, 48, 86, 115, 125, 157, 168, 169, 176
   Colonel, commanding DET 101   214, 227, 229, 287, 288, 300
"Penny Farthing"   243
Pete   106, 107
Pittard, Lieutenant   155, 156
Ploesti oilfields   289
POEN   271
Pratt, George   196
Primbs, Dr. Max   274, 276, 277
"principle of three"   144
"Professor Moriarty"   90, 93, 94, 95, 100

Q

Quinn, Patrick   135
Quoc, Nguyen Ai   311, 312. *See also* Ho Chi Minh

R

Rackett, Sergeant Mel   166, 167
Raiss, Captain John   105, 106
Ravensbruck prison   309
"Rebecca-Eureka"   143
Reddick, Willis   194, 198
Reichenau prison   276
Rhea, CWO Bob   166, 167, 220, 231
Rhee, Syngman   48, 168
Richmond, Wally   66, 68, 69, 128, 130, 132, 133, 187, 189
Richter, Sergeant Alan   46, 88, 89, 108, 113, 146
Ringling, John   179
Ripper, Captain Baron Rudolf von   281
Roberts, George   18, 186, 187
Robinson, Colonel Henson L.   179, 187
Romer, Joy   304
Rommel, Field Marshal Irwin   97
Roosevelt, Franklin D.   4, 5, 7, 8, 9, 17, 30, 31, 33, 40, 41, 51, 54, 76,
   78, 90, 91, 94, 100, 179, 183, 184, 215, 265, 290
   authorizes preemptive bombing of Japan   17
Rossi, Italian Ambassador   10
Rostow, Walt   179
Rotary   195

S

SACO   284, 285
Sadler, General P. L.   210
Saw Dhee Htu   268
Scharf, Ed   156
Schlesinger, Arthur   179
Schmahl, Horace   40
Schools and Training Branch   179
Schreiner, Sergeant Sam   133
Scones, Lieutenant General   108
Scorge, Richard   303

338